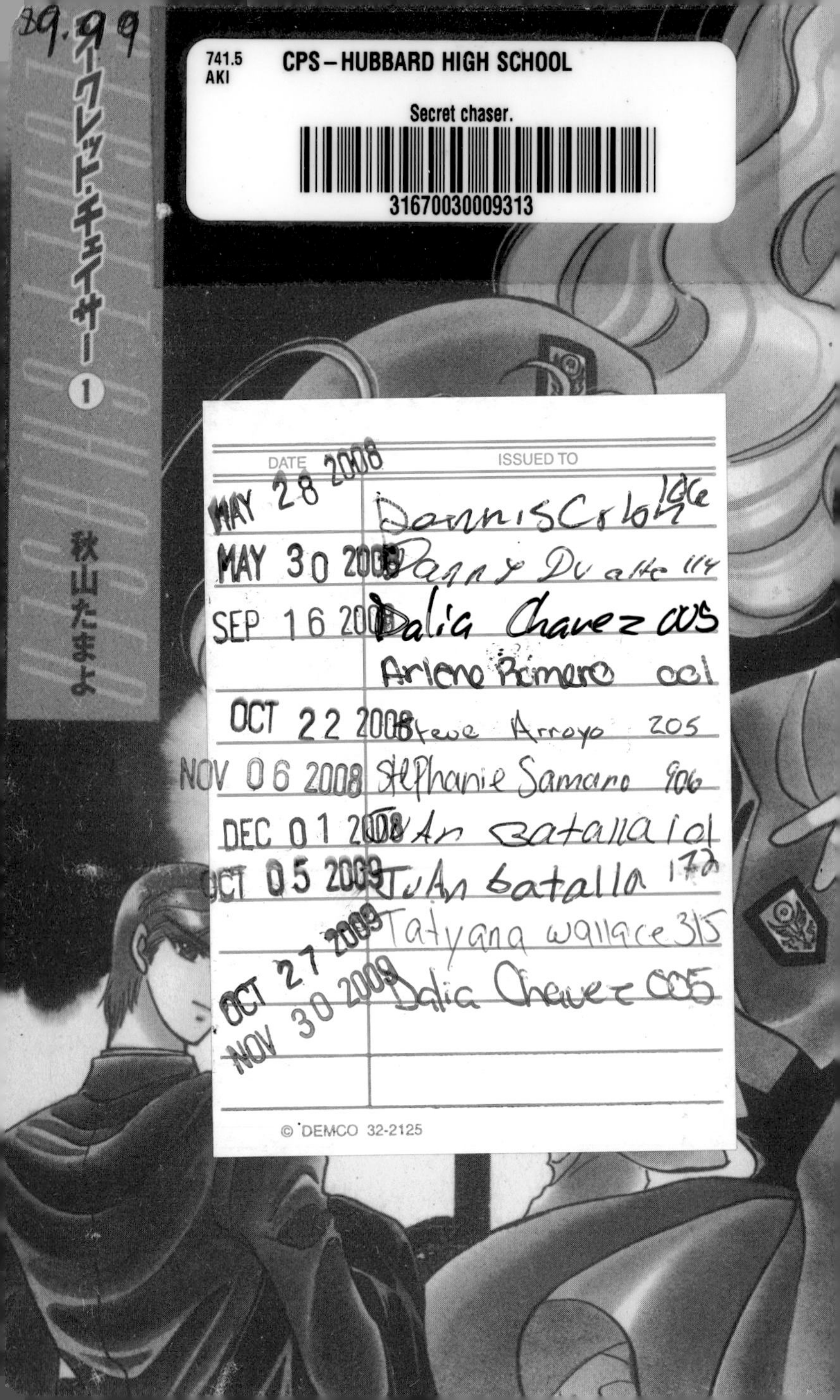
ークレット・チェイサー①
秋山たまよ

SECRET CHASER

Volume 1

Tamayo Akiyama

TOKYOPOP®

HAMBURG // LONDON // LOS ANGELES // TOKYO

741.5
AKI
31670030009313

Secret Chaser Vol. 1
created by Tamayo Akiyama

Translation - Ray Yoshimoto
English Adaptation - Patrick Neighly
Copy Editor - Hope Donovan
Retouch and Lettering - Alyson Stetz
Production Artist - Alyson Stetz
Cover Design - Kyle Plummer

Editor - Bryce P. Coleman
Digital Imaging Manager - Chris Buford
Managing Editor - Lindsey Johnston
VP of Production - Ron Klamert
Editor-in-Chief - Rob Tokar
Publisher - Mike Kiley
President and C.O.O. - John Parker
C.E.O. and Chief Creative Officer - Stuart Levy

A  Manga

TOKYOPOP Inc.
5900 Wilshire Blvd. Suite 2000
Los Angeles, CA 90036

E-mail: info@TOKYOPOP.com
Come visit us online at www.TOKYOPOP.com

ISBN: 1-59816-341-8
First TOKYOPOP printing: June 2006
10 9 8 7 6 5 4 3 2
Printed in the USA

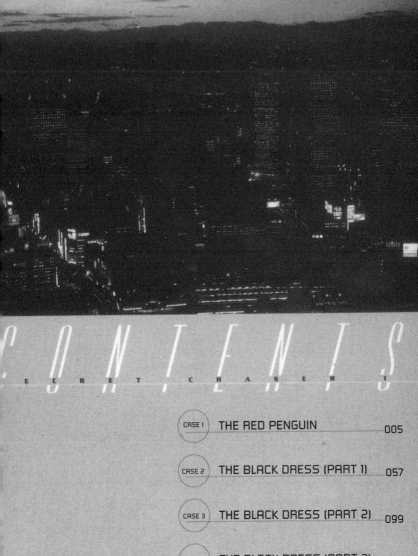

CONTENTS

SECRET CHASER 1

oto/ Nakada Masumi, Sekai Bunka Photo

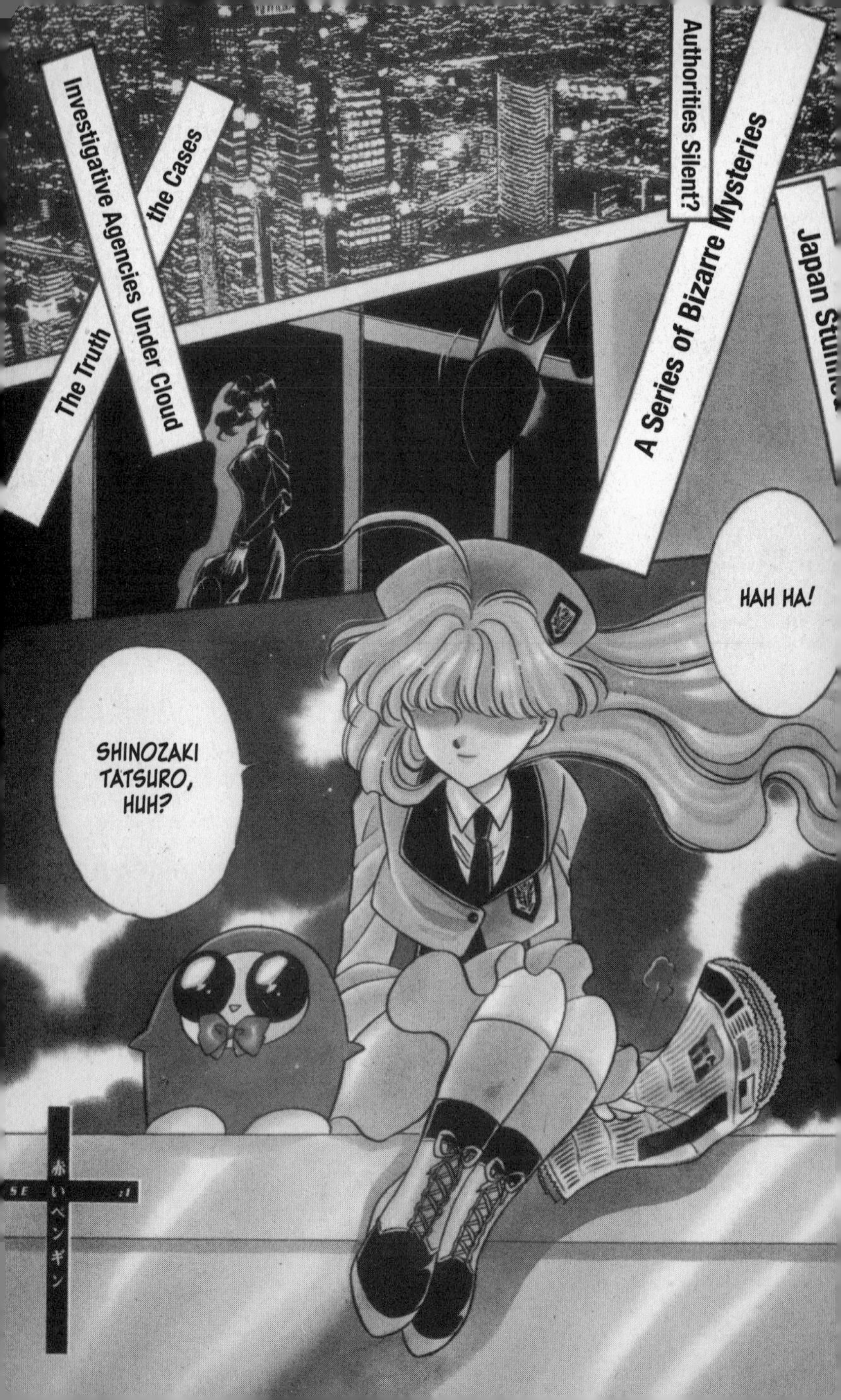
Japan Stunn
A Series of Bizarre Mysteries
Authorities Silent?
the Cases
Investigative Agencies Under Cloud
The Truth
HAH HA!
SHINOZAKI TATSURO, HUH?
赤いペンギン

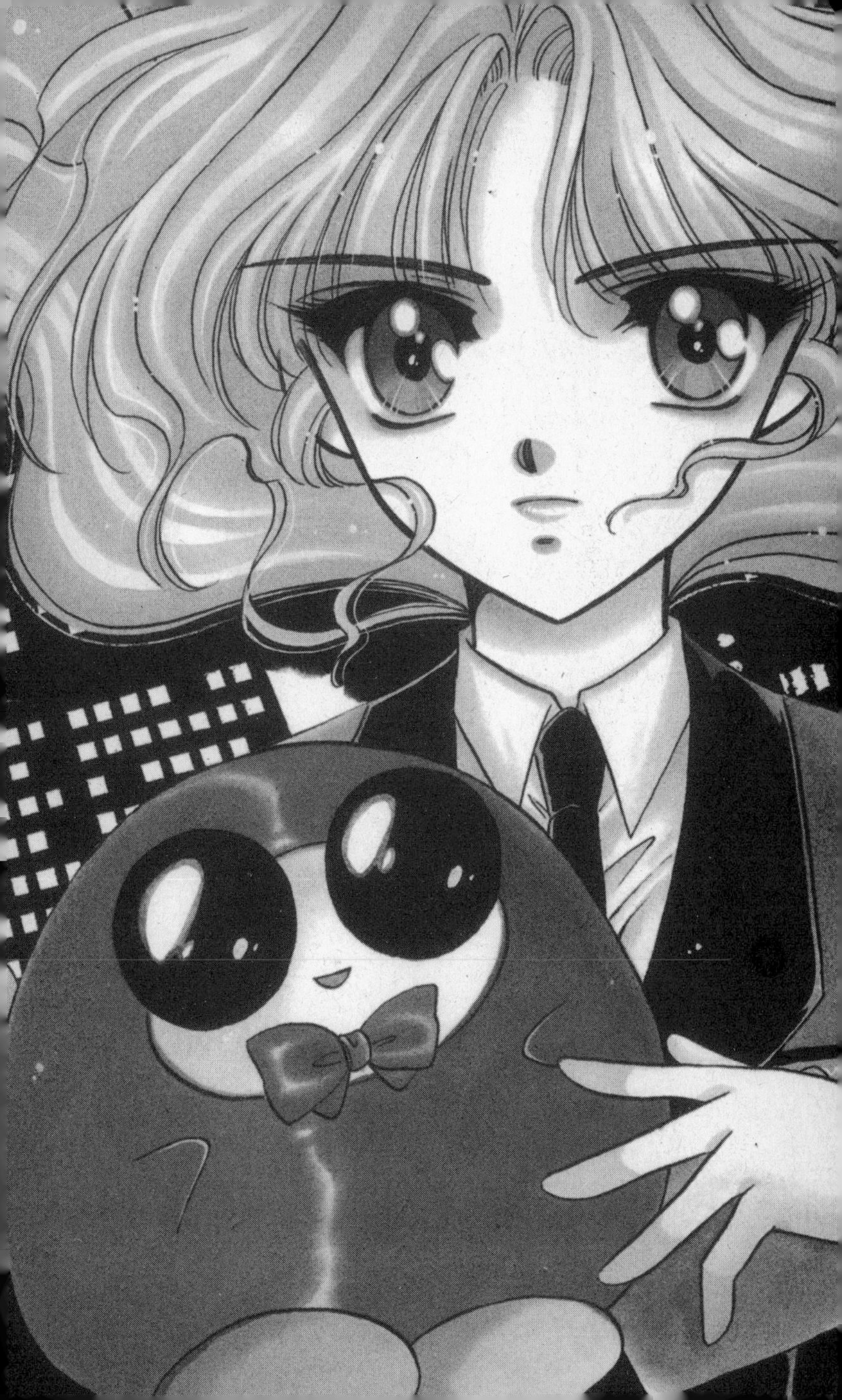

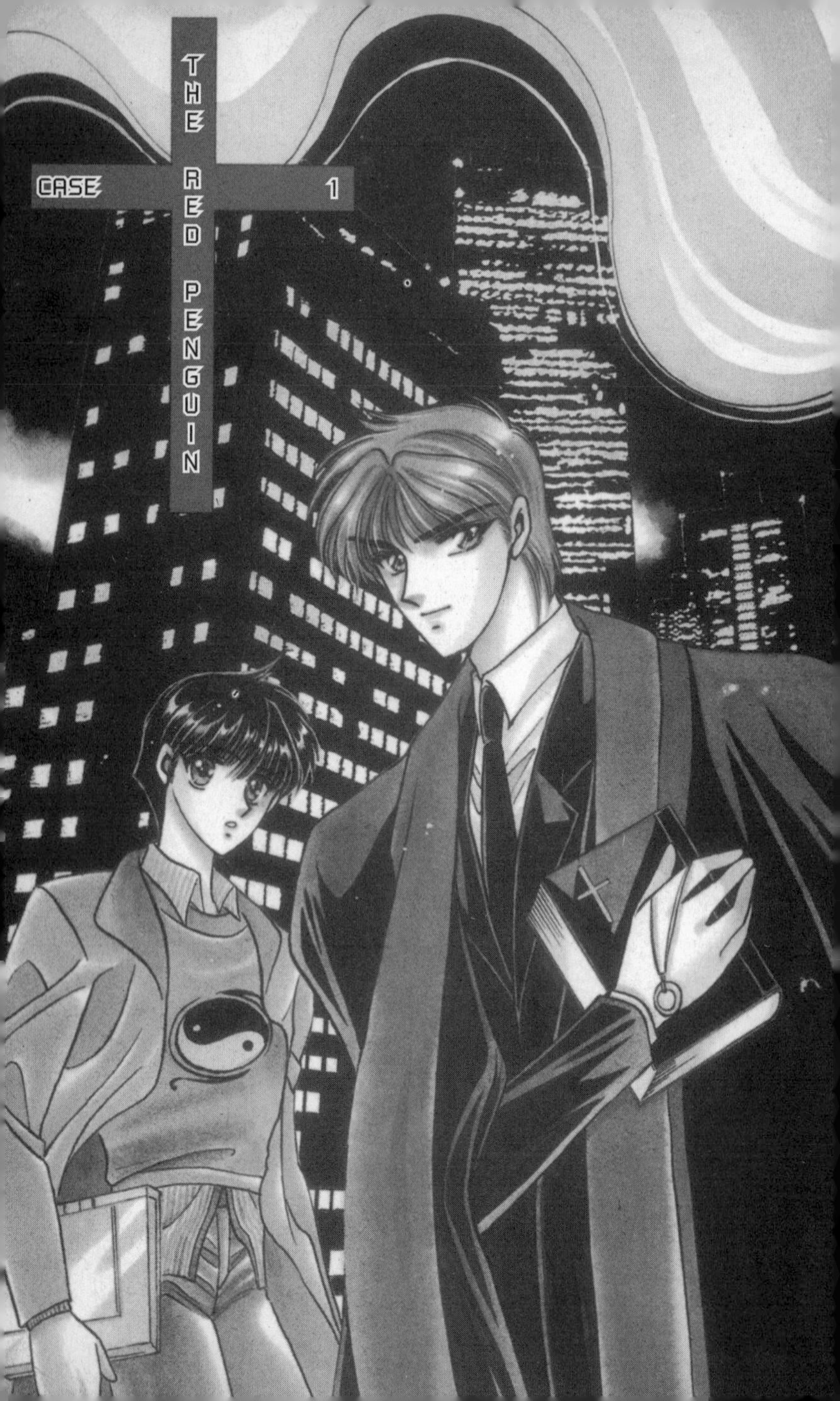
CASE 1
THE RED PENGUIN

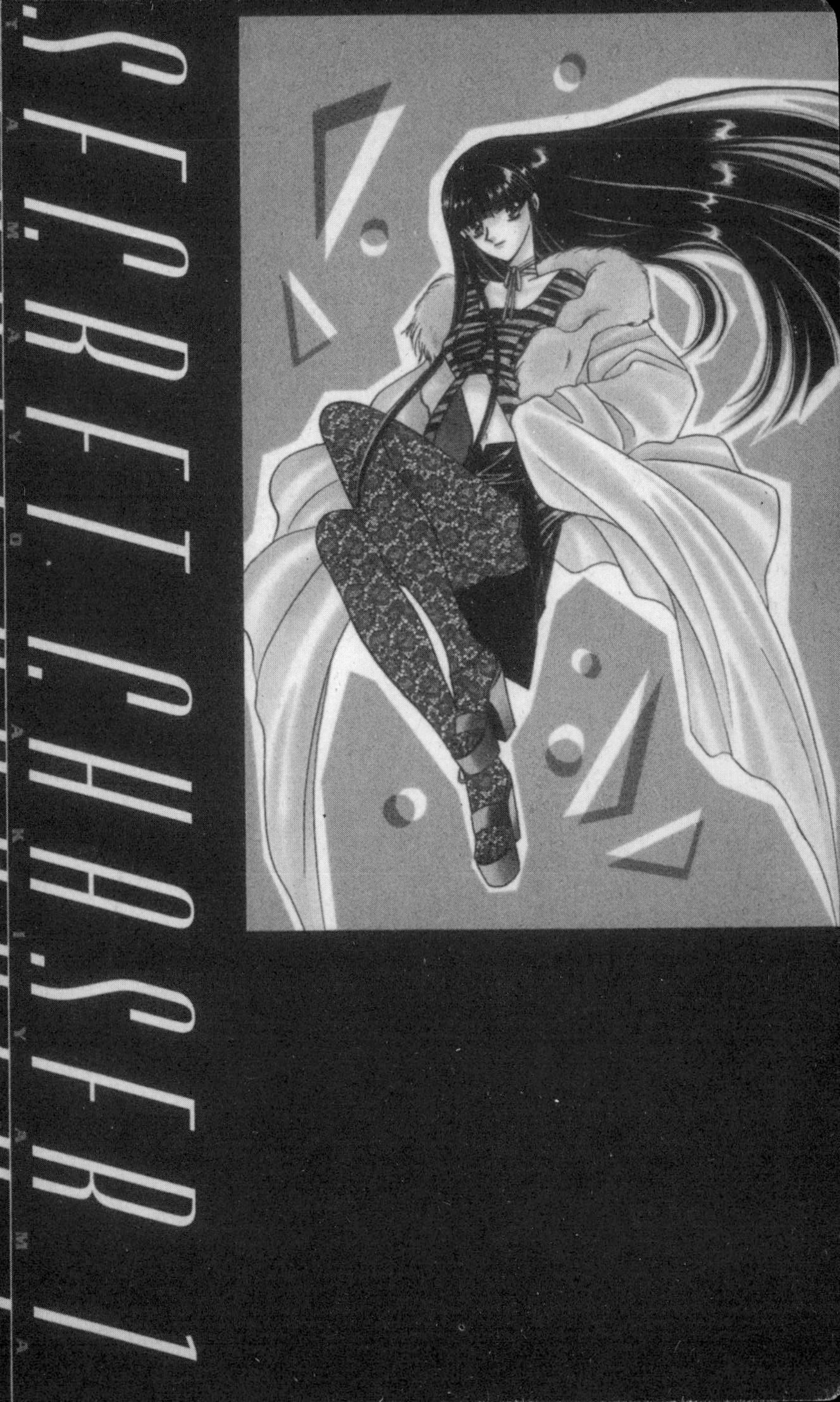

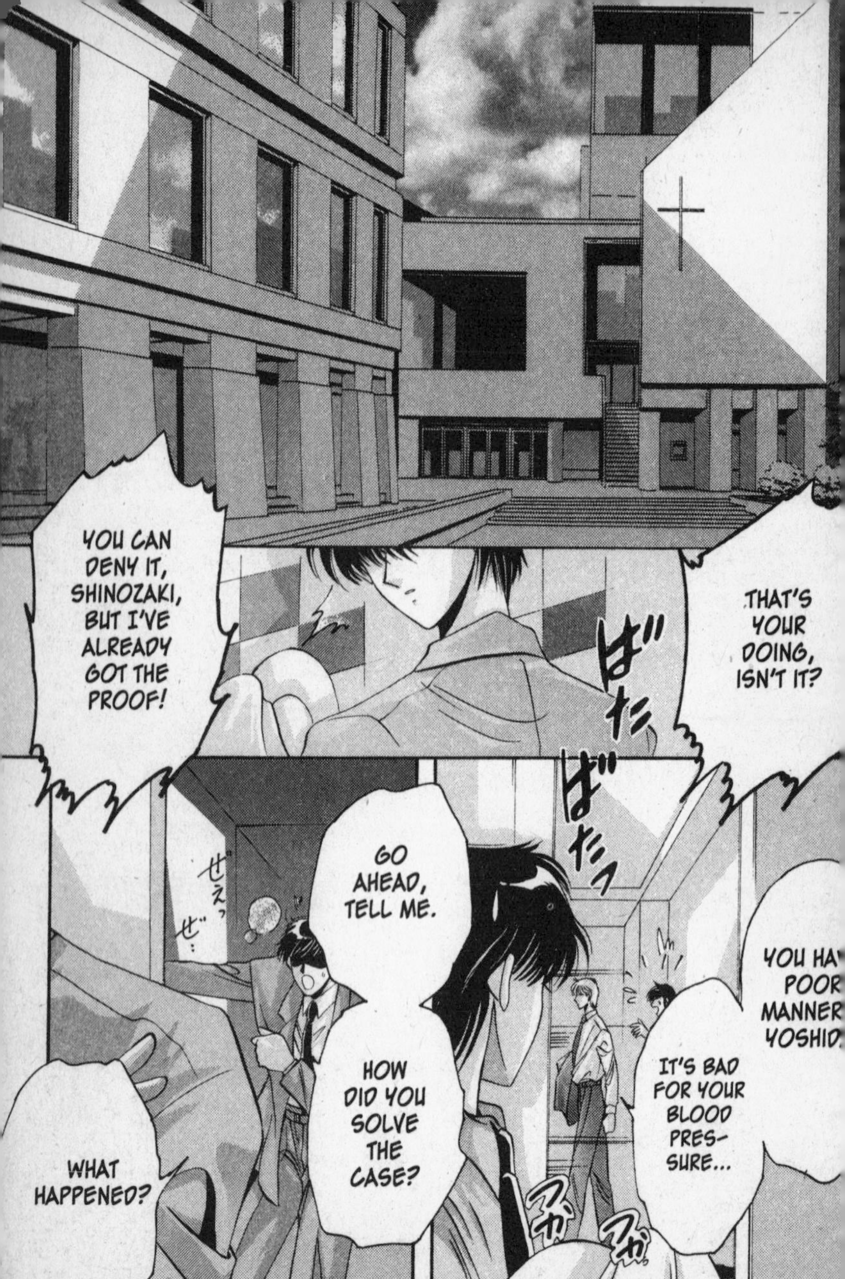

THAT'S YOUR DOING, ISN'T IT?
ばた ばたっ
YOU CAN DENY IT, SHINOZAKI, BUT I'VE ALREADY GOT THE PROOF!
YOU HA POOR MANNER YOSHID
IT'S BAD FOR YOUR BLOOD PRES-SURE...
GO AHEAD, TELL ME.
HOW DID YOU SOLVE THE CASE?
ぜえっ
ぜ
WHAT HAPPENED?

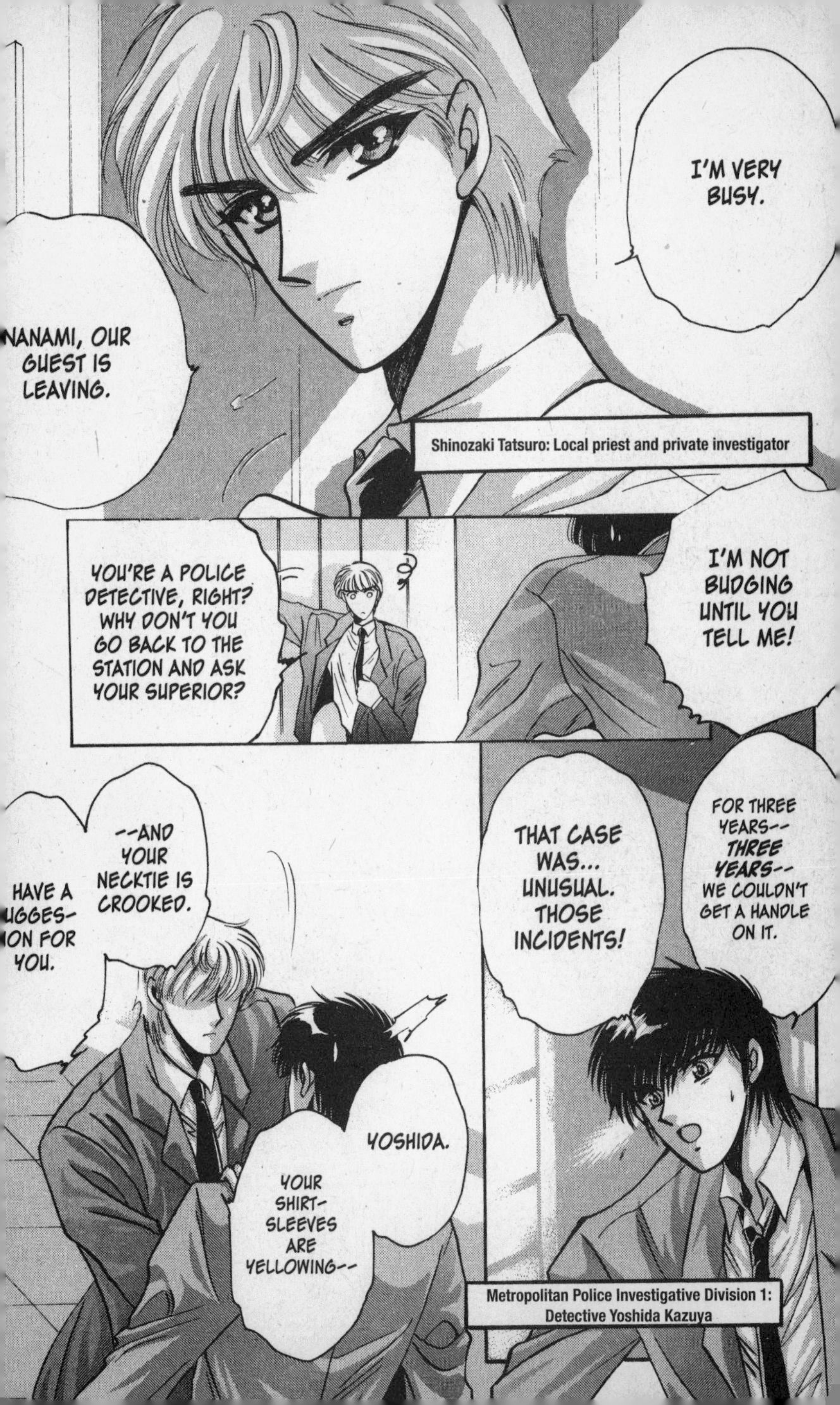

I'M VERY BUSY.
NANAMI, OUR GUEST IS LEAVING.
Shinozaki Tatsuro: Local priest and private investigator
I'M NOT BUDGING UNTIL YOU TELL ME!
YOU'RE A POLICE DETECTIVE, RIGHT? WHY DON'T YOU GO BACK TO THE STATION AND ASK YOUR SUPERIOR?
FOR THREE YEARS-- THREE YEARS-- WE COULDN'T GET A HANDLE ON IT.
THAT CASE WAS... UNUSUAL. THOSE INCIDENTS!
Metropolitan Police Investigative Division 1: Detective Yoshida Kazuya
YOSHIDA.
YOUR SHIRT-SLEEVES ARE YELLOWING--
--AND YOUR NECKTIE IS CROOKED.
HAVE A UGGES- ION FOR YOU.

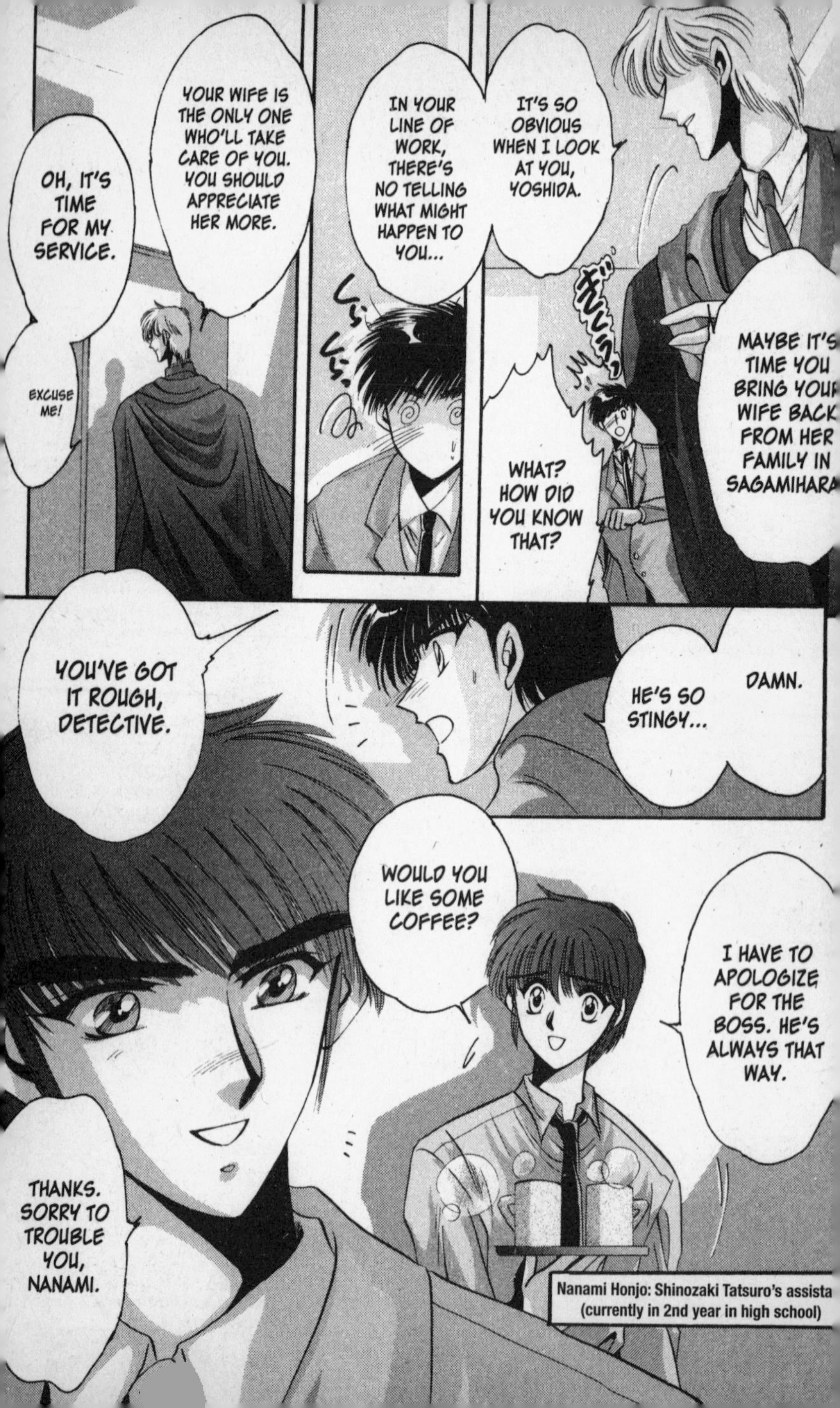
MAYBE IT'S TIME YOU BRING YOUR WIFE BACK FROM HER FAMILY IN SAGAMIHARA
WHAT? HOW DID YOU KNOW THAT?
IT'S SO OBVIOUS WHEN I LOOK AT YOU, YOSHIDA.
IN YOUR LINE OF WORK, THERE'S NO TELLING WHAT MIGHT HAPPEN TO YOU...
YOUR WIFE IS THE ONLY ONE WHO'LL TAKE CARE OF YOU. YOU SHOULD APPRECIATE HER MORE.
OH, IT'S TIME FOR MY SERVICE.
EXCUSE ME!
DAMN.
HE'S SO STINGY...
YOU'VE GOT IT ROUGH, DETECTIVE.
I HAVE TO APOLOGIZE FOR THE BOSS. HE'S ALWAYS THAT WAY.
WOULD YOU LIKE SOME COFFEE?
THANKS. SORRY TO TROUBLE YOU, NANAMI.
Nanami Honjo: Shinozaki Tatsuro's assista
(currently in 2nd year in high school)

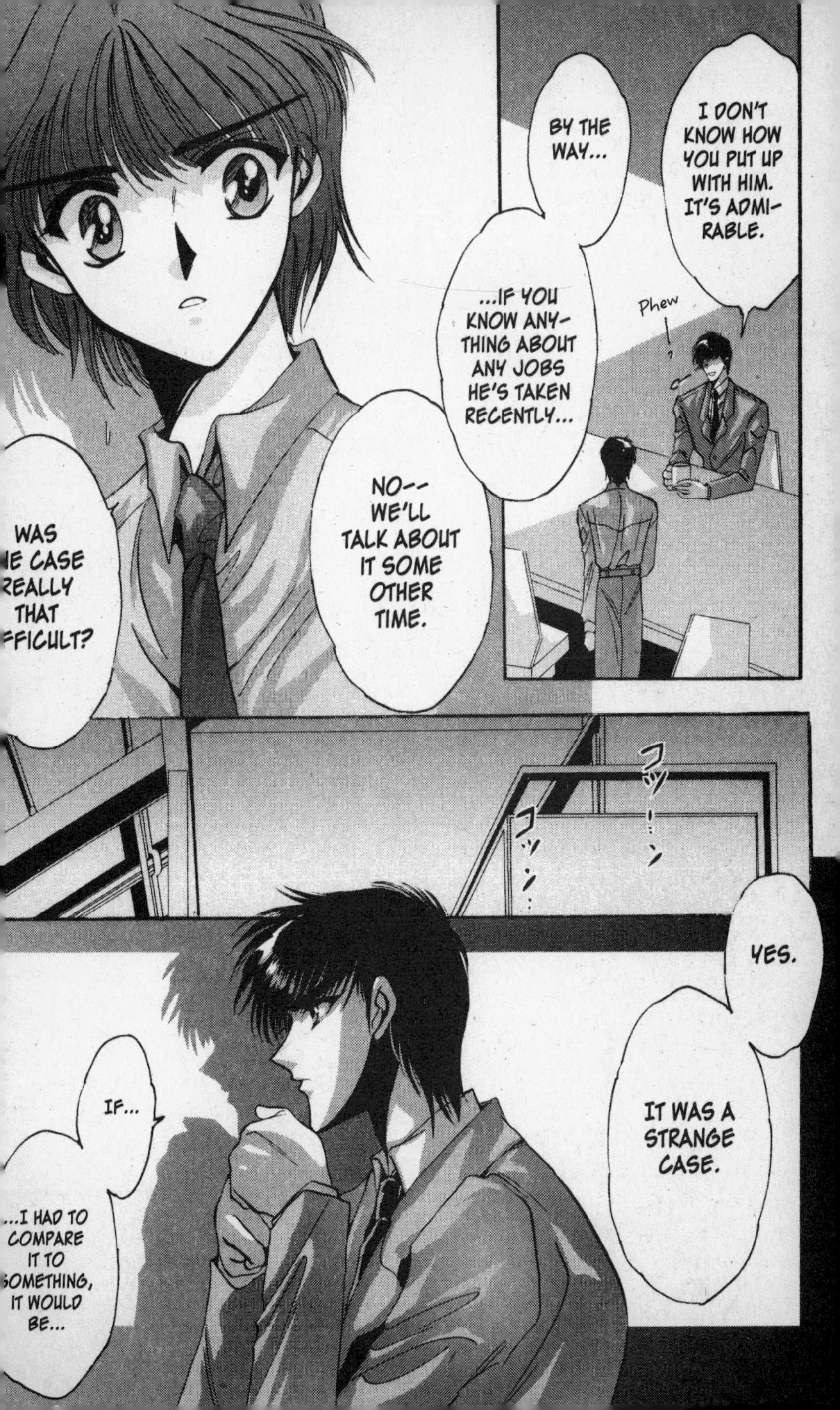

I DON'T KNOW HOW YOU PUT UP WITH HIM. IT'S ADMI-RABLE.
Phew
BY THE WAY...
...IF YOU KNOW ANY-THING ABOUT ANY JOBS HE'S TAKEN RECENTLY...
NO-- WE'LL TALK ABOUT IT SOME OTHER TIME.
WAS E CASE EALLY THAT FFICULT?
コツ…ン
コツ…ン
YES.
IT WAS A STRANGE CASE.
IF...
...I HAD TO COMPARE IT TO OMETHING, IT WOULD BE...

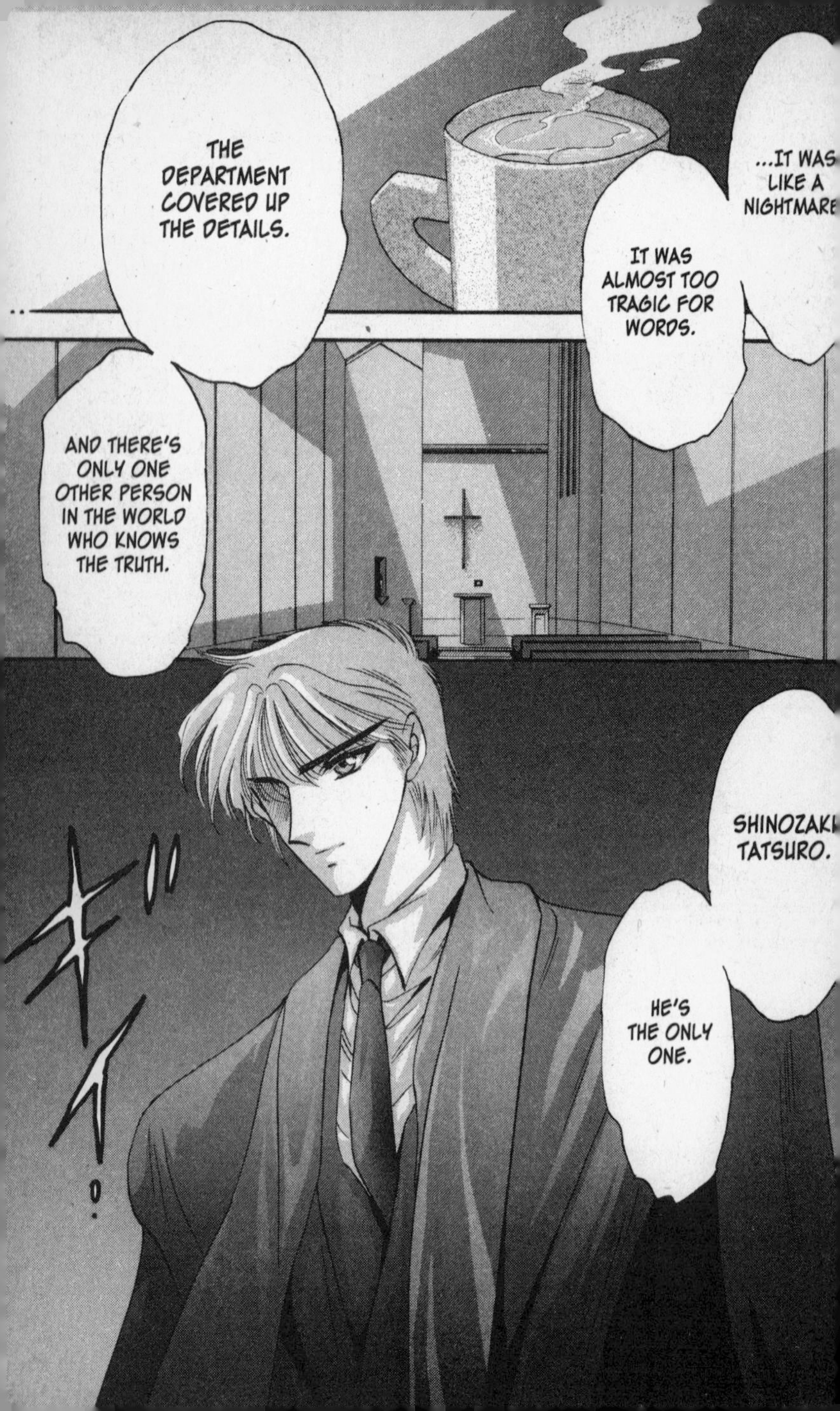

...IT WAS LIKE A NIGHTMARE
IT WAS ALMOST TOO TRAGIC FOR WORDS.
THE DEPARTMENT COVERED UP THE DETAILS.
AND THERE'S ONLY ONE OTHER PERSON IN THE WORLD WHO KNOWS THE TRUTH.
SHINOZAKI TATSURO.
HE'S THE ONLY ONE.

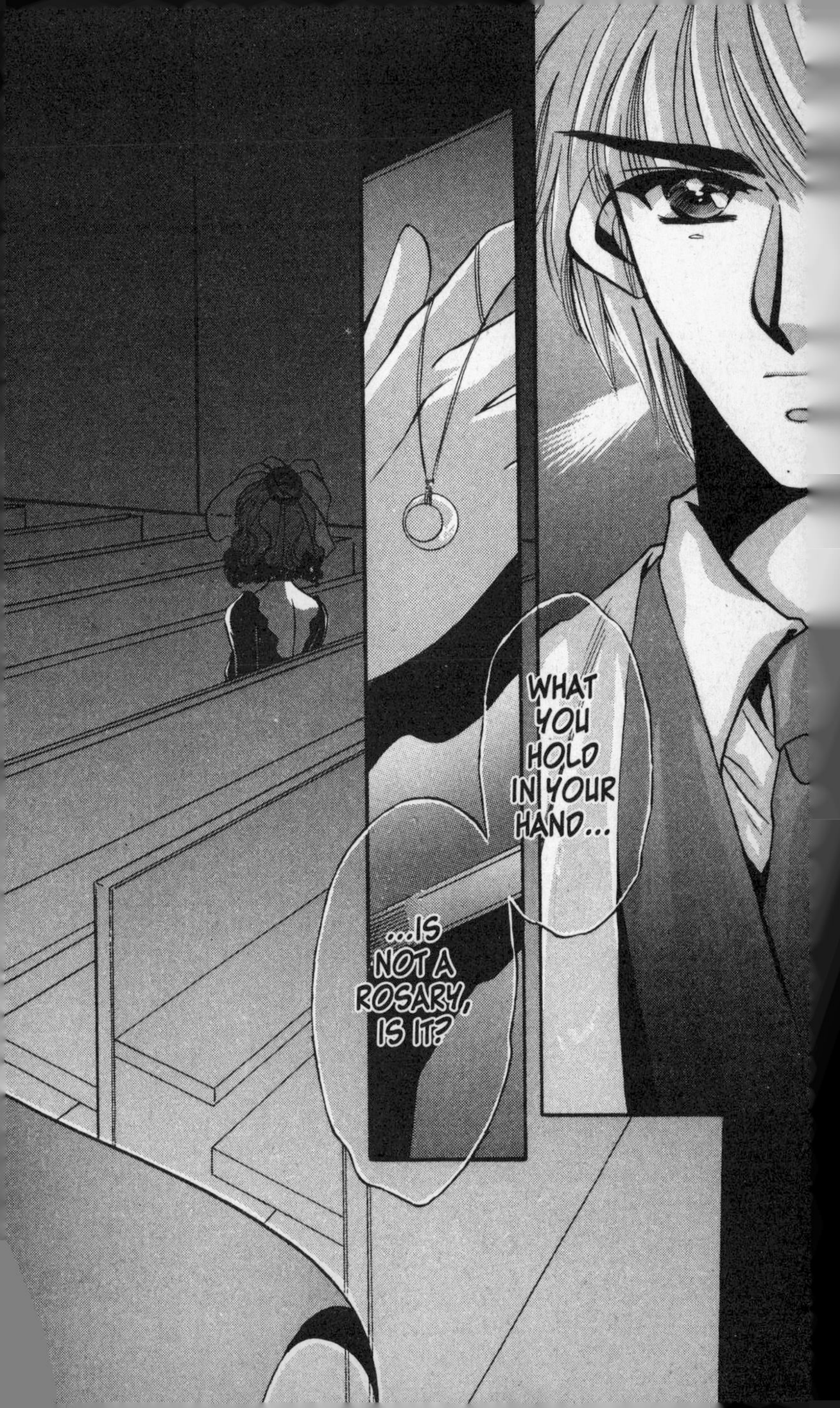
WHAT YOU HOLD IN YOUR HAND...
...IS NOT A ROSARY, IS IT?

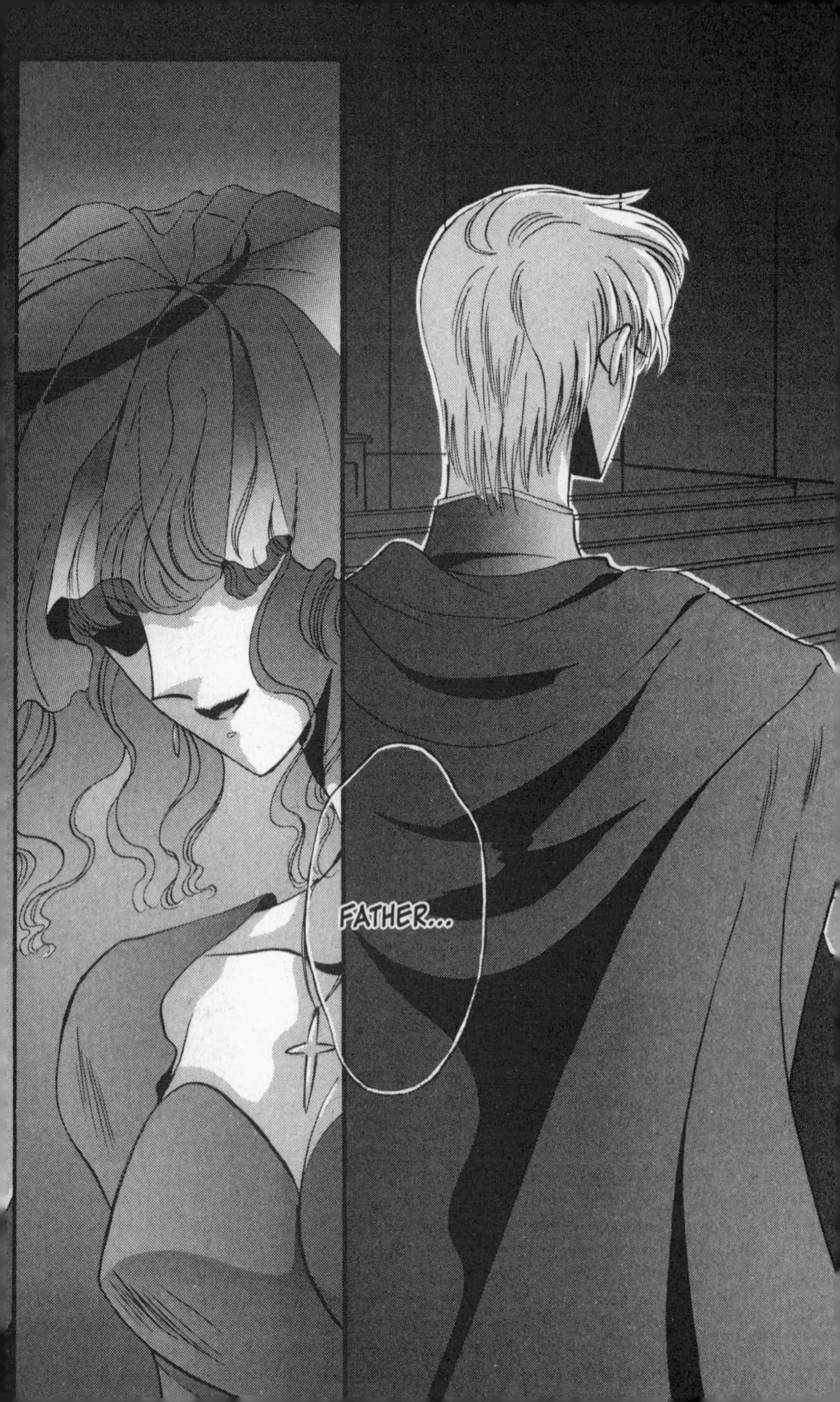
FATHER...

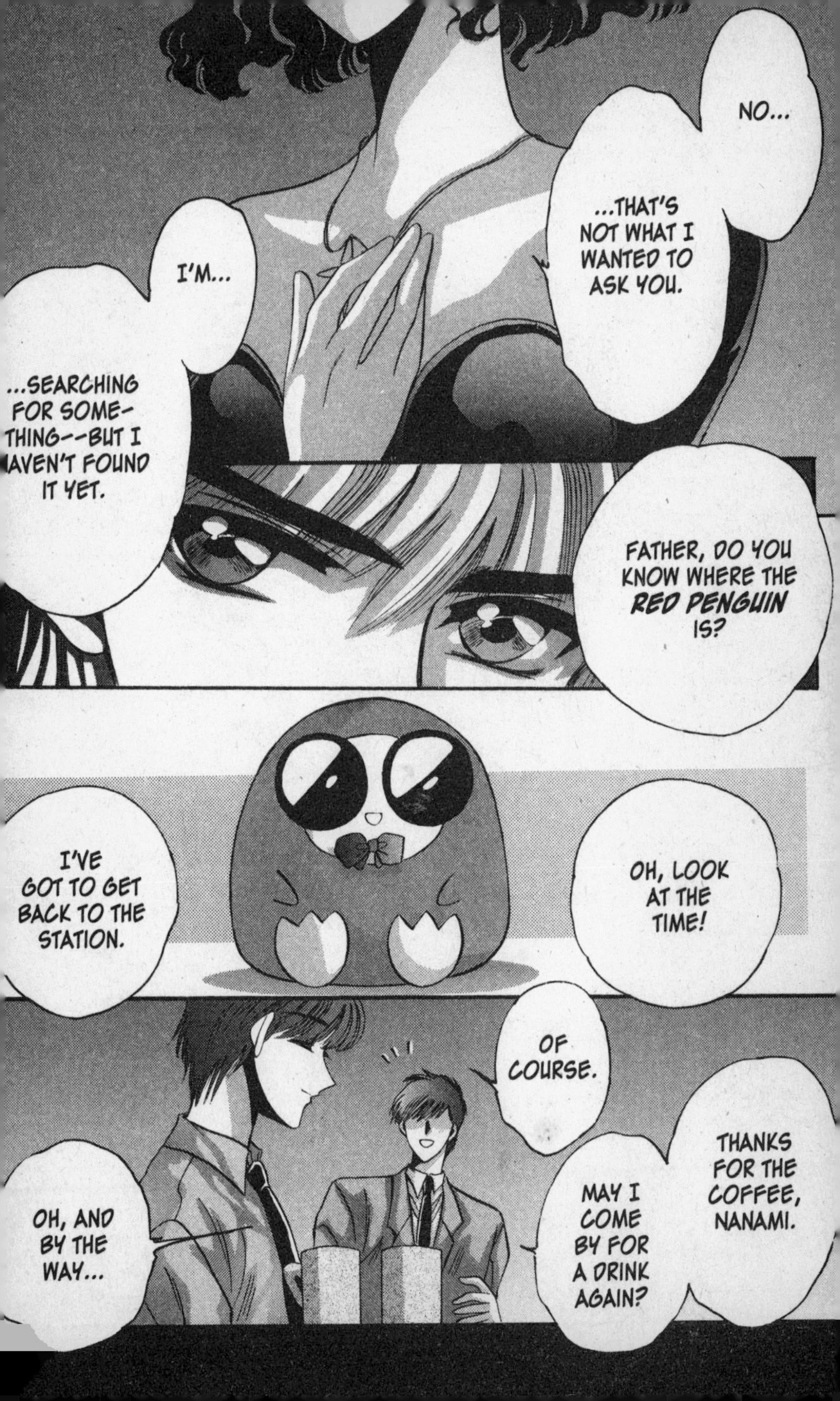
NO...
...THAT'S NOT WHAT I WANTED TO ASK YOU.
I'M...
...SEARCHING FOR SOME-THING--BUT I AVEN'T FOUND IT YET.
FATHER, DO YOU KNOW WHERE THE *RED PENGUIN* IS?
OH, LOOK AT THE TIME!
I'VE GOT TO GET BACK TO THE STATION.
THANKS FOR THE COFFEE, NANAMI.
MAY I COME BY FOR A DRINK AGAIN?
OF COURSE.
OH, AND BY THE WAY...

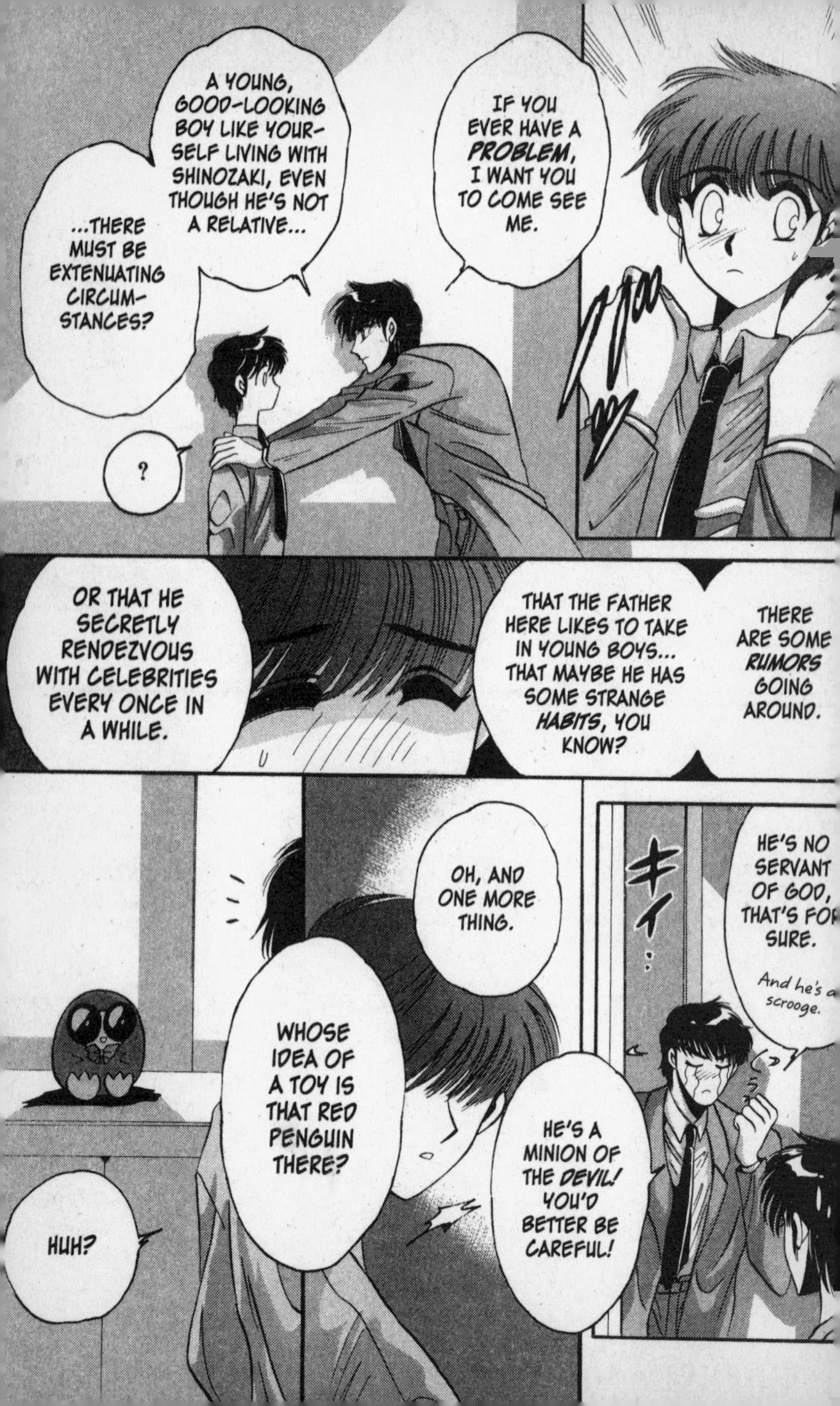
IF YOU EVER HAVE A PROBLEM, I WANT YOU TO COME SEE ME.
A YOUNG, GOOD-LOOKING BOY LIKE YOURSELF LIVING WITH SHINOZAKI, EVEN THOUGH HE'S NOT A RELATIVE...
...THERE MUST BE EXTENUATING CIRCUMSTANCES?
?
THERE ARE SOME RUMORS GOING AROUND.
THAT THE FATHER HERE LIKES TO TAKE IN YOUNG BOYS... THAT MAYBE HE HAS SOME STRANGE HABITS, YOU KNOW?
OR THAT HE SECRETLY RENDEZVOUS WITH CELEBRITIES EVERY ONCE IN A WHILE.
HE'S NO SERVANT OF GOD, THAT'S FOR SURE.
And he's a scrooge.
キイ…
HE'S A MINION OF THE DEVIL! YOU'D BETTER BE CAREFUL!
OH, AND ONE MORE THING.
WHOSE IDEA OF A TOY IS THAT RED PENGUIN THERE?
HUH?

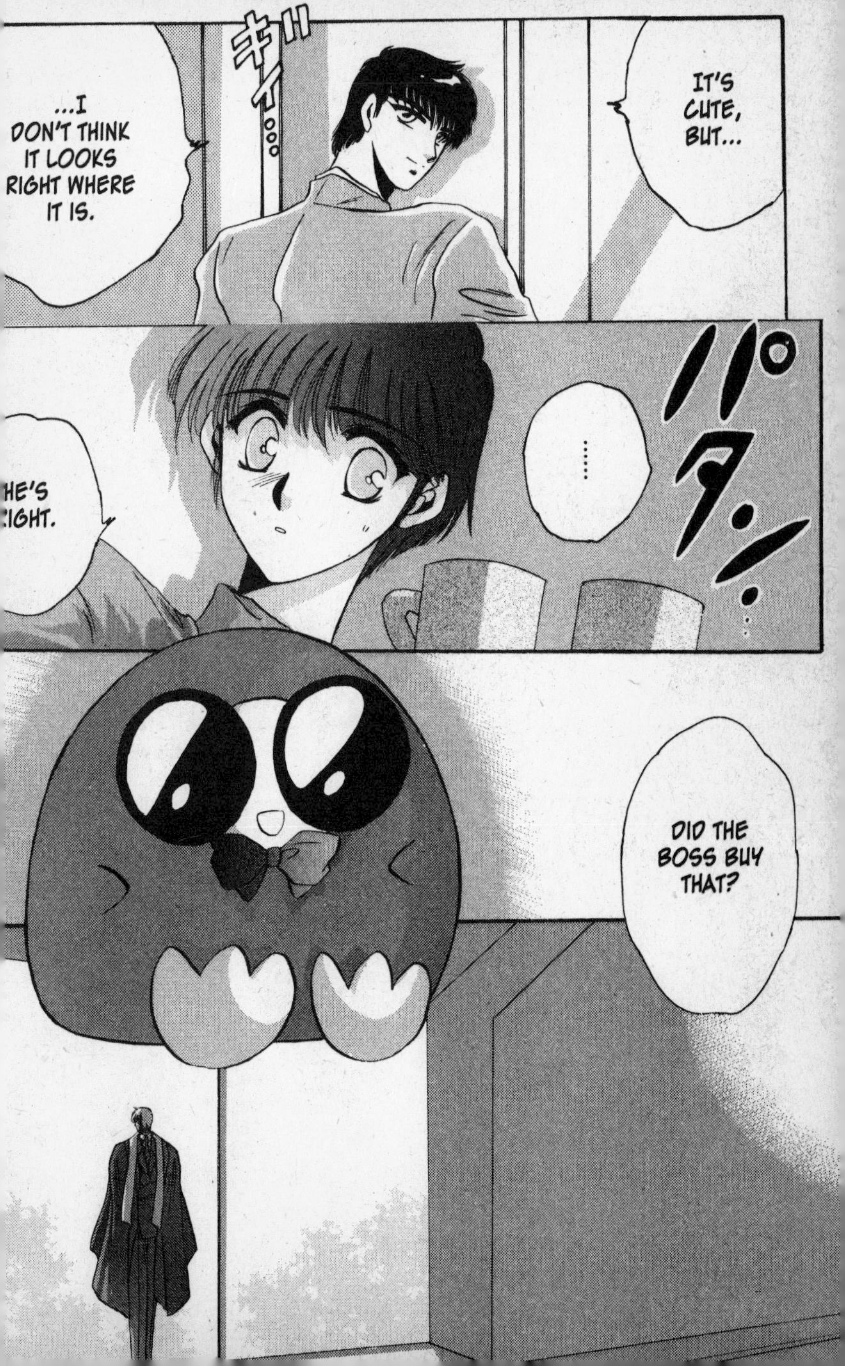
IT'S CUTE, BUT...
ギィ
...I DON'T THINK IT LOOKS RIGHT WHERE IT IS.
パタン!
......
HE'S
IGHT.
DID THE BOSS BUY THAT?

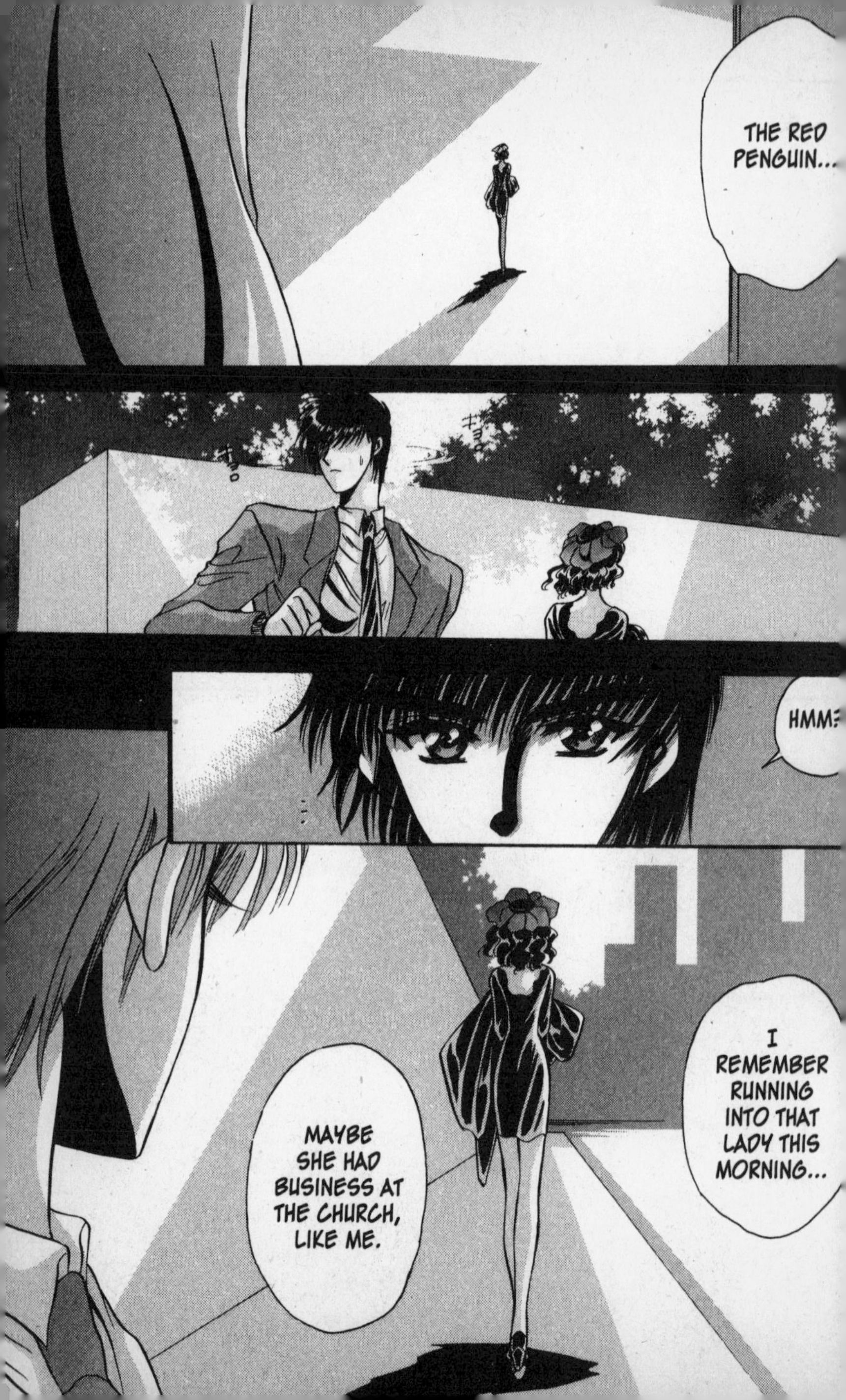
THE RED PENGUIN...
HMM?
I REMEMBER RUNNING INTO THAT LADY THIS MORNING...
MAYBE SHE HAD BUSINESS AT THE CHURCH, LIKE ME.

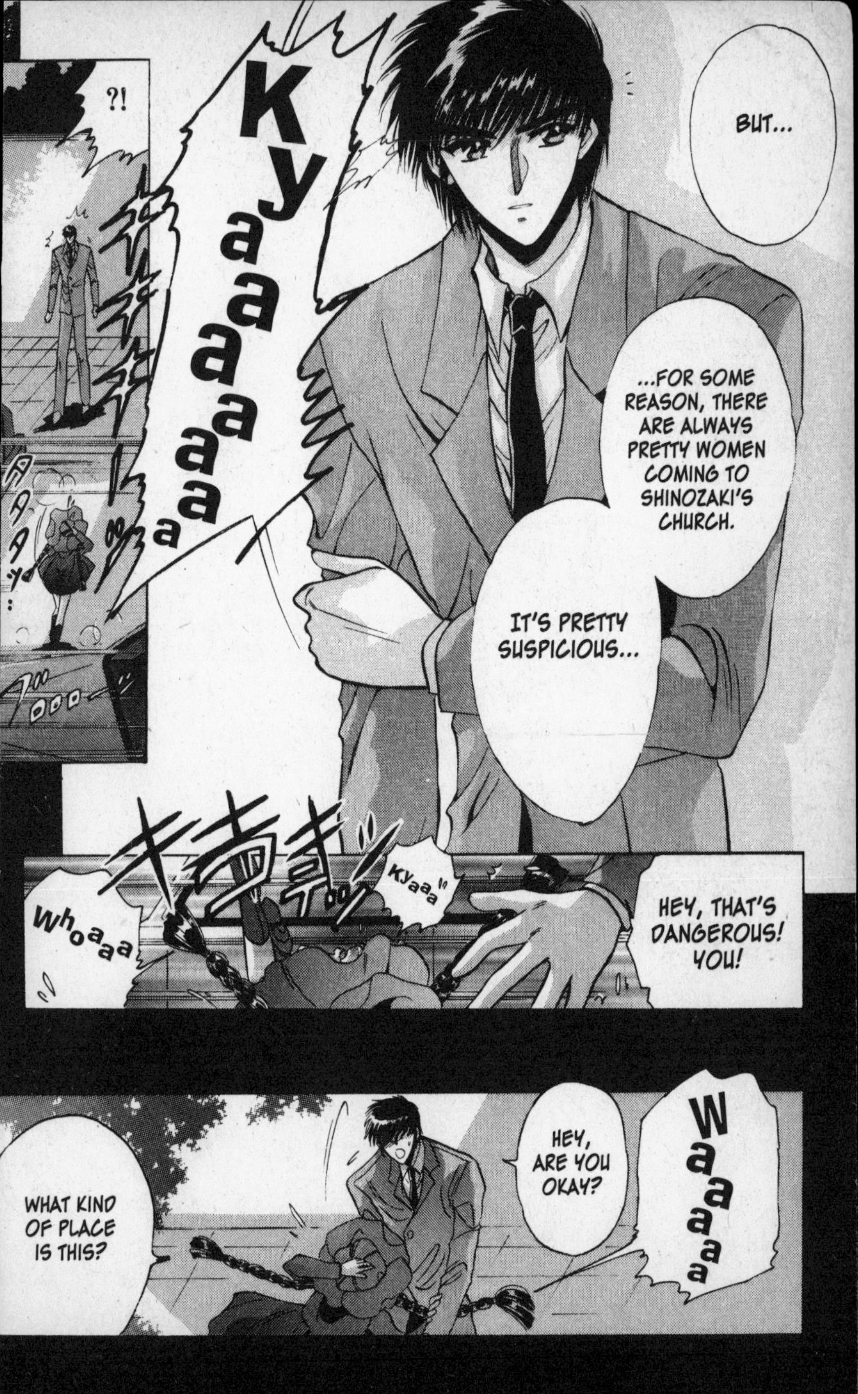
BUT...
...FOR SOME REASON, THERE ARE ALWAYS PRETTY WOMEN COMING TO SHINOZAKI'S CHURCH.
IT'S PRETTY SUSPICIOUS...
?!
Kyaaaaaaaa
HEY, THAT'S DANGEROUS! YOU!
Kyaaa
Whoaaa
Waaaaaa
HEY, ARE YOU OKAY?
WHAT KIND OF PLACE IS THIS?

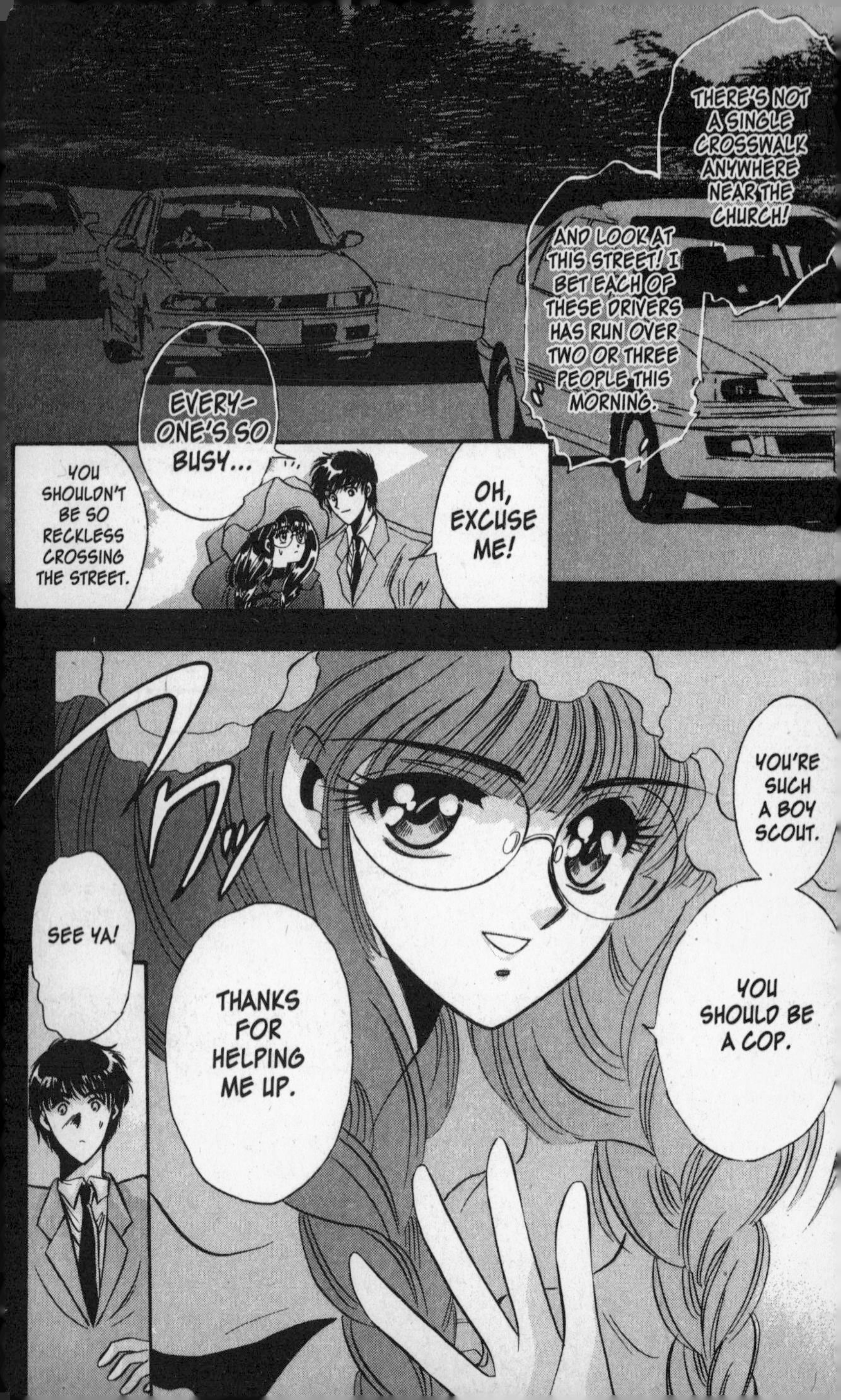
THERE'S NOT A SINGLE CROSSWALK ANYWHERE NEAR THE CHURCH!
AND LOOK AT THIS STREET! I BET EACH OF THESE DRIVERS HAS RUN OVER TWO OR THREE PEOPLE THIS MORNING.
EVERY-ONE'S SO BUSY...
OH, EXCUSE ME!
YOU SHOULDN'T BE SO RECKLESS CROSSING THE STREET.
YOU'RE SUCH A BOY SCOUT.
YOU SHOULD BE A COP.
THANKS FOR HELPING ME UP.
SEE YA!

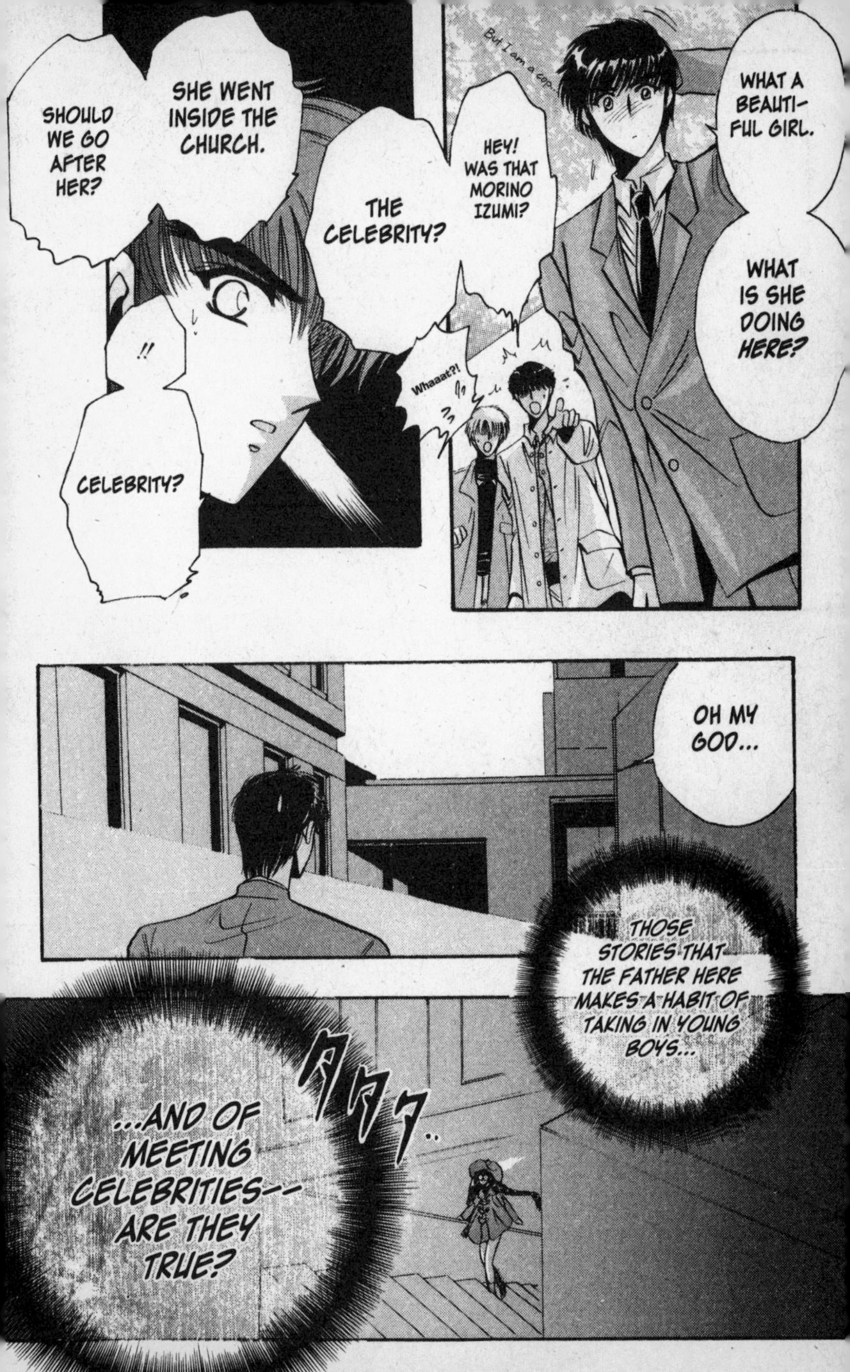
WHAT A BEAUTIFUL GIRL.
But I am a cop.
WHAT IS SHE DOING HERE?
HEY! WAS THAT MORINO IZUMI?
THE CELEBRITY?
Whaaat?!
SHE WENT INSIDE THE CHURCH.
SHOULD WE GO AFTER HER?
!!
CELEBRITY?
OH MY GOD...
THOSE STORIES THAT THE FATHER HERE MAKES A HABIT OF TAKING IN YOUNG BOYS...
...AND OF MEETING CELEBRITIES--ARE THEY TRUE?

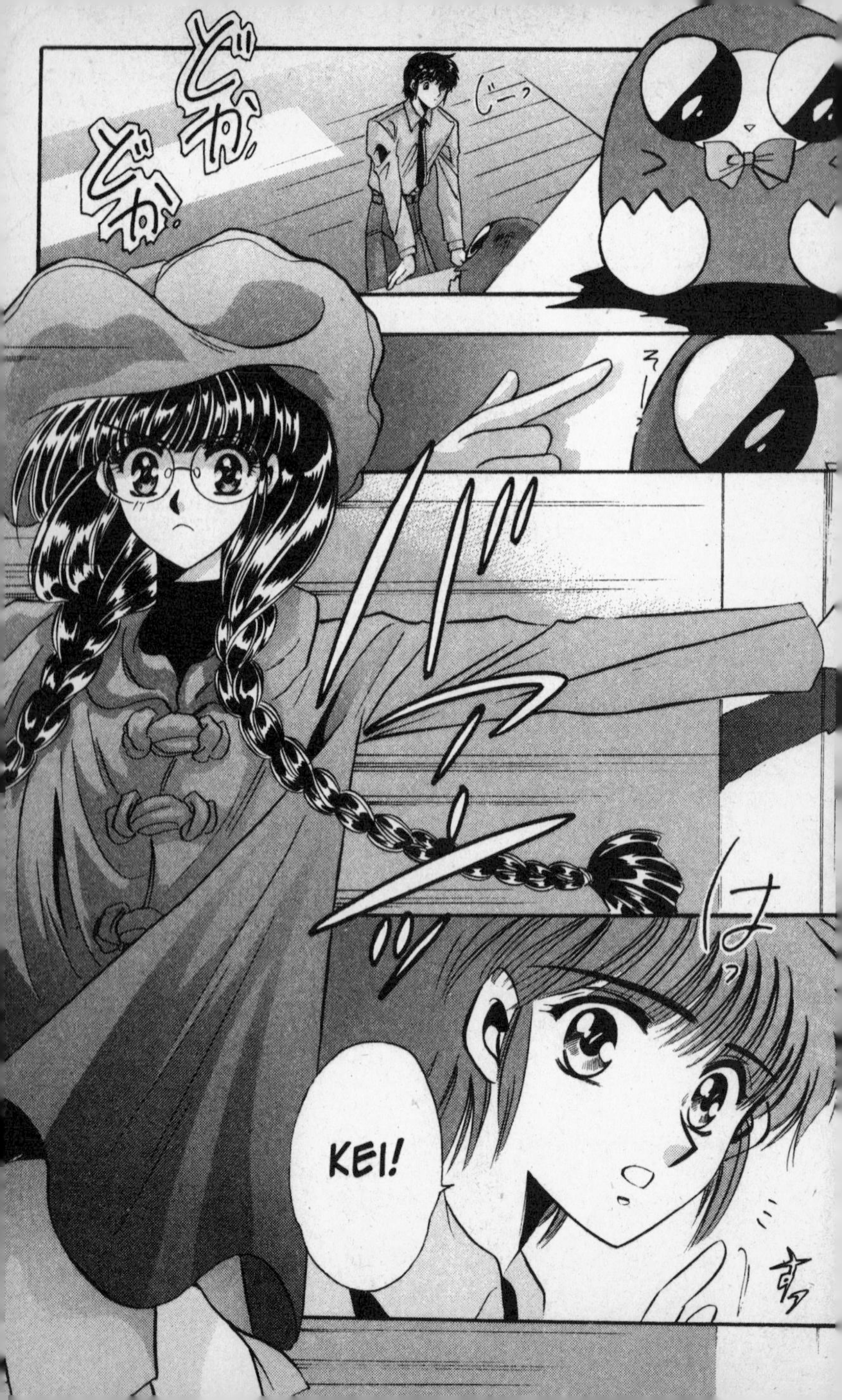

じーっ
そーっ
はっ
KEI!

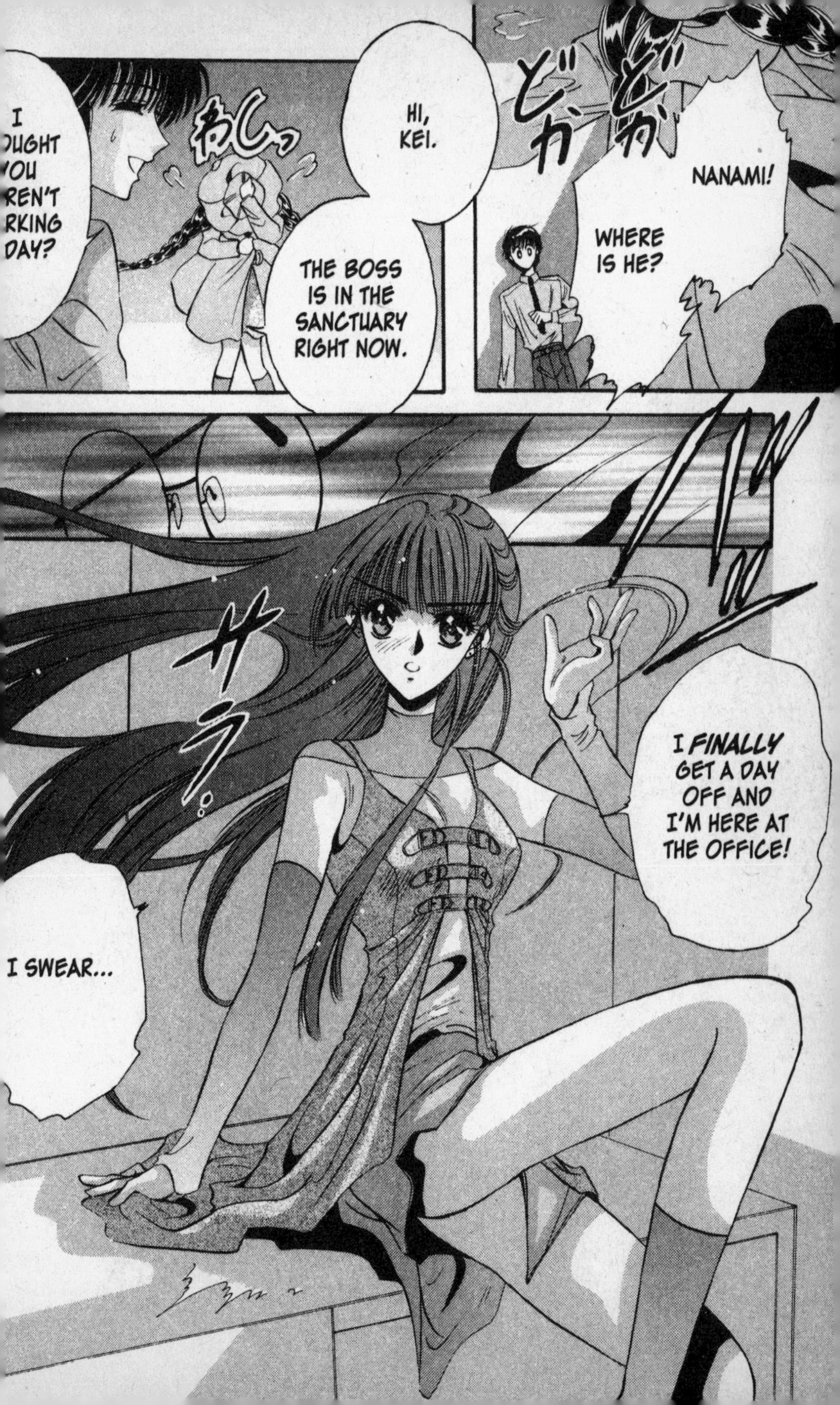
NANAMI!
WHERE IS HE?
HI, KEI.
THE BOSS IS IN THE SANCTUARY RIGHT NOW.
I OUGHT OU REN'T RKING DAY?
I *FINALLY* GET A DAY OFF AND I'M HERE AT THE OFFICE!
I SWEAR...

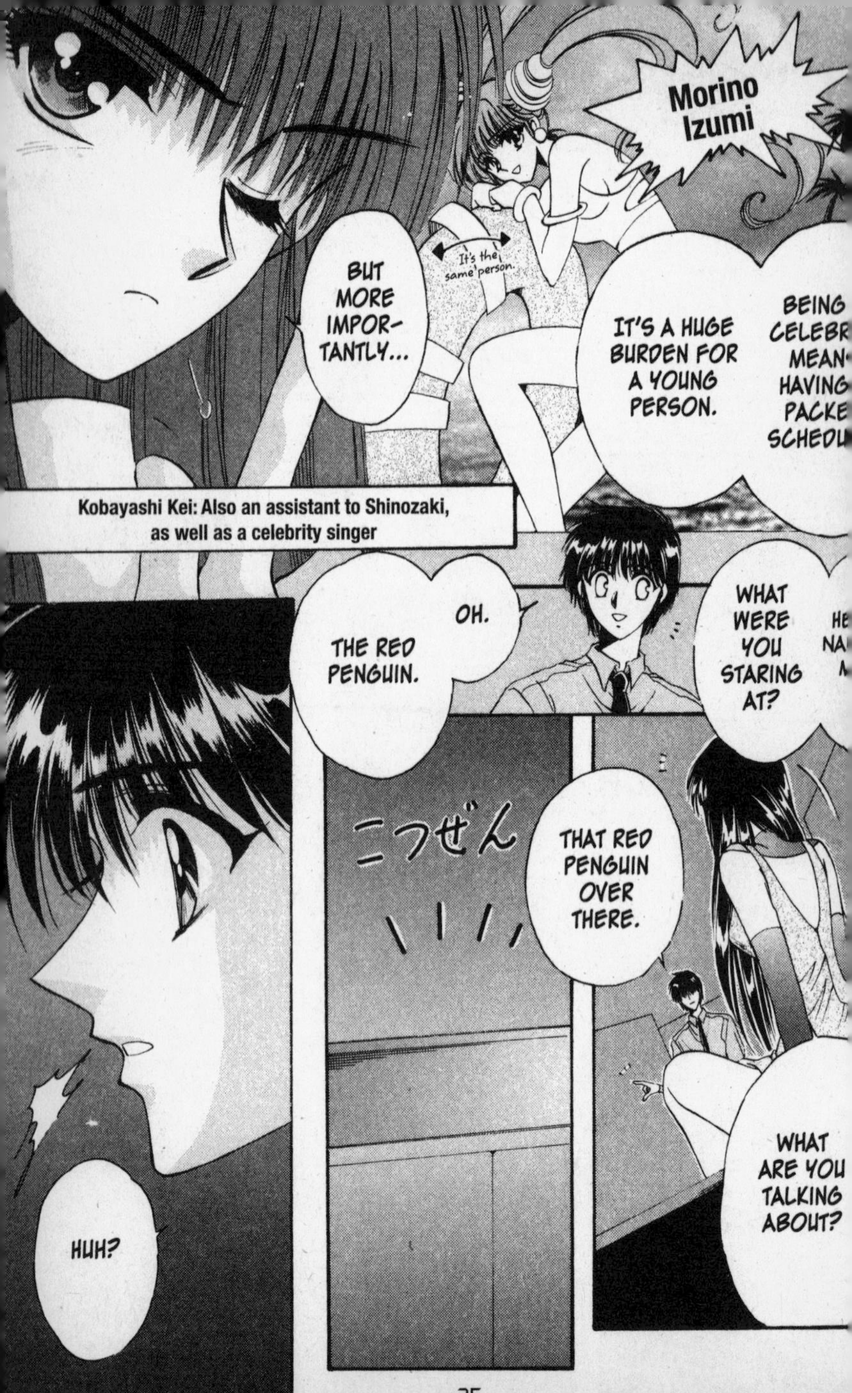
Morino Izumi
BEING CELEBR MEAN HAVING PACKE SCHEDU
IT'S A HUGE BURDEN FOR A YOUNG PERSON.
It's the same person.
BUT MORE IMPOR-TANTLY...
Kobayashi Kei: Also an assistant to Shinozaki, as well as a celebrity singer
WHAT WERE YOU STARING AT?
OH.
THE RED PENGUIN.
WHAT ARE YOU TALKING ABOUT?
THAT RED PENGUIN OVER THERE.
こつぜん
HUH?

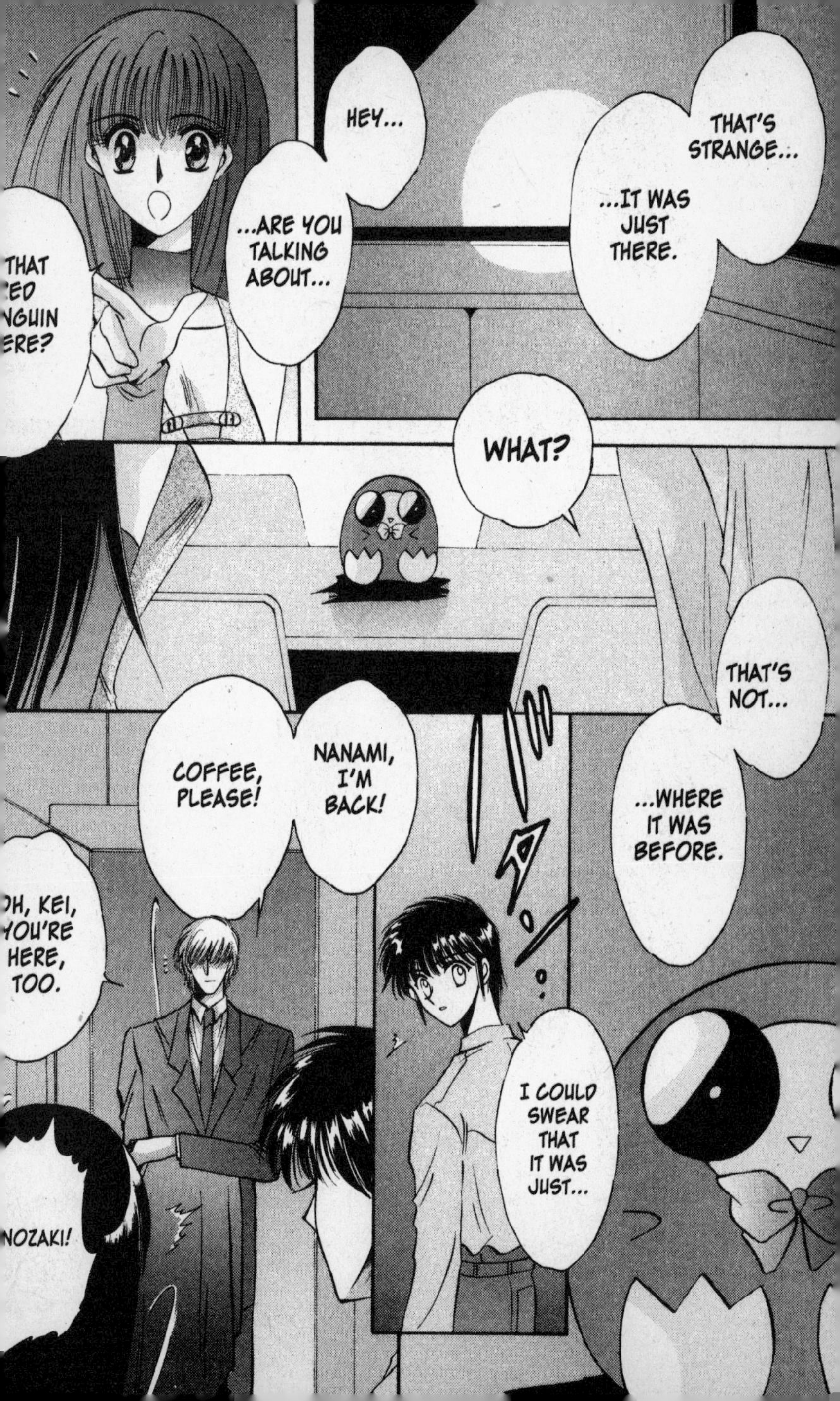
THAT'S STRANGE...
...IT WAS JUST THERE.
HEY...
...ARE YOU TALKING ABOUT...
THAT ED NGUIN ERE?
WHAT?
THAT'S NOT...
...WHERE IT WAS BEFORE.
I COULD SWEAR THAT IT WAS JUST...
NANAMI, I'M BACK!
COFFEE, PLEASE!
H, KEI, OU'RE HERE, TOO.
NOZAKI!

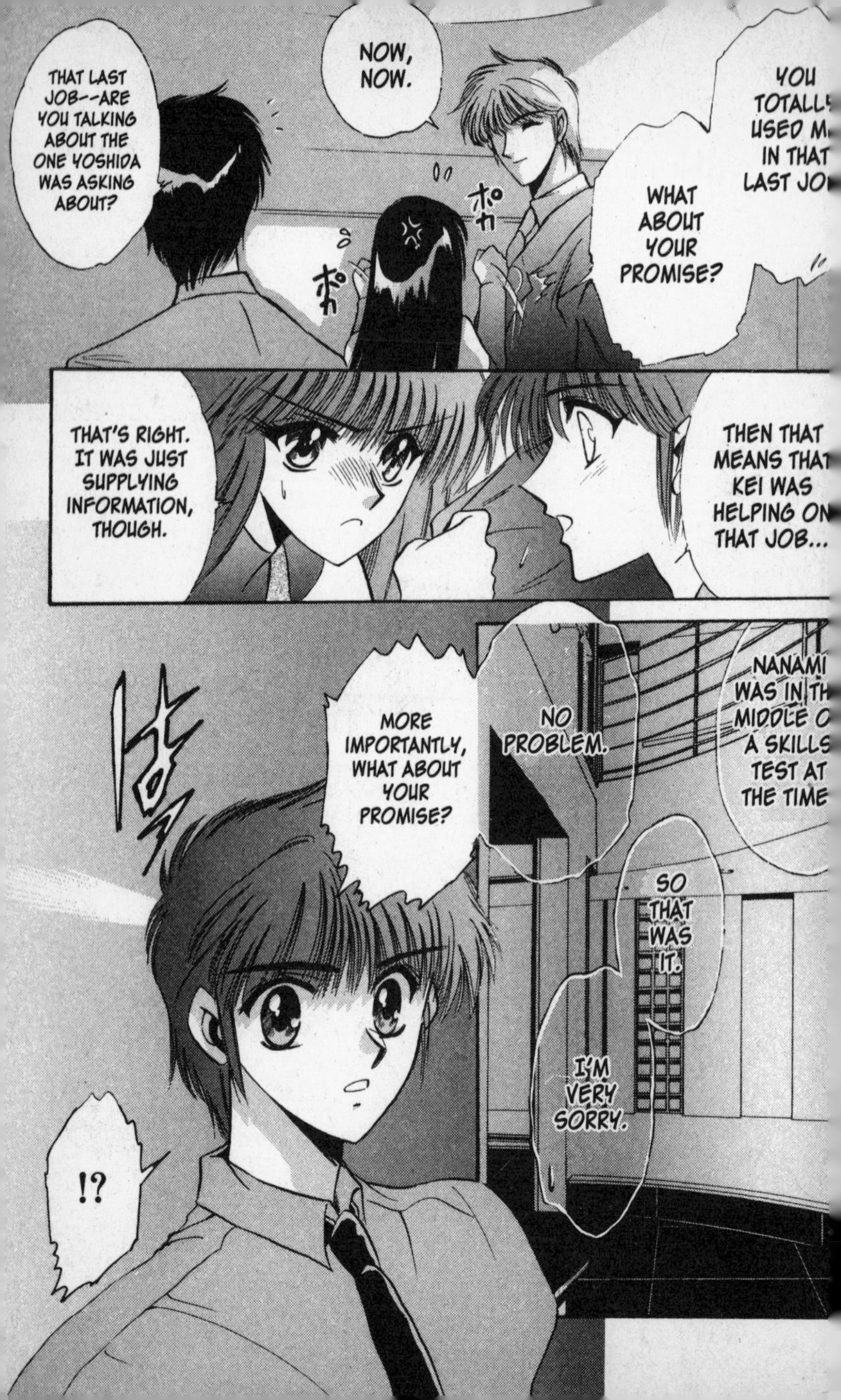
YOU TOTALL USED M IN THAT LAST JO
WHAT ABOUT YOUR PROMISE?
NOW, NOW.
ポカ
ポカ
THAT LAST JOB--ARE YOU TALKING ABOUT THE ONE YOSHIDA WAS ASKING ABOUT?
THEN THAT MEANS THA KEI WAS HELPING ON THAT JOB...
THAT'S RIGHT. IT WAS JUST SUPPLYING INFORMATION, THOUGH.
NANAMI WAS IN TH MIDDLE O A SKILLS TEST AT THE TIME
NO PROBLEM.
SO THAT WAS IT.
I'M VERY SORRY.
MORE IMPORTANTLY, WHAT ABOUT YOUR PROMISE?
はっ
!?

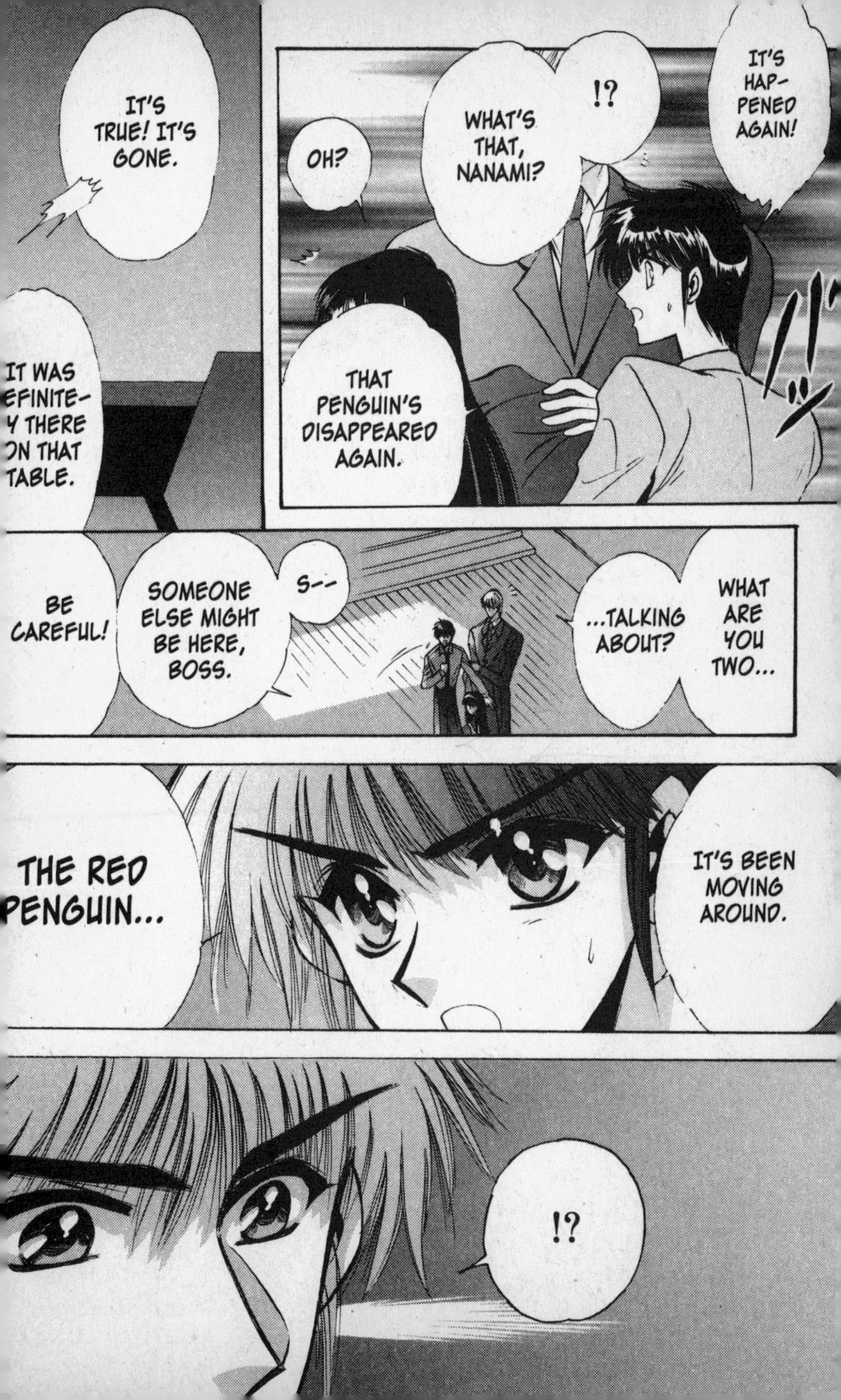
IT'S HAPPENED AGAIN!
!?
WHAT'S THAT, NANAMI?
OH?
THAT PENGUIN'S DISAPPEARED AGAIN.
IT'S TRUE! IT'S GONE.
IT WAS EFINITE-Y THERE ON THAT TABLE.
WHAT ARE YOU TWO...
...TALKING ABOUT?
S--
SOMEONE ELSE MIGHT BE HERE, BOSS.
BE CAREFUL!
IT'S BEEN MOVING AROUND.
THE RED PENGUIN...
!?

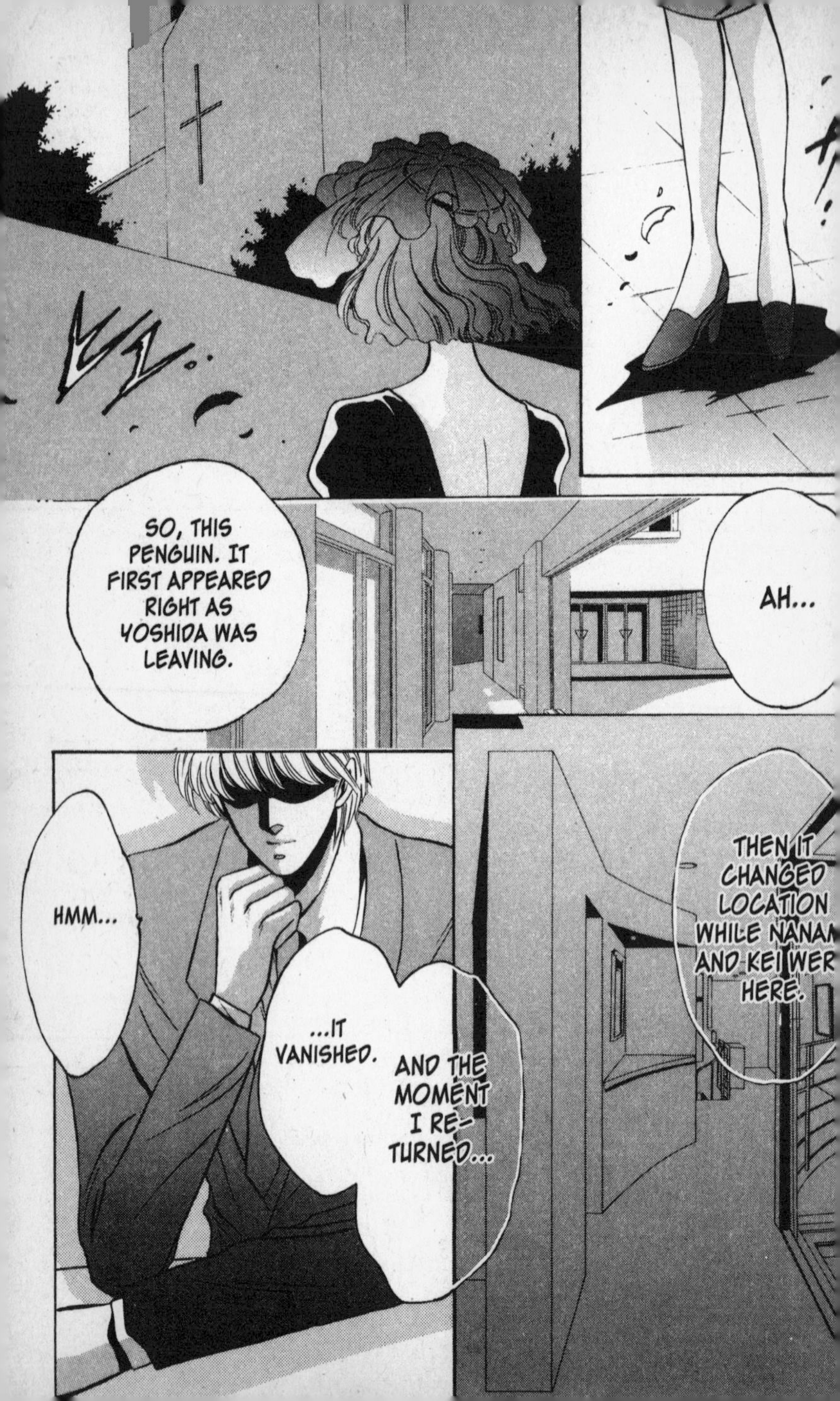
AH...
SO, THIS PENGUIN. IT FIRST APPEARED RIGHT AS YOSHIDA WAS LEAVING.
THEN IT CHANGED LOCATION WHILE NANAM AND KEI WER HERE.
AND THE MOMENT I RE-TURNED...
...IT VANISHED.
HMM...

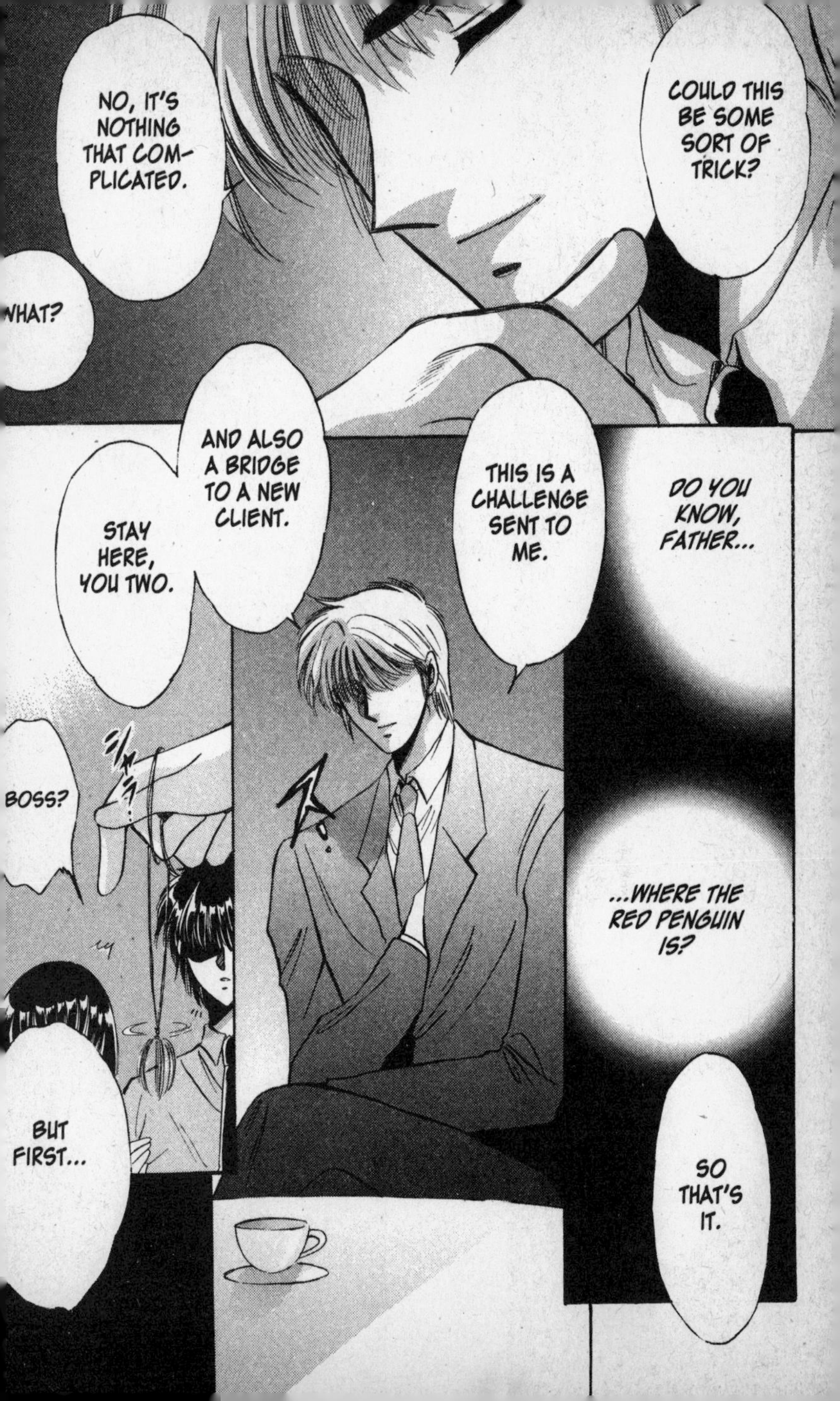
COULD THIS BE SOME SORT OF TRICK?
NO, IT'S NOTHING THAT COM-PLICATED.
WHAT?
DO YOU KNOW, FATHER...
...WHERE THE RED PENGUIN IS?
SO THAT'S IT.
THIS IS A CHALLENGE SENT TO ME.
AND ALSO A BRIDGE TO A NEW CLIENT.
STAY HERE, YOU TWO.
BOSS?
BUT FIRST...

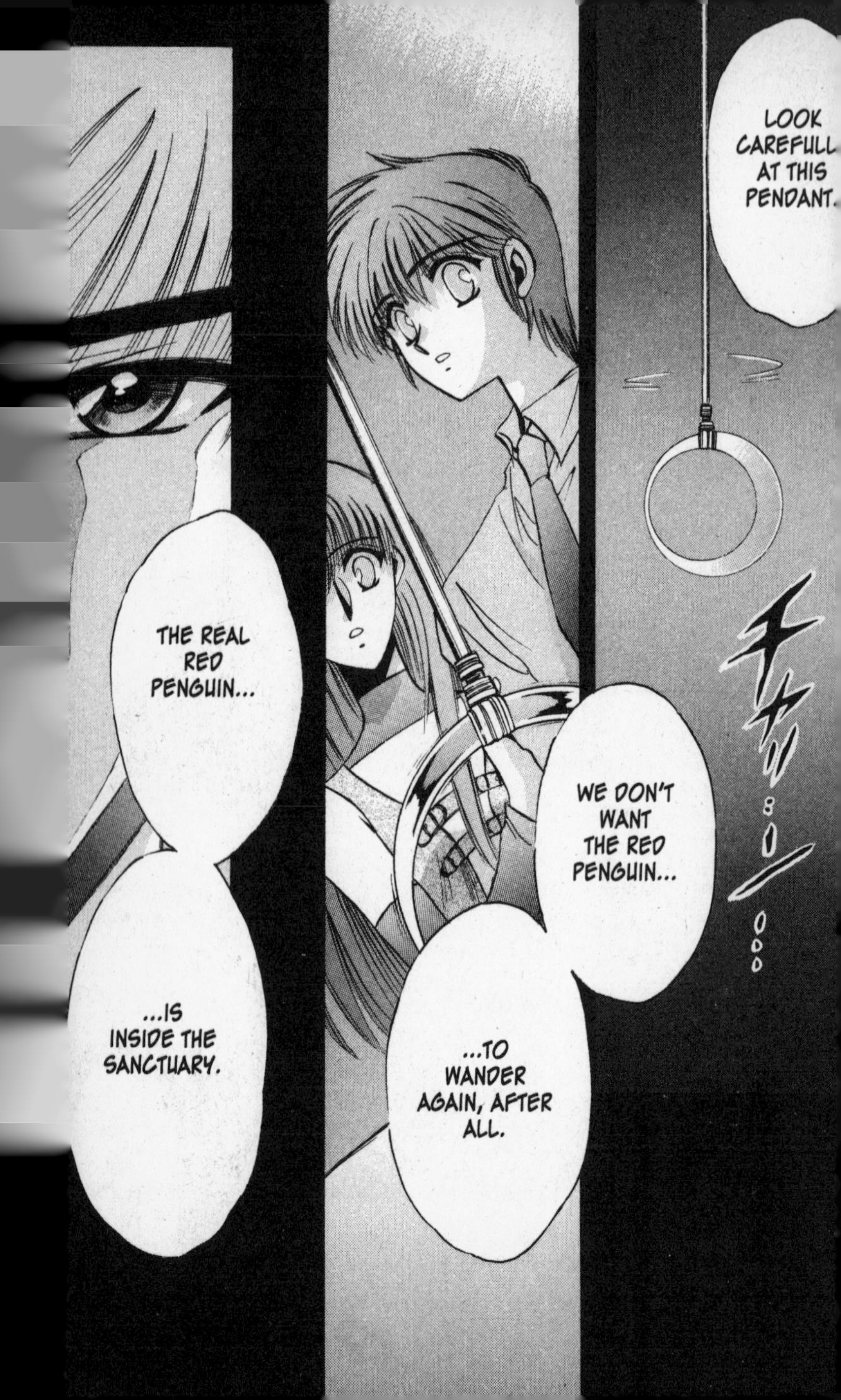
LOOK CAREFULL AT THIS PENDANT.
チャリ…
WE DON'T WANT THE RED PENGUIN...
...TO WANDER AGAIN, AFTER ALL.
THE REAL RED PENGUIN...
...IS INSIDE THE SANCTUARY.

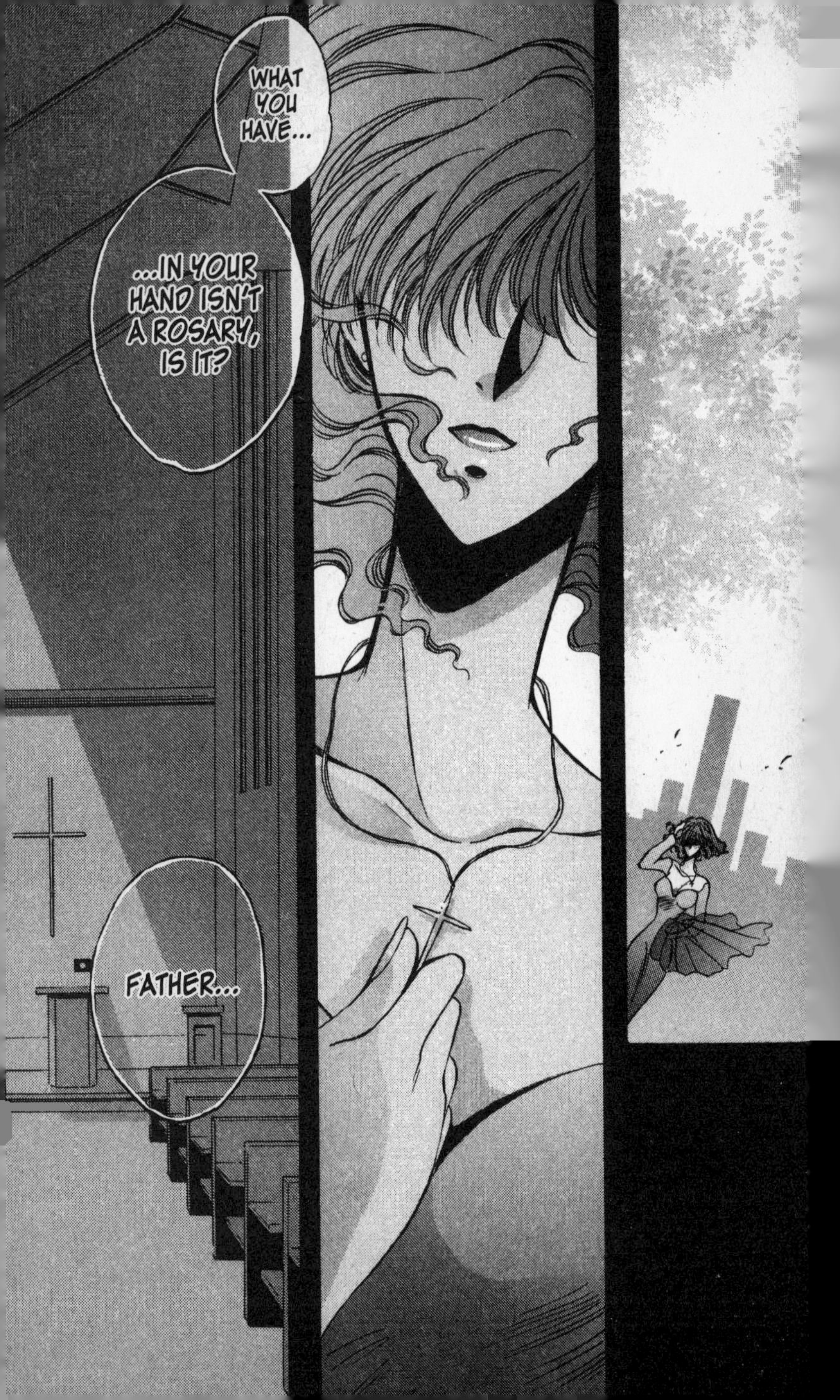
WHAT YOU HAVE...
...IN YOUR HAND ISN'T A ROSARY, IS IT?
FATHER...

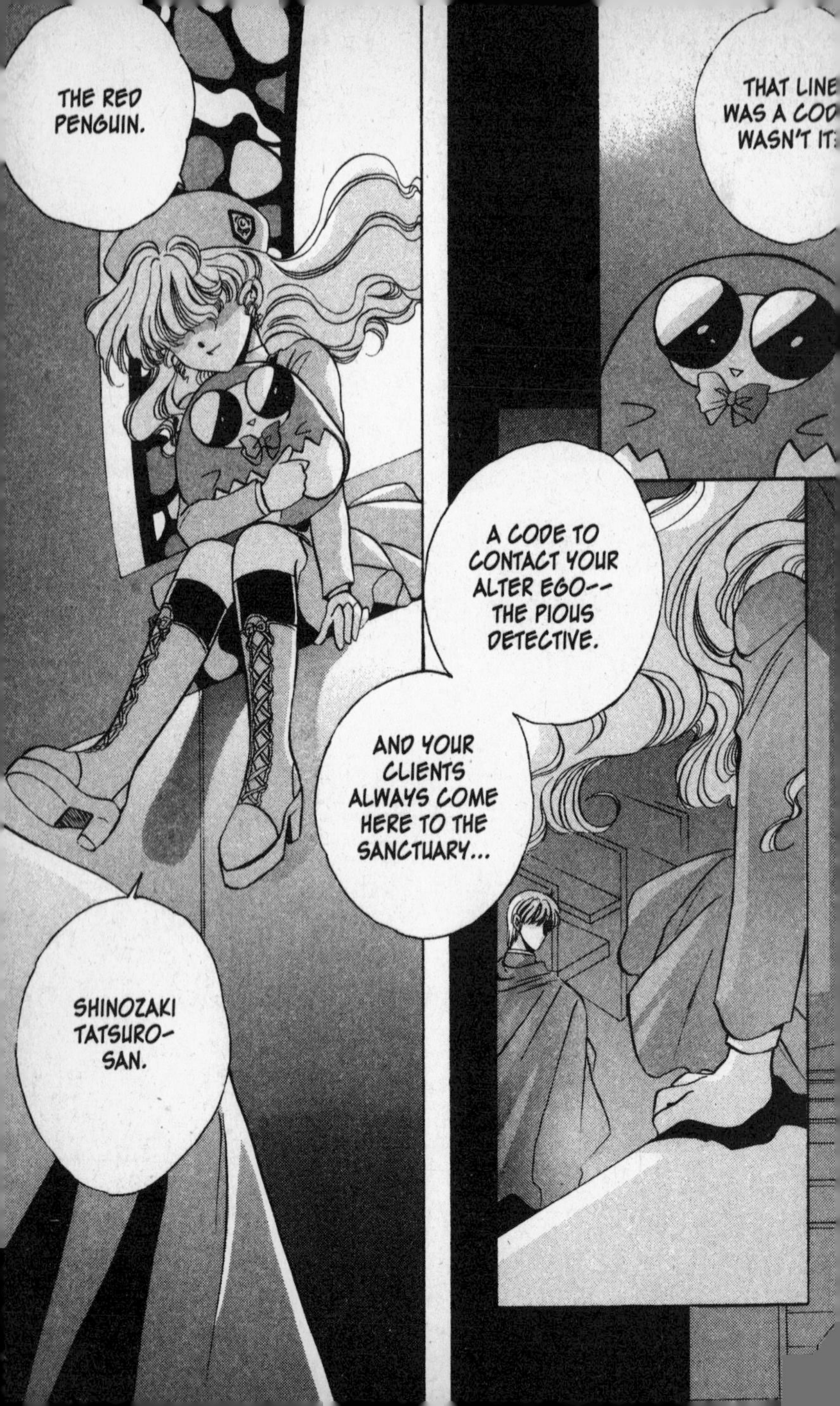
THAT LINE WAS A COD WASN'T IT
A CODE TO CONTACT YOUR ALTER EGO-- THE PIOUS DETECTIVE.
AND YOUR CLIENTS ALWAYS COME HERE TO THE SANCTUARY...
THE RED PENGUIN.
SHINOZAKI TATSURO-SAN.

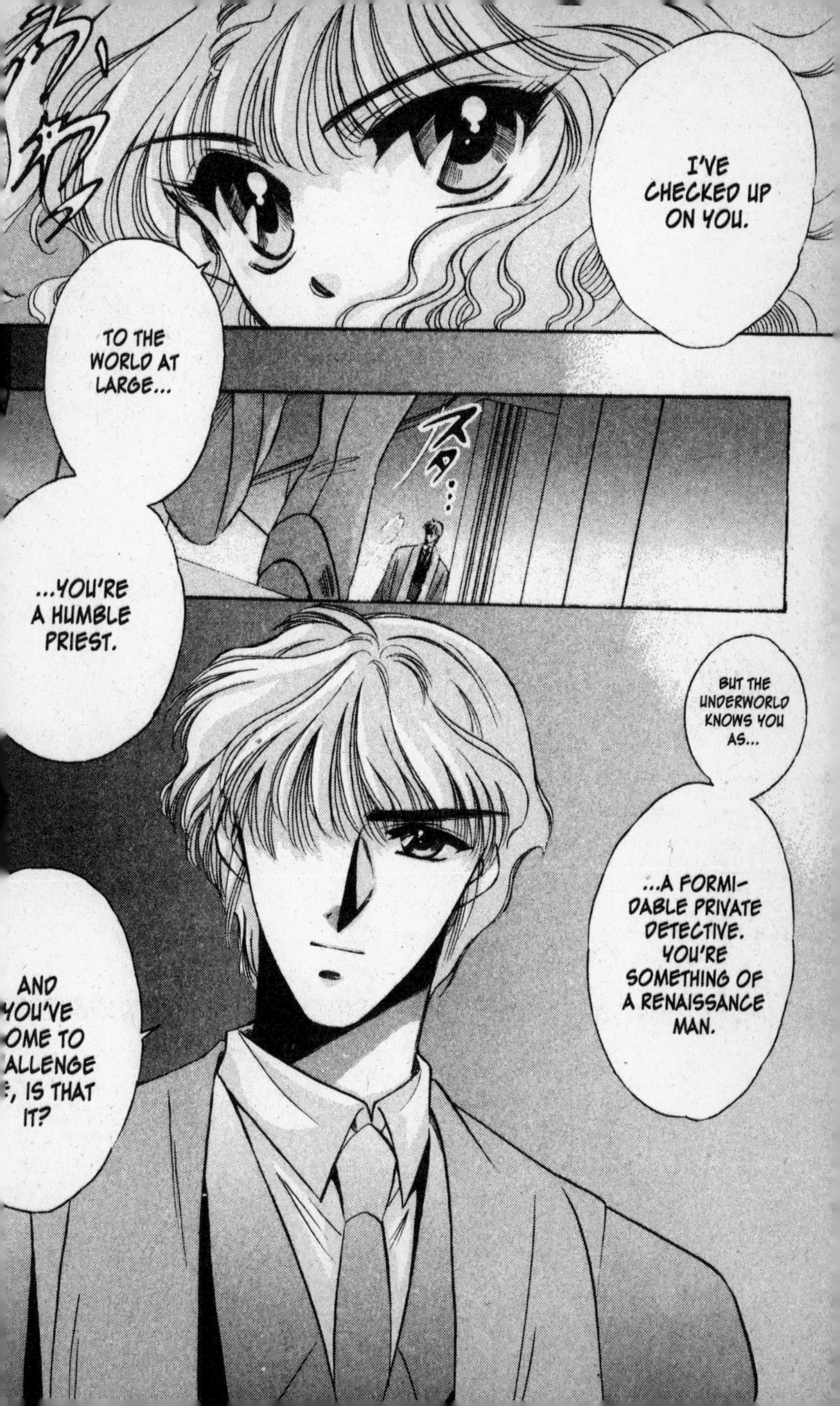
I'VE CHECKED UP ON YOU.
TO THE WORLD AT LARGE...
...YOU'RE A HUMBLE PRIEST.
BUT THE UNDERWORLD KNOWS YOU AS...
...A FORMIDABLE PRIVATE DETECTIVE. YOU'RE SOMETHING OF A RENAISSANCE MAN.
AND YOU'VE OME TO ALLENGE E, IS THAT IT?

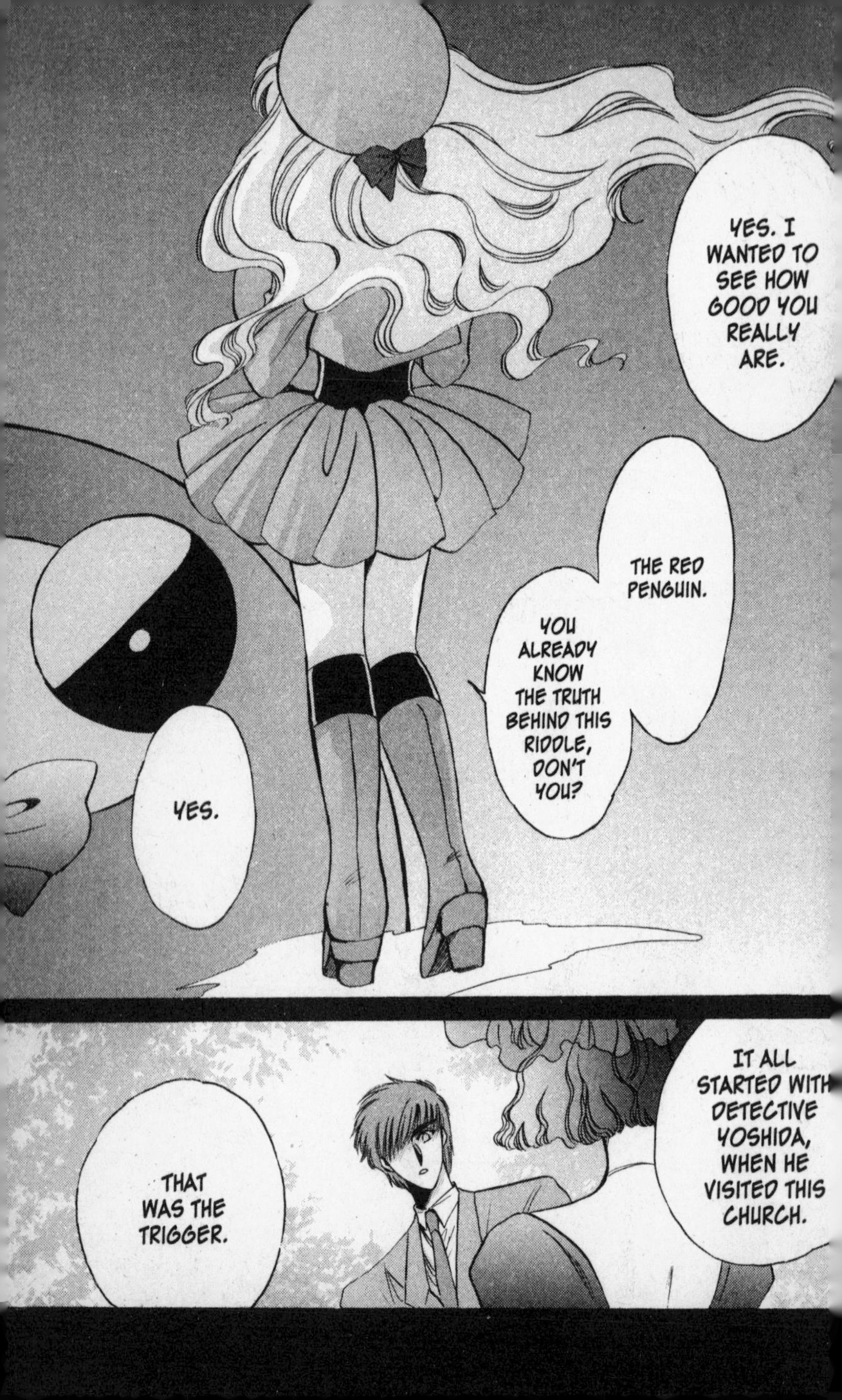
YES. I WANTED TO SEE HOW GOOD YOU REALLY ARE.
THE RED PENGUIN.
YOU ALREADY KNOW THE TRUTH BEHIND THIS RIDDLE, DON'T YOU?
YES.
IT ALL STARTED WITH DETECTIVE YOSHIDA, WHEN HE VISITED THIS CHURCH.
THAT WAS THE TRIGGER.

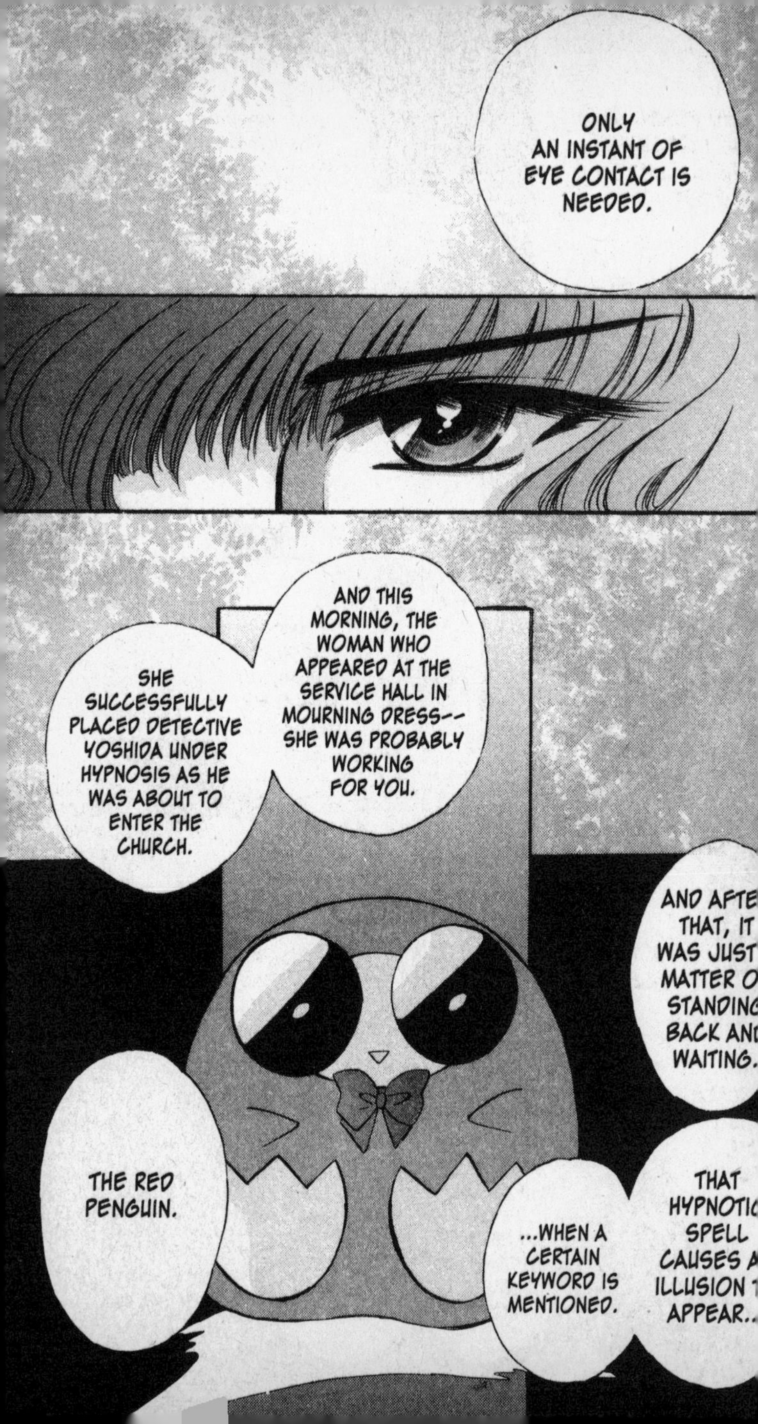
ONLY AN INSTANT OF EYE CONTACT IS NEEDED.
AND THIS MORNING, THE WOMAN WHO APPEARED AT THE SERVICE HALL IN MOURNING DRESS-- SHE WAS PROBABLY WORKING FOR YOU.
SHE SUCCESSFULLY PLACED DETECTIVE YOSHIDA UNDER HYPNOSIS AS HE WAS ABOUT TO ENTER THE CHURCH.
AND AFTE THAT, IT WAS JUST MATTER O STANDING BACK AND WAITING.
THAT HYPNOTIC SPELL CAUSES A ILLUSION APPEAR...
...WHEN A CERTAIN KEYWORD IS MENTIONED.
THE RED PENGUIN.

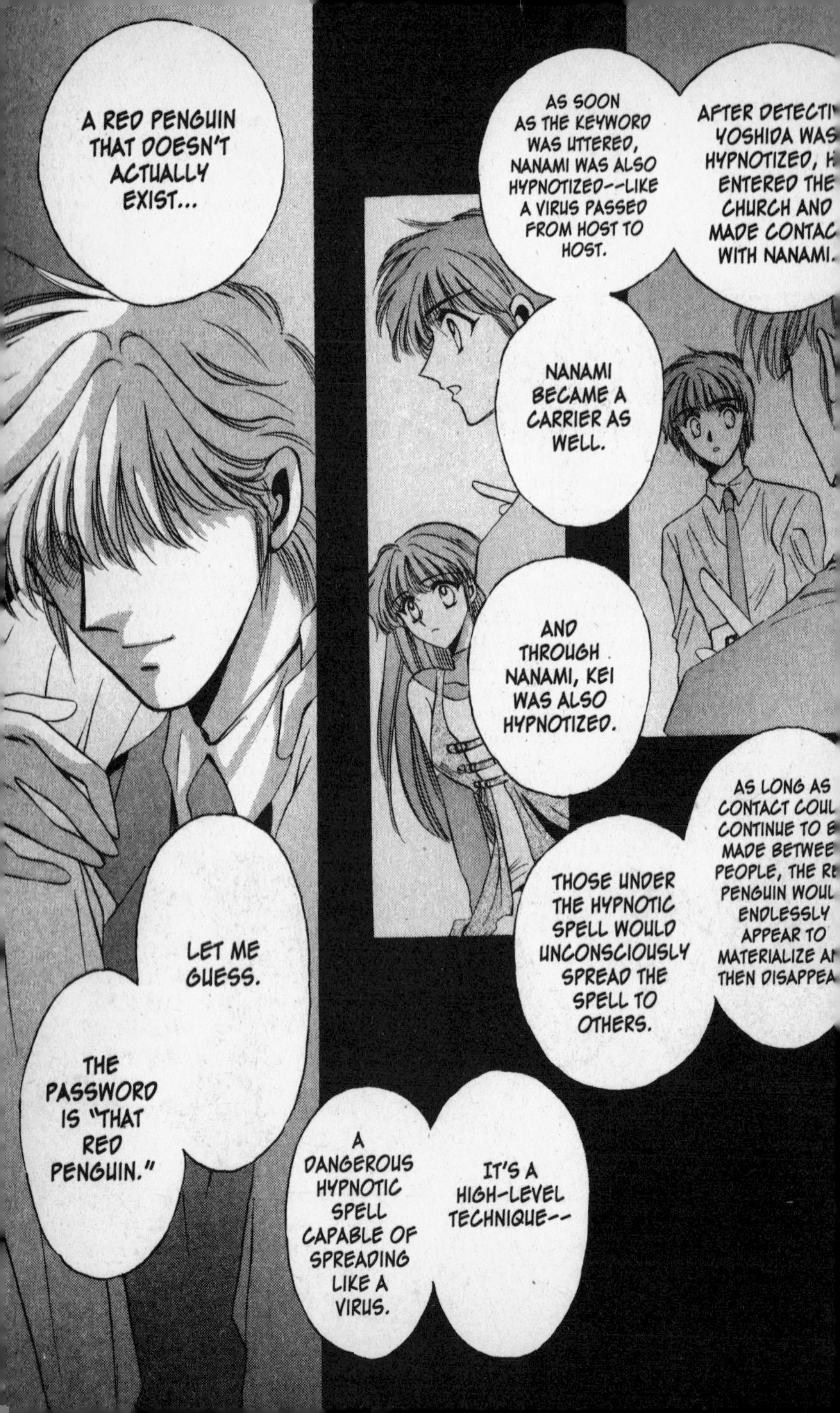
AFTER DETECTI YOSHIDA WAS HYPNOTIZED, H ENTERED THE CHURCH AND MADE CONTAC WITH NANAMI.
AS SOON AS THE KEYWORD WAS UTTERED, NANAMI WAS ALSO HYPNOTIZED--LIKE A VIRUS PASSED FROM HOST TO HOST.
NANAMI BECAME A CARRIER AS WELL.
AND THROUGH NANAMI, KEI WAS ALSO HYPNOTIZED.
AS LONG AS CONTACT COUL CONTINUE TO B MADE BETWEE PEOPLE, THE R PENGUIN WOUL ENDLESSLY APPEAR TO MATERIALIZE A THEN DISAPPEA
THOSE UNDER THE HYPNOTIC SPELL WOULD UNCONSCIOUSLY SPREAD THE SPELL TO OTHERS.
IT'S A HIGH-LEVEL TECHNIQUE--
A DANGEROUS HYPNOTIC SPELL CAPABLE OF SPREADING LIKE A VIRUS.
A RED PENGUIN THAT DOESN'T ACTUALLY EXIST...
LET ME GUESS.
THE PASSWORD IS "THAT RED PENGUIN."

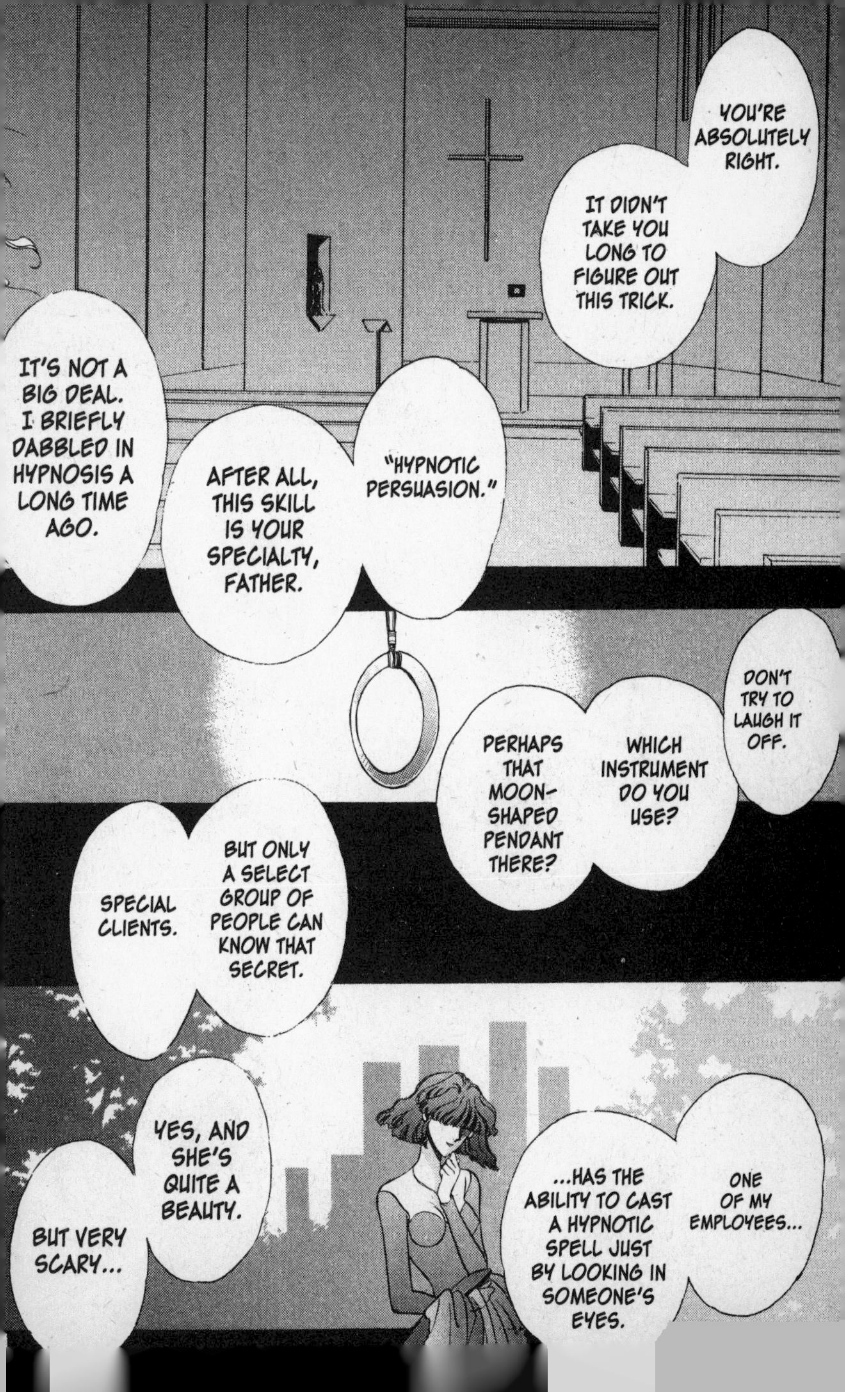
YOU'RE ABSOLUTELY RIGHT.
IT DIDN'T TAKE YOU LONG TO FIGURE OUT THIS TRICK.
"HYPNOTIC PERSUASION."
AFTER ALL, THIS SKILL IS YOUR SPECIALTY, FATHER.
IT'S NOT A BIG DEAL. I BRIEFLY DABBLED IN HYPNOSIS A LONG TIME AGO.
DON'T TRY TO LAUGH IT OFF.
WHICH INSTRUMENT DO YOU USE?
PERHAPS THAT MOON-SHAPED PENDANT THERE?
BUT ONLY A SELECT GROUP OF PEOPLE CAN KNOW THAT SECRET.
SPECIAL CLIENTS.
ONE OF MY EMPLOYEES...
...HAS THE ABILITY TO CAST A HYPNOTIC SPELL JUST BY LOOKING IN SOMEONE'S EYES.
YES, AND SHE'S QUITE A BEAUTY.
BUT VERY SCARY...

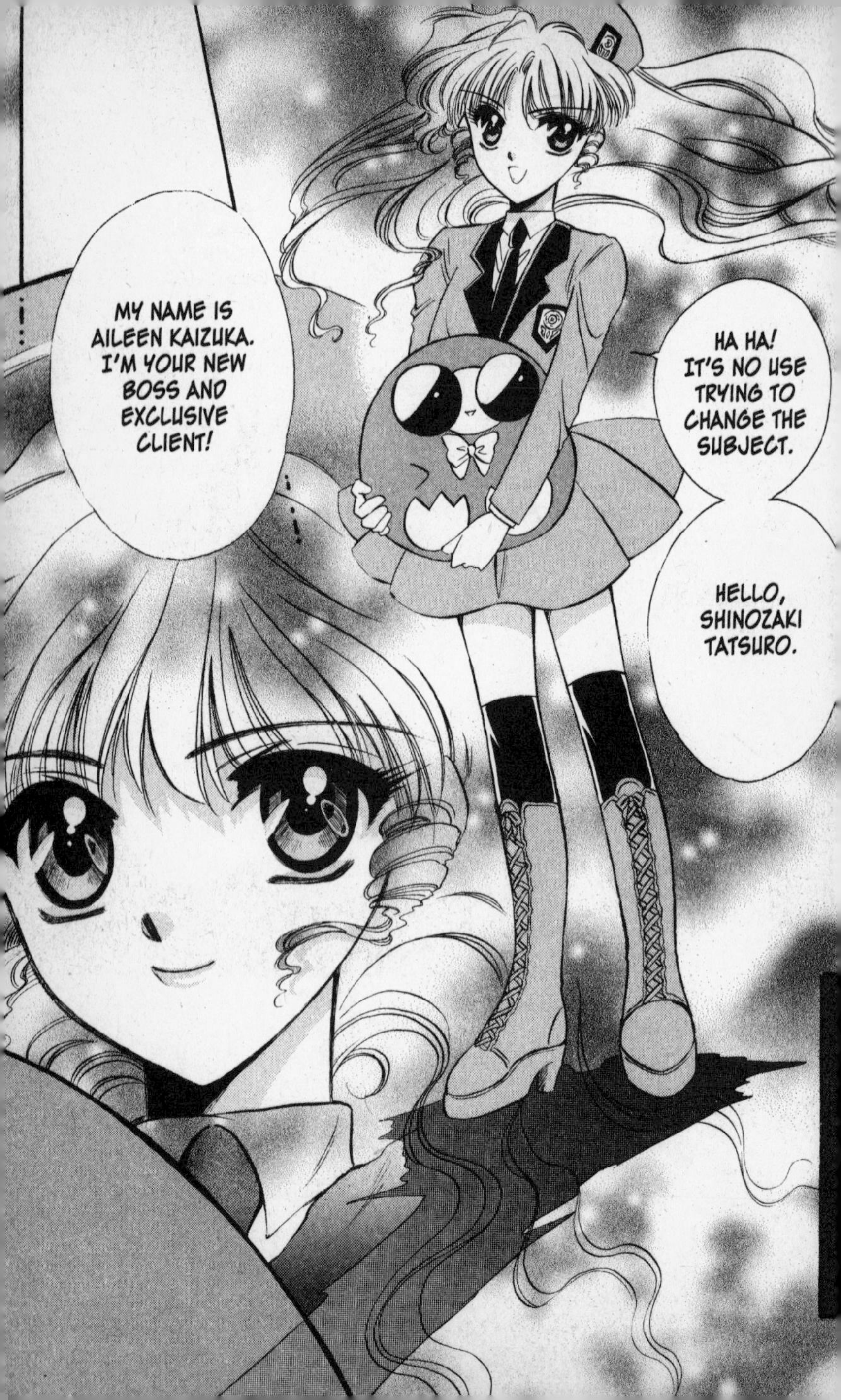
HA HA! IT'S NO USE TRYING TO CHANGE THE SUBJECT.
HELLO, SHINOZAKI TATSURO.
MY NAME IS AILEEN KAIZUKA. I'M YOUR NEW BOSS AND EXCLUSIVE CLIENT!

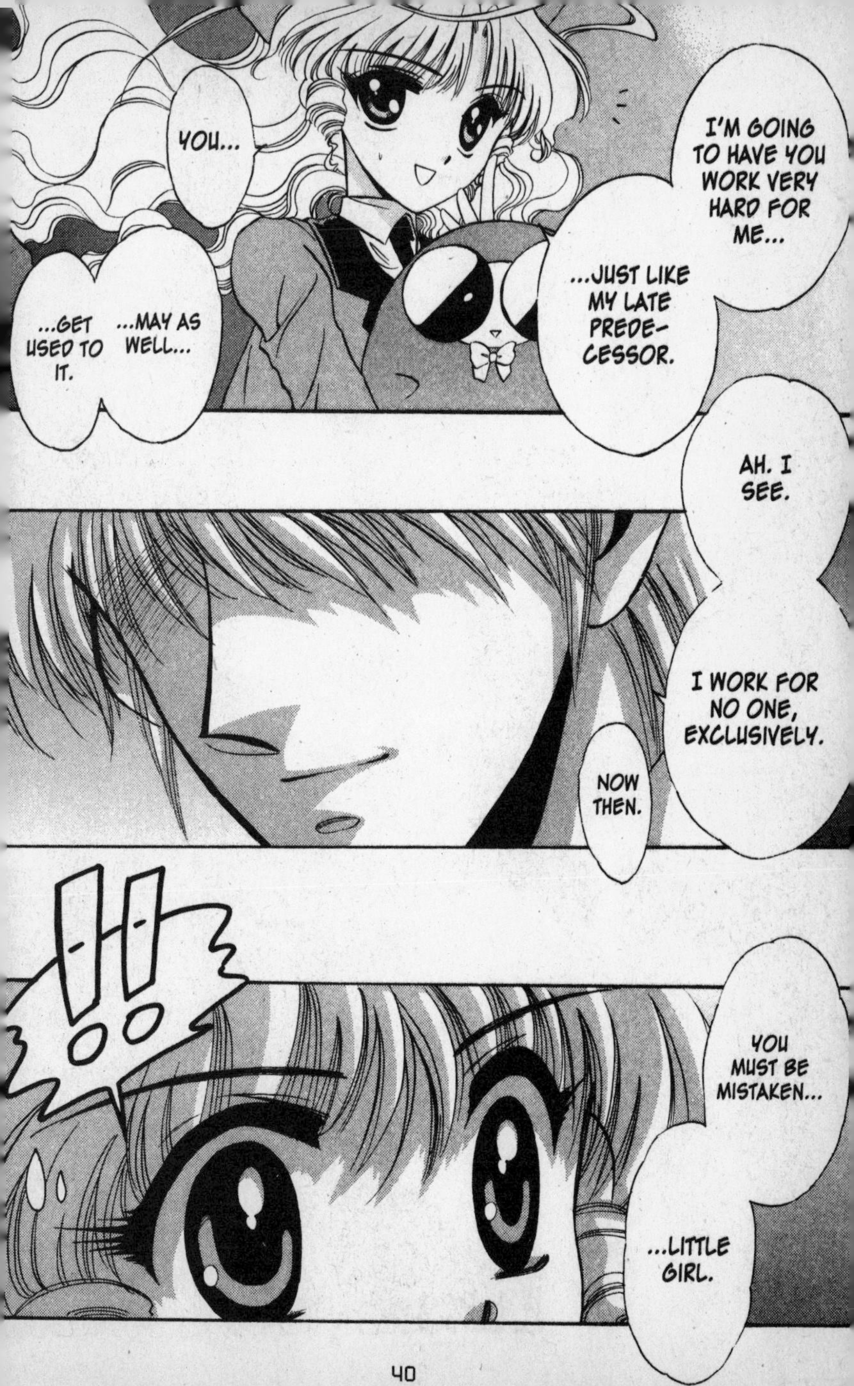

I'M GOING TO HAVE YOU WORK VERY HARD FOR ME...
...JUST LIKE MY LATE PREDE-CESSOR.
YOU...
...MAY AS WELL...
...GET USED TO IT.
AH. I SEE.
I WORK FOR NO ONE, EXCLUSIVELY.
NOW THEN.
YOU MUST BE MISTAKEN...
...LITTLE GIRL.
!!

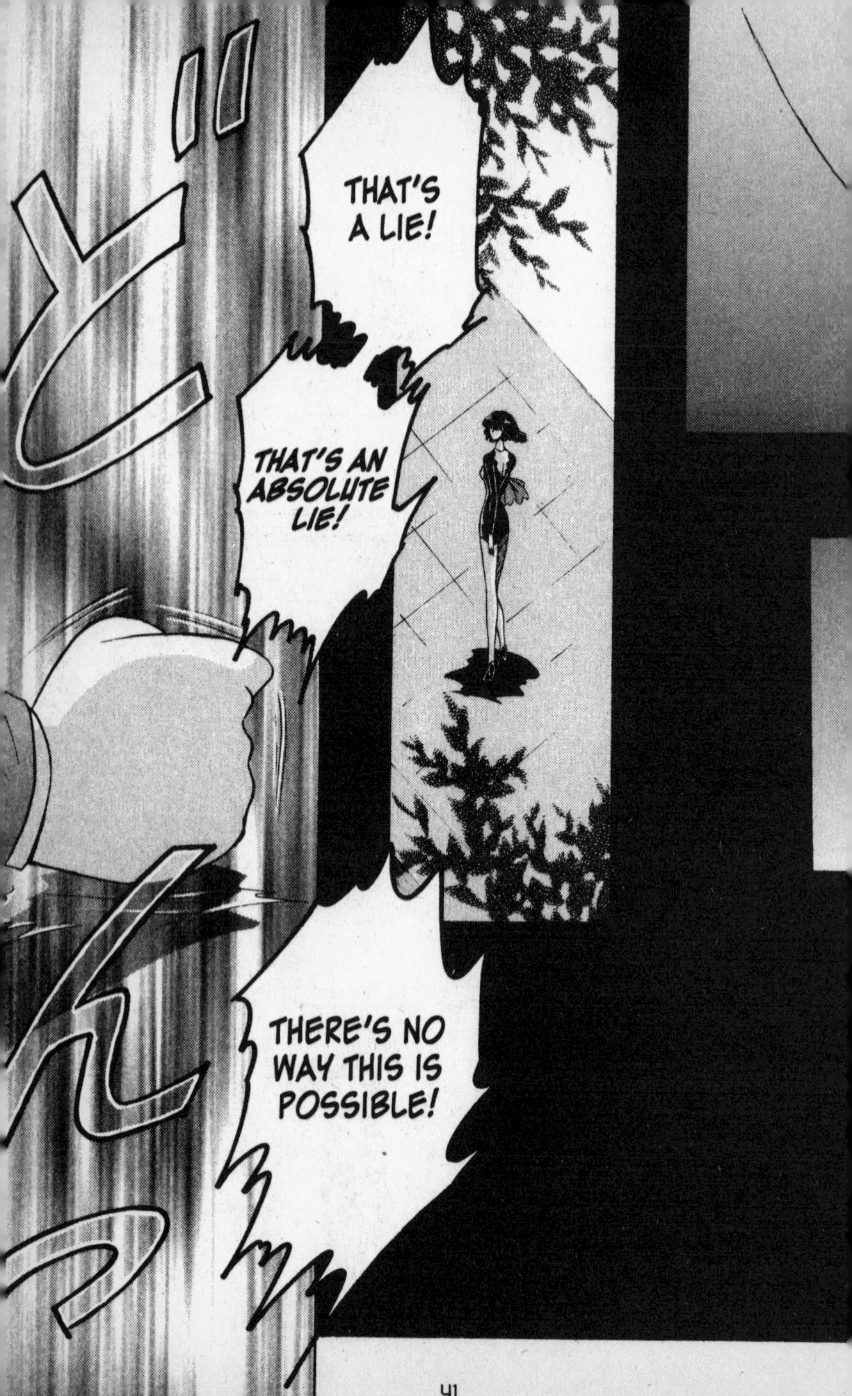
THAT'S A LIE!
THAT'S AN ABSOLUTE LIE!
THERE'S NO WAY THIS IS POSSIBLE!

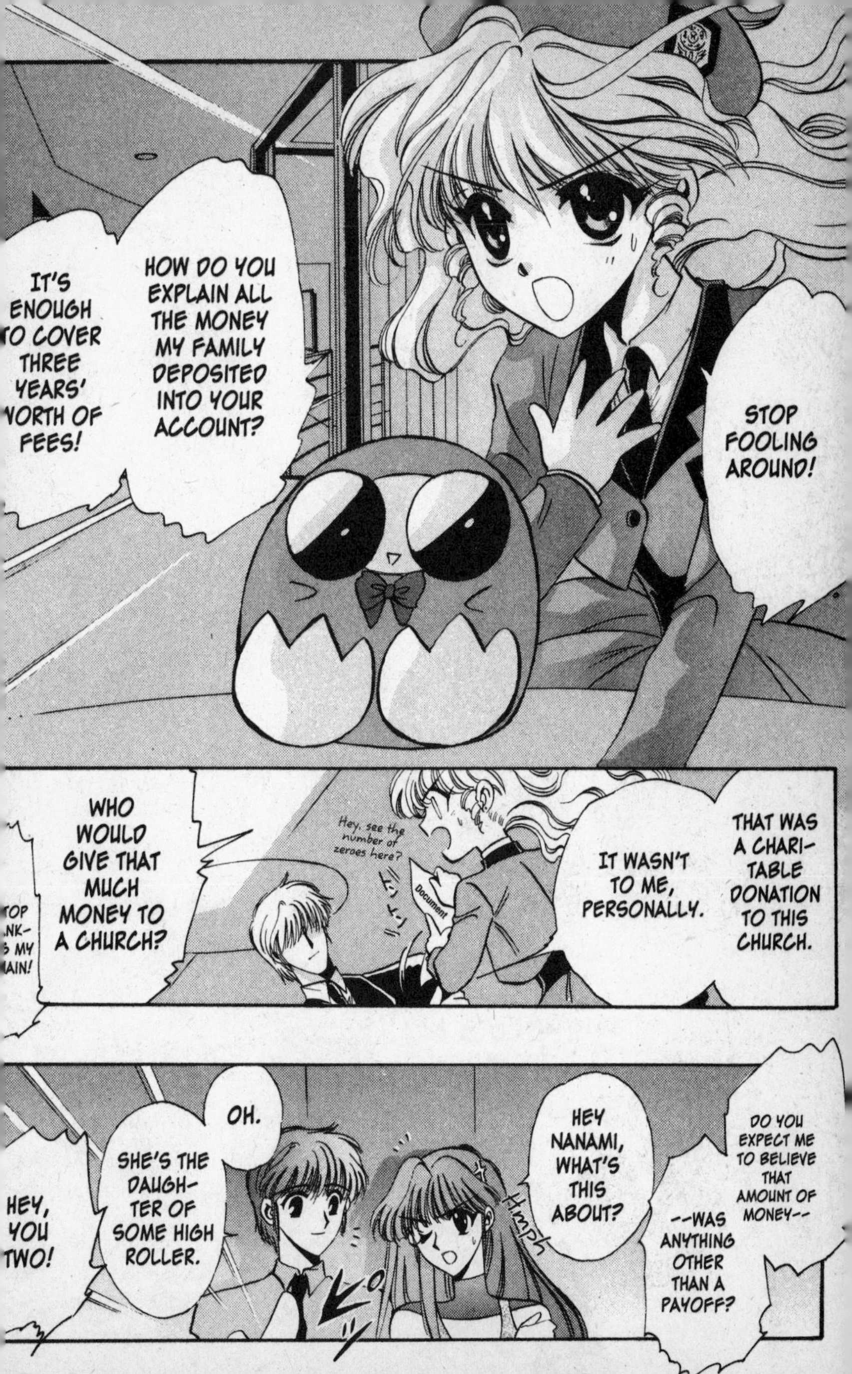
STOP FOOLING AROUND!
HOW DO YOU EXPLAIN ALL THE MONEY MY FAMILY DEPOSITED INTO YOUR ACCOUNT?
IT'S ENOUGH TO COVER THREE YEARS' WORTH OF FEES!
THAT WAS A CHARI-TABLE DONATION TO THIS CHURCH.
IT WASN'T TO ME, PERSONALLY.
Hey, see the number of zeroes here?
Document
WHO WOULD GIVE THAT MUCH MONEY TO A CHURCH?
DO YOU EXPECT ME TO BELIEVE THAT AMOUNT OF MONEY--
--WAS ANYTHING OTHER THAN A PAYOFF?
HEY NANAMI, WHAT'S THIS ABOUT?
Hmph
OH.
SHE'S THE DAUGH-TER OF SOME HIGH ROLLER.
HEY, YOU TWO!

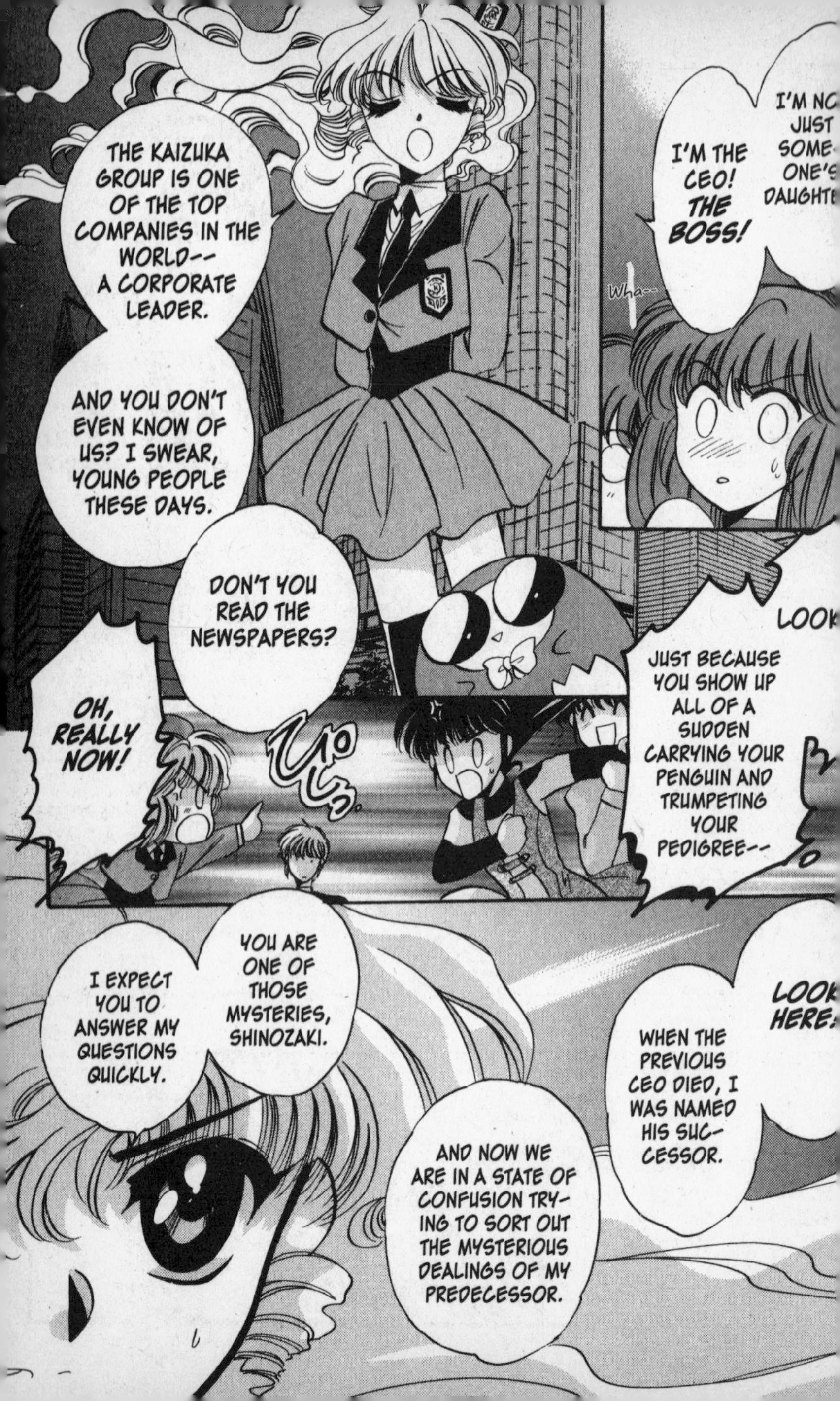
I'M NO JUST SOME-ONE'S DAUGHTE
I'M THE CEO! THE BOSS!
Wha--
THE KAIZUKA GROUP IS ONE OF THE TOP COMPANIES IN THE WORLD-- A CORPORATE LEADER.
AND YOU DON'T EVEN KNOW OF US? I SWEAR, YOUNG PEOPLE THESE DAYS.
DON'T YOU READ THE NEWSPAPERS?
LOOK
JUST BECAUSE YOU SHOW UP ALL OF A SUDDEN CARRYING YOUR PENGUIN AND TRUMPETING YOUR PEDIGREE--
OH, REALLY NOW!
LOOK HERE:
WHEN THE PREVIOUS CEO DIED, I WAS NAMED HIS SUC-CESSOR.
AND NOW WE ARE IN A STATE OF CONFUSION TRY-ING TO SORT OUT THE MYSTERIOUS DEALINGS OF MY PREDECESSOR.
YOU ARE ONE OF THOSE MYSTERIES, SHINOZAKI.
I EXPECT YOU TO ANSWER MY QUESTIONS QUICKLY.

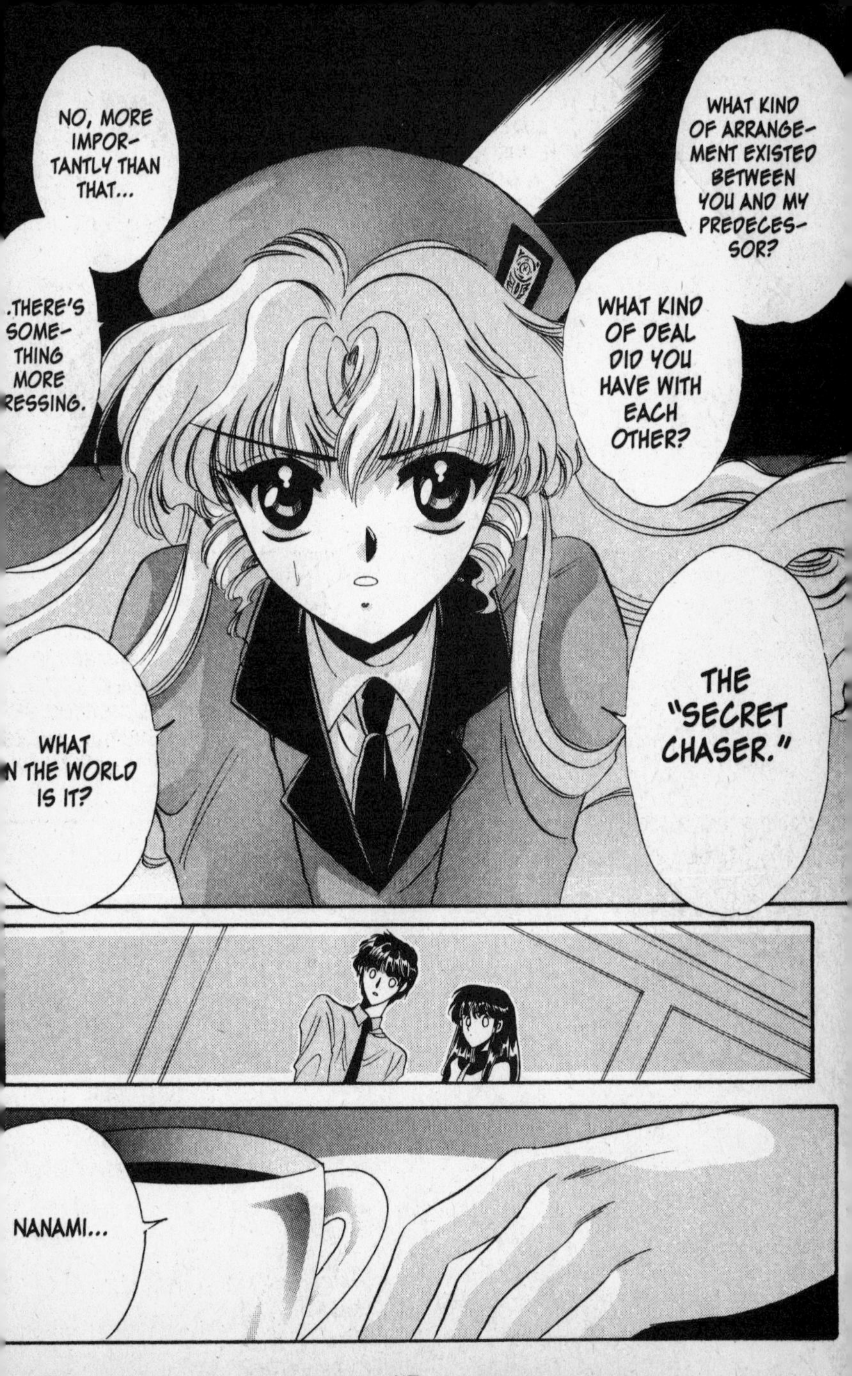
WHAT KIND OF ARRANGEMENT EXISTED BETWEEN YOU AND MY PREDECESSOR?
WHAT KIND OF DEAL DID YOU HAVE WITH EACH OTHER?
NO, MORE IMPORTANTLY THAN THAT...
.THERE'S SOMETHING MORE RESSING.
THE "SECRET CHASER."
WHAT N THE WORLD IS IT?
NANAMI...

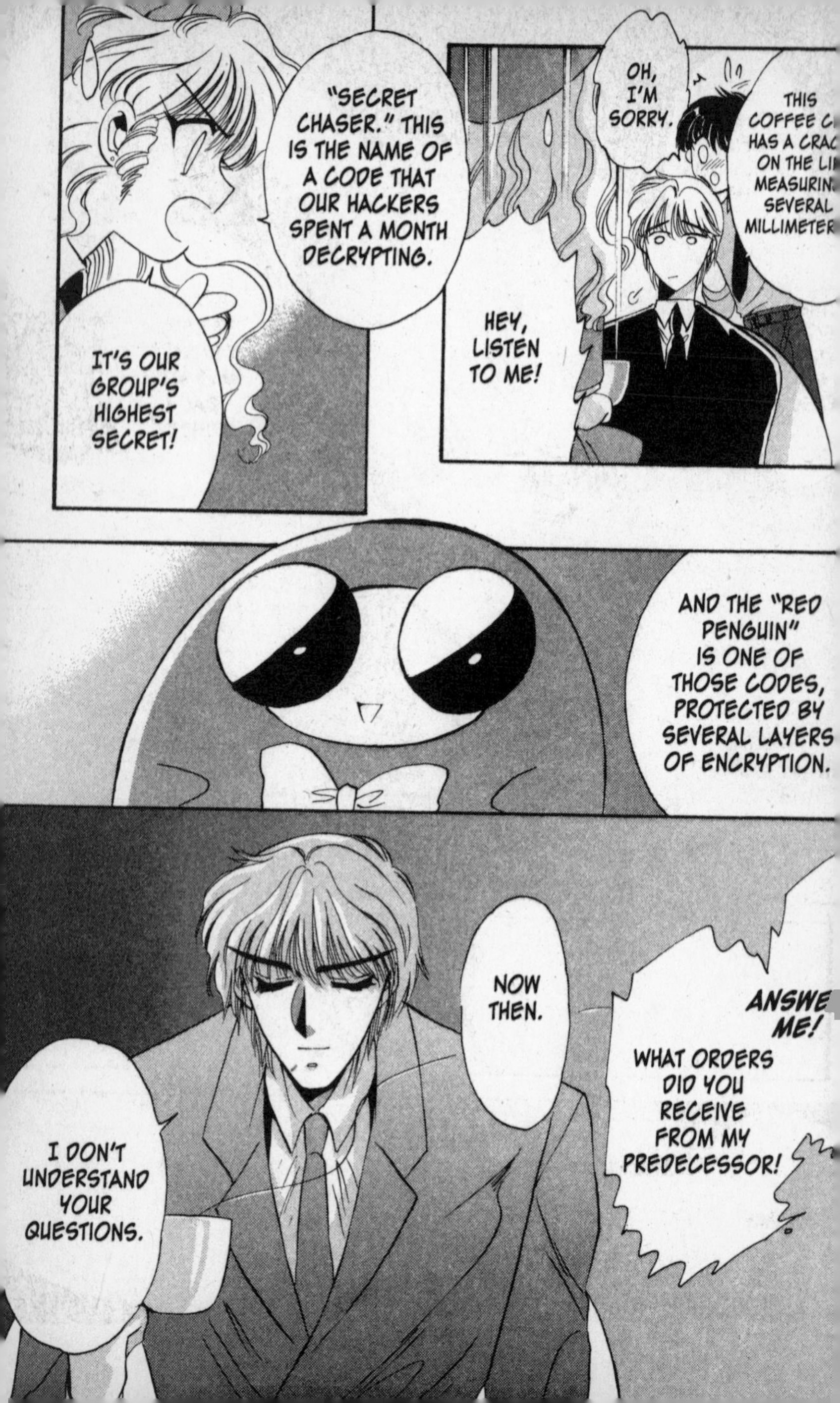
THIS COFFEE C HAS A CRAC ON THE LI MEASURIN SEVERAL MILLIMETER
OH, I'M SORRY.
HEY, LISTEN TO ME!
"SECRET CHASER." THIS IS THE NAME OF A CODE THAT OUR HACKERS SPENT A MONTH DECRYPTING.
IT'S OUR GROUP'S HIGHEST SECRET!
AND THE "RED PENGUIN" IS ONE OF THOSE CODES, PROTECTED BY SEVERAL LAYERS OF ENCRYPTION.
ANSWE ME!
WHAT ORDERS DID YOU RECEIVE FROM MY PREDECESSOR!
NOW THEN.
I DON'T UNDERSTAND YOUR QUESTIONS.

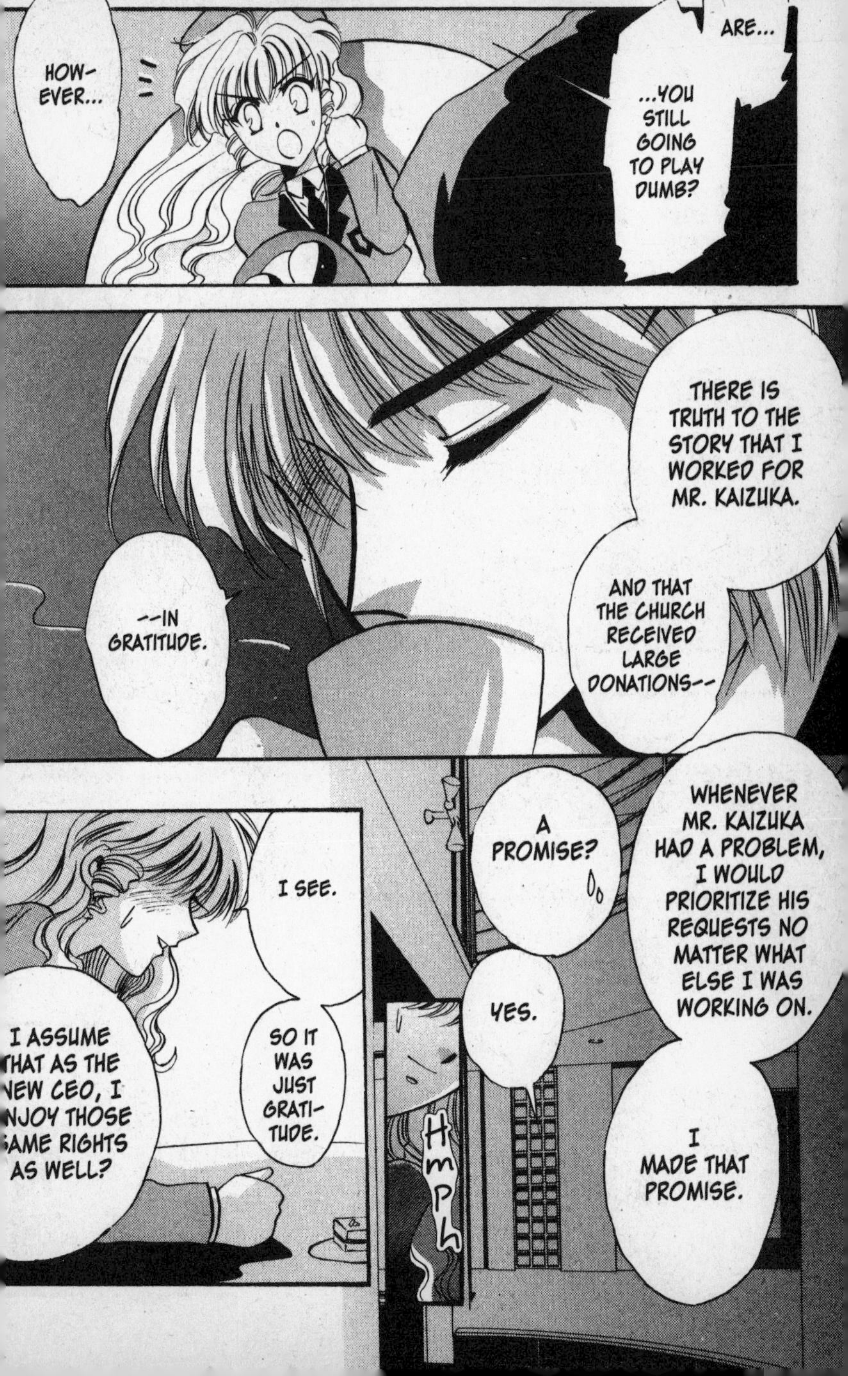
ARE...
...YOU STILL GOING TO PLAY DUMB?
HOW-EVER...
THERE IS TRUTH TO THE STORY THAT I WORKED FOR MR. KAIZUKA.
AND THAT THE CHURCH RECEIVED LARGE DONATIONS--
--IN GRATITUDE.
WHENEVER MR. KAIZUKA HAD A PROBLEM, I WOULD PRIORITIZE HIS REQUESTS NO MATTER WHAT ELSE I WAS WORKING ON.
I MADE THAT PROMISE.
A PROMISE?
YES.
Hmph
I SEE.
SO IT WAS JUST GRATI-TUDE.
I ASSUME THAT AS THE NEW CEO, I ENJOY THOSE SAME RIGHTS AS WELL?

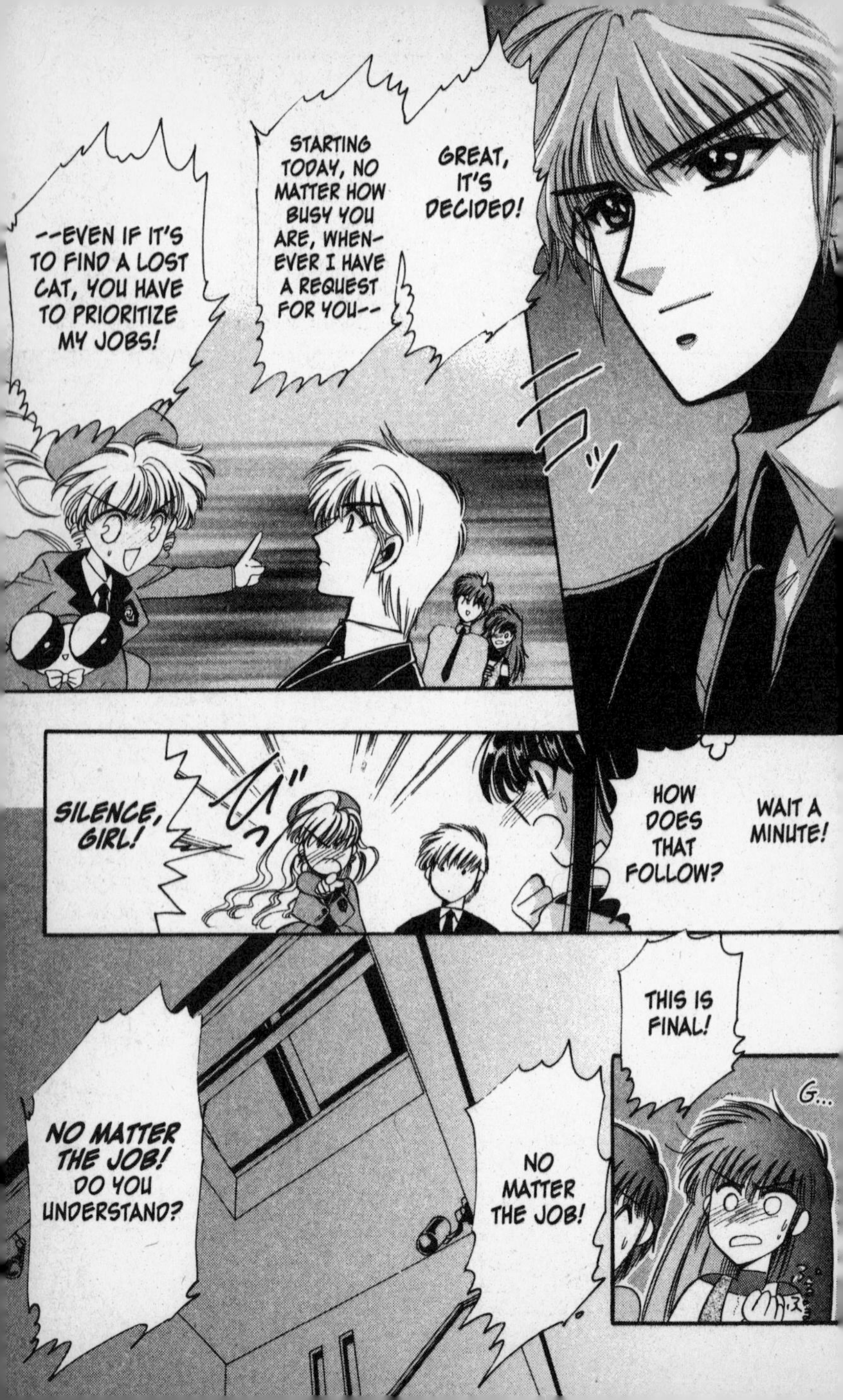
GREAT, IT'S DECIDED!
STARTING TODAY, NO MATTER HOW BUSY YOU ARE, WHEN-EVER I HAVE A REQUEST FOR YOU--
--EVEN IF IT'S TO FIND A LOST CAT, YOU HAVE TO PRIORITIZE MY JOBS!
WAIT A MINUTE!
HOW DOES THAT FOLLOW?
SILENCE, GIRL!
THIS IS FINAL!
G...
NO MATTER THE JOB!
NO MATTER THE JOB! DO YOU UNDERSTAND?

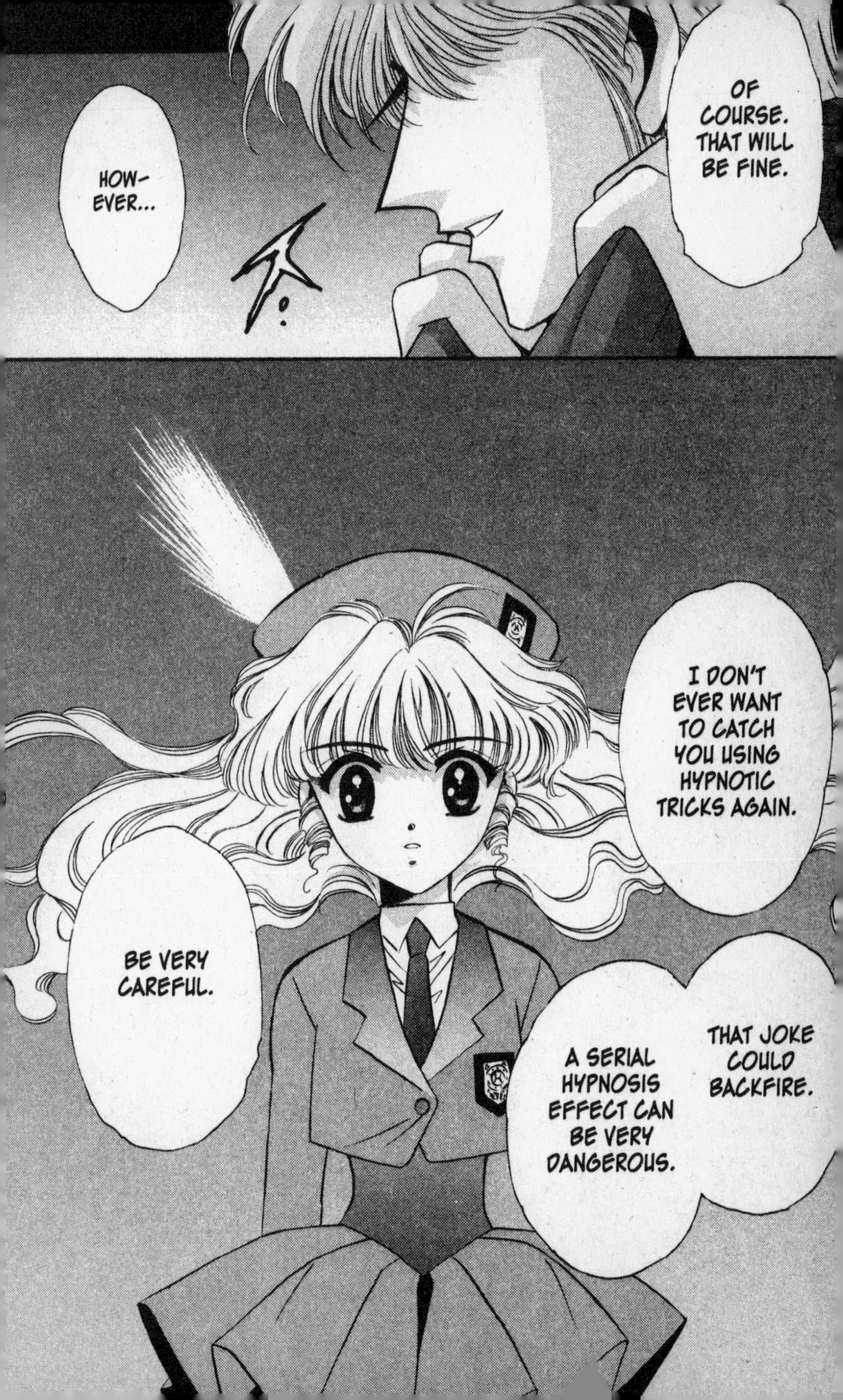
OF COURSE. THAT WILL BE FINE.
HOW-EVER...
I DON'T EVER WANT TO CATCH YOU USING HYPNOTIC TRICKS AGAIN.
THAT JOKE COULD BACKFIRE.
A SERIAL HYPNOSIS EFFECT CAN BE VERY DANGEROUS.
BE VERY CAREFUL.

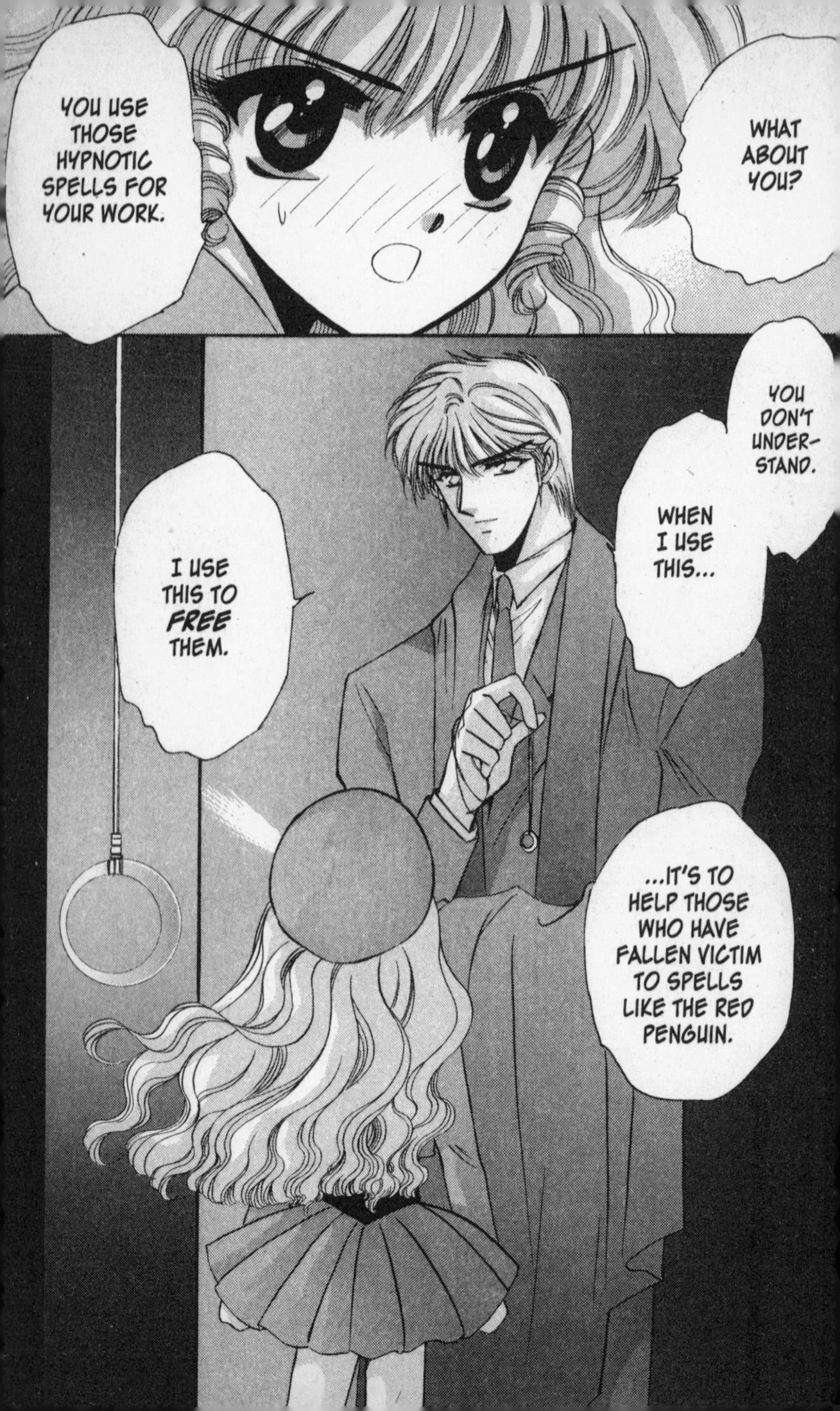
WHAT ABOUT YOU?
YOU USE THOSE HYPNOTIC SPELLS FOR YOUR WORK.
YOU DON'T UNDER-STAND.
WHEN I USE THIS...
...IT'S TO HELP THOSE WHO HAVE FALLEN VICTIM TO SPELLS LIKE THE RED PENGUIN.
I USE THIS TO ***FREE*** THEM.

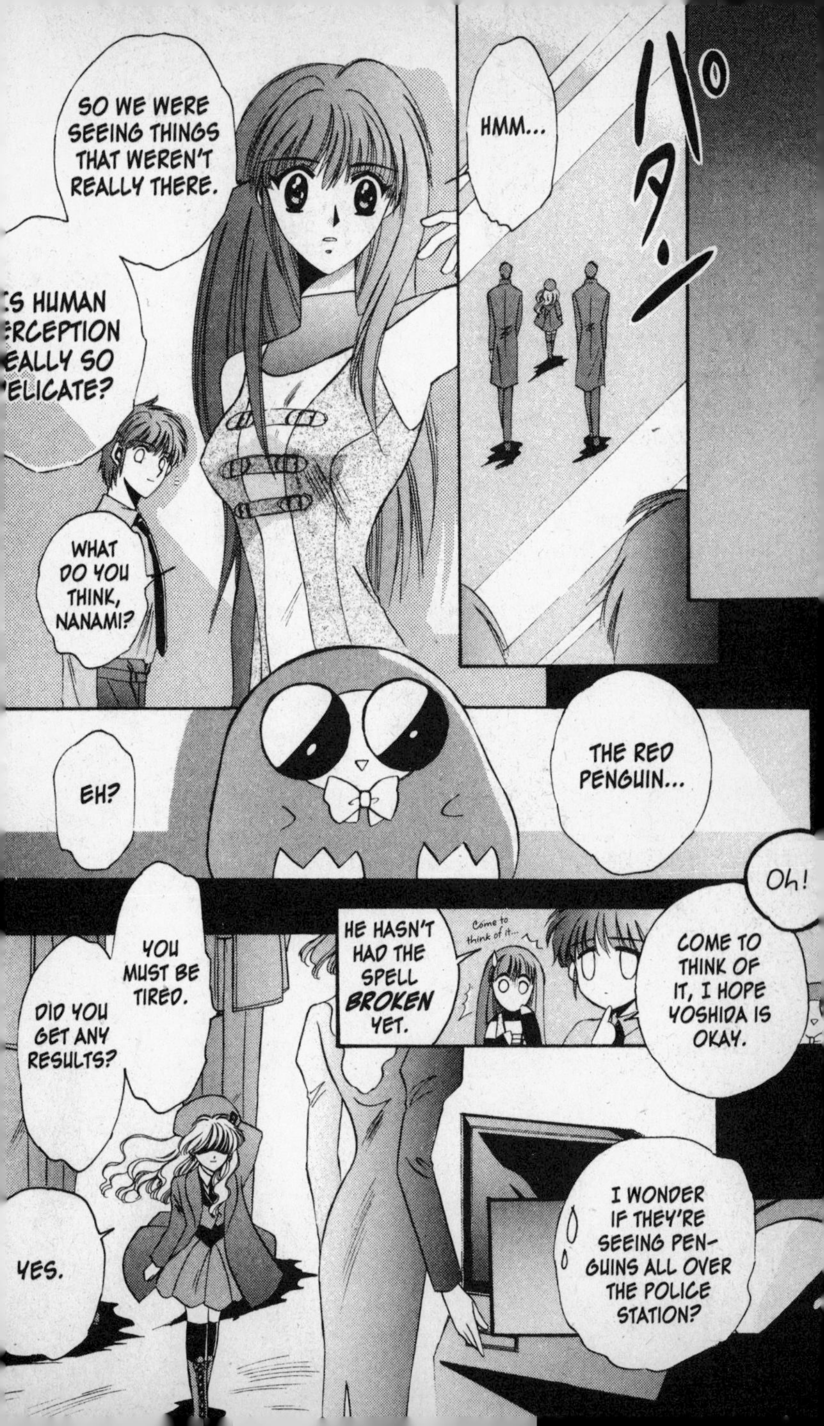
HMM...
パタン
SO WE WERE SEEING THINGS THAT WEREN'T REALLY THERE.
S HUMAN RCEPTION EALLY SO ELICATE?
WHAT DO YOU THINK, NANAMI?
THE RED PENGUIN...
EH?
Oh!
COME TO THINK OF IT, I HOPE YOSHIDA IS OKAY.
Come to think of it...
HE HASN'T HAD THE SPELL BROKEN YET.
I WONDER IF THEY'RE SEEING PEN-GUINS ALL OVER THE POLICE STATION?
YOU MUST BE TIRED.
DID YOU GET ANY RESULTS?
YES.

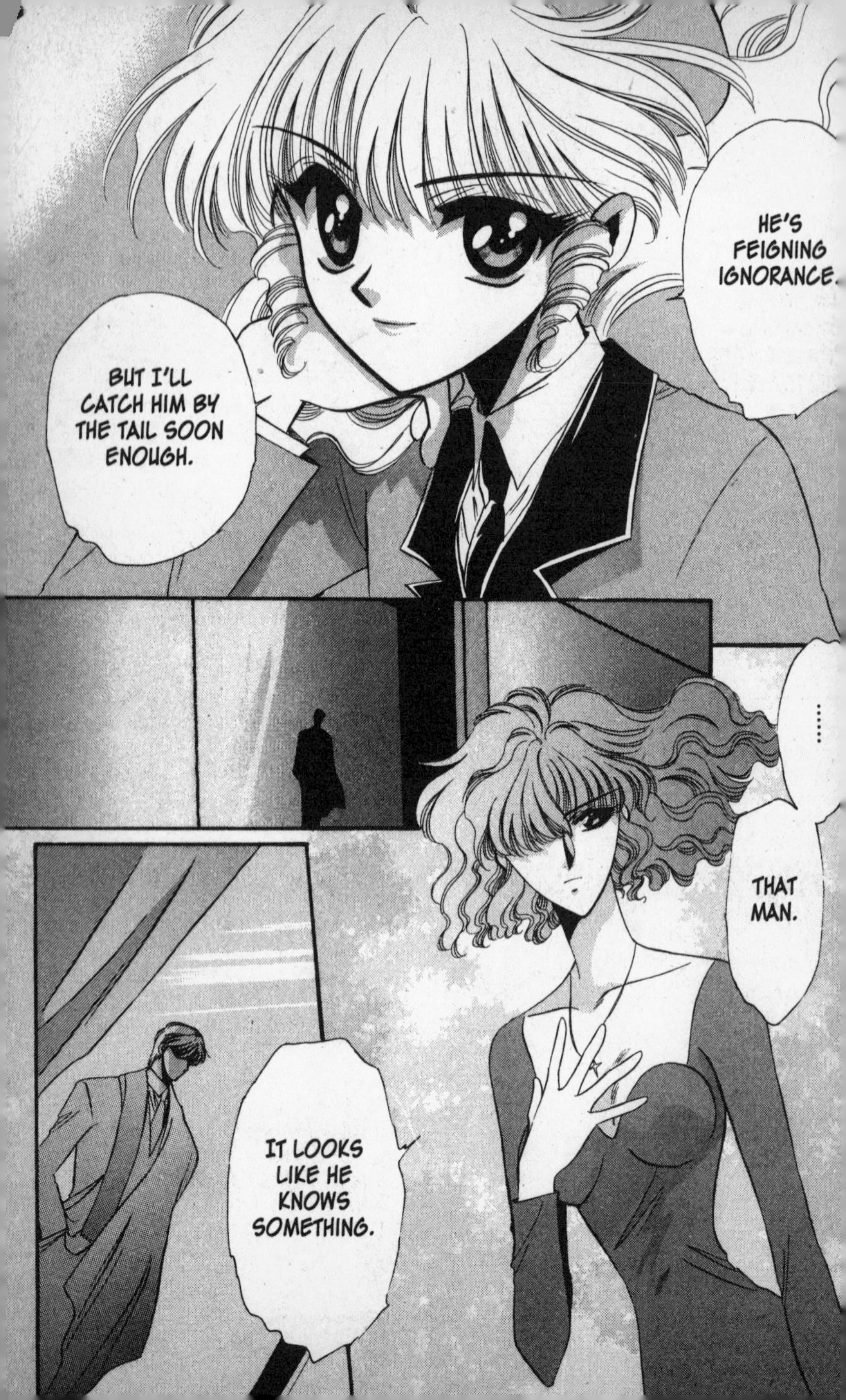
HE'S FEIGNING IGNORANCE.
BUT I'LL CATCH HIM BY THE TAIL SOON ENOUGH.
......
THAT MAN.
IT LOOKS LIKE HE KNOWS SOMETHING.

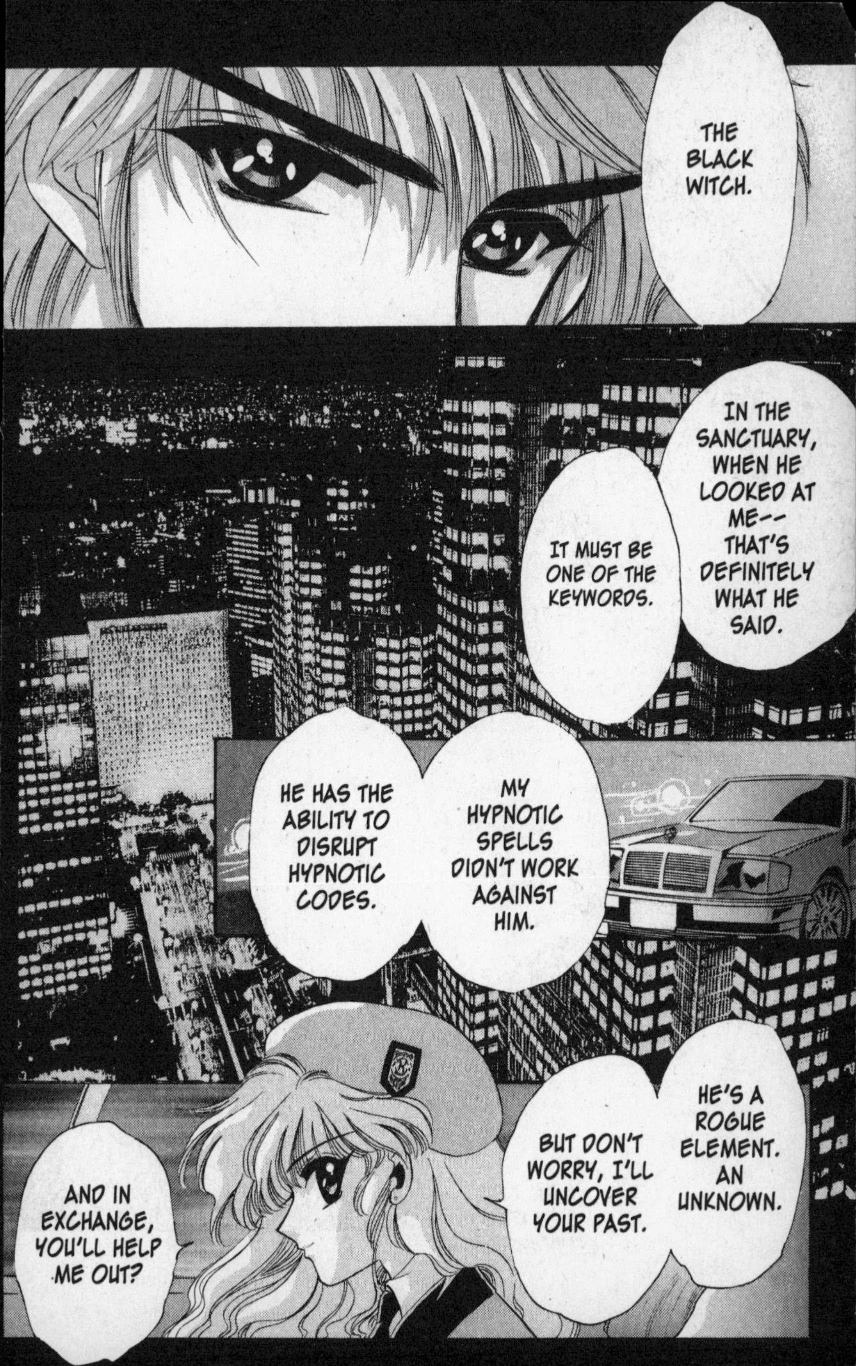
THE BLACK WITCH.
IN THE SANCTUARY, WHEN HE LOOKED AT ME--THAT'S DEFINITELY WHAT HE SAID.
IT MUST BE ONE OF THE KEYWORDS.
MY HYPNOTIC SPELLS DIDN'T WORK AGAINST HIM.
HE HAS THE ABILITY TO DISRUPT HYPNOTIC CODES.
HE'S A ROGUE ELEMENT. AN UNKNOWN.
BUT DON'T WORRY, I'LL UNCOVER YOUR PAST.
AND IN EXCHANGE, YOU'LL HELP ME OUT?

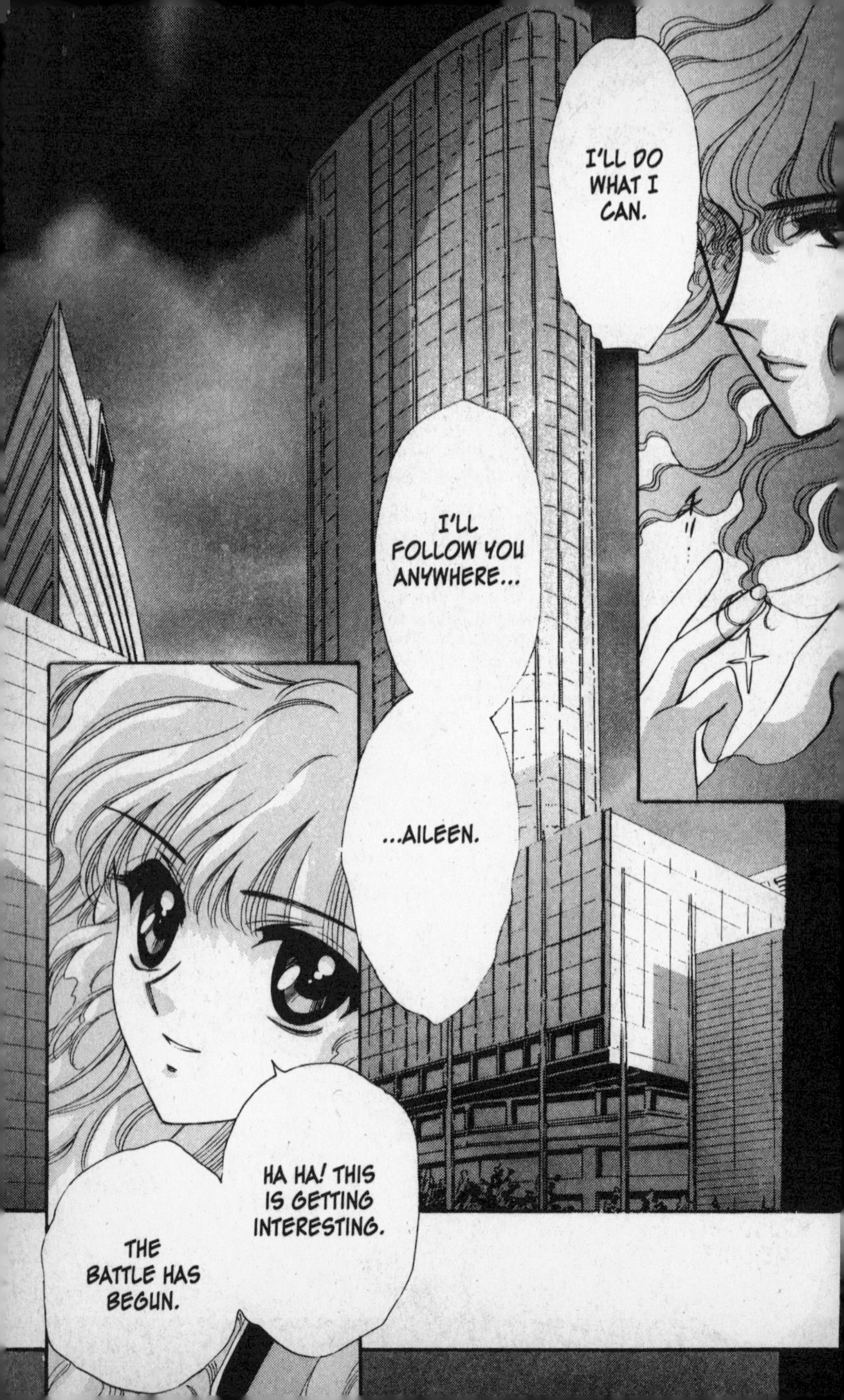
I'LL DO WHAT I CAN.
I'LL FOLLOW YOU ANYWHERE...
...AILEEN.
HA HA! THIS IS GETTING INTERESTING.
THE BATTLE HAS BEGUN.

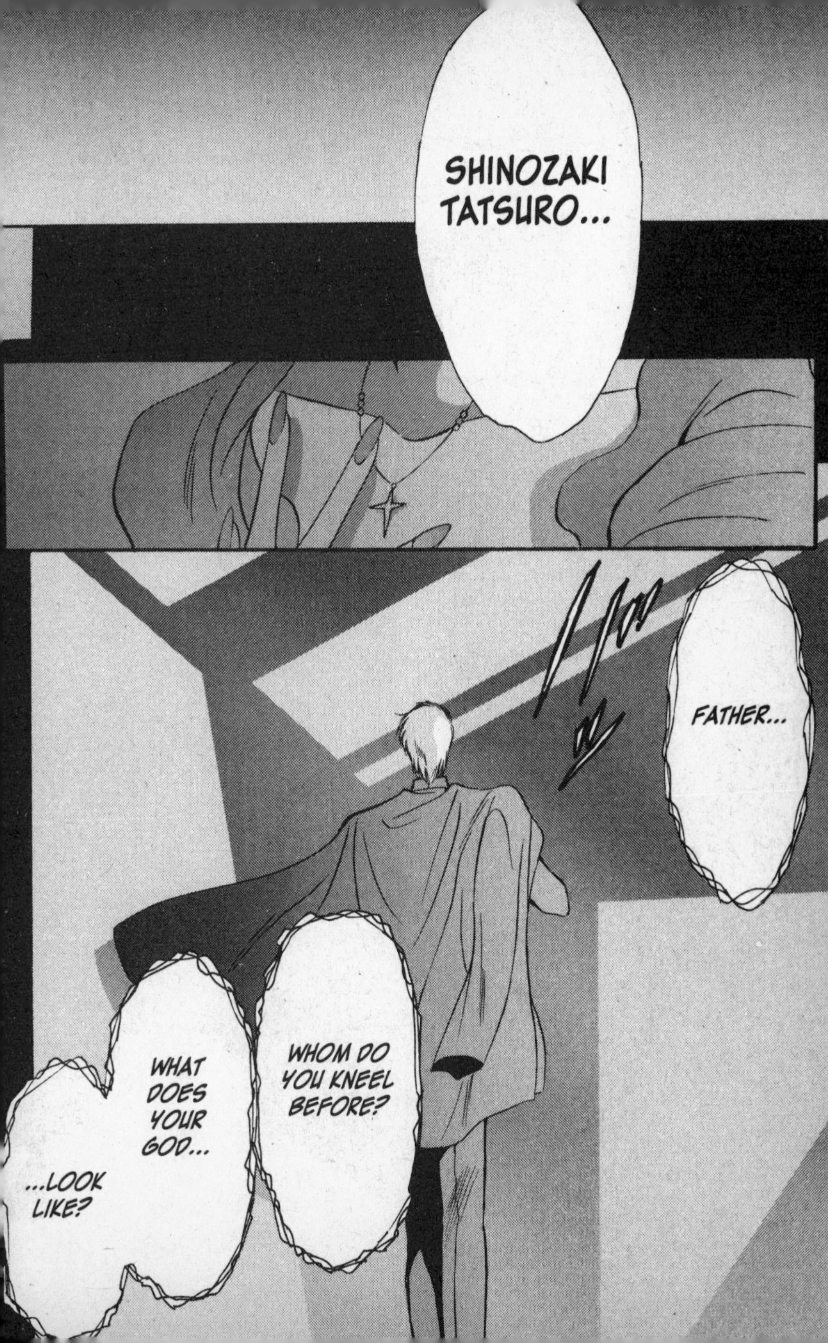
SHINOZAKI TATSURO...
FATHER...
WHOM DO YOU KNEEL BEFORE?
WHAT DOES YOUR GOD...
...LOOK LIKE?

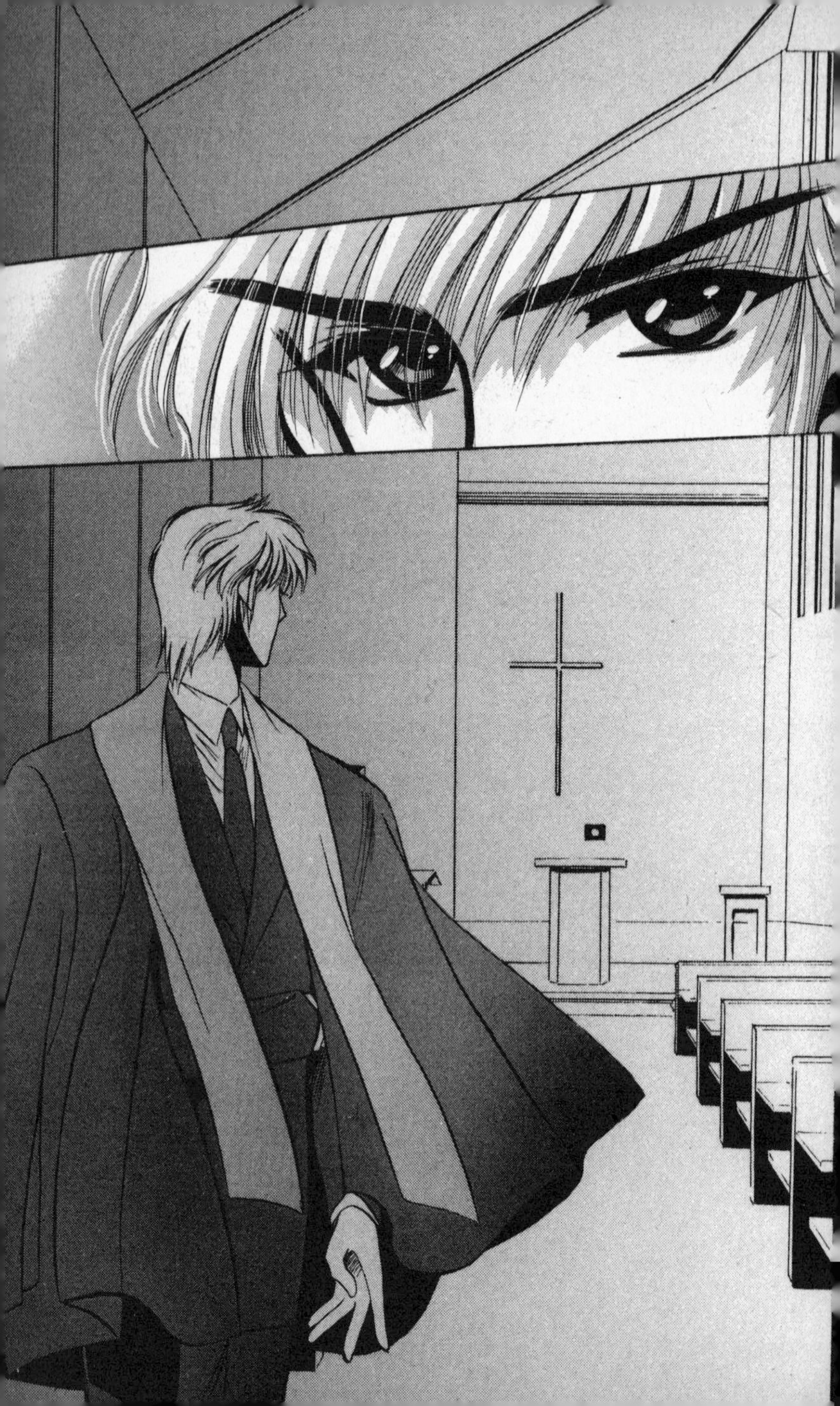

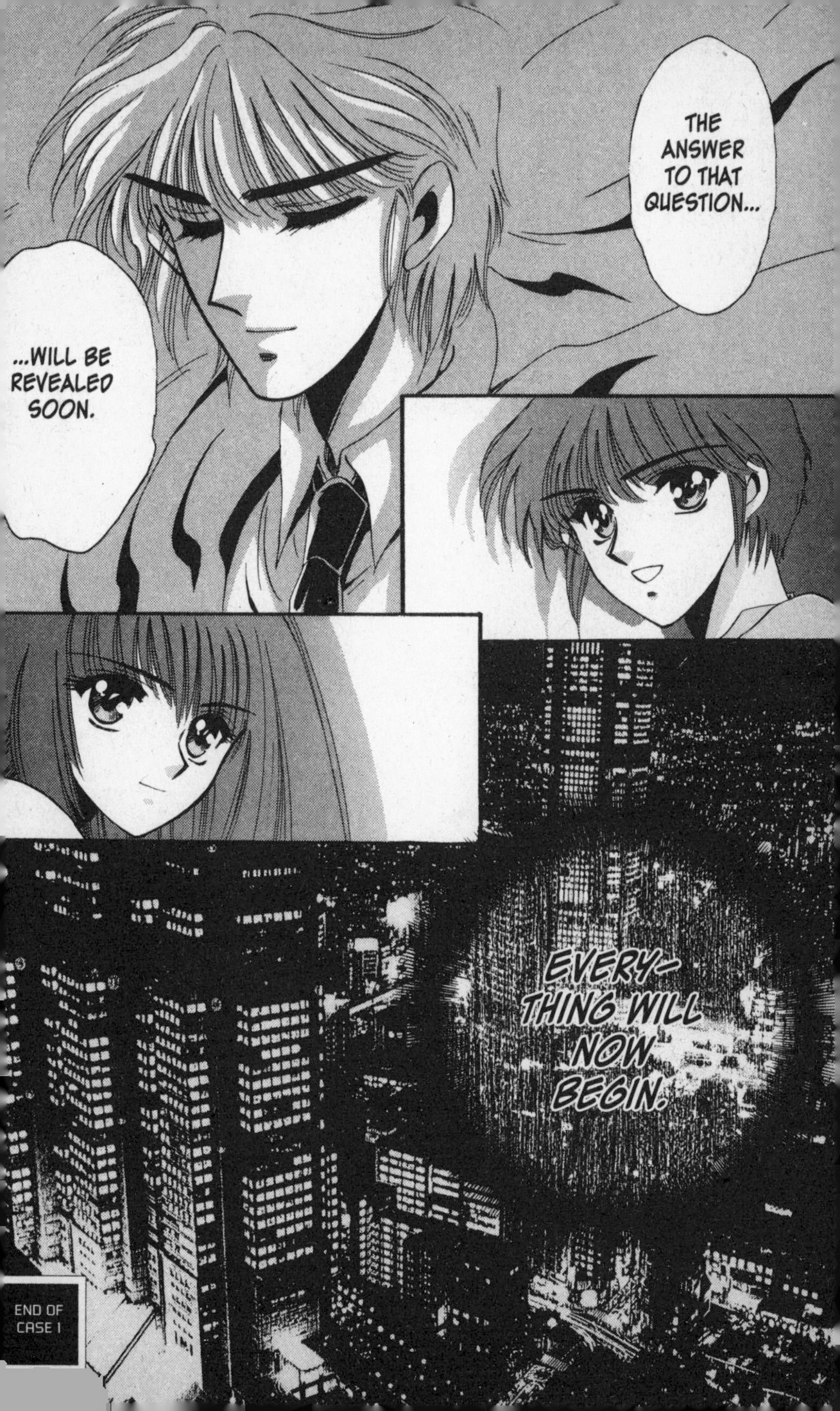
THE ANSWER TO THAT QUESTION...
...WILL BE REVEALED SOON.
EVERY-THING WILL NOW BEGIN.
END OF CASE 1

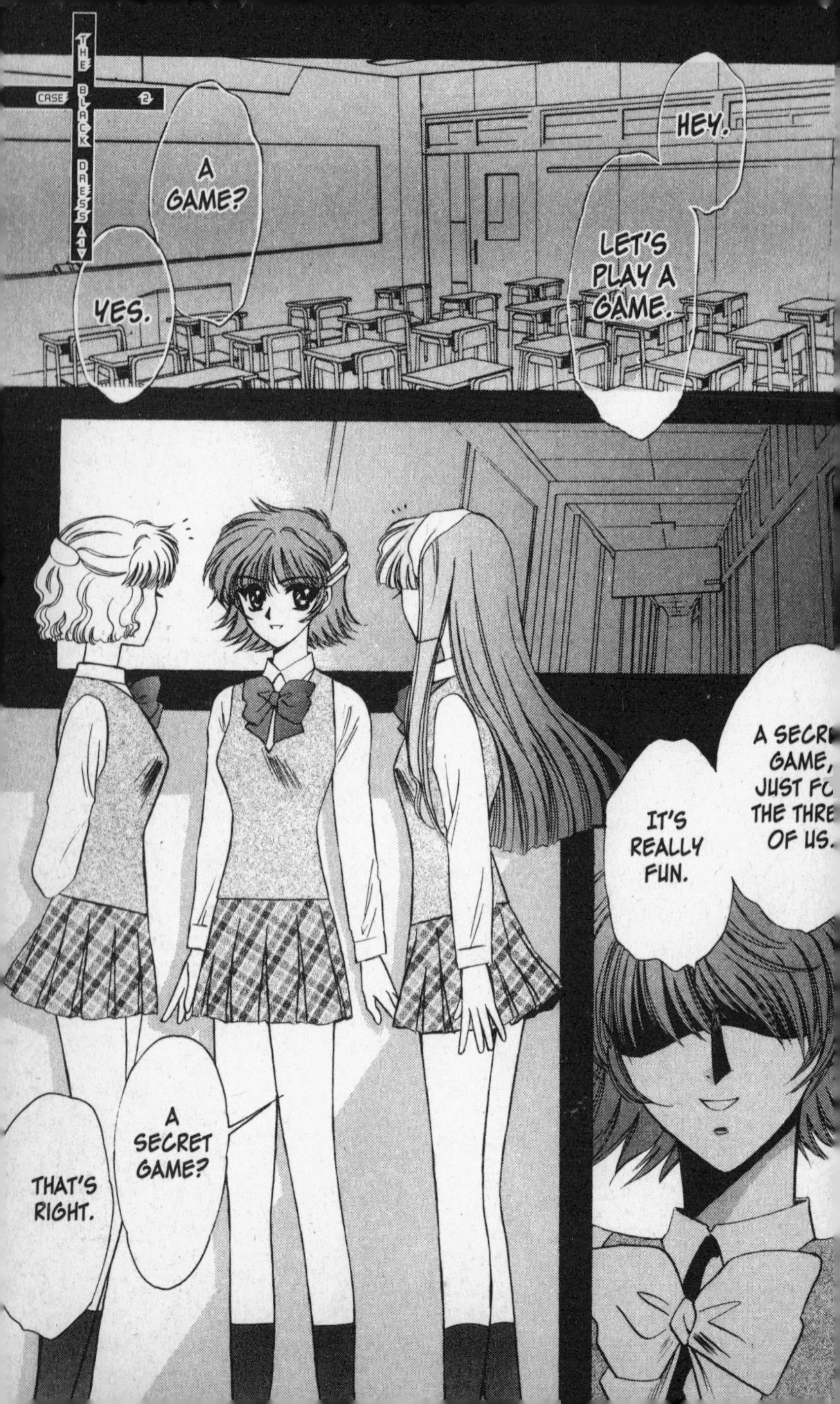
HEY.
LET'S PLAY A GAME.
A GAME?
YES.
A SECR GAME, JUST FO THE THRE OF US.
IT'S REALLY FUN.
A SECRET GAME?
THAT'S RIGHT.

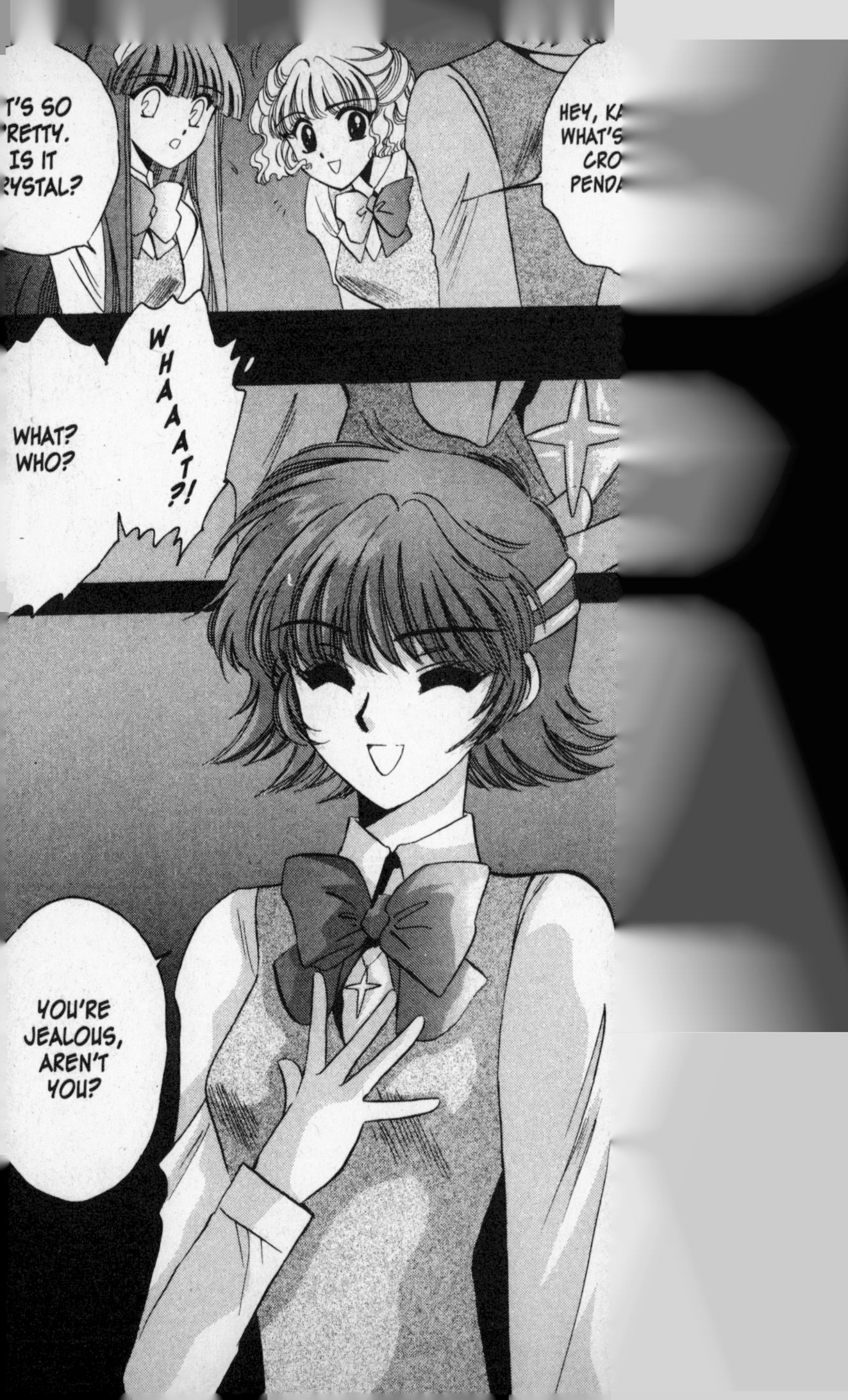
HEY, KA WHAT'S CRO PENDA
T'S SO RETTY. IS IT RYSTAL?
WHAAAAT?!
WHAT? WHO?
YOU'RE JEALOUS, AREN'T YOU?

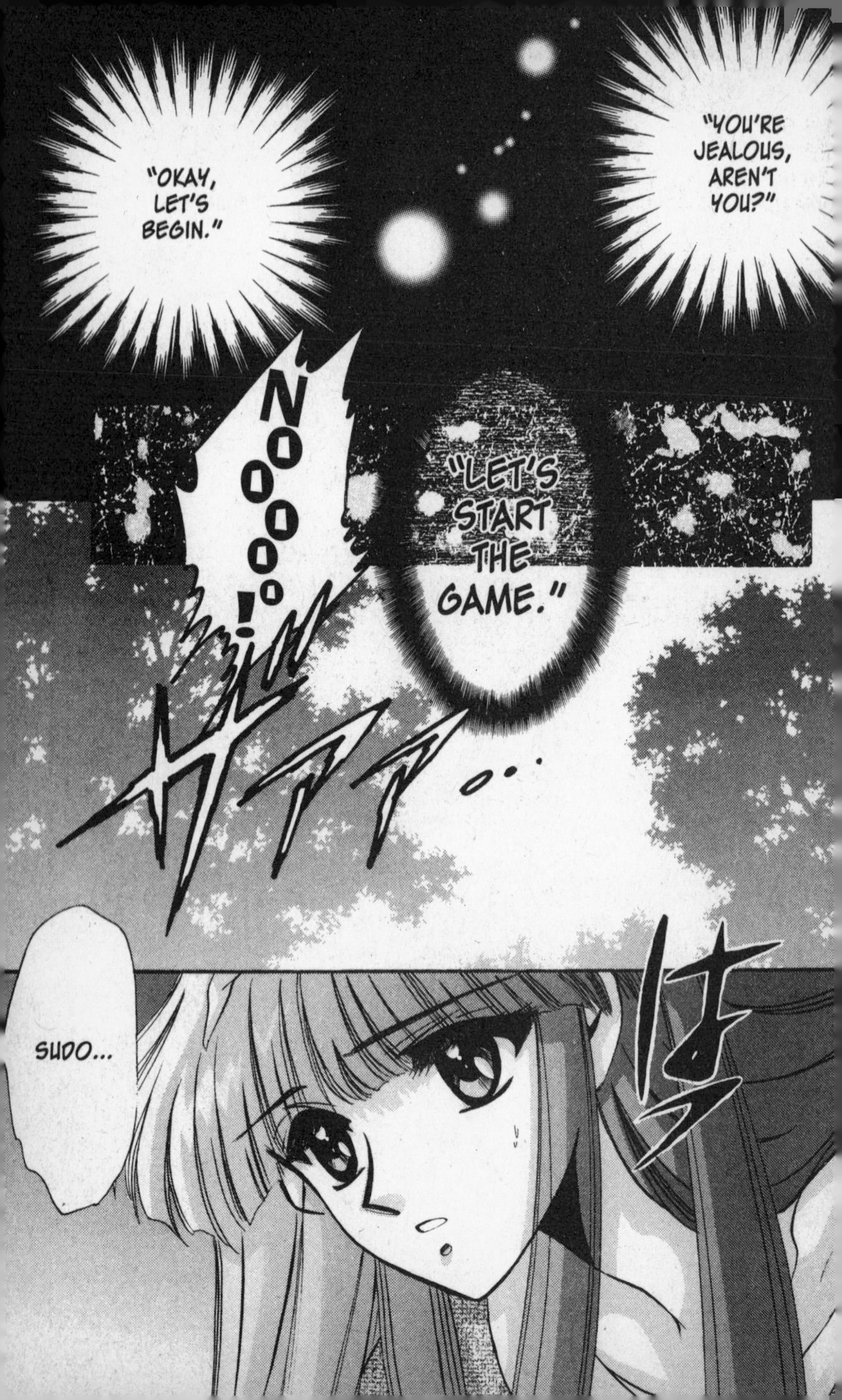
"YOU'RE JEALOUS, AREN'T YOU?"
"OKAY, LET'S BEGIN."
"LET'S START THE GAME."
NOOOOO!
SUDO...

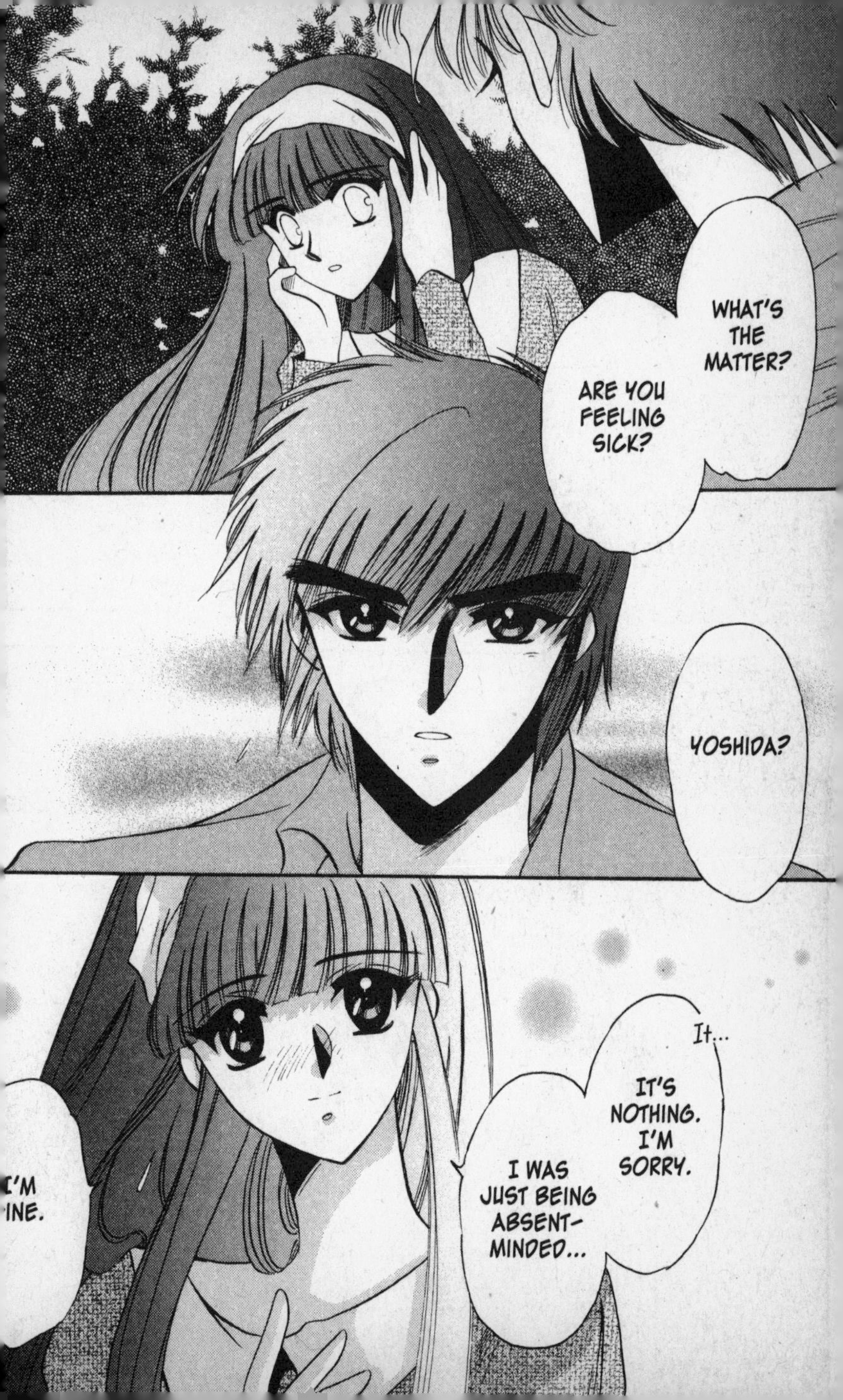
WHAT'S THE MATTER?
ARE YOU FEELING SICK?
YOSHIDA?
It...
IT'S NOTHING. I'M SORRY.
I WAS JUST BEING ABSENT-MINDED...
I'M INE.

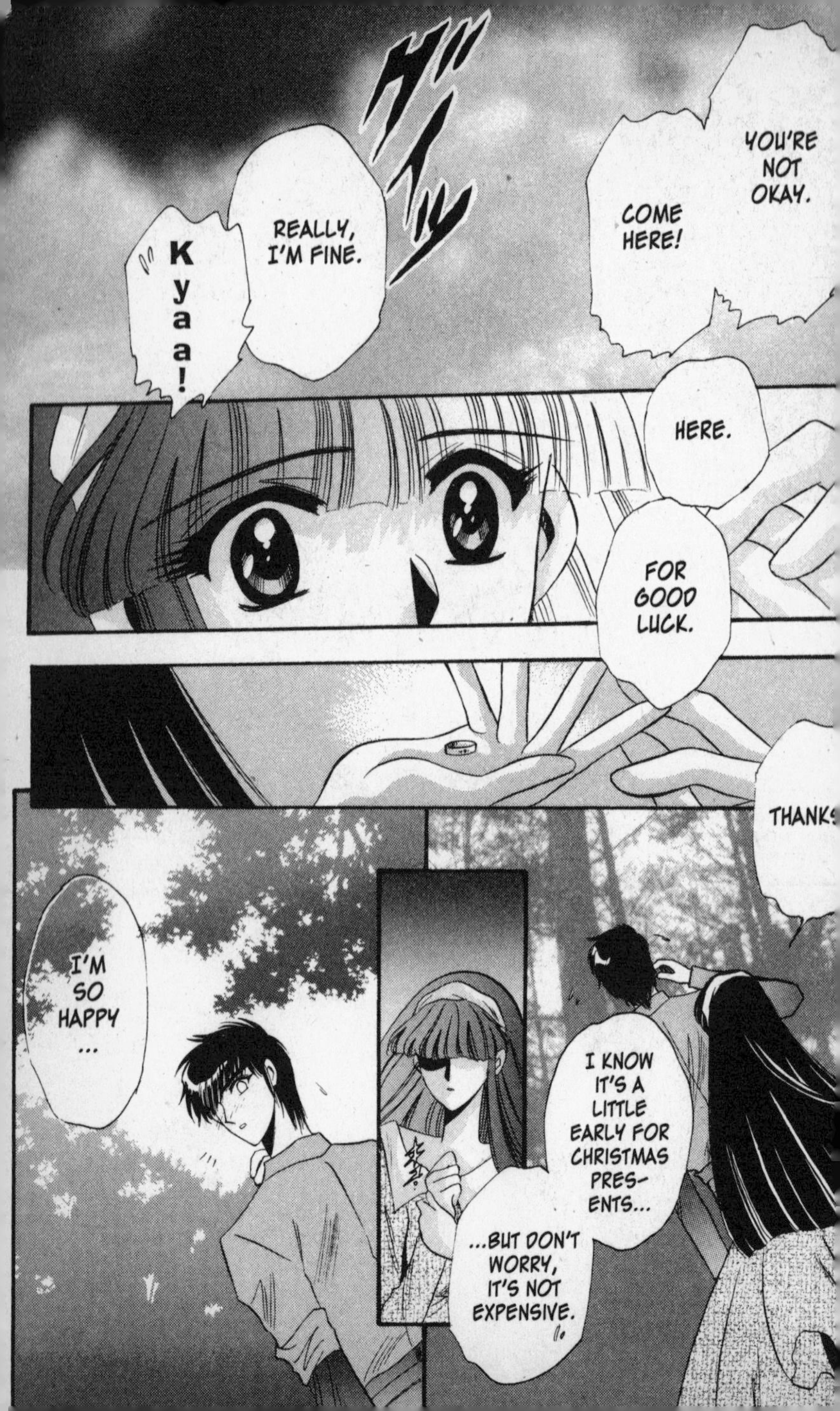
YOU'RE NOT OKAY.
COME HERE!
REALLY, I'M FINE.
Kyaa!
HERE.
FOR GOOD LUCK.
THANKS
I KNOW IT'S A LITTLE EARLY FOR CHRISTMAS PRES-ENTS...
...BUT DON'T WORRY, IT'S NOT EXPENSIVE.
I'M SO HAPPY ...

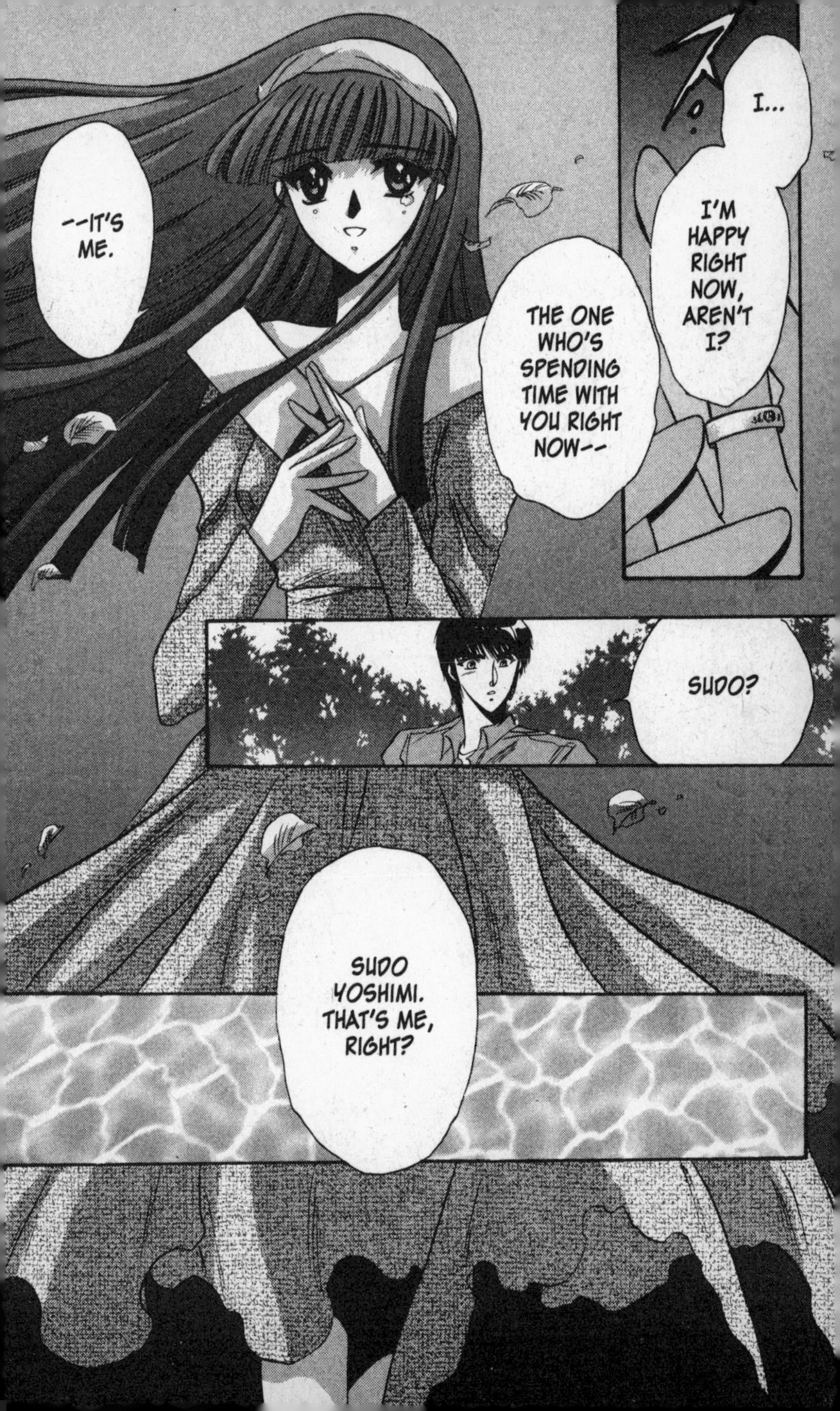

I...
I'M HAPPY RIGHT NOW, AREN'T I?
THE ONE WHO'S SPENDING TIME WITH YOU RIGHT NOW--
--IT'S ME.
SUDO?
SUDO YOSHIMI. THAT'S ME, RIGHT?

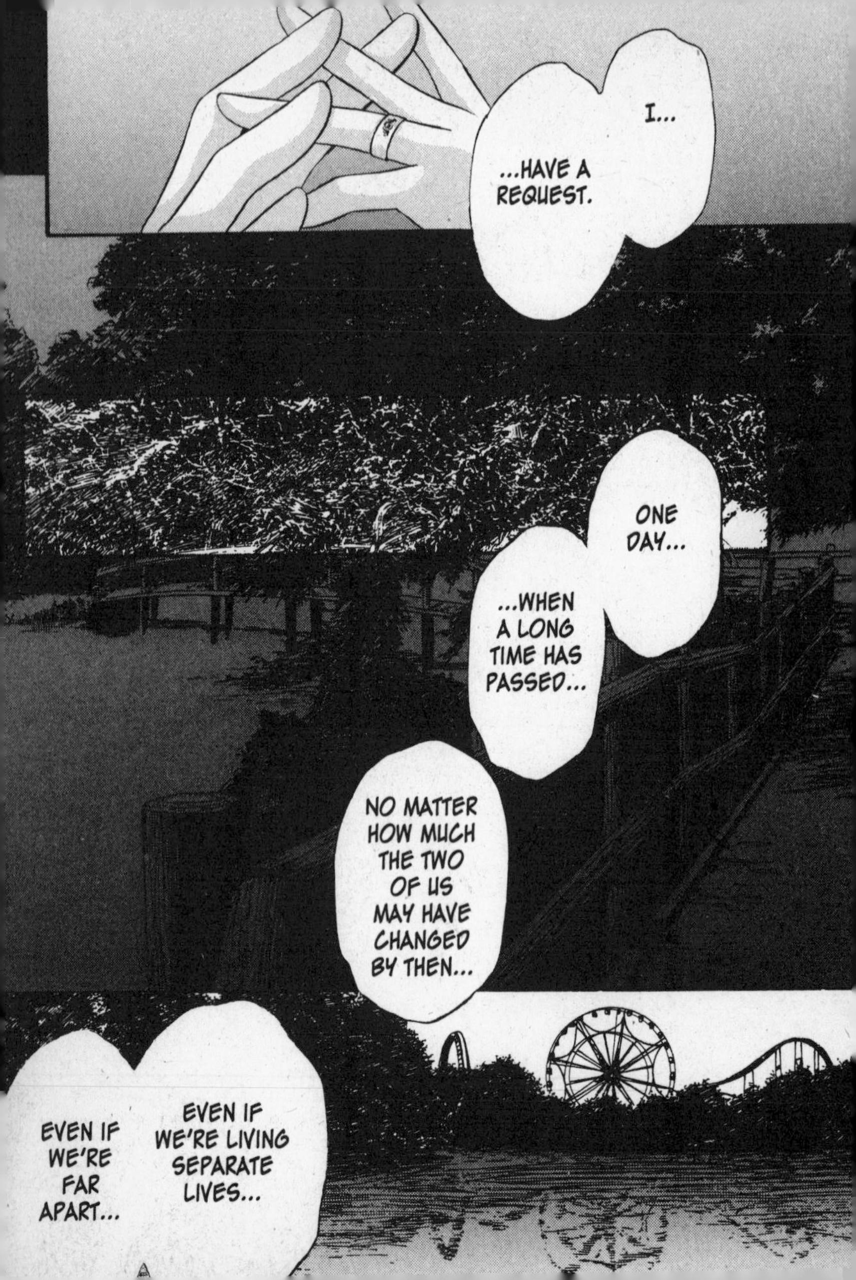
I...
...HAVE A REQUEST.
ONE DAY...
...WHEN A LONG TIME HAS PASSED...
NO MATTER HOW MUCH THE TWO OF US MAY HAVE CHANGED BY THEN...
EVEN IF WE'RE LIVING SEPARATE LIVES...
EVEN IF WE'RE FAR APART...

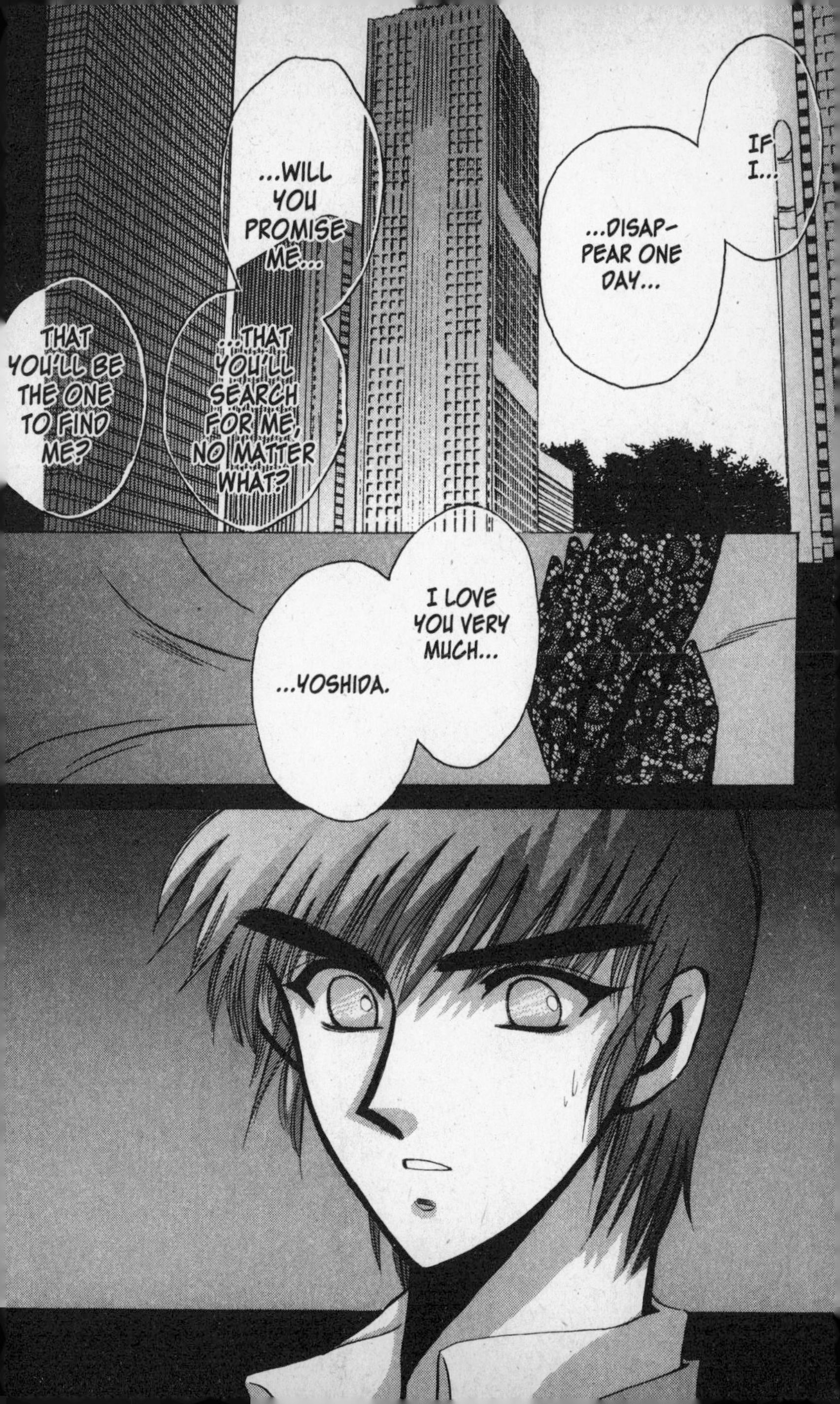
IF I...
...DISAP-PEAR ONE DAY...
...WILL YOU PROMISE ME...
...THAT YOU'LL SEARCH FOR ME, NO MATTER WHAT?
THAT YOU'LL BE THE ONE TO FIND ME?
I LOVE YOU VERY MUCH...
...YOSHIDA.

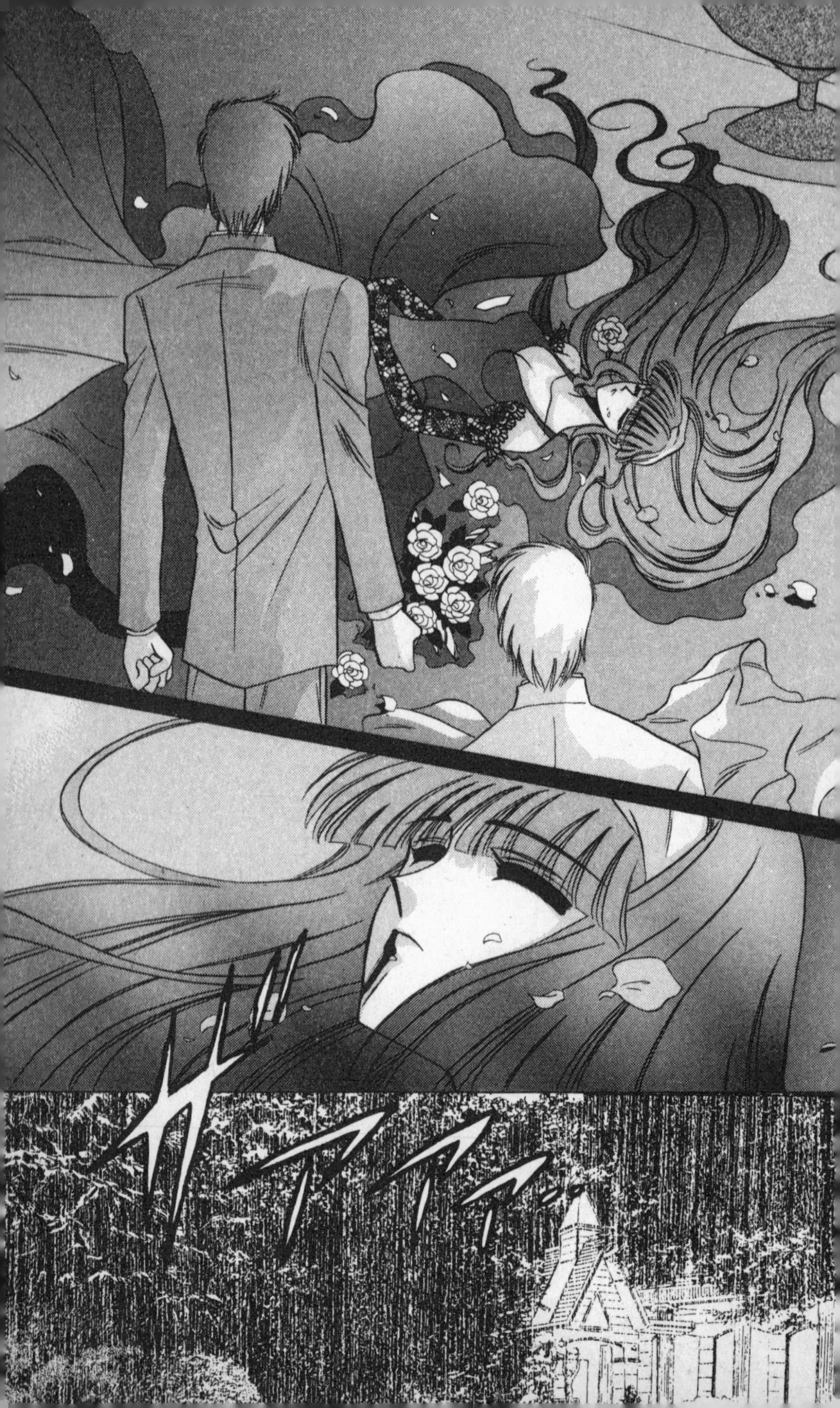
ザアアア

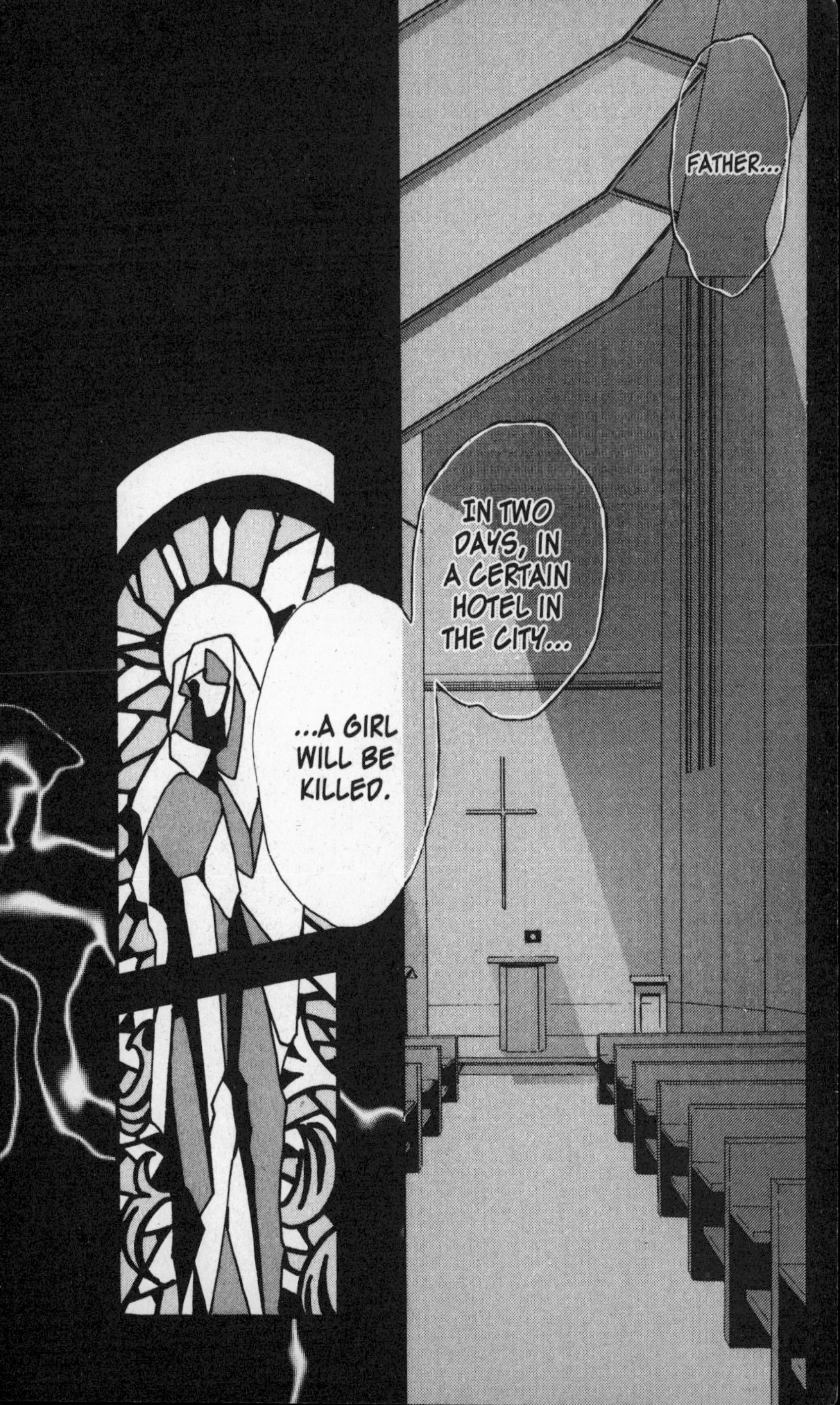
FATHER...
IN TWO DAYS, IN A CERTAIN HOTEL IN THE CITY...
...A GIRL WILL BE KILLED.

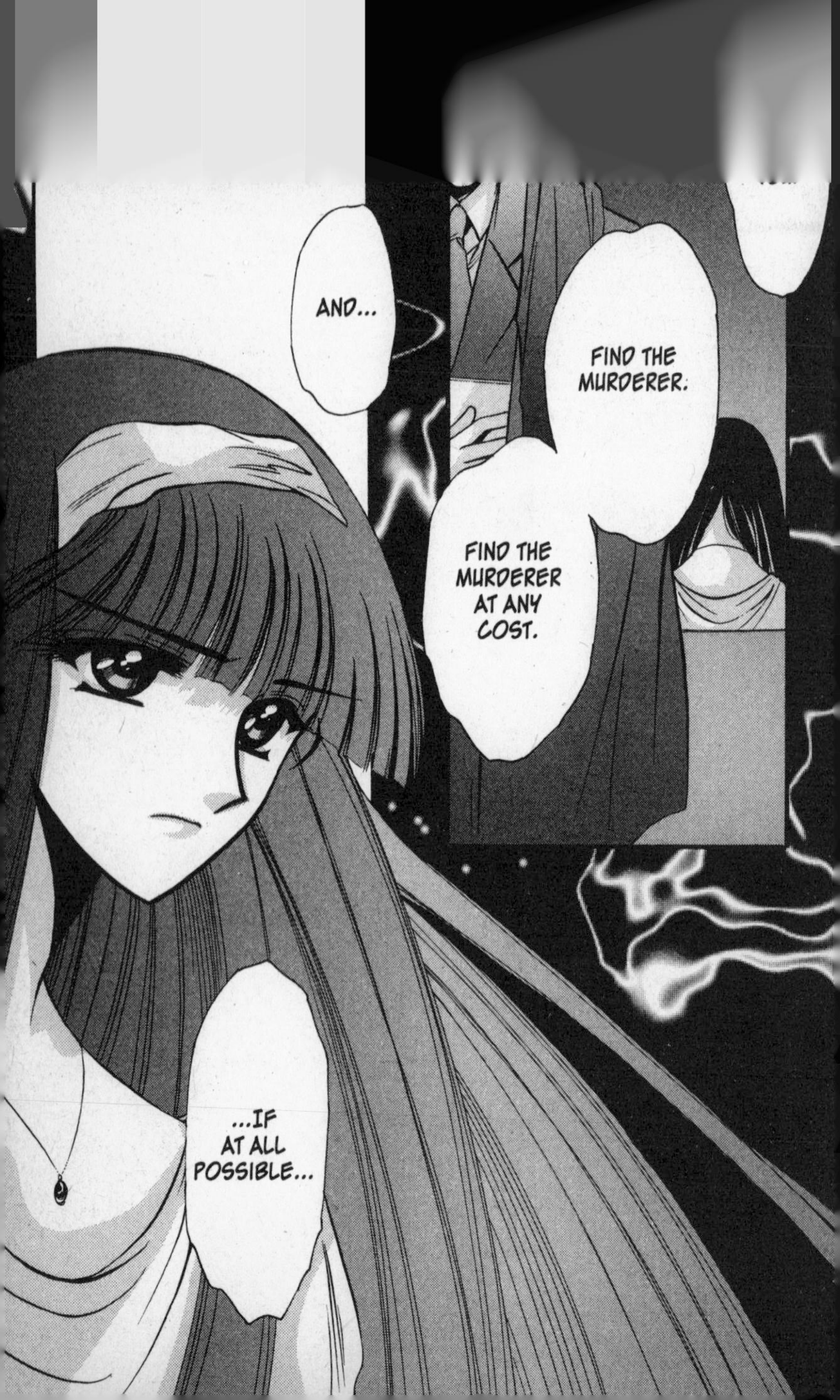
FIND THE MURDERER.
FIND THE MURDERER AT ANY COST.
AND...
...IF AT ALL POSSIBLE...

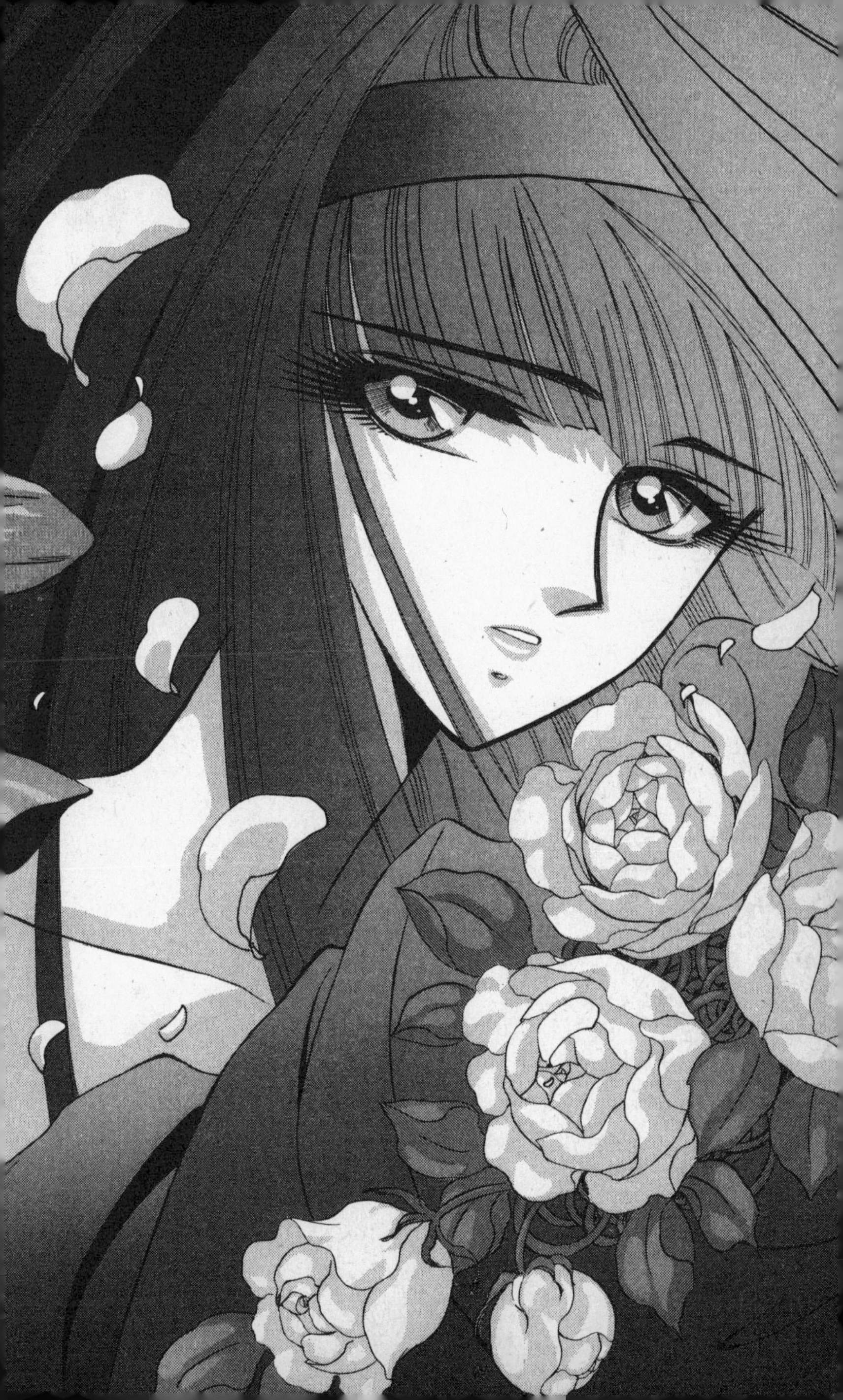

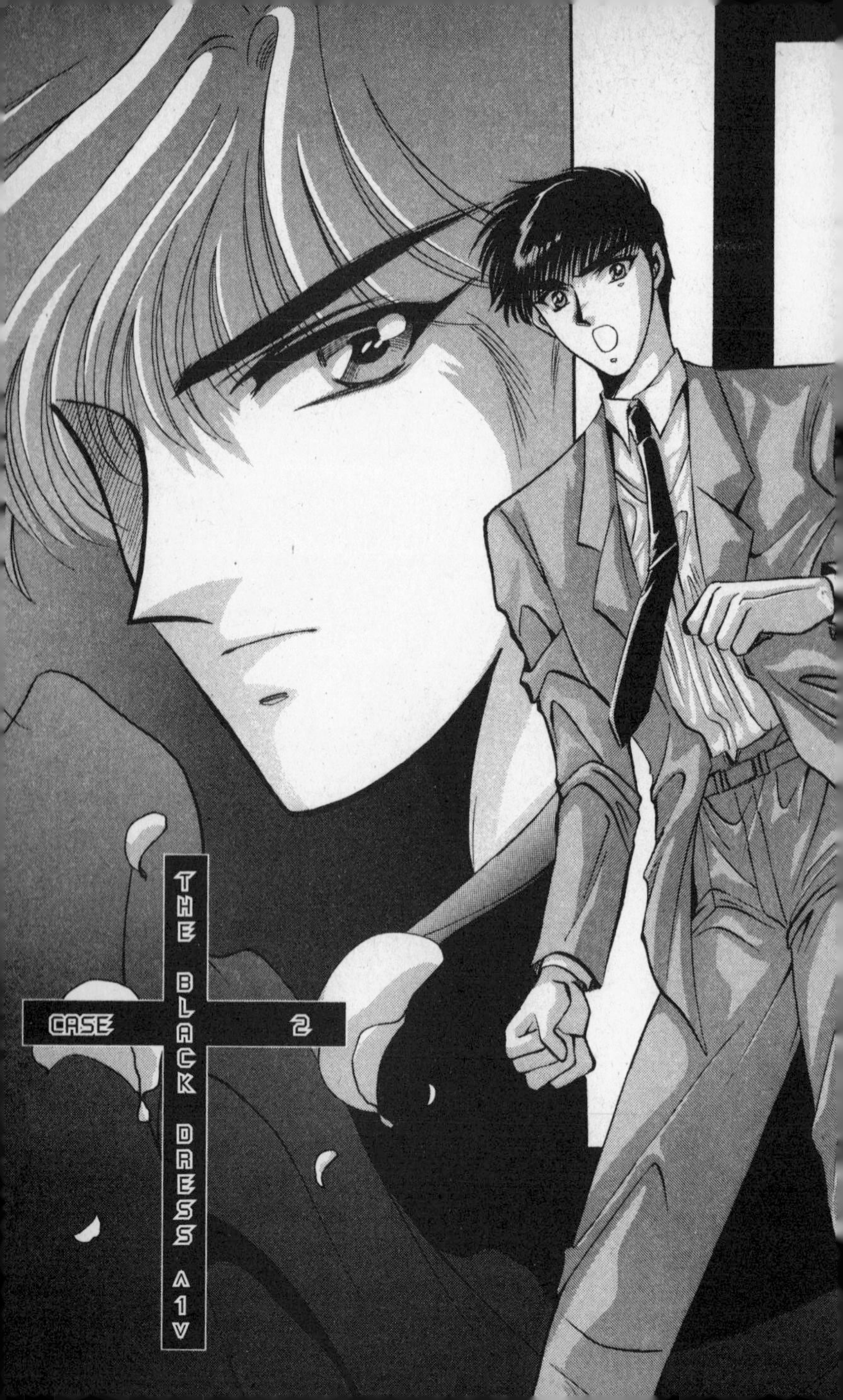
CASE 2
THE BLACK DRESS <1>

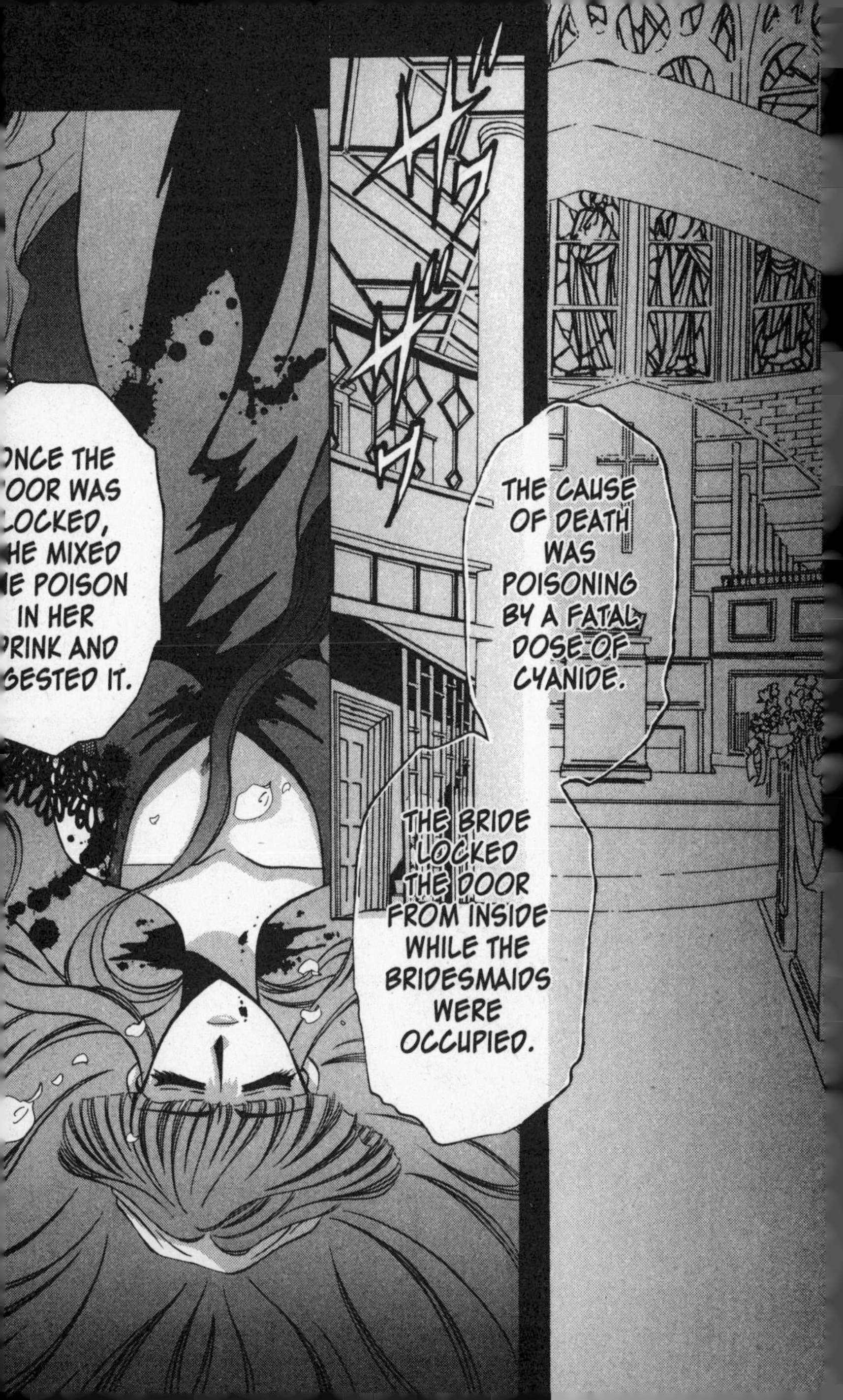
THE CAUSE OF DEATH WAS POISONING BY A FATAL DOSE OF CYANIDE.
THE BRIDE LOCKED THE DOOR FROM INSIDE WHILE THE BRIDESMAIDS WERE OCCUPIED.
NCE THE OOR WAS OCKED, HE MIXED E POISON IN HER RINK AND GESTED IT.

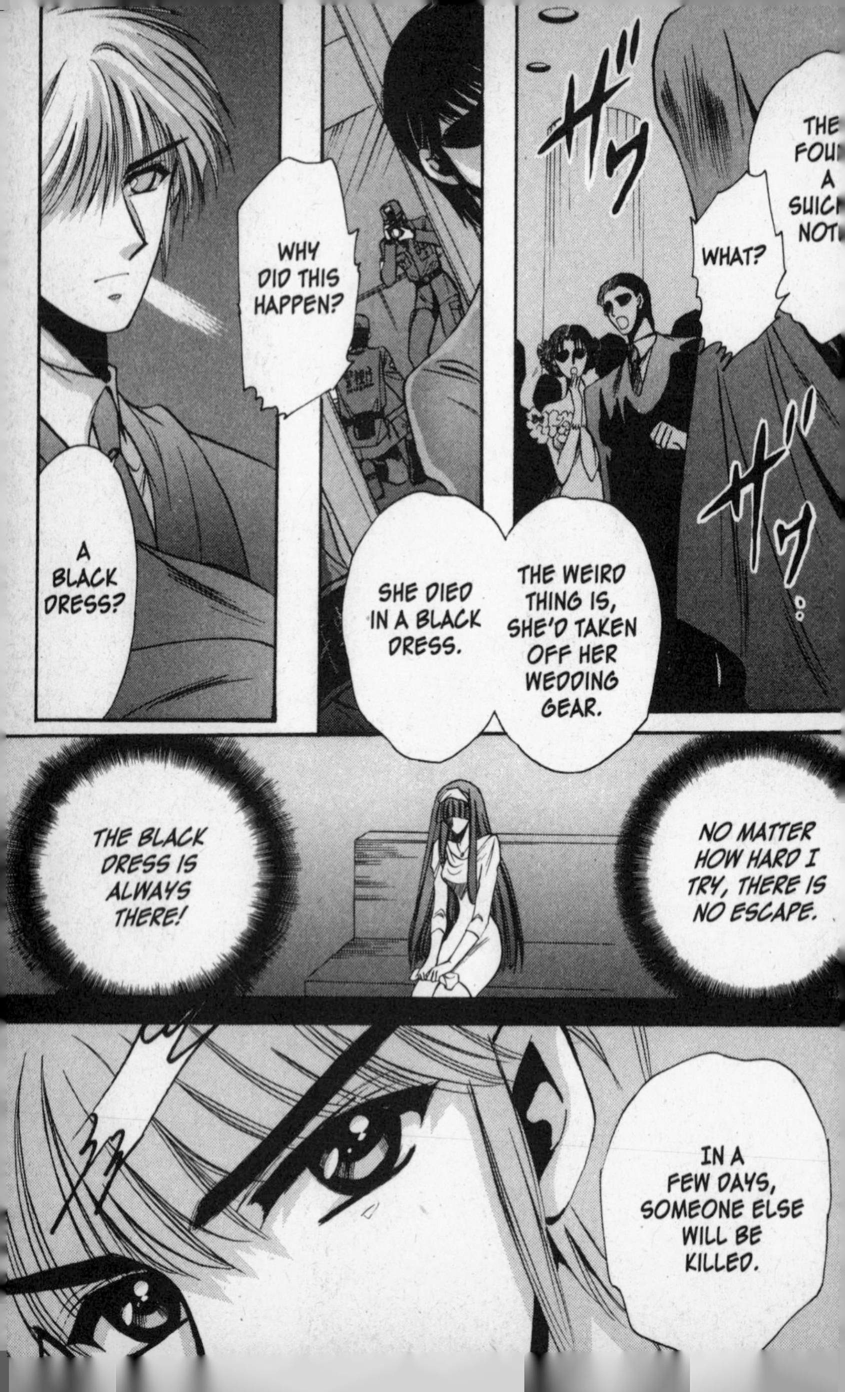
THE FOU A SUIC NOT
WHAT?
ザワ
ザワ
WHY DID THIS HAPPEN?
THE WEIRD THING IS, SHE'D TAKEN OFF HER WEDDING GEAR.
SHE DIED IN A BLACK DRESS.
A BLACK DRESS?
NO MATTER HOW HARD I TRY, THERE IS NO ESCAPE.
THE BLACK DRESS IS ALWAYS THERE!
IN A FEW DAYS, SOMEONE ELSE WILL BE KILLED.

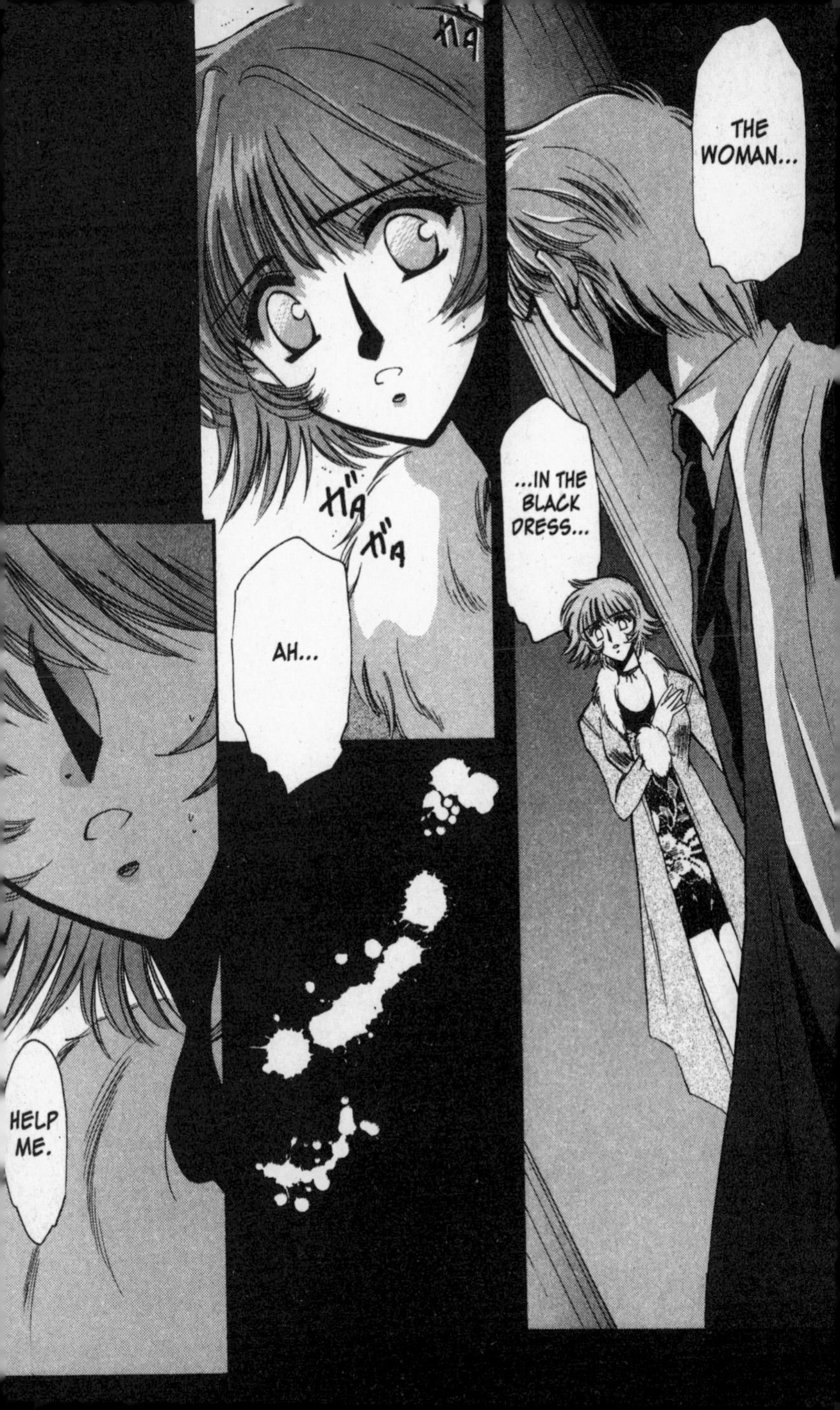
THE WOMAN...
...IN THE BLACK DRESS...
AH...
HELP ME.

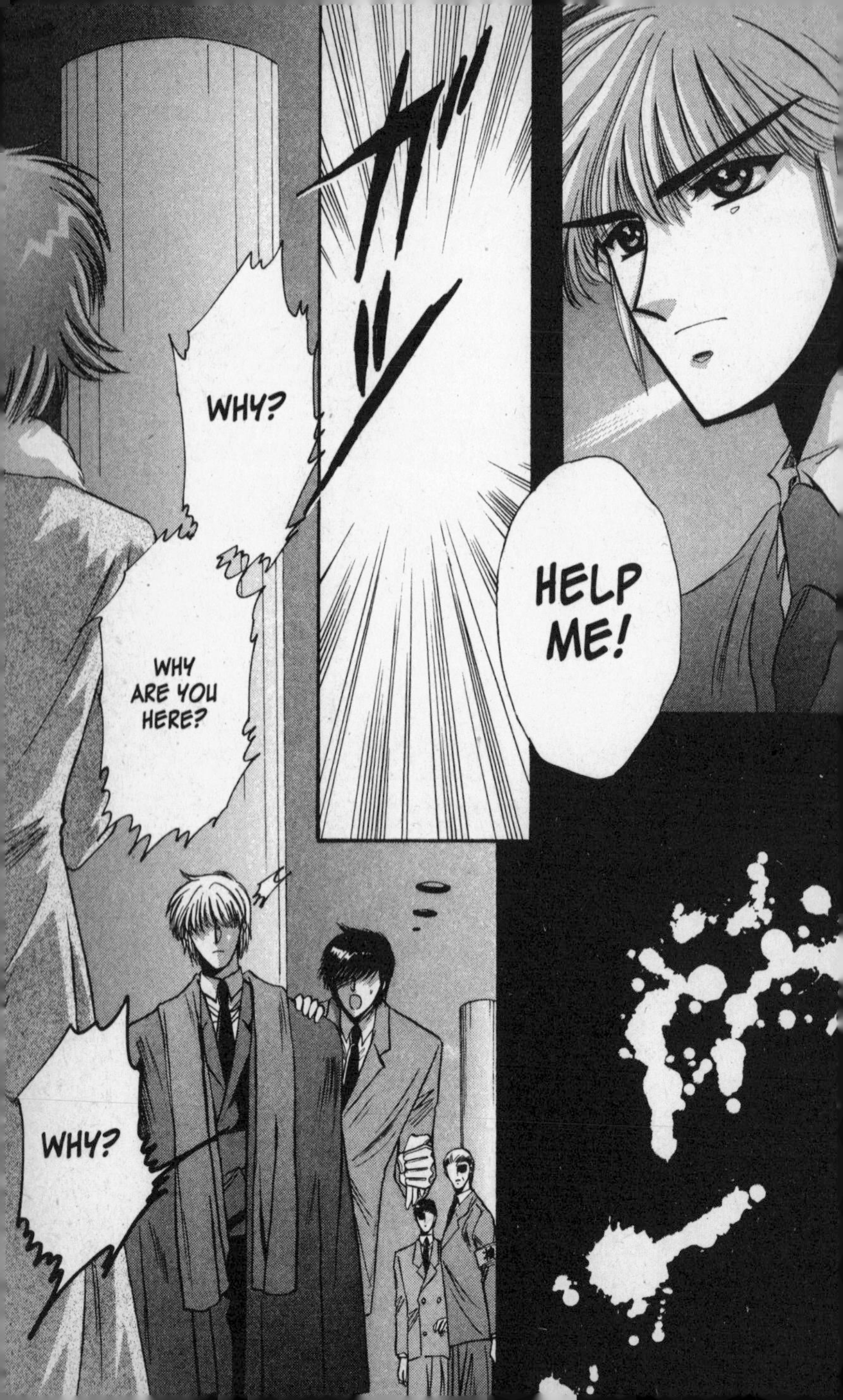
HELP ME!
ガッ
WHY?
WHY ARE YOU HERE?
WHY?

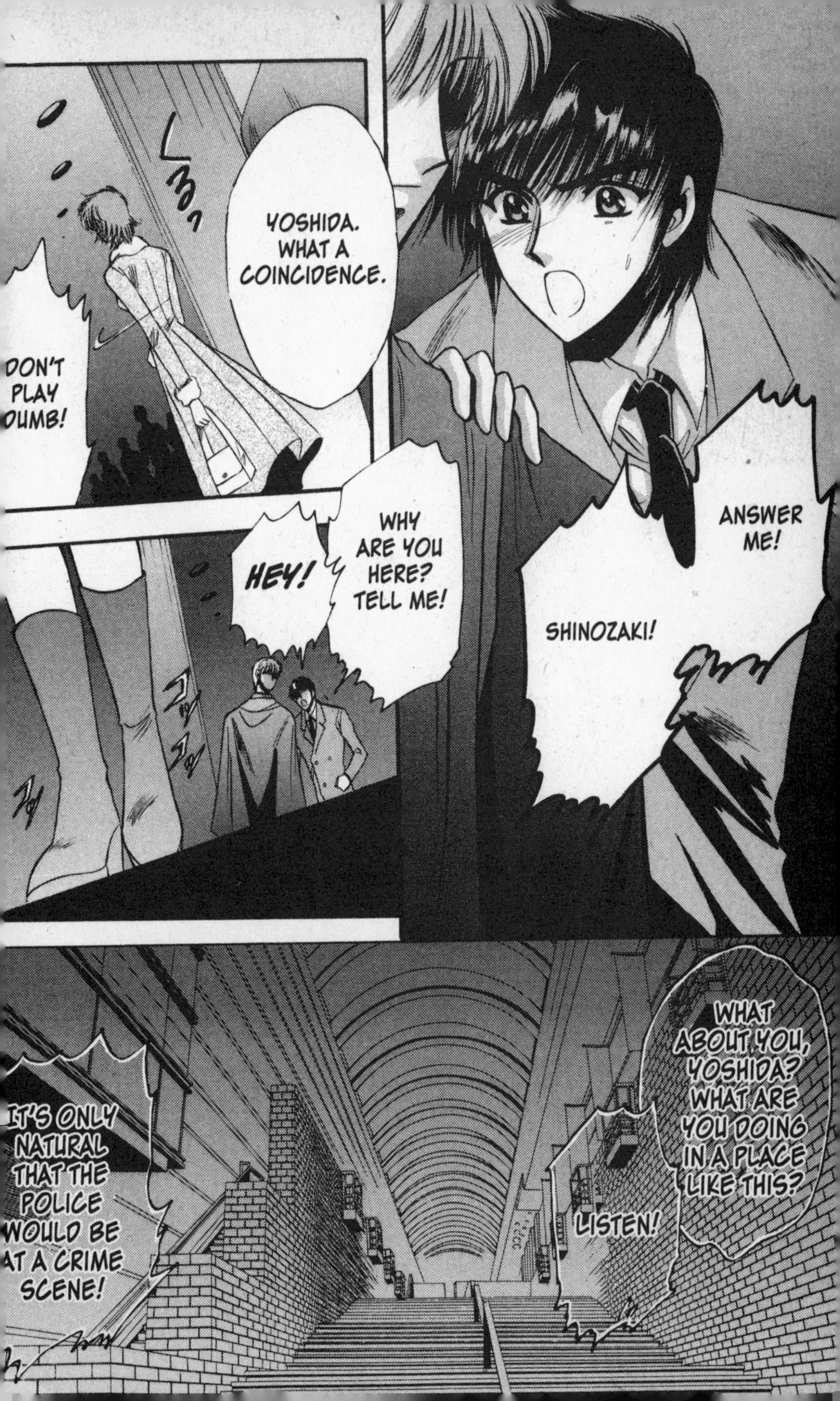
YOSHIDA. WHAT A COINCIDENCE.
DON'T PLAY DUMB!
HEY!
WHY ARE YOU HERE? TELL ME!
ANSWER ME!
SHINOZAKI!
WHAT ABOUT YOU, YOSHIDA? WHAT ARE YOU DOING IN A PLACE LIKE THIS?
LISTEN!
IT'S ONLY NATURAL THAT THE POLICE WOULD BE AT A CRIME SCENE!

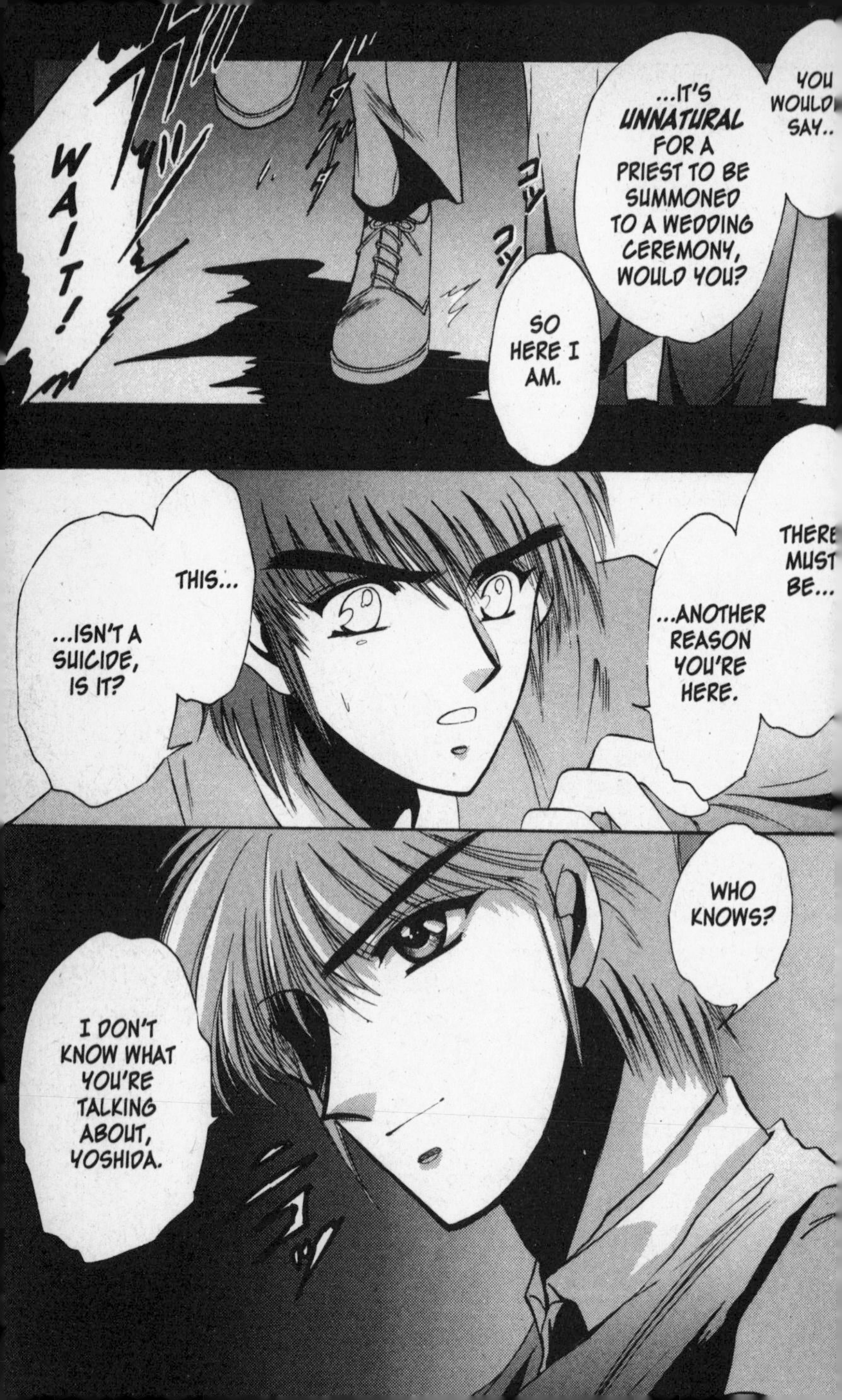
YOU WOULD SAY..
...IT'S UNNATURAL FOR A PRIEST TO BE SUMMONED TO A WEDDING CEREMONY, WOULD YOU?
SO HERE I AM.
WAIT!
THERE MUST BE...
...ANOTHER REASON YOU'RE HERE.
THIS...
...ISN'T A SUICIDE, IS IT?
WHO KNOWS?
I DON'T KNOW WHAT YOU'RE TALKING ABOUT, YOSHIDA.

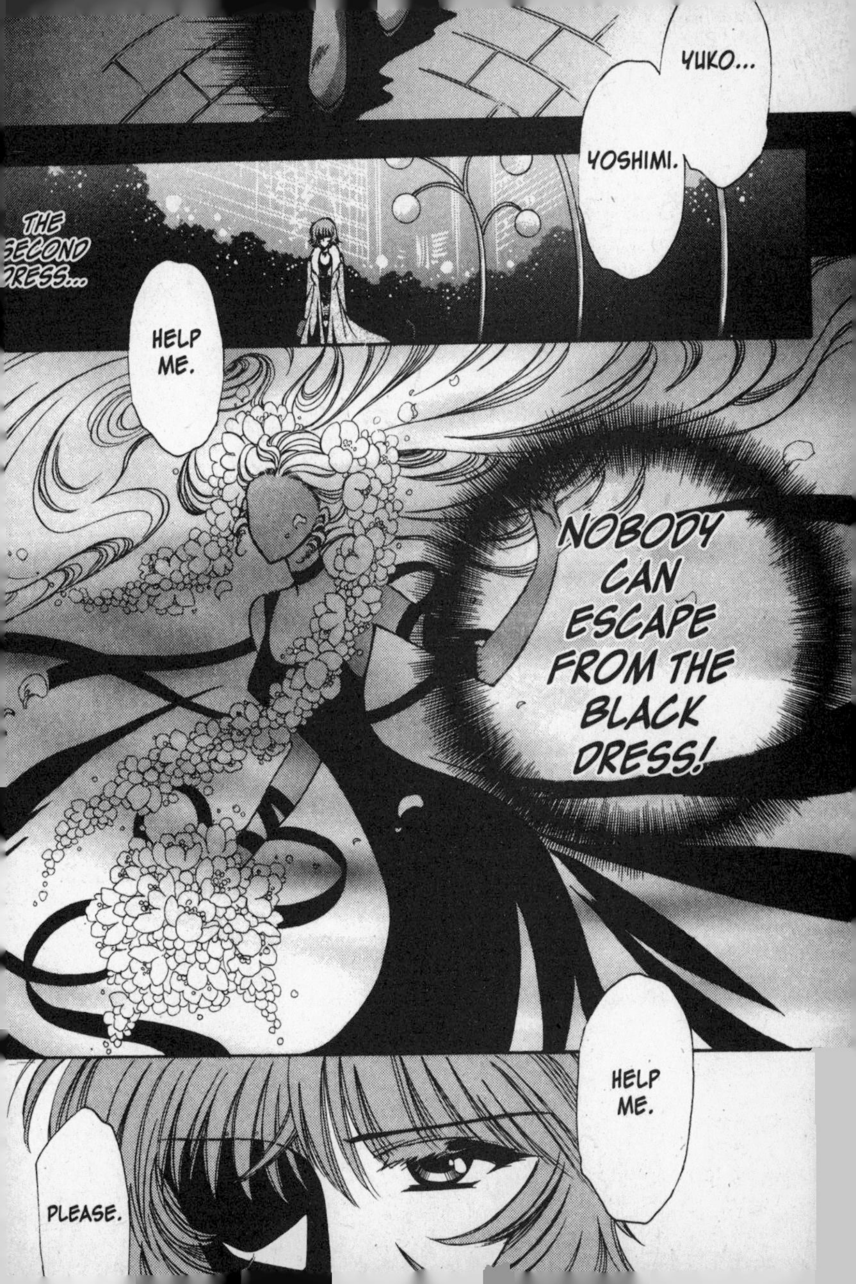
YUKO...
YOSHIMI.
THE SECOND DRESS...
HELP ME.
NOBODY CAN ESCAPE FROM THE BLACK DRESS!
HELP ME.
PLEASE.

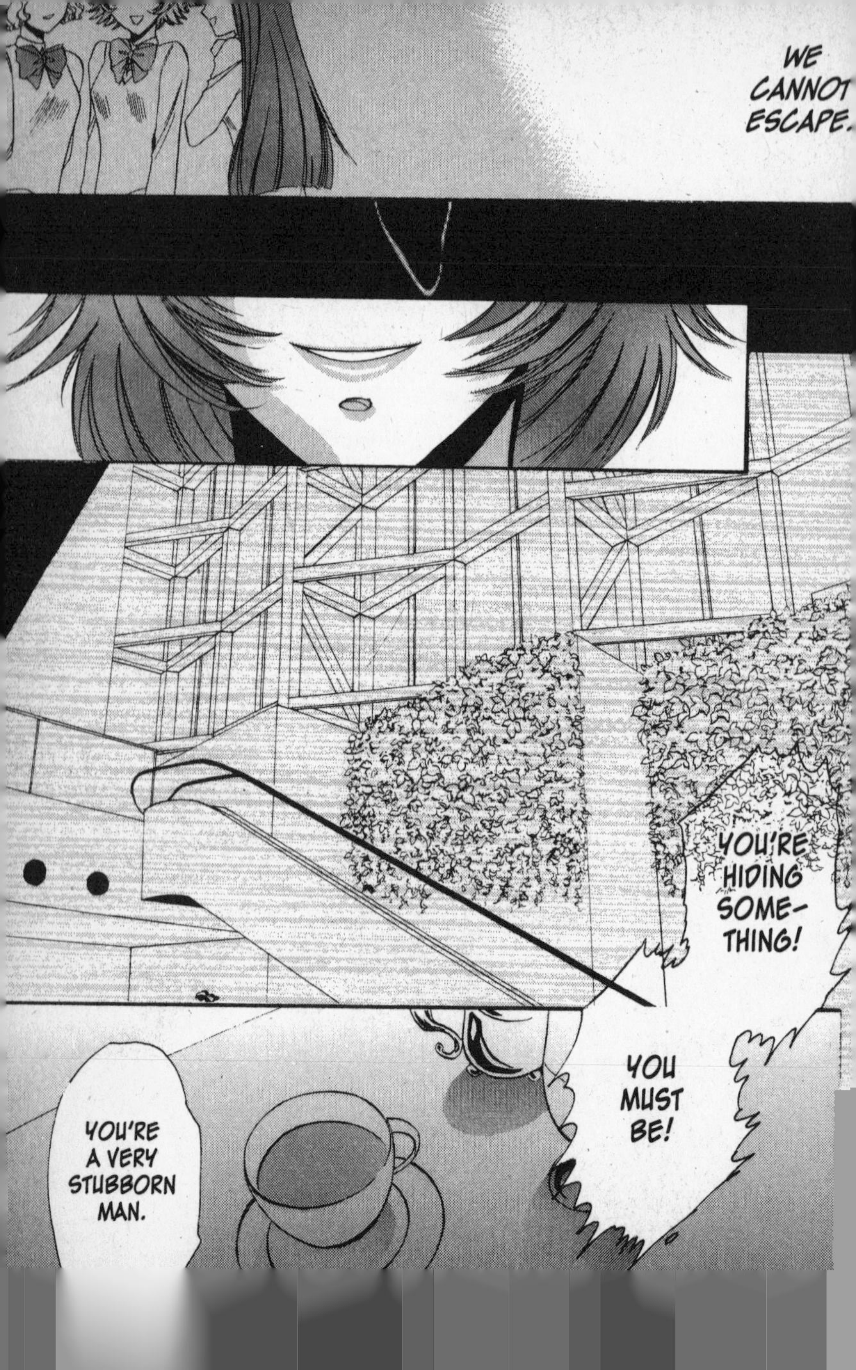
WE CANNOT ESCAPE.
YOU'RE HIDING SOME-THING!
...
YOU MUST BE!
YOU'RE A VERY STUBBORN MAN.

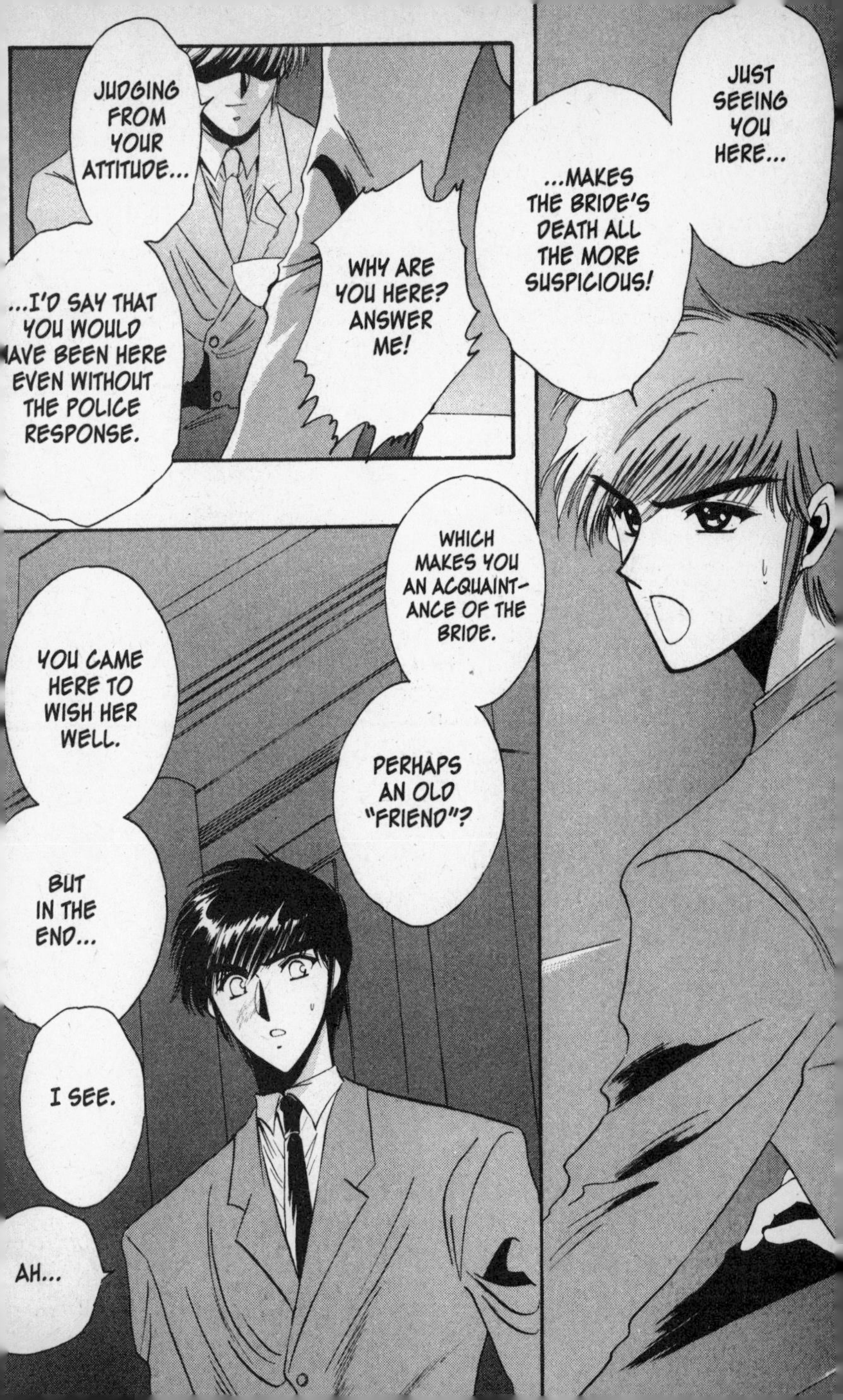

JUST SEEING YOU HERE...
...MAKES THE BRIDE'S DEATH ALL THE MORE SUSPICIOUS!
WHY ARE YOU HERE? ANSWER ME!
JUDGING FROM YOUR ATTITUDE...
...I'D SAY THAT YOU WOULD AVE BEEN HERE EVEN WITHOUT THE POLICE RESPONSE.
WHICH MAKES YOU AN ACQUAINT-ANCE OF THE BRIDE.
PERHAPS AN OLD "FRIEND"?
YOU CAME HERE TO WISH HER WELL.
BUT IN THE END...
I SEE.
AH...

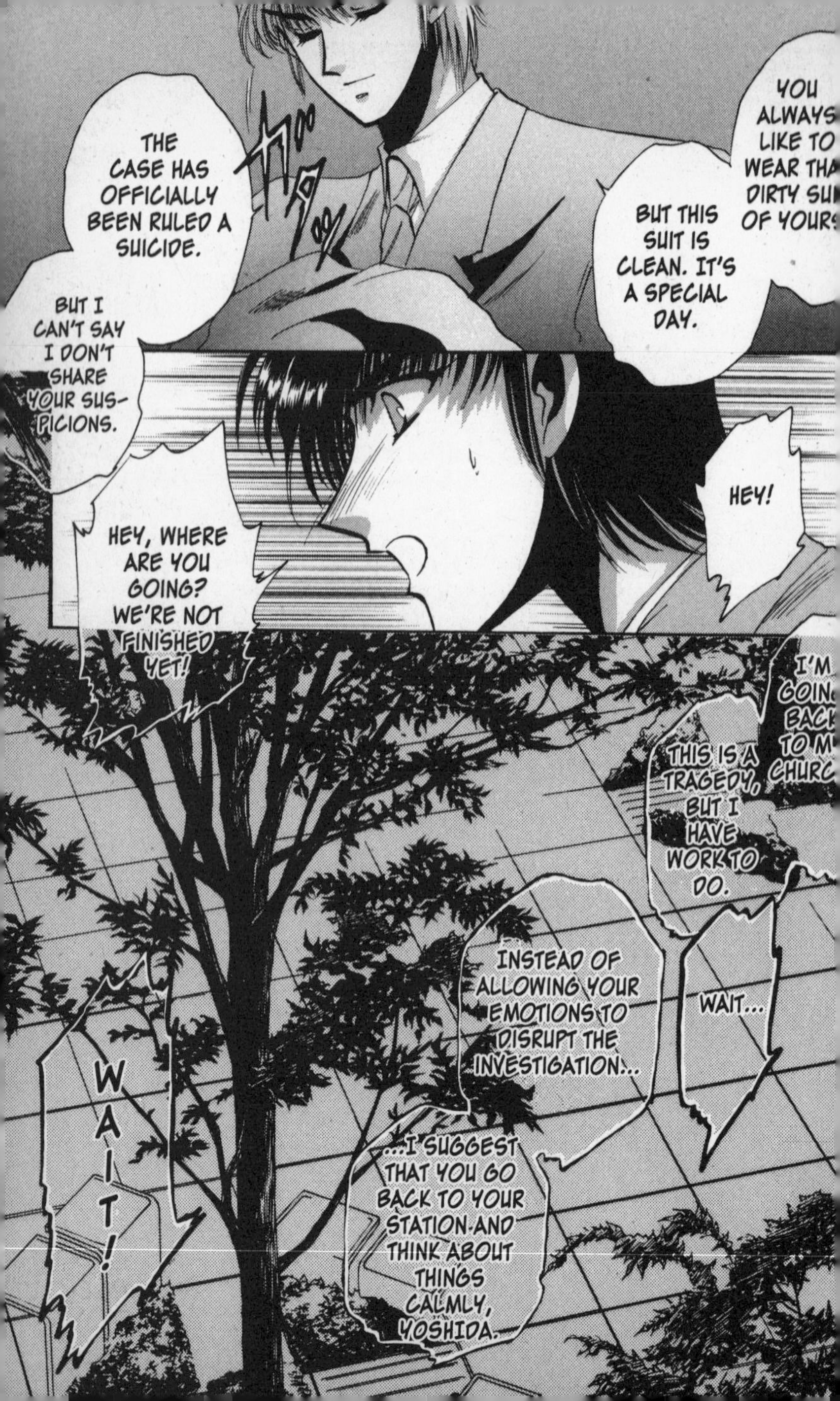

YOU ALWAYS LIKE TO WEAR THA DIRTY SU OF YOURS
BUT THIS SUIT IS CLEAN. IT'S A SPECIAL DAY.
THE CASE HAS OFFICIALLY BEEN RULED A SUICIDE.
BUT I CAN'T SAY I DON'T SHARE YOUR SUSPICIONS.
HEY!
HEY, WHERE ARE YOU GOING? WE'RE NOT FINISHED YET!
I'M GOIN BACK TO M CHURC
THIS IS A TRAGEDY, BUT I HAVE WORK TO DO.
WAIT...
INSTEAD OF ALLOWING YOUR EMOTIONS TO DISRUPT THE INVESTIGATION...
...I SUGGEST THAT YOU GO BACK TO YOUR STATION AND THINK ABOUT THINGS CALMLY, YOSHIDA.
WAIT!

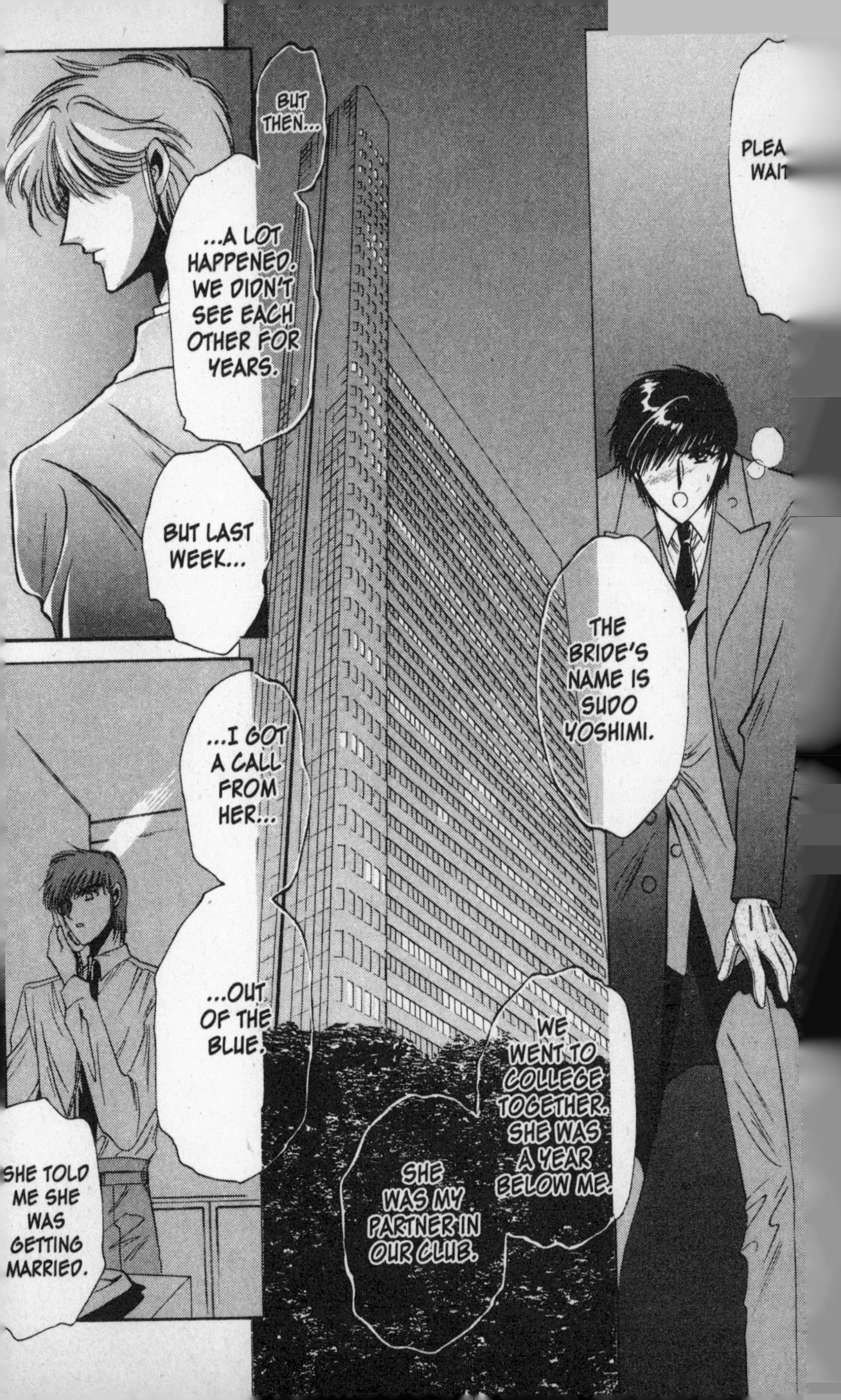
PLEA WAIT
THE BRIDE'S NAME IS SUDO YOSHIMI.
WE WENT TO COLLEGE TOGETHER. SHE WAS A YEAR BELOW ME.
SHE WAS MY PARTNER IN OUR CLUB.
BUT THEN...
...A LOT HAPPENED. WE DIDN'T SEE EACH OTHER FOR YEARS.
BUT LAST WEEK...
...I GOT A CALL FROM HER...
...OUT OF THE BLUE.
SHE TOLD ME SHE WAS GETTING MARRIED.

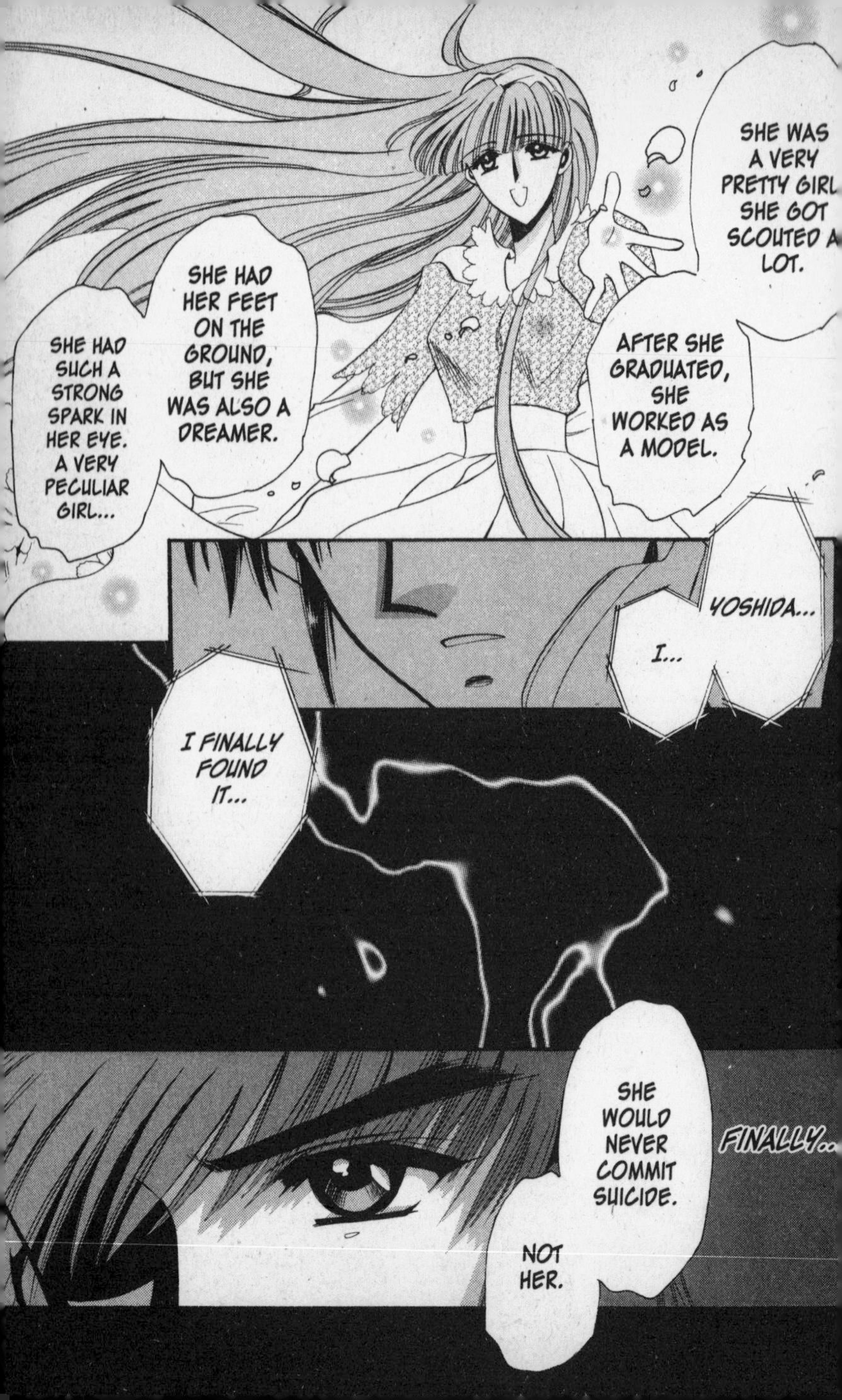

SHE WAS A VERY PRETTY GIRL. SHE GOT SCOUTED A LOT.
AFTER SHE GRADUATED, SHE WORKED AS A MODEL.
SHE HAD HER FEET ON THE GROUND, BUT SHE WAS ALSO A DREAMER.
SHE HAD SUCH A STRONG SPARK IN HER EYE. A VERY PECULIAR GIRL...
YOSHIDA...
I...
I FINALLY FOUND IT...
FINALLY...
SHE WOULD NEVER COMMIT SUICIDE.
NOT HER.

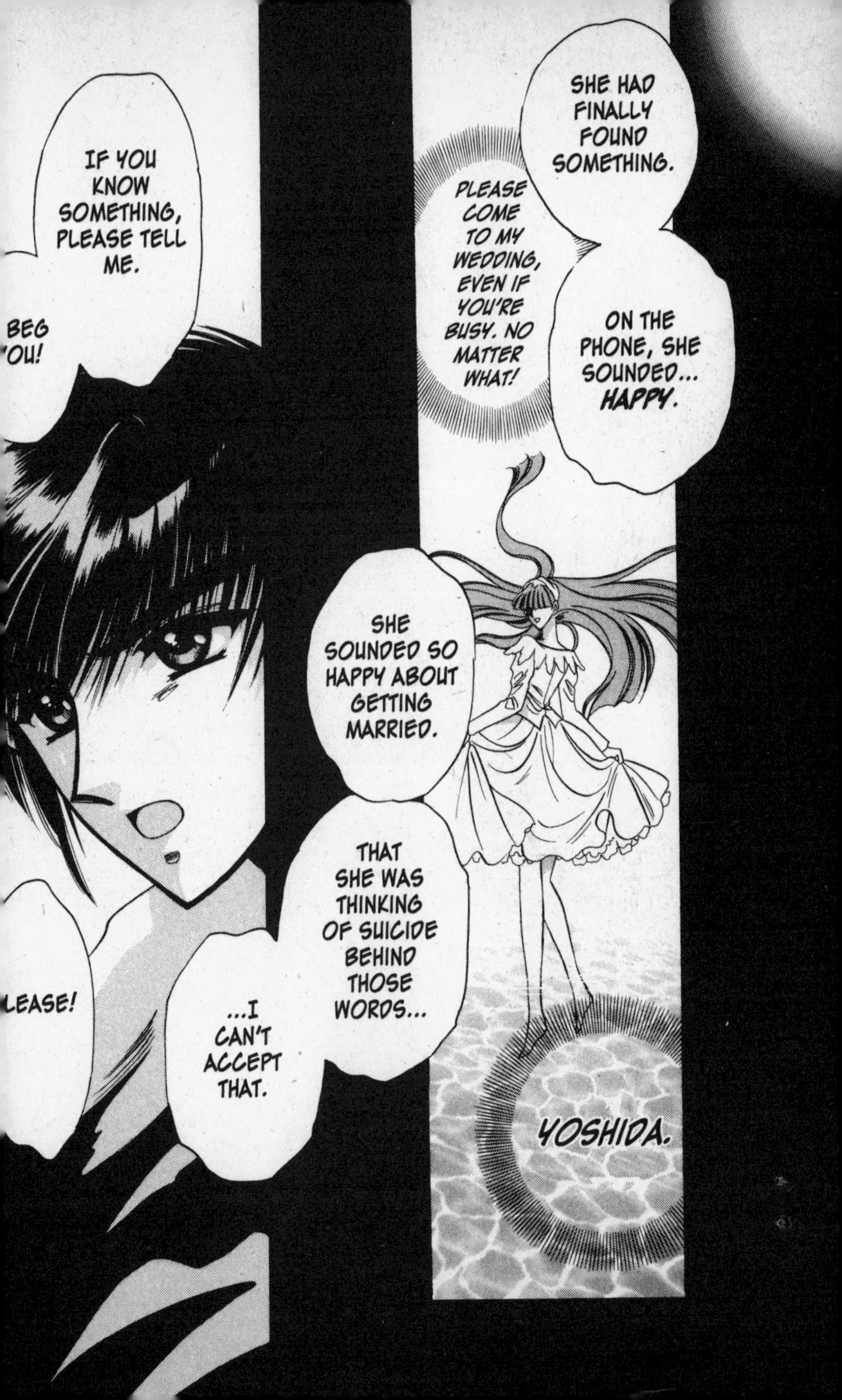
SHE HAD FINALLY FOUND SOMETHING.
PLEASE COME TO MY WEDDING, EVEN IF YOU'RE BUSY. NO MATTER WHAT!
ON THE PHONE, SHE SOUNDED... *HAPPY*.
SHE SOUNDED SO HAPPY ABOUT GETTING MARRIED.
THAT SHE WAS THINKING OF SUICIDE BEHIND THOSE WORDS...
...I CAN'T ACCEPT THAT.
YOSHIDA.
IF YOU KNOW SOMETHING, PLEASE TELL ME.
BEG 'OU!
LEASE!

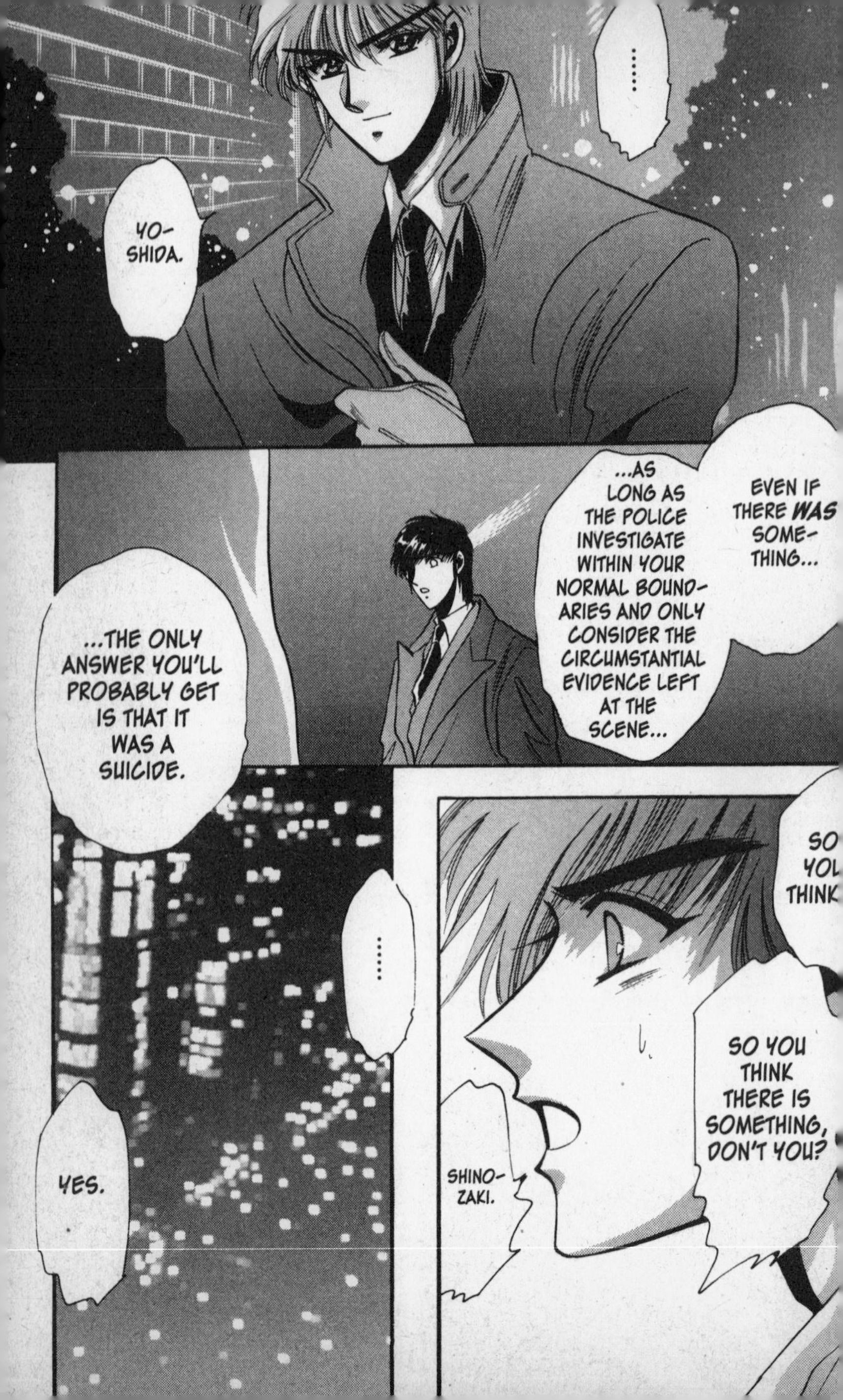
……
YO-SHIDA.
EVEN IF THERE **WAS** SOME-THING...
...AS LONG AS THE POLICE INVESTIGATE WITHIN YOUR NORMAL BOUND-ARIES AND ONLY CONSIDER THE CIRCUMSTANTIAL EVIDENCE LEFT AT THE SCENE...
...THE ONLY ANSWER YOU'LL PROBABLY GET IS THAT IT WAS A SUICIDE.
SO YOU THINK
SO YOU THINK THERE IS SOMETHING, DON'T YOU?
SHINO-ZAKI.
……
YES.

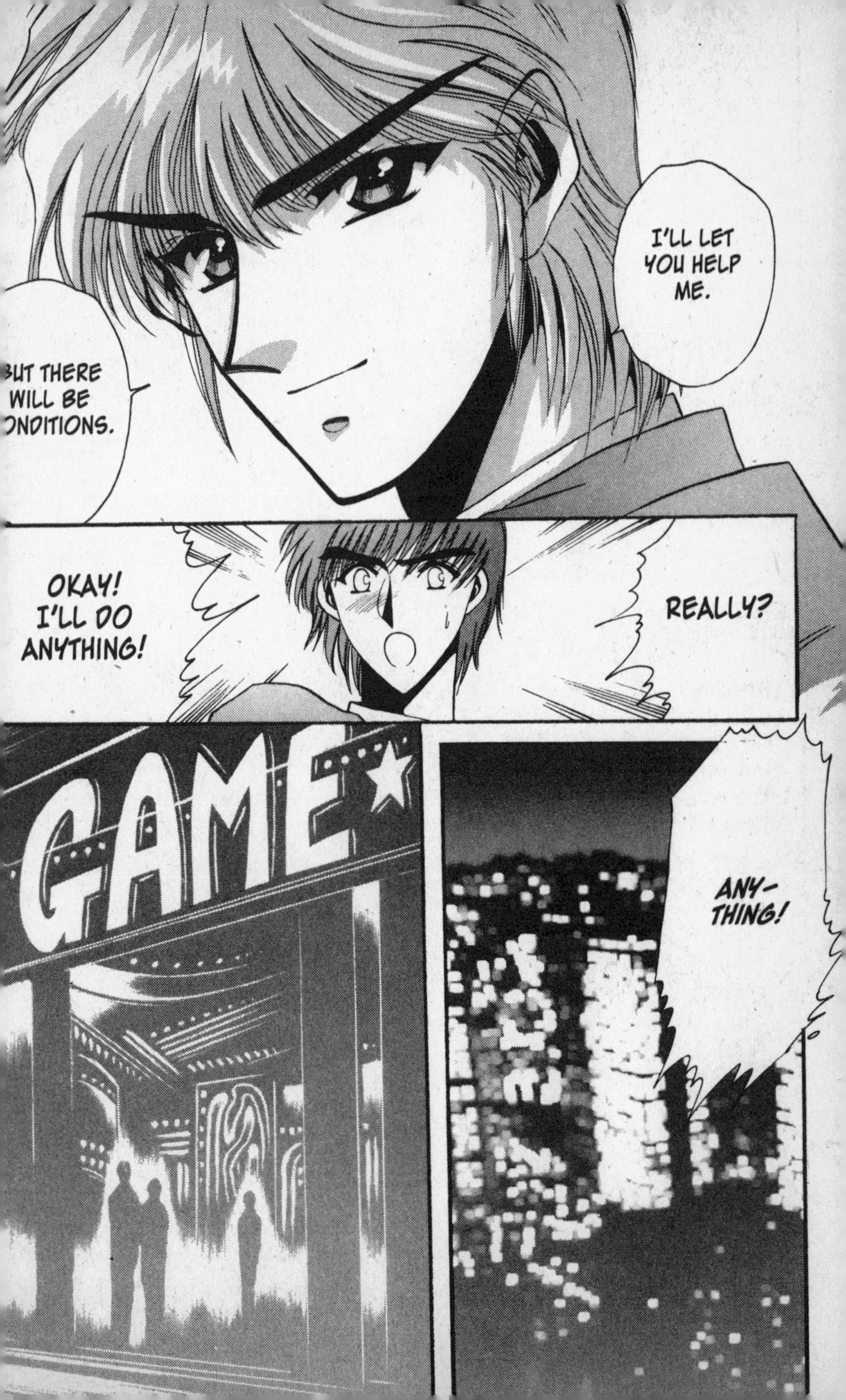
I'LL LET YOU HELP ME.
UT THERE WILL BE ONDITIONS.
REALLY?
OKAY! I'LL DO ANYTHING!
ANY- THING!

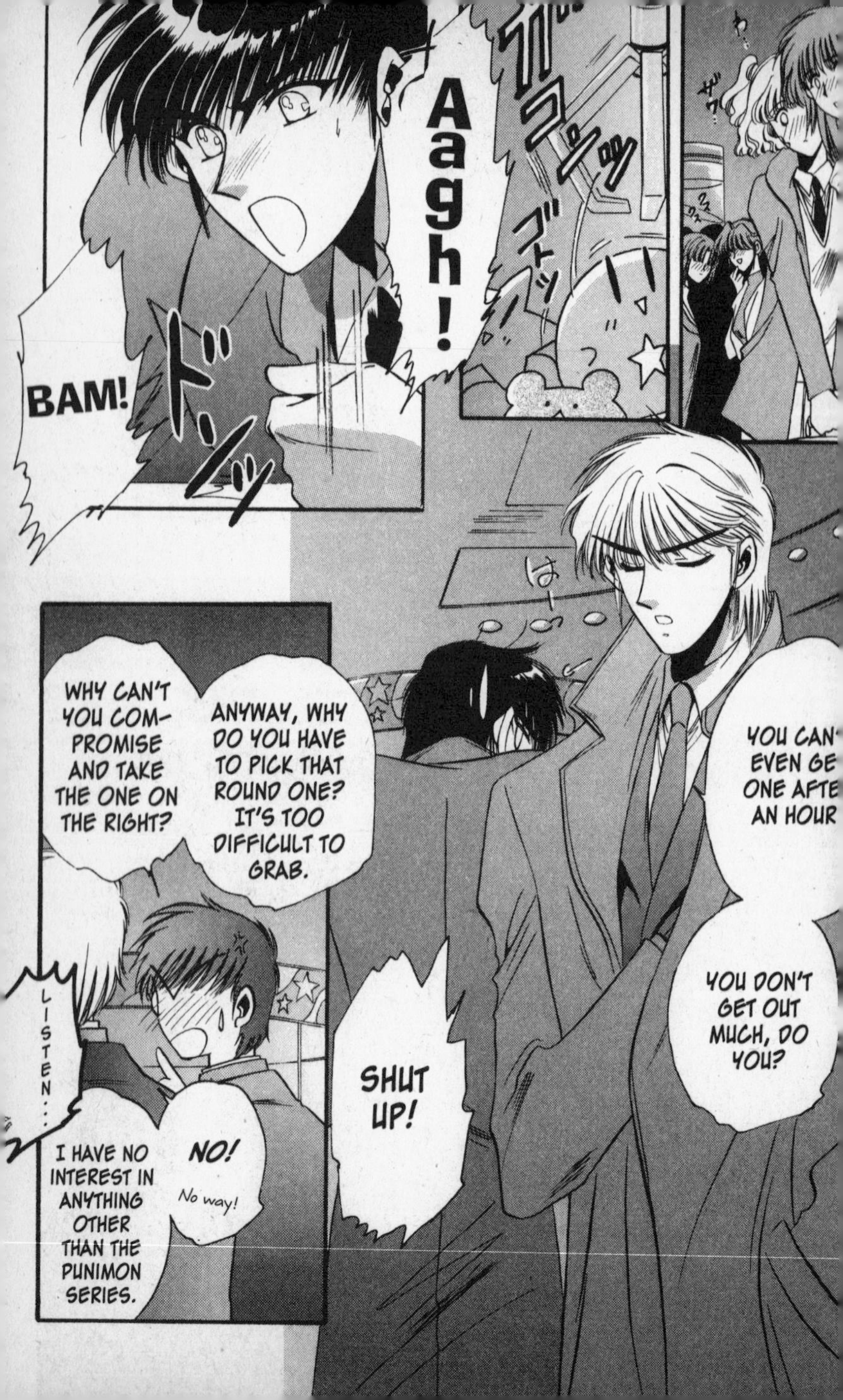

Aagh!
BAM!
YOU CAN
EVEN GE
ONE AFTE
AN HOUR
YOU DON'T GET OUT MUCH, DO YOU?
SHUT UP!
ANYWAY, WHY DO YOU HAVE TO PICK THAT ROUND ONE? IT'S TOO DIFFICULT TO GRAB.
WHY CAN'T YOU COM-PROMISE AND TAKE THE ONE ON THE RIGHT?
NO!
No way!
I HAVE NO INTEREST IN ANYTHING OTHER THAN THE PUNIMON SERIES.
LISTEN...

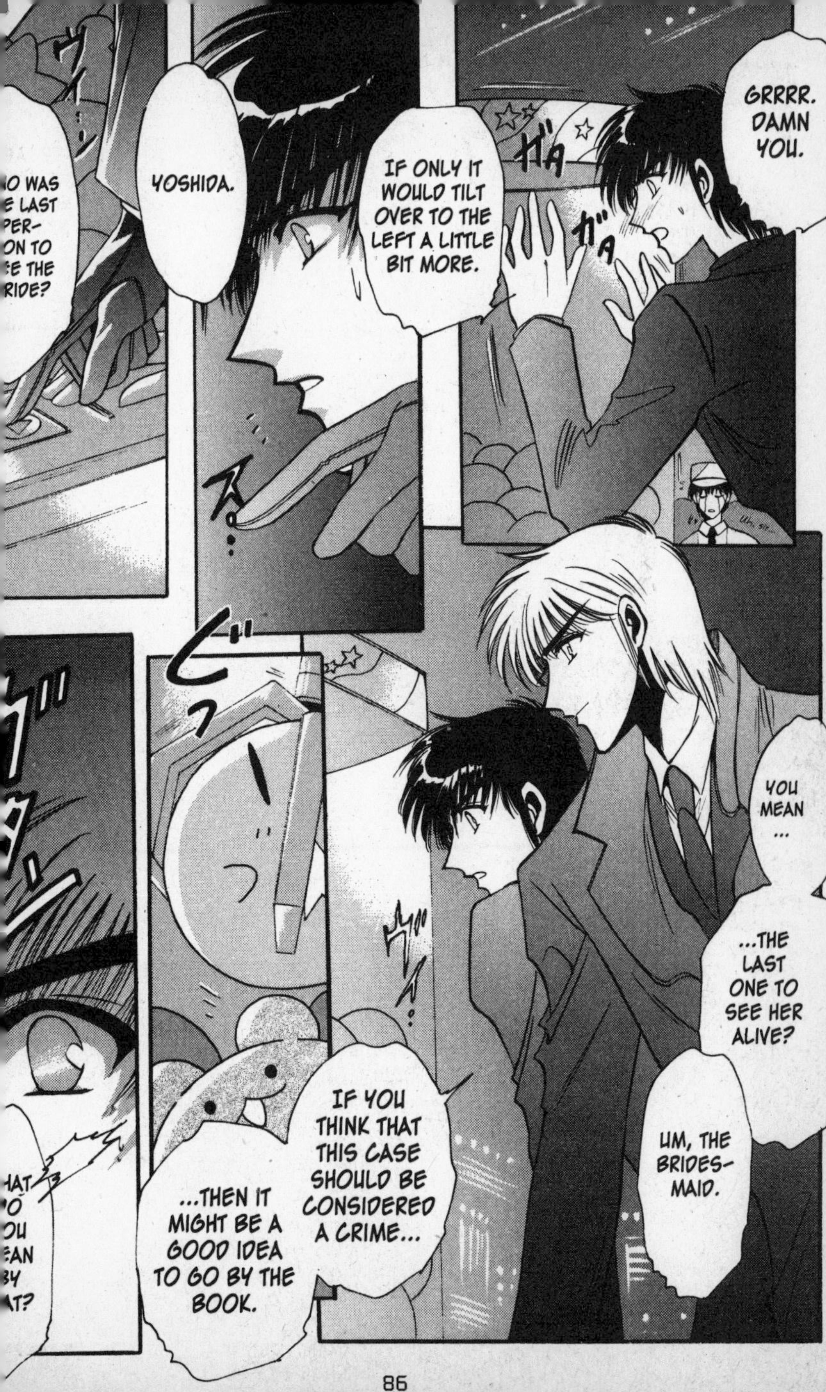
GRRRR. DAMN YOU.
IF ONLY IT WOULD TILT OVER TO THE LEFT A LITTLE BIT MORE.
YOSHIDA.
YOU MEAN ...
...THE LAST ONE TO SEE HER ALIVE?
UM, THE BRIDES-MAID.
IF YOU THINK THAT THIS CASE SHOULD BE CONSIDERED A CRIME...
...THEN IT MIGHT BE A GOOD IDEA TO GO BY THE BOOK.

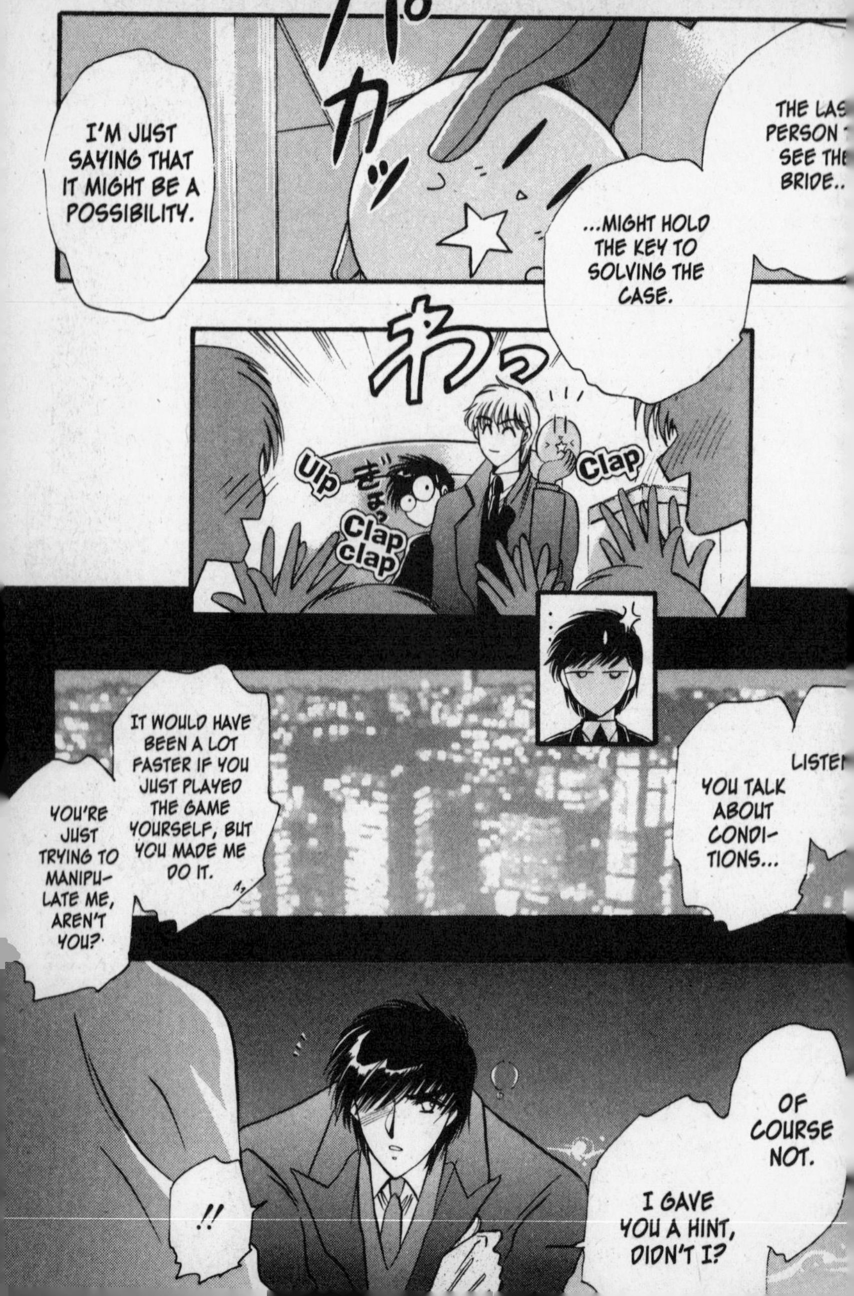

パカッ
THE LAS PERSON T SEE THE BRIDE..
...MIGHT HOLD THE KEY TO SOLVING THE CASE.
I'M JUST SAYING THAT IT MIGHT BE A POSSIBILITY.
わっ
Clap
Ulp
ぎょっ
Clap clap
LISTE
YOU TALK ABOUT CONDI-TIONS...
IT WOULD HAVE BEEN A LOT FASTER IF YOU JUST PLAYED THE GAME YOURSELF, BUT YOU MADE ME DO IT.
YOU'RE JUST TRYING TO MANIPU-LATE ME, AREN'T YOU?
OF COURSE NOT.
I GAVE YOU A HINT, DIDN'T I?
!!

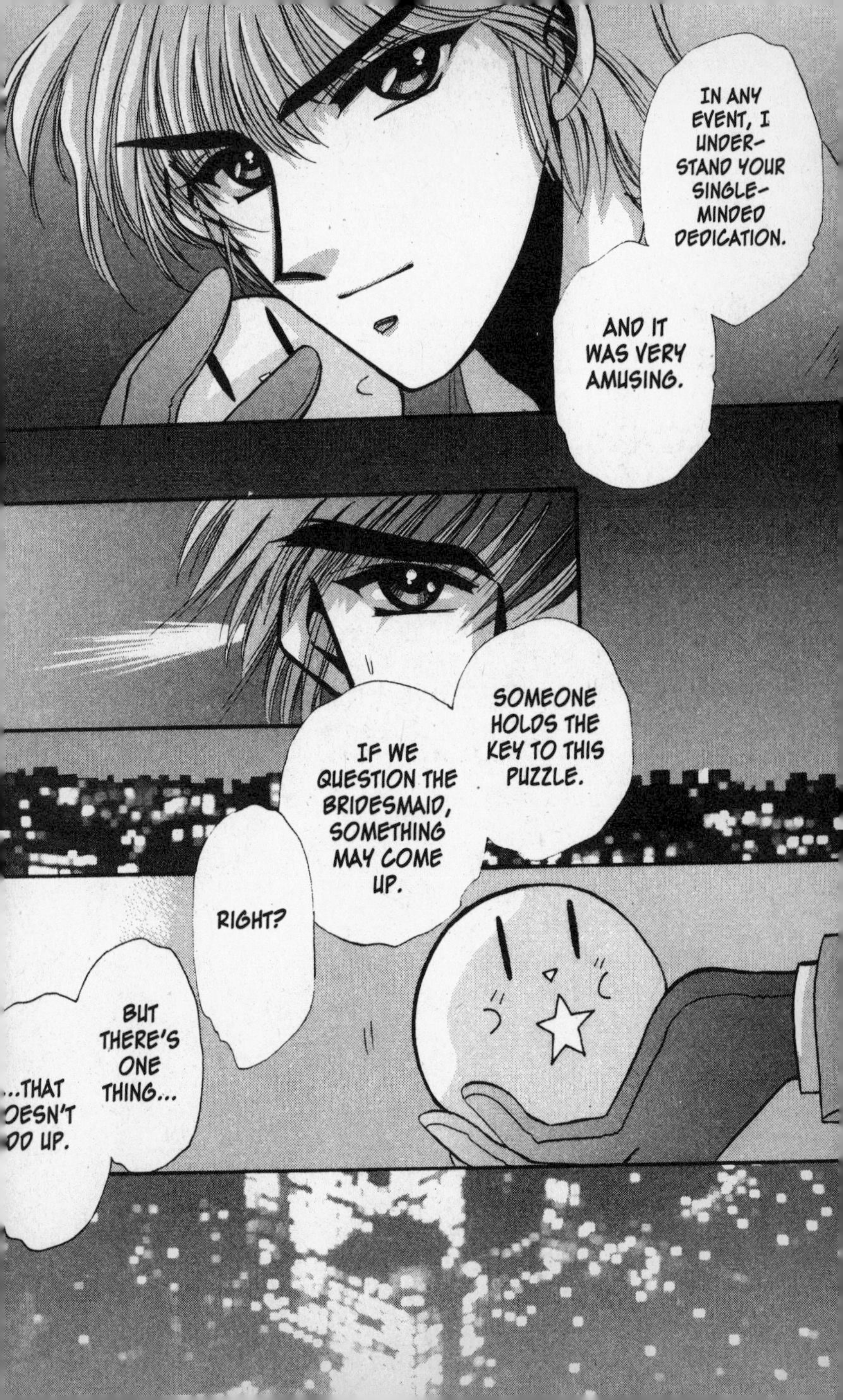
IN ANY EVENT, I UNDER-STAND YOUR SINGLE-MINDED DEDICATION.
AND IT WAS VERY AMUSING.
SOMEONE HOLDS THE KEY TO THIS PUZZLE.
IF WE QUESTION THE BRIDESMAID, SOMETHING MAY COME UP.
RIGHT?
BUT THERE'S ONE THING...
...THAT OESN'T OD UP.

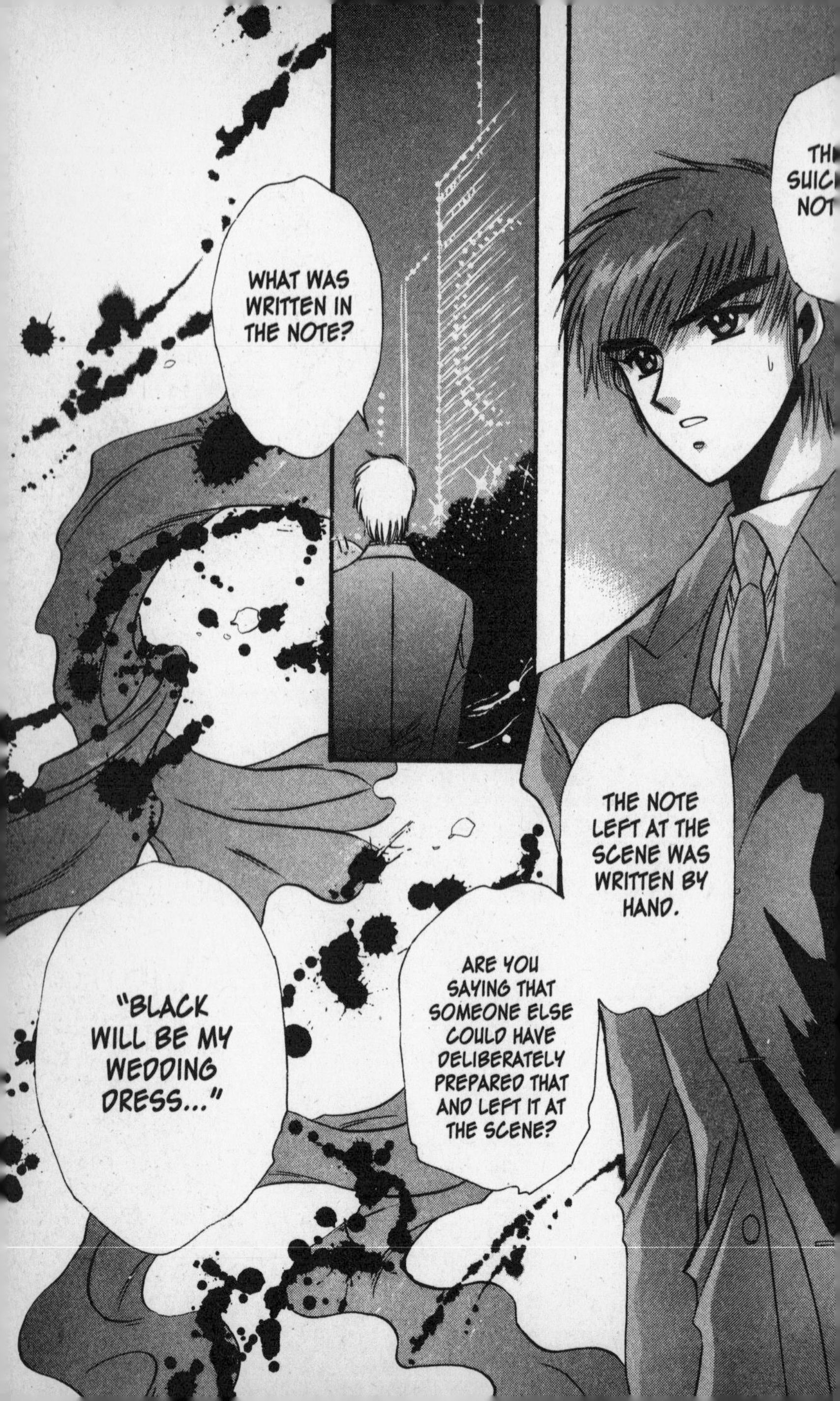
WHAT WAS WRITTEN IN THE NOTE?
"BLACK WILL BE MY WEDDING DRESS..."
THE NOTE LEFT AT THE SCENE WAS WRITTEN BY HAND.
ARE YOU SAYING THAT SOMEONE ELSE COULD HAVE DELIBERATELY PREPARED THAT AND LEFT IT AT THE SCENE?

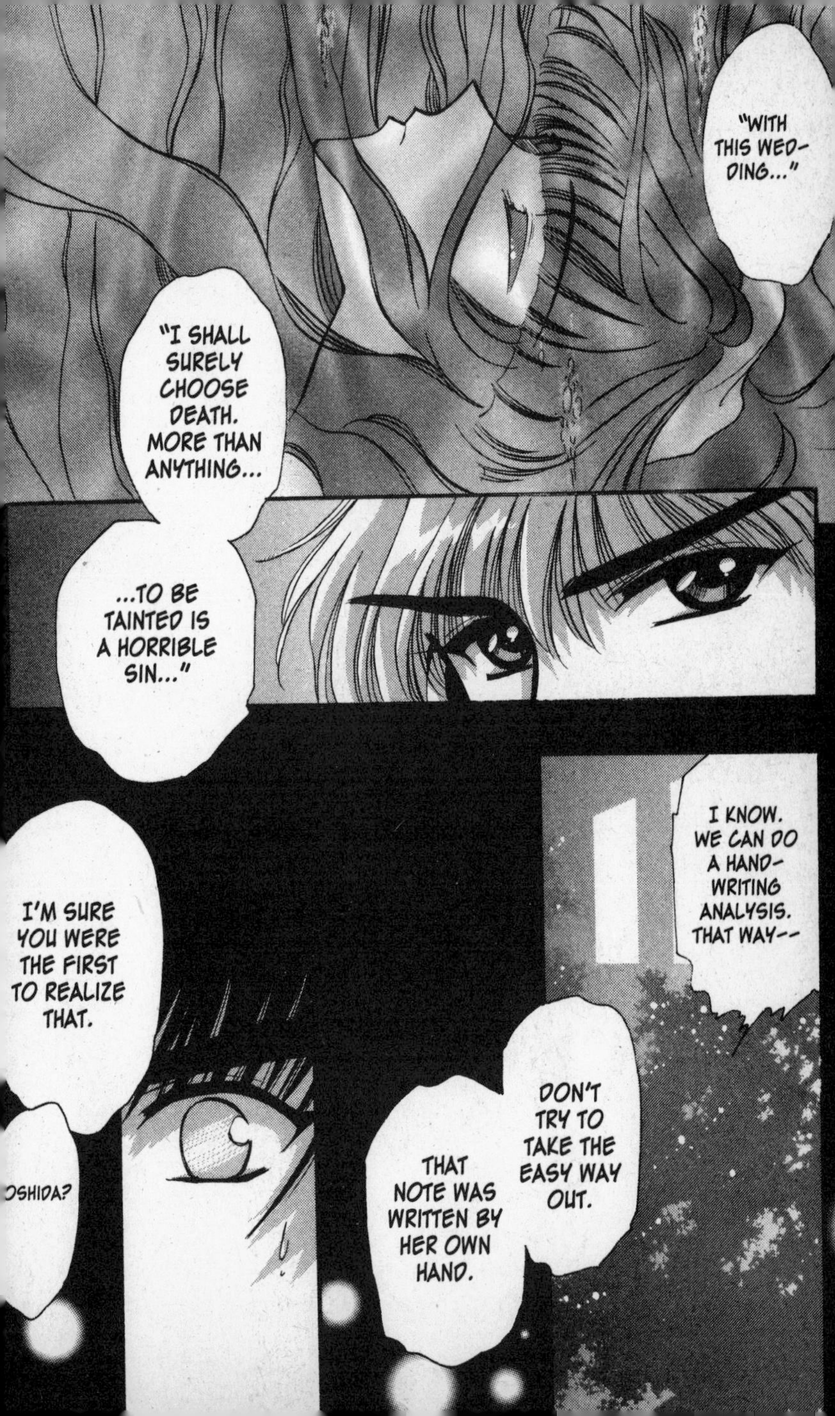
"WITH THIS WED-DING..."
"I SHALL SURELY CHOOSE DEATH. MORE THAN ANYTHING...
...TO BE TAINTED IS A HORRIBLE SIN..."
I KNOW. WE CAN DO A HAND-WRITING ANALYSIS. THAT WAY--
DON'T TRY TO TAKE THE EASY WAY OUT.
THAT NOTE WAS WRITTEN BY HER OWN HAND.
I'M SURE YOU WERE THE FIRST TO REALIZE THAT.
OSHIDA?

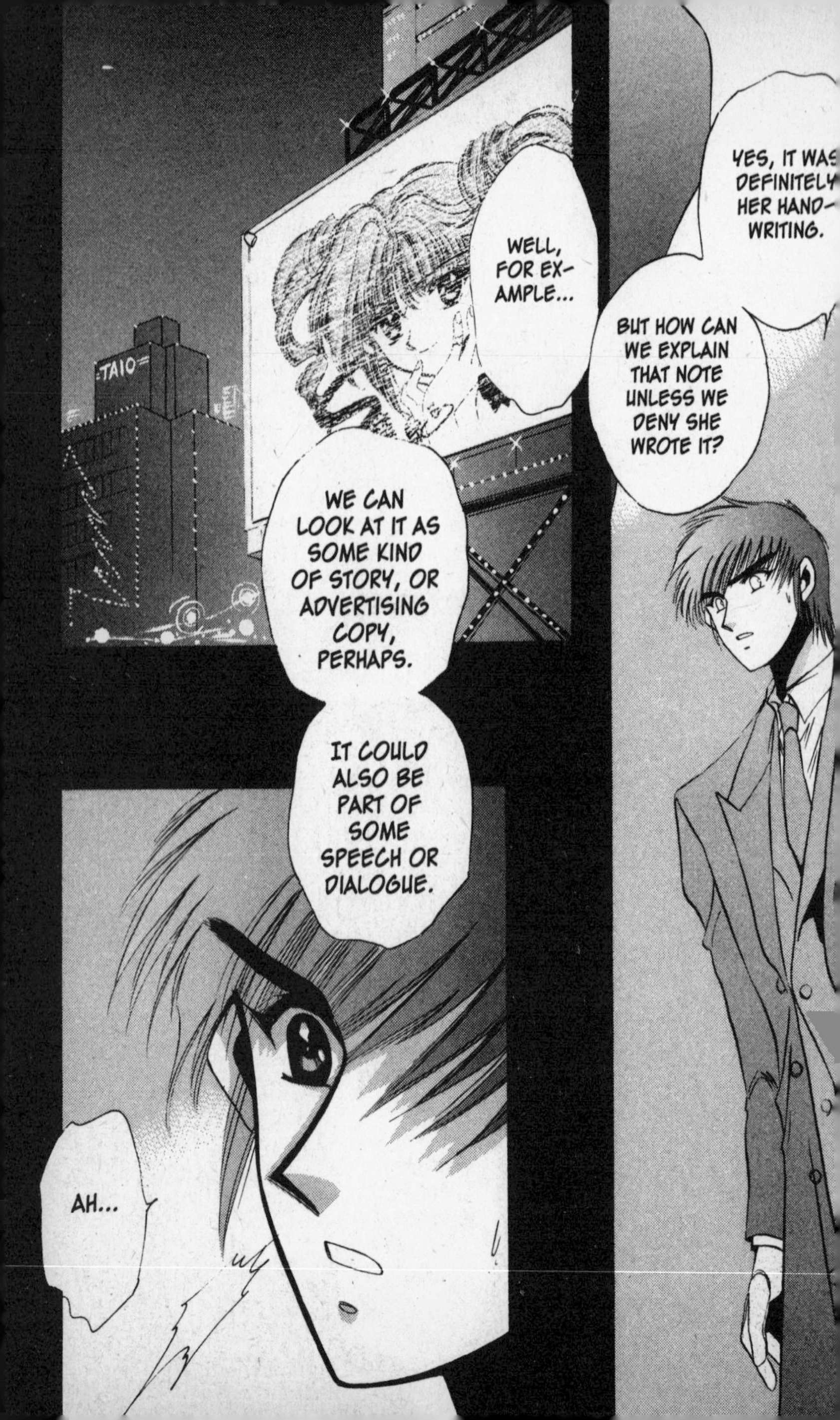
YES, IT WAS DEFINITELY HER HAND-WRITING.
BUT HOW CAN WE EXPLAIN THAT NOTE UNLESS WE DENY SHE WROTE IT?
TAIO
WELL, FOR EX-AMPLE...
WE CAN LOOK AT IT AS SOME KIND OF STORY, OR ADVERTISING COPY, PERHAPS.
IT COULD ALSO BE PART OF SOME SPEECH OR DIALOGUE.
AH...

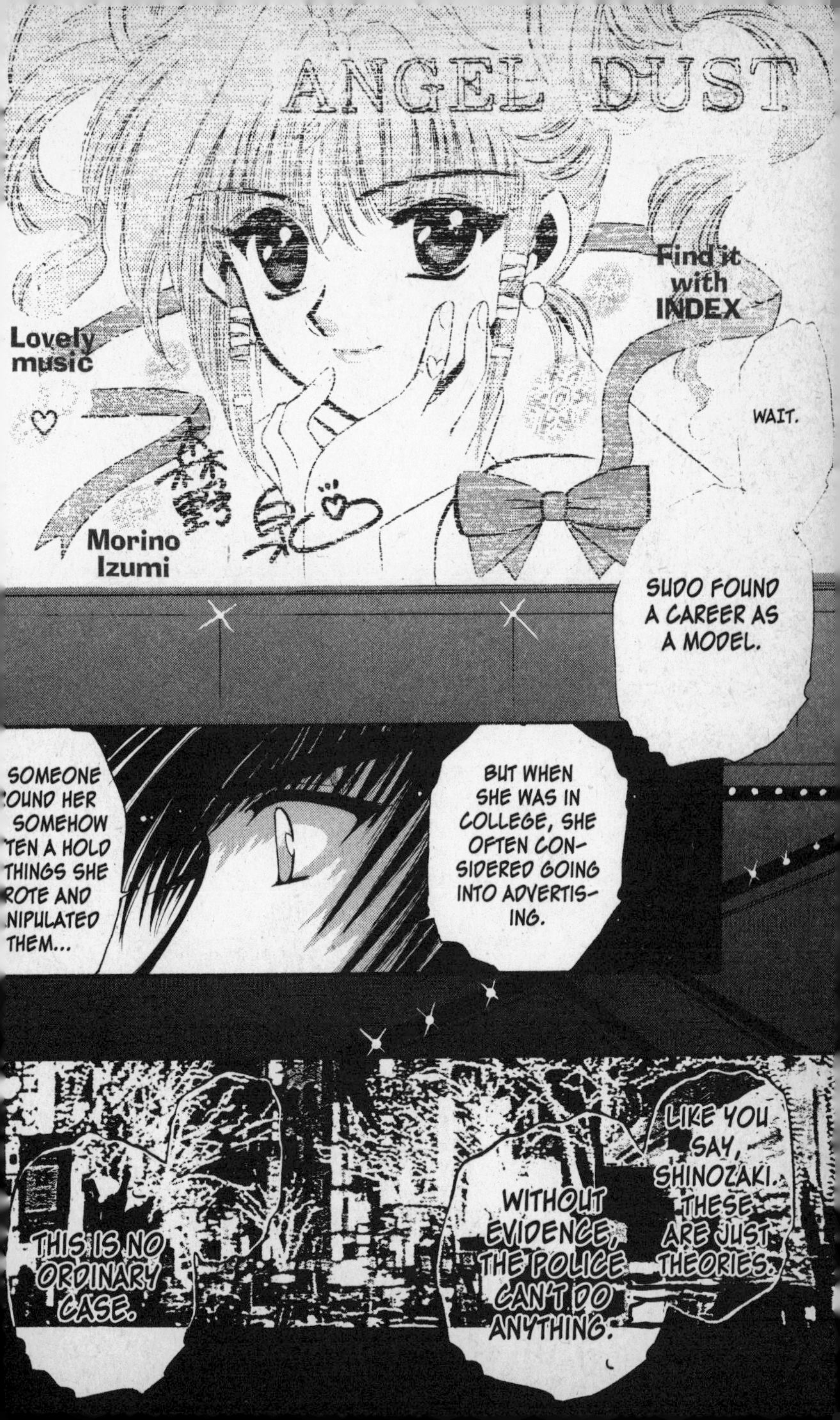
ANGEL DUST
Find it with INDEX
Lovely music
Morino Izumi
WAIT.
SUDO FOUND A CAREER AS A MODEL.
BUT WHEN SHE WAS IN COLLEGE, SHE OFTEN CON-SIDERED GOING INTO ADVERTIS-ING.
SOMEONE OUND HER SOMEHOW TEN A HOLD THINGS SHE ROTE AND NIPULATED THEM...
LIKE YOU SAY, SHINOZAKI. THESE ARE JUST THEORIES.
WITHOUT EVIDENCE, THE POLICE CAN'T DO ANYTHING.
THIS IS NO ORDINARY CASE.

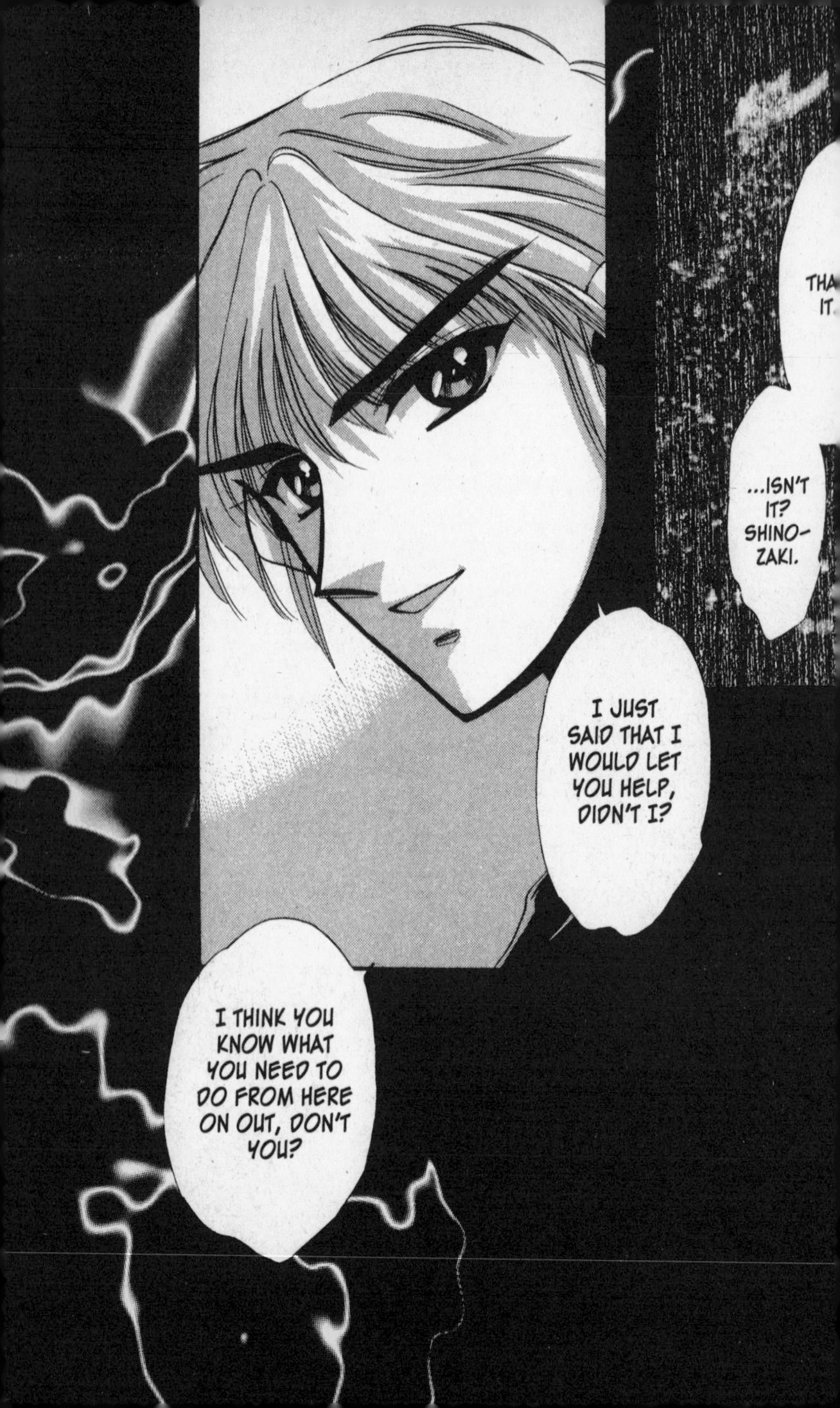
THA IT.
...ISN'T IT? SHINO-ZAKI.
I JUST SAID THAT I WOULD LET YOU HELP, DIDN'T I?
I THINK YOU KNOW WHAT YOU NEED TO DO FROM HERE ON OUT, DON'T YOU?

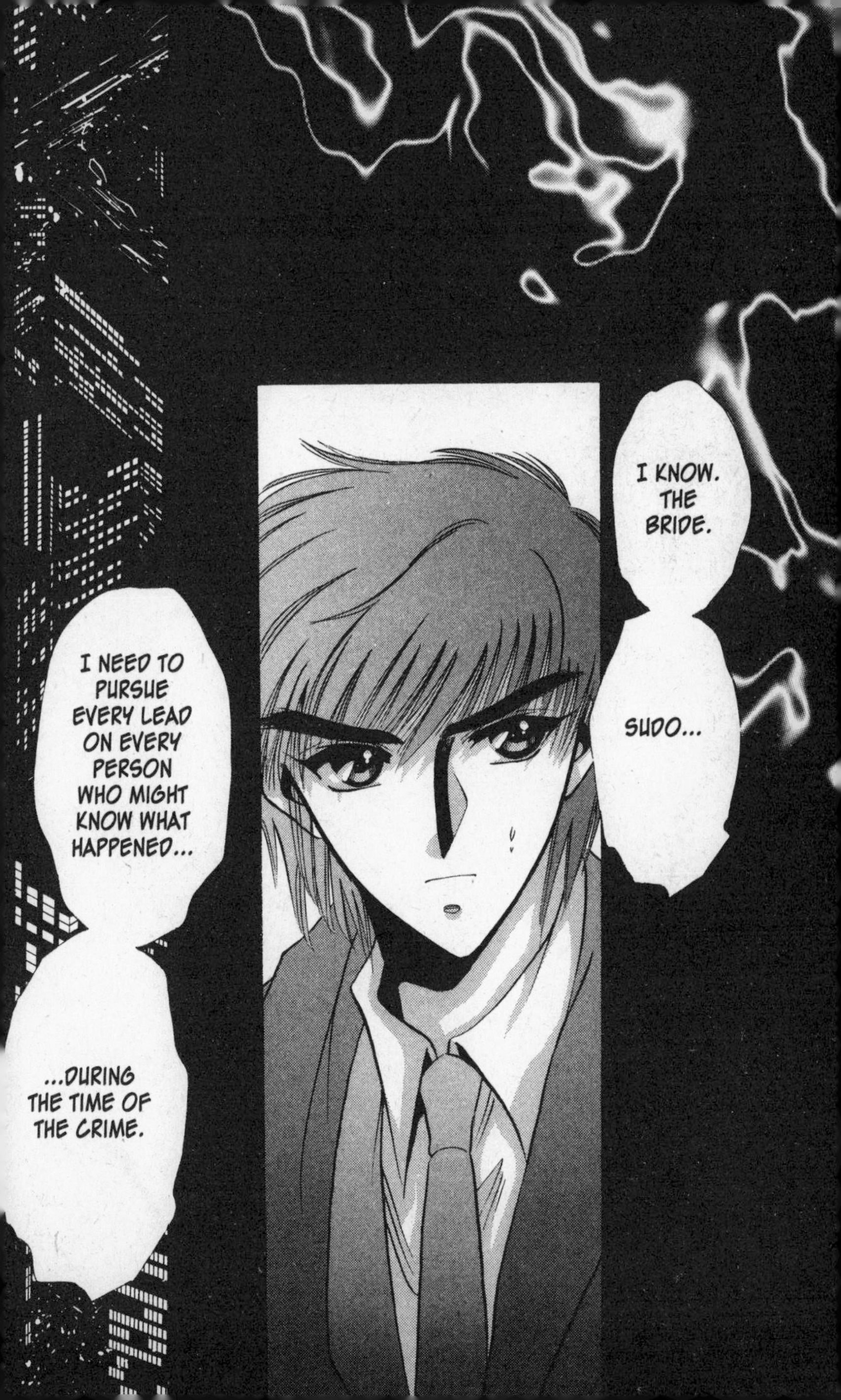
I KNOW. THE BRIDE.
SUDO...
I NEED TO PURSUE EVERY LEAD ON EVERY PERSON WHO MIGHT KNOW WHAT HAPPENED...
...DURING THE TIME OF THE CRIME.

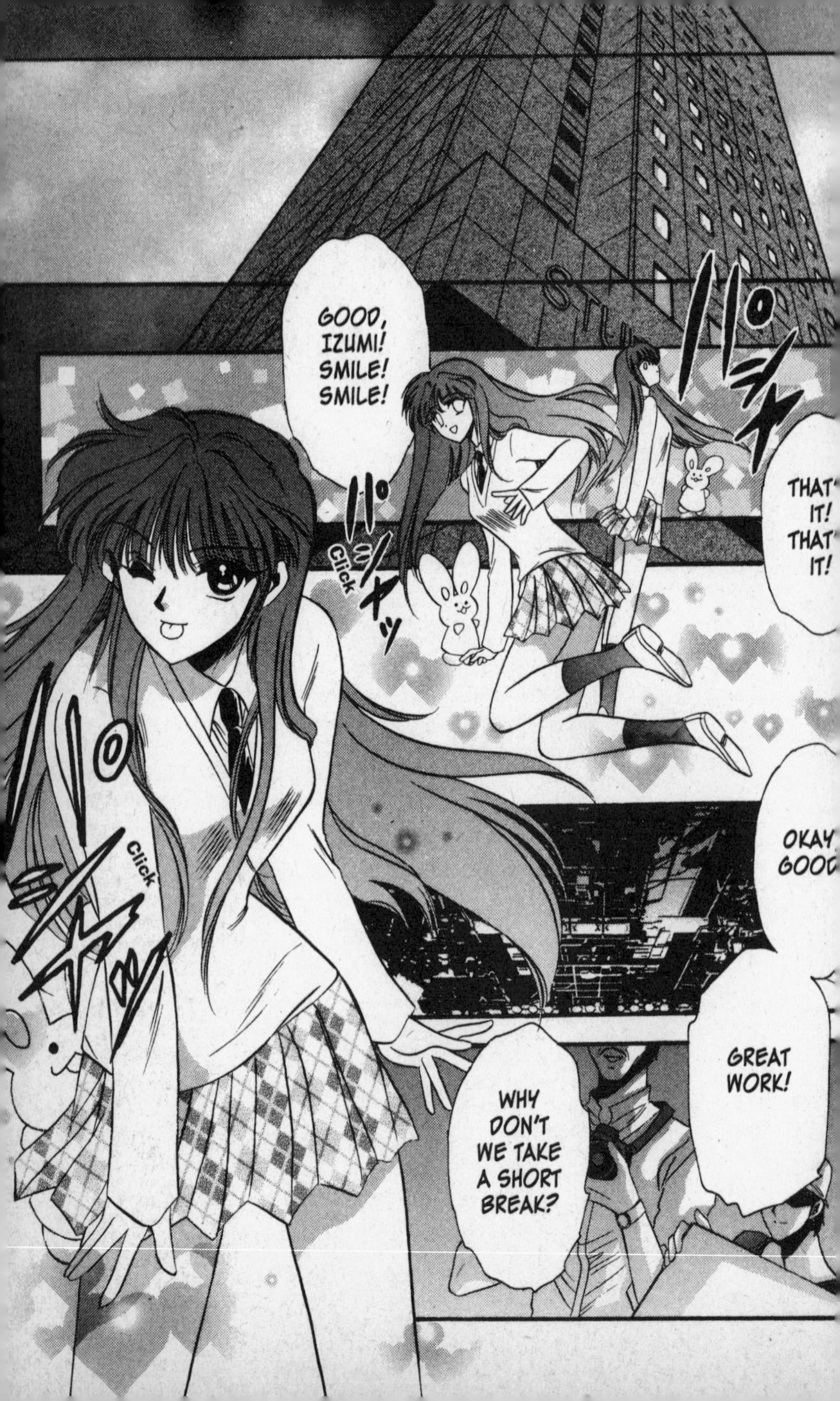
THAT IT! THAT IT!
GOOD, IZUMI! SMILE! SMILE!
Click
OKAY GOOD
GREAT WORK!
WHY DON'T WE TAKE A SHORT BREAK?
Click

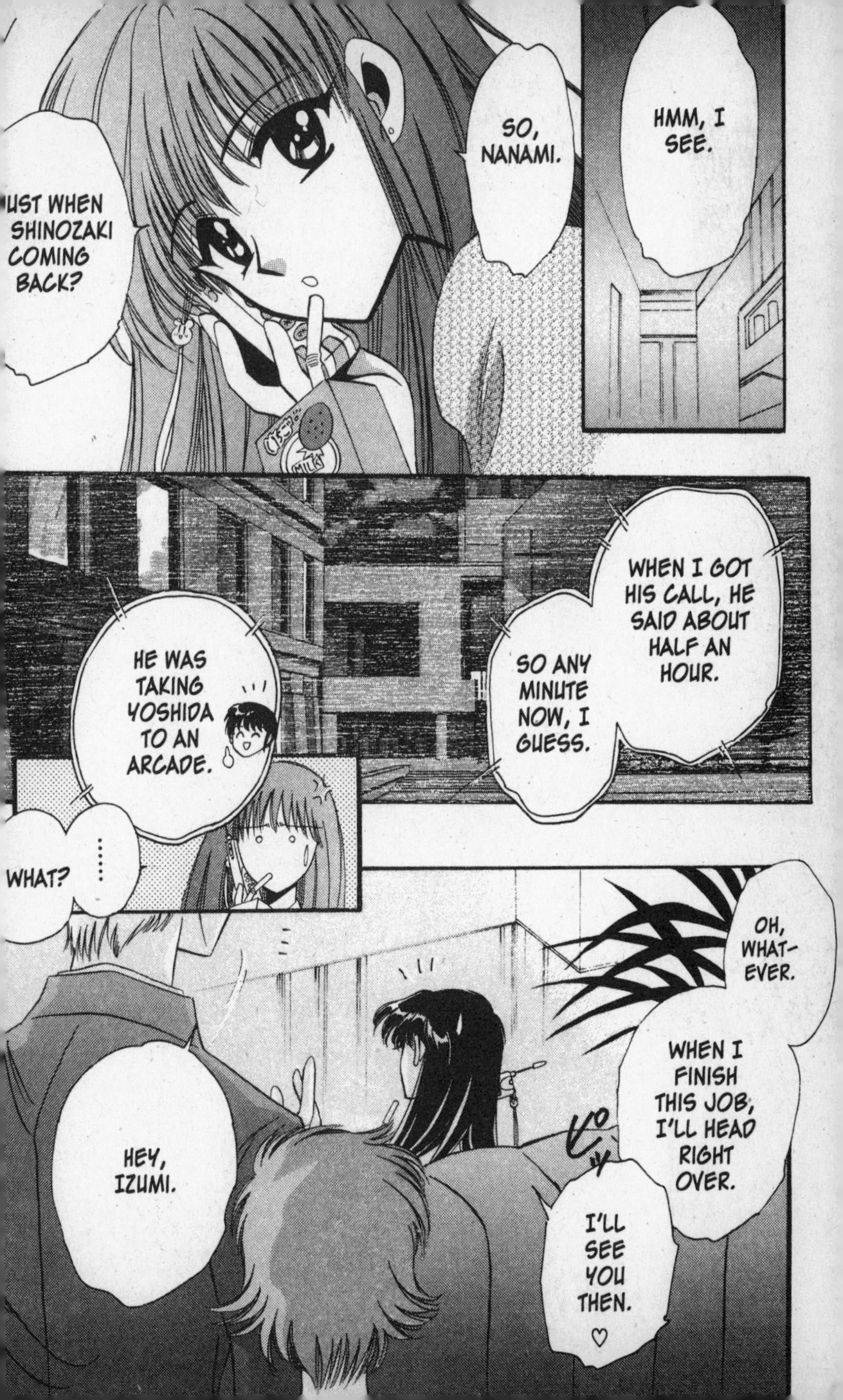
HMM, I SEE.
SO, NANAMI.
UST WHEN SHINOZAKI COMING BACK?
WHEN I GOT HIS CALL, HE SAID ABOUT HALF AN HOUR.
SO ANY MINUTE NOW, I GUESS.
HE WAS TAKING YOSHIDA TO AN ARCADE.
......
WHAT?
OH, WHAT-EVER.
WHEN I FINISH THIS JOB, I'LL HEAD RIGHT OVER.
I'LL SEE YOU THEN. ♡
HEY, IZUMI.

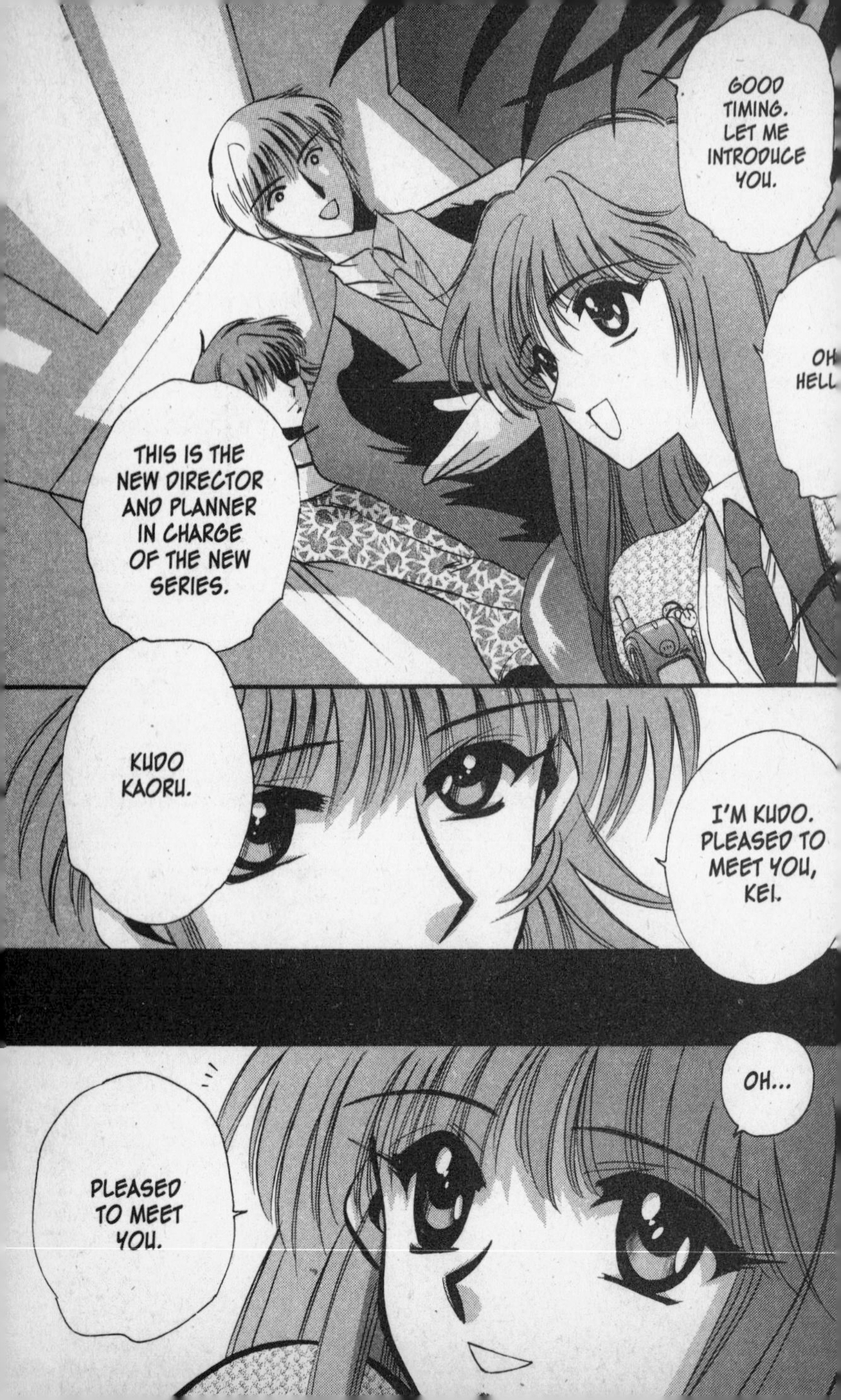

GOOD TIMING. LET ME INTRODUCE YOU.
OH HELL
THIS IS THE NEW DIRECTOR AND PLANNER IN CHARGE OF THE NEW SERIES.
KUDO KAORU.
I'M KUDO. PLEASED TO MEET YOU, KEI.
OH...
PLEASED TO MEET YOU.

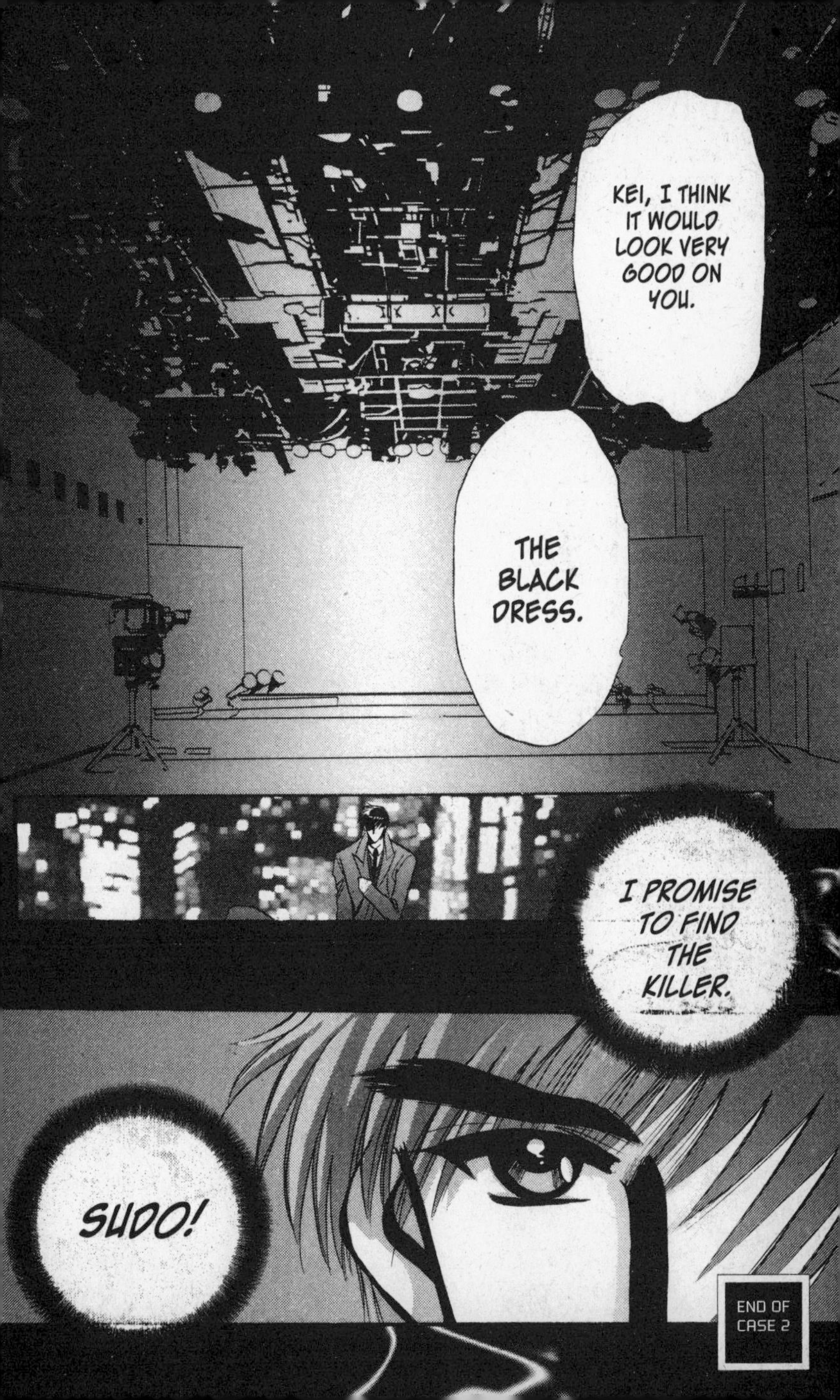
KEI, I THINK IT WOULD LOOK VERY GOOD ON YOU.
THE BLACK DRESS.
I PROMISE TO FIND THE KILLER.
SUDO!
END OF CASE 2

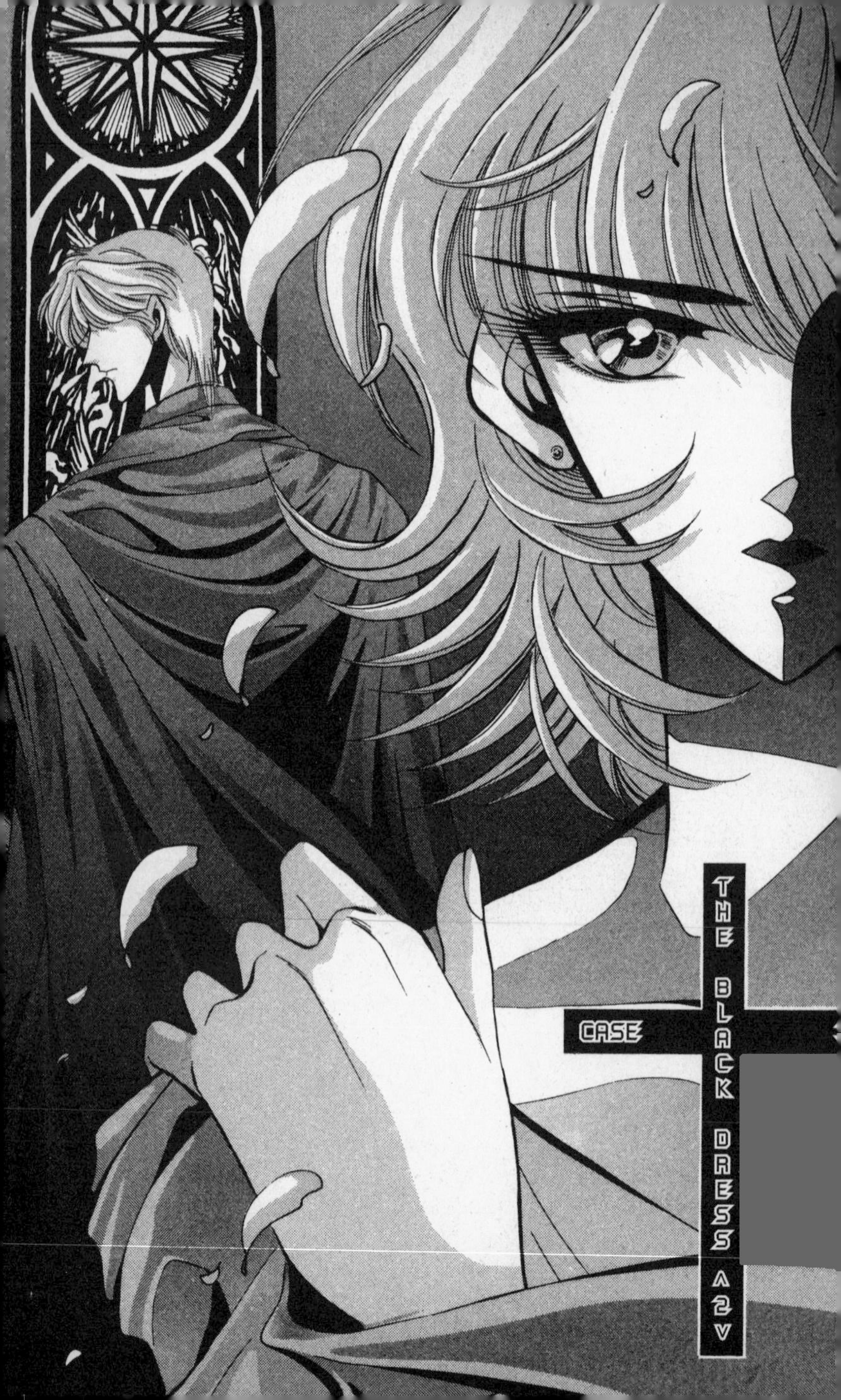
CASE
THE BLACK DRESS <2>

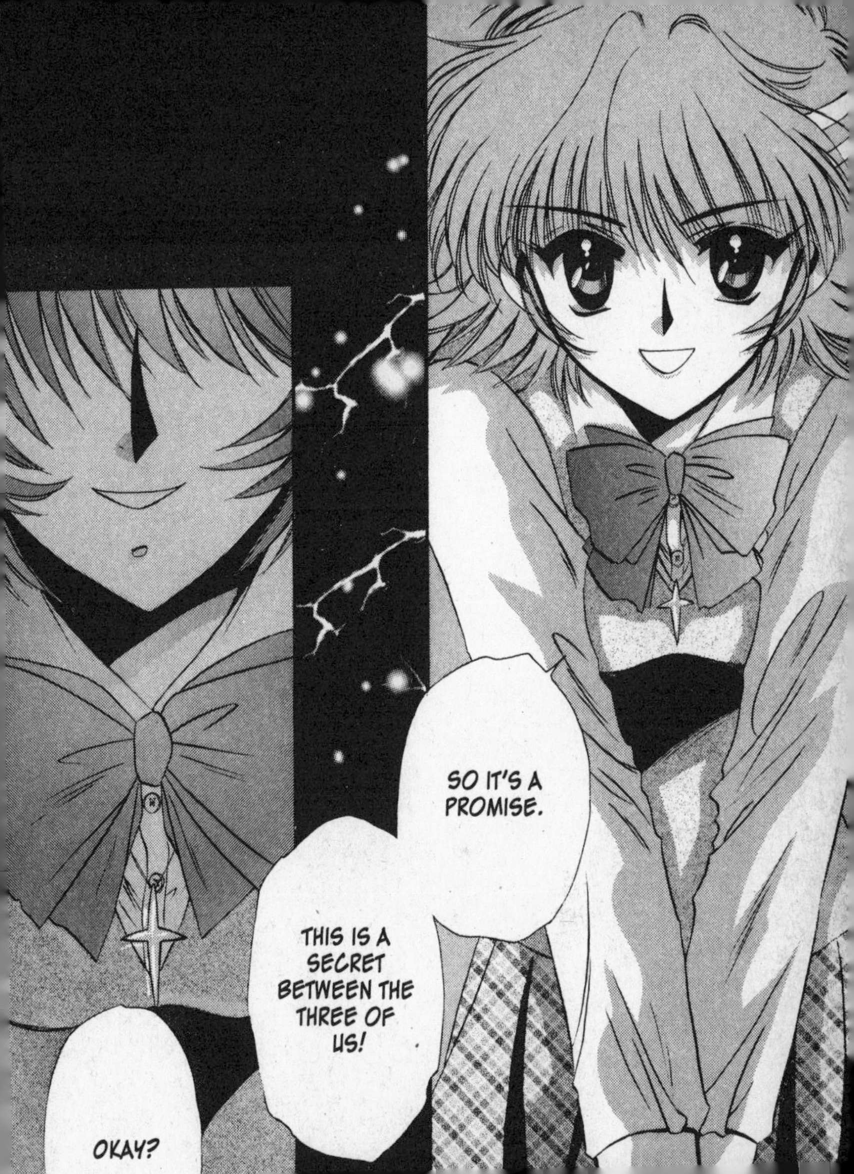
SO IT'S A PROMISE.
THIS IS A SECRET BETWEEN THE THREE OF US!
OKAY?

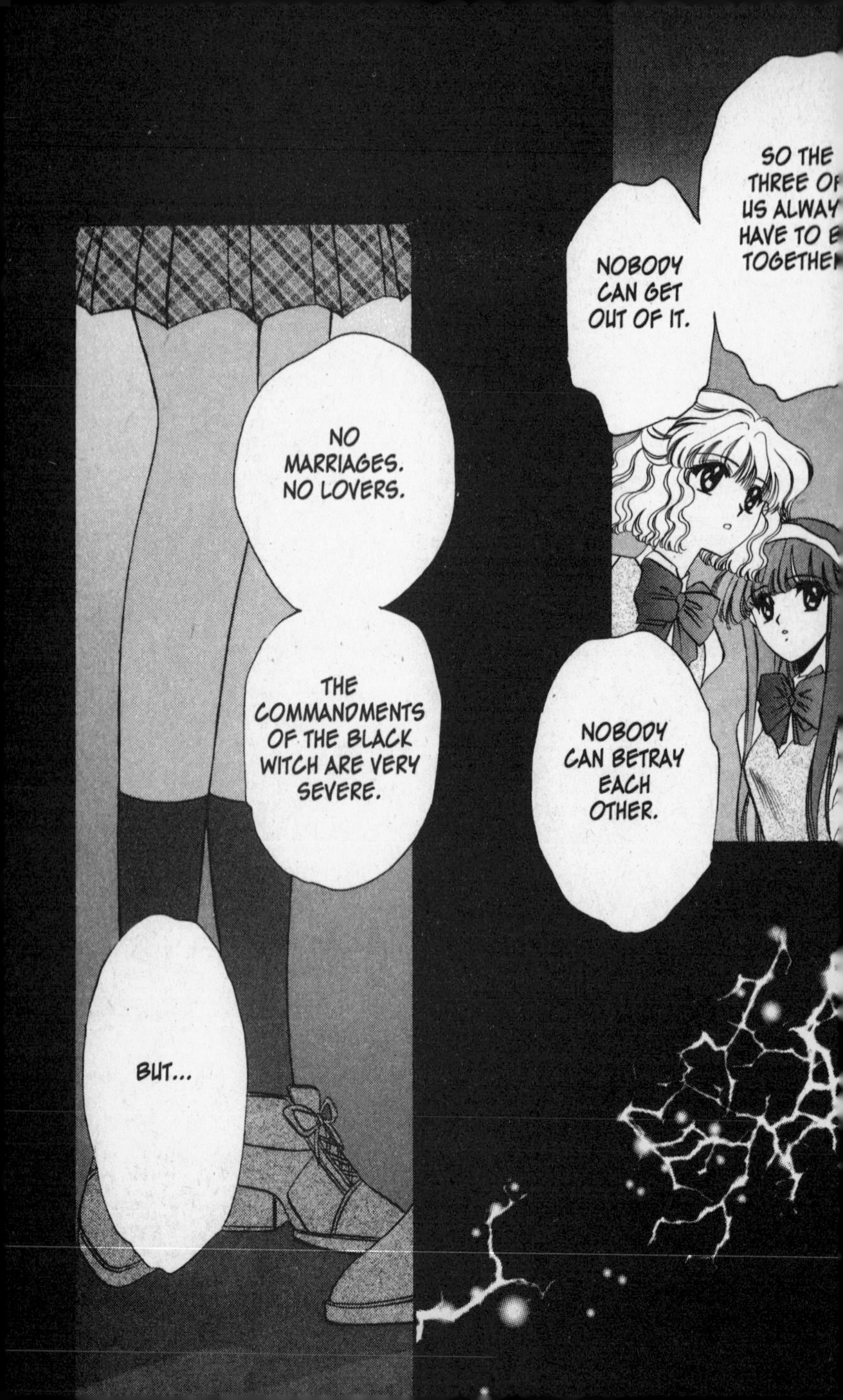
SO THE THREE OF US ALWAY HAVE TO B TOGETHE
NOBODY CAN GET OUT OF IT.
NOBODY CAN BETRAY EACH OTHER.
NO MARRIAGES. NO LOVERS.
THE COMMANDMENTS OF THE BLACK WITCH ARE VERY SEVERE.
BUT...

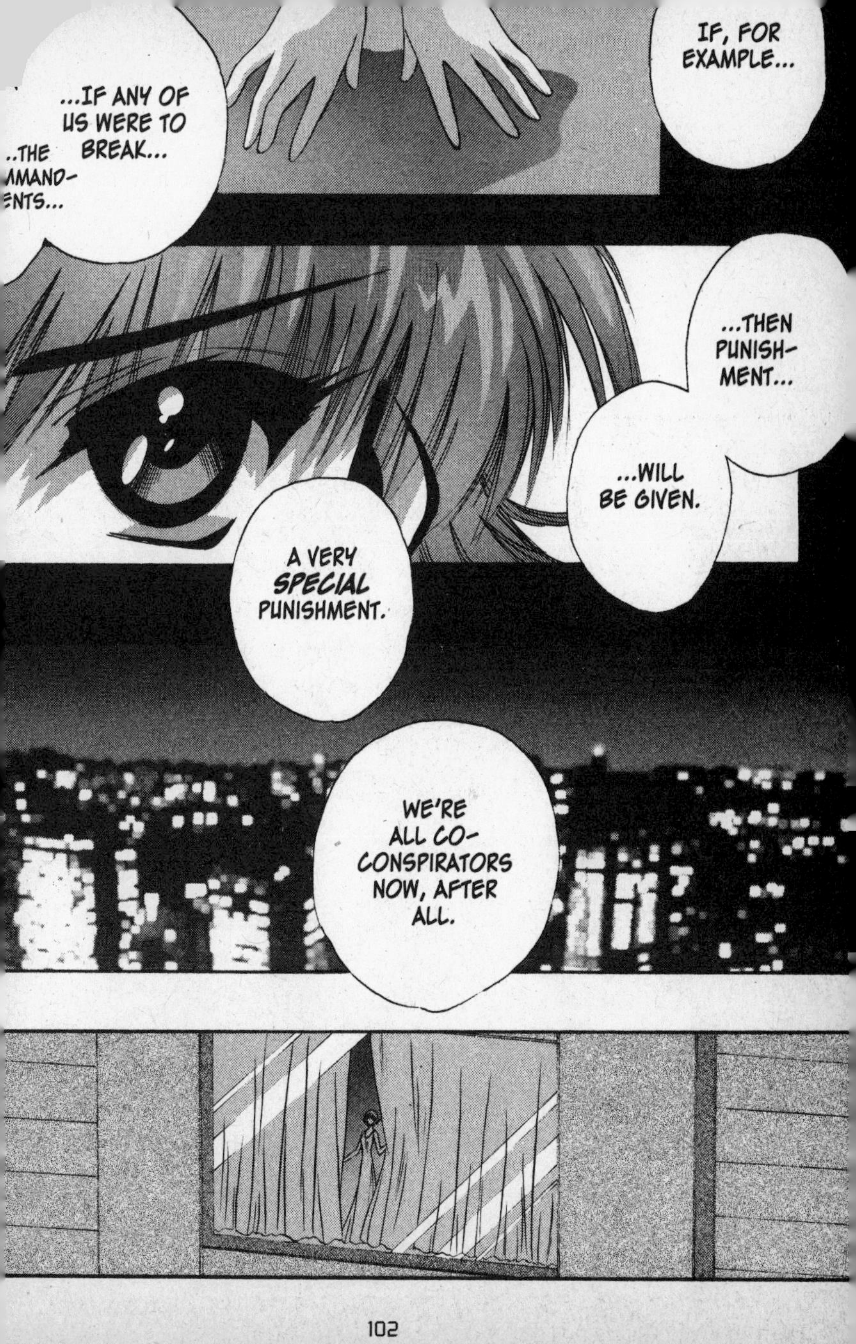

IF, FOR EXAMPLE...
...IF ANY OF US WERE TO BREAK...
..THE
MMAND-
ENTS...
...THEN PUNISHMENT...
...WILL BE GIVEN.
A VERY SPECIAL PUNISHMENT.
WE'RE ALL CO-CONSPIRATORS NOW, AFTER ALL.

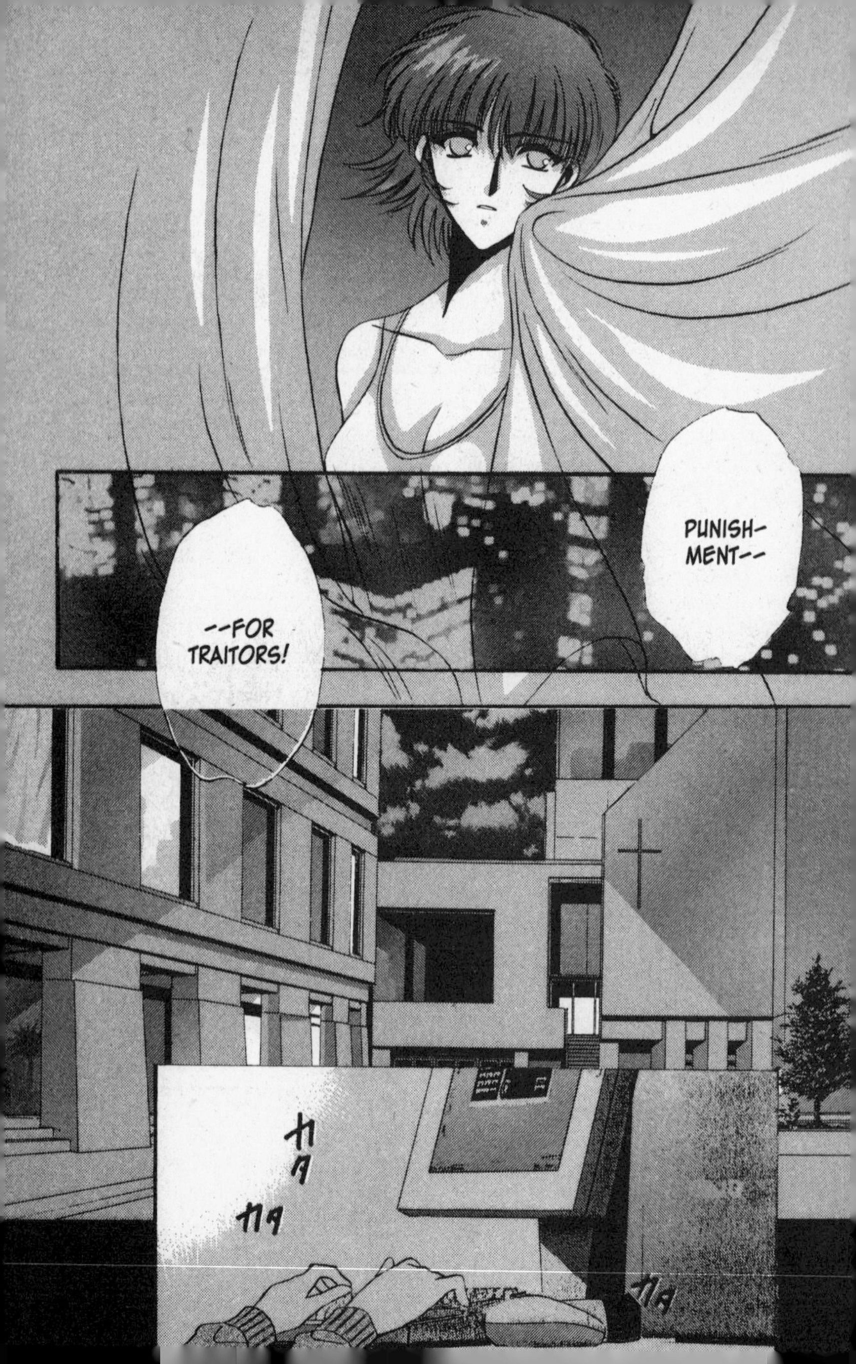
PUNISH-
MENT--
--FOR
TRAITORS!
カタ
カタ
カタ

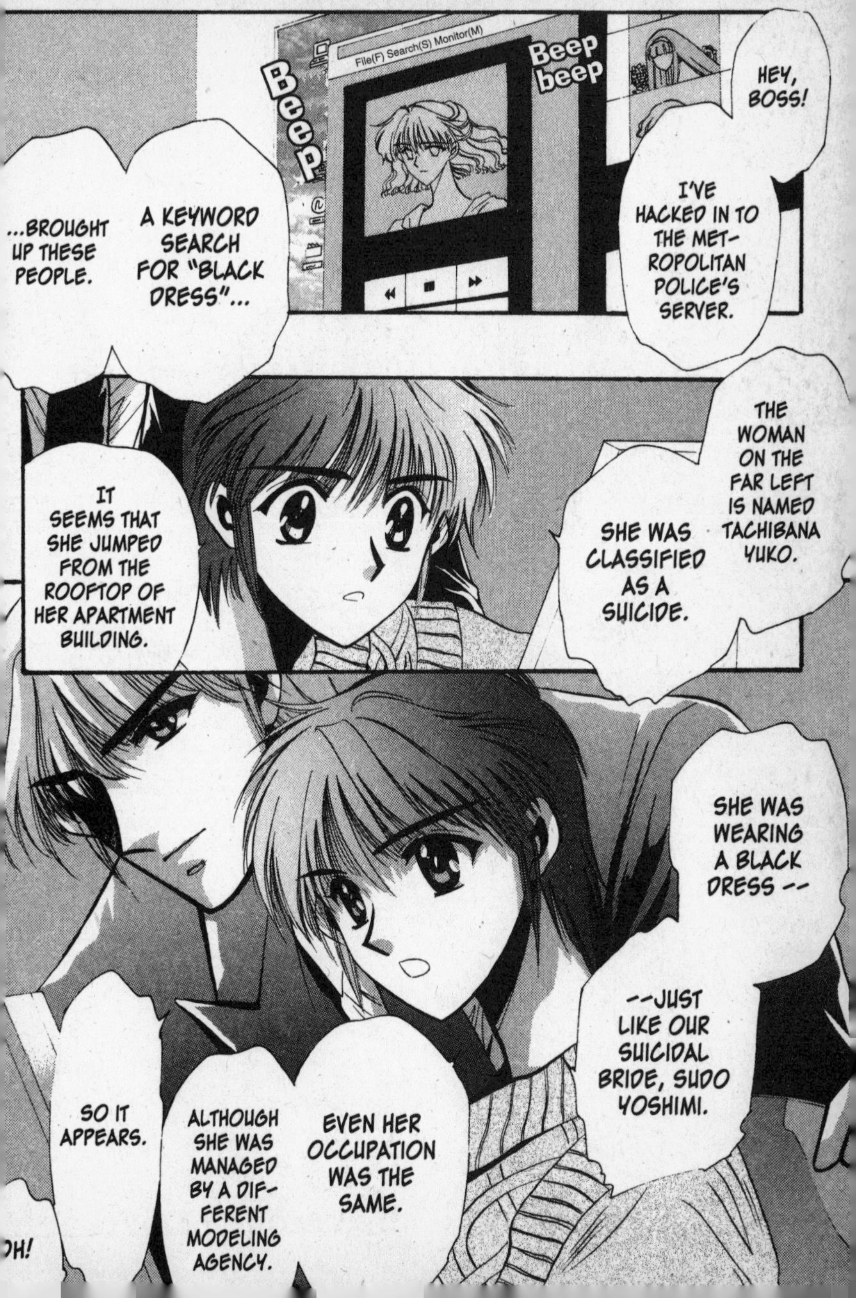
HEY, BOSS!
I'VE HACKED IN TO THE MET-ROPOLITAN POLICE'S SERVER.
Beep beep
File(F) Search(S) Monitor(M)
Beep
A KEYWORD SEARCH FOR "BLACK DRESS"...
...BROUGHT UP THESE PEOPLE.
THE WOMAN ON THE FAR LEFT IS NAMED TACHIBANA YUKO.
SHE WAS CLASSIFIED AS A SUICIDE.
IT SEEMS THAT SHE JUMPED FROM THE ROOFTOP OF HER APARTMENT BUILDING.
SHE WAS WEARING A BLACK DRESS --
--JUST LIKE OUR SUICIDAL BRIDE, SUDO YOSHIMI.
EVEN HER OCCUPATION WAS THE SAME.
ALTHOUGH SHE WAS MANAGED BY A DIF-FERENT MODELING AGENCY.
SO IT APPEARS.

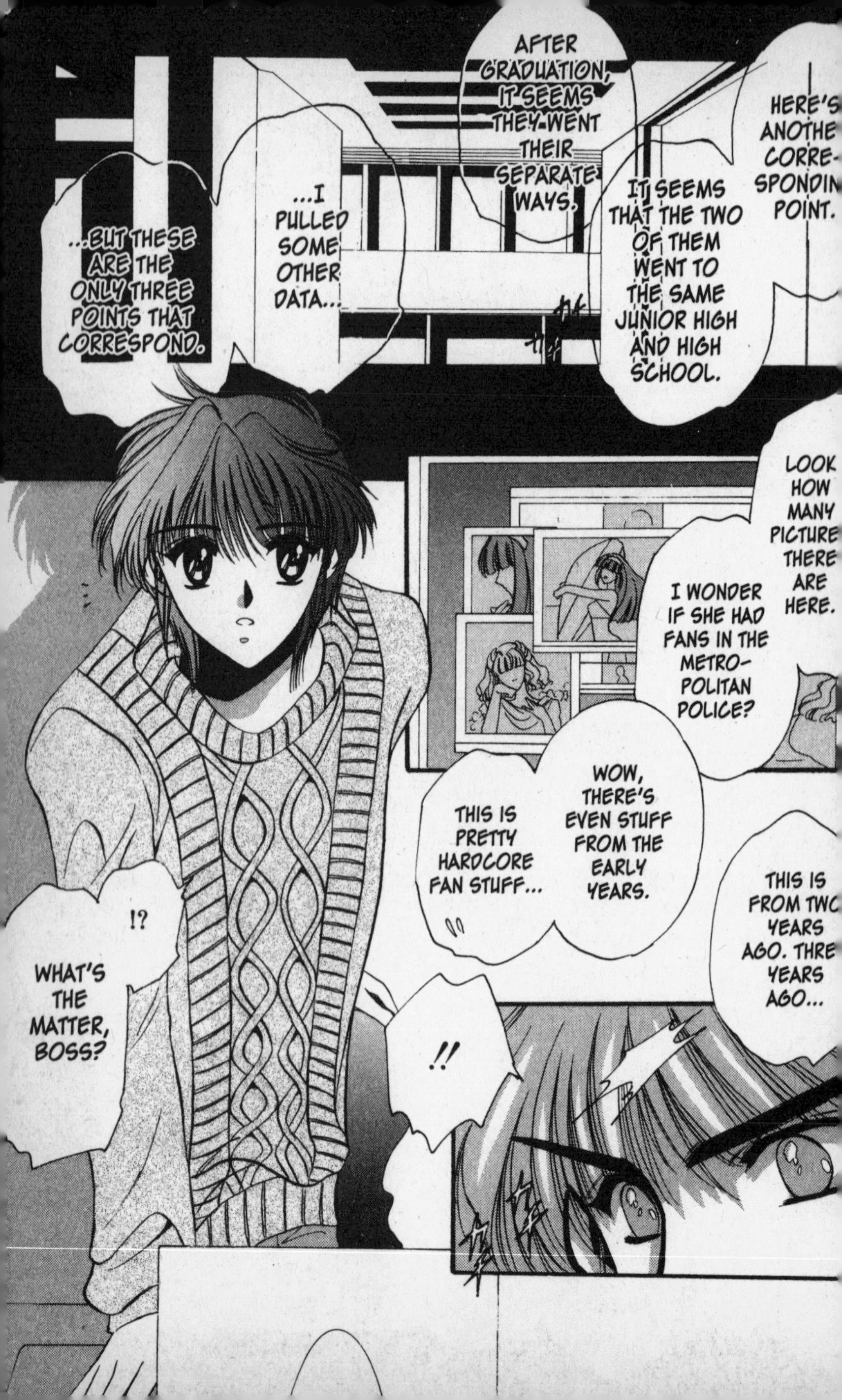
HERE'S ANOTHE CORRE-SPONDIN POINT.
IT SEEMS THAT THE TWO OF THEM WENT TO THE SAME JUNIOR HIGH AND HIGH SCHOOL.
AFTER GRADUATION, IT SEEMS THEY WENT THEIR SEPARATE WAYS.
...I PULLED SOME OTHER DATA...
...BUT THESE ARE THE ONLY THREE POINTS THAT CORRESPOND.
LOOK HOW MANY PICTURE THERE ARE HERE.
I WONDER IF SHE HAD FANS IN THE METRO-POLITAN POLICE?
WOW, THERE'S EVEN STUFF FROM THE EARLY YEARS.
THIS IS PRETTY HARDCORE FAN STUFF...
THIS IS FROM TWO YEARS AGO. THRE YEARS AGO...
!!
!?
WHAT'S THE MATTER, BOSS?

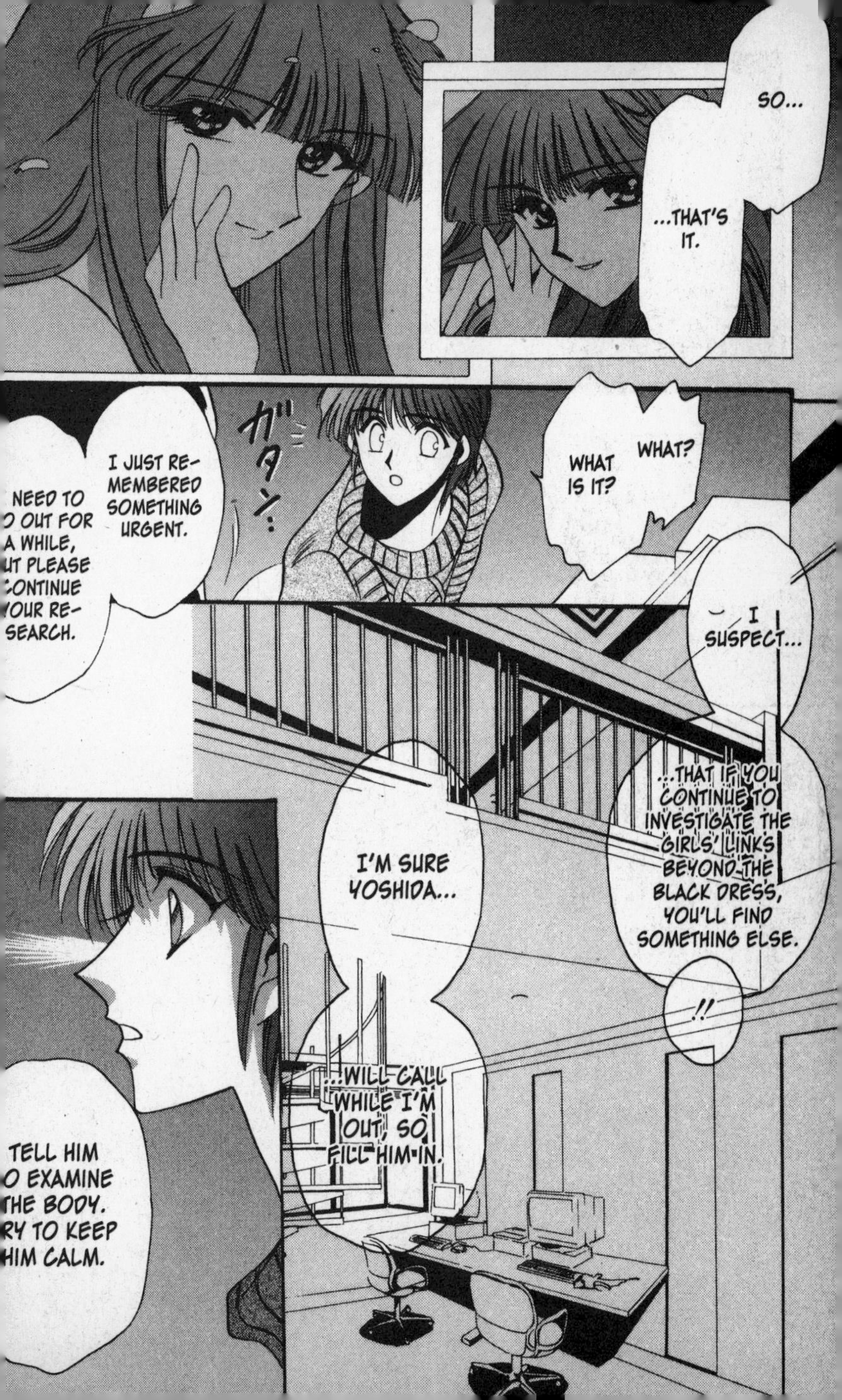
SO...
...THAT'S IT.
WHAT?
WHAT IS IT?
ガタン
I JUST RE-MEMBERED SOMETHING URGENT.
NEED TO
O OUT FOR
A WHILE,
UT PLEASE
ONTINUE
OUR RE-
SEARCH.
I SUSPECT...
...THAT IF YOU CONTINUE TO INVESTIGATE THE GIRLS' LINKS BEYOND THE BLACK DRESS, YOU'LL FIND SOMETHING ELSE.
!!
I'M SURE YOSHIDA...
...WILL CALL WHILE I'M OUT, SO FILL HIM IN.
TELL HIM
O EXAMINE
THE BODY.
RY TO KEEP
HIM CALM.

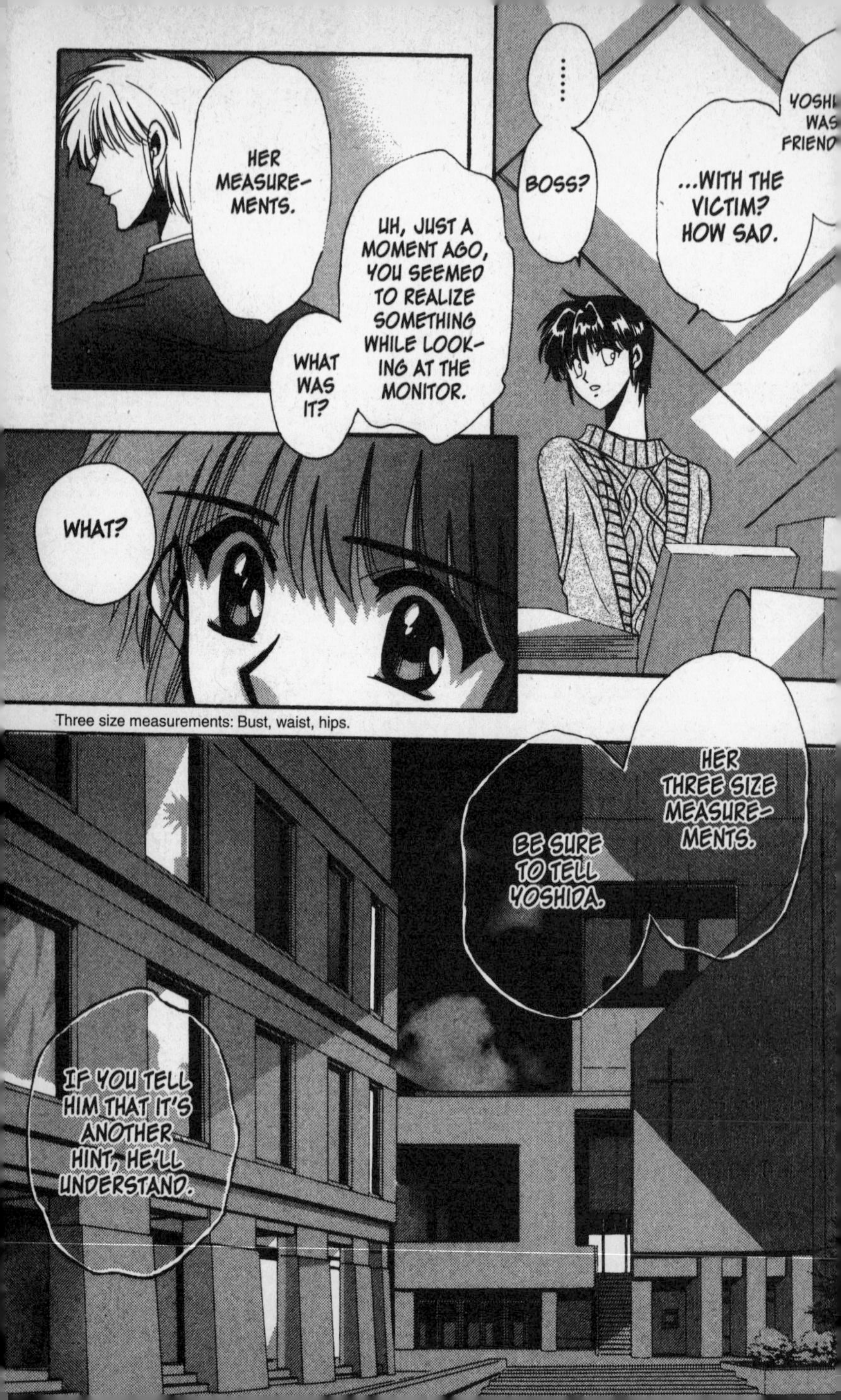
YOSHI WAS FRIEND
...WITH THE VICTIM? HOW SAD.
......
BOSS?
UH, JUST A MOMENT AGO, YOU SEEMED TO REALIZE SOMETHING WHILE LOOKING AT THE MONITOR.
WHAT WAS IT?
HER MEASUREMENTS.
WHAT?
HER THREE SIZE MEASUREMENTS.
BE SURE TO TELL YOSHIDA.
IF YOU TELL HIM THAT IT'S ANOTHER HINT, HE'LL UNDERSTAND.

Three size measurements: Bust, waist, hips.

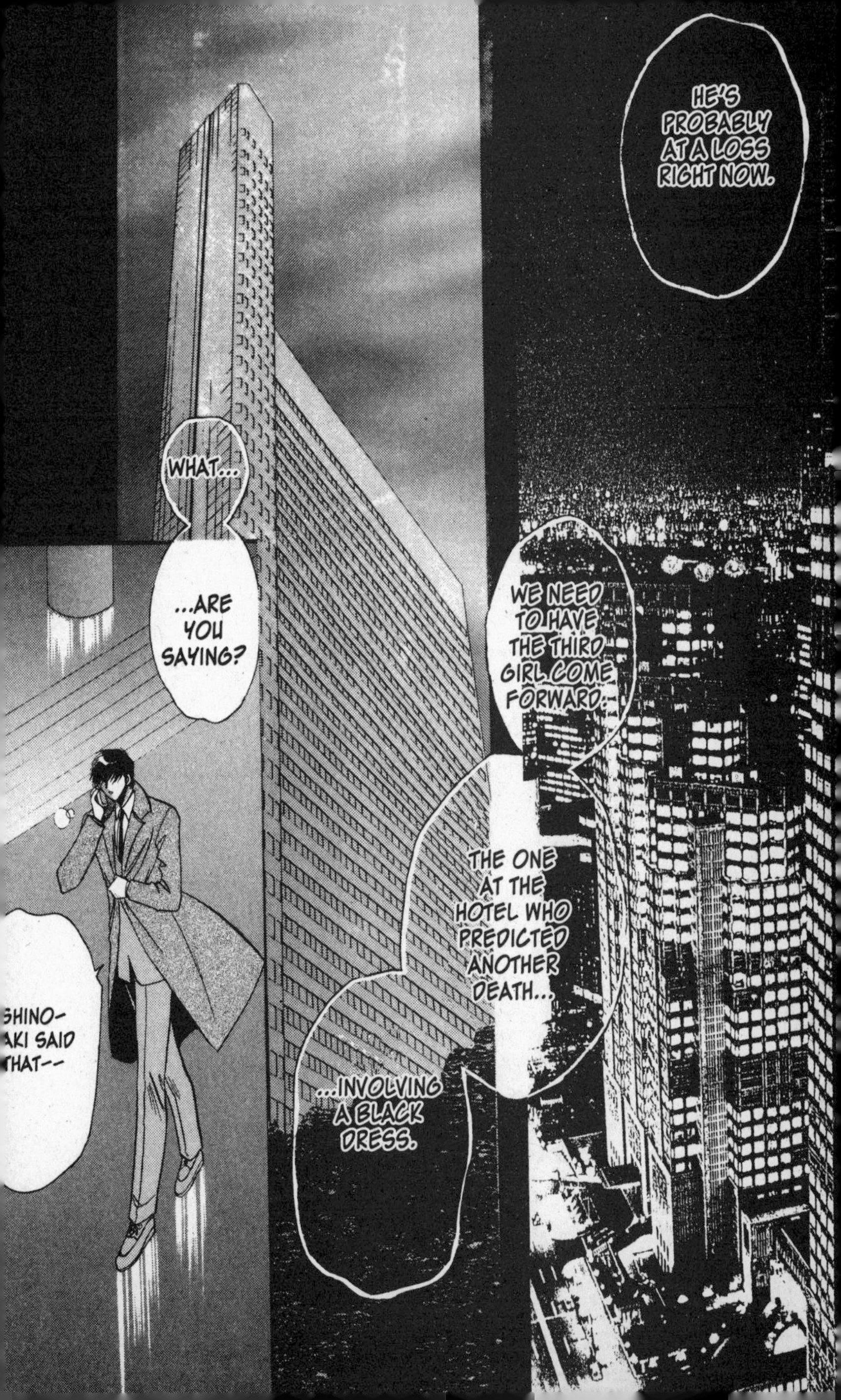
HE'S PROBABLY AT A LOSS RIGHT NOW.
WE NEED TO HAVE THE THIRD GIRL COME FORWARD.
THE ONE AT THE HOTEL WHO PREDICTED ANOTHER DEATH...
...INVOLVING A BLACK DRESS.
WHAT...
...ARE YOU SAYING?
SHINO-
AKI SAID
THAT--

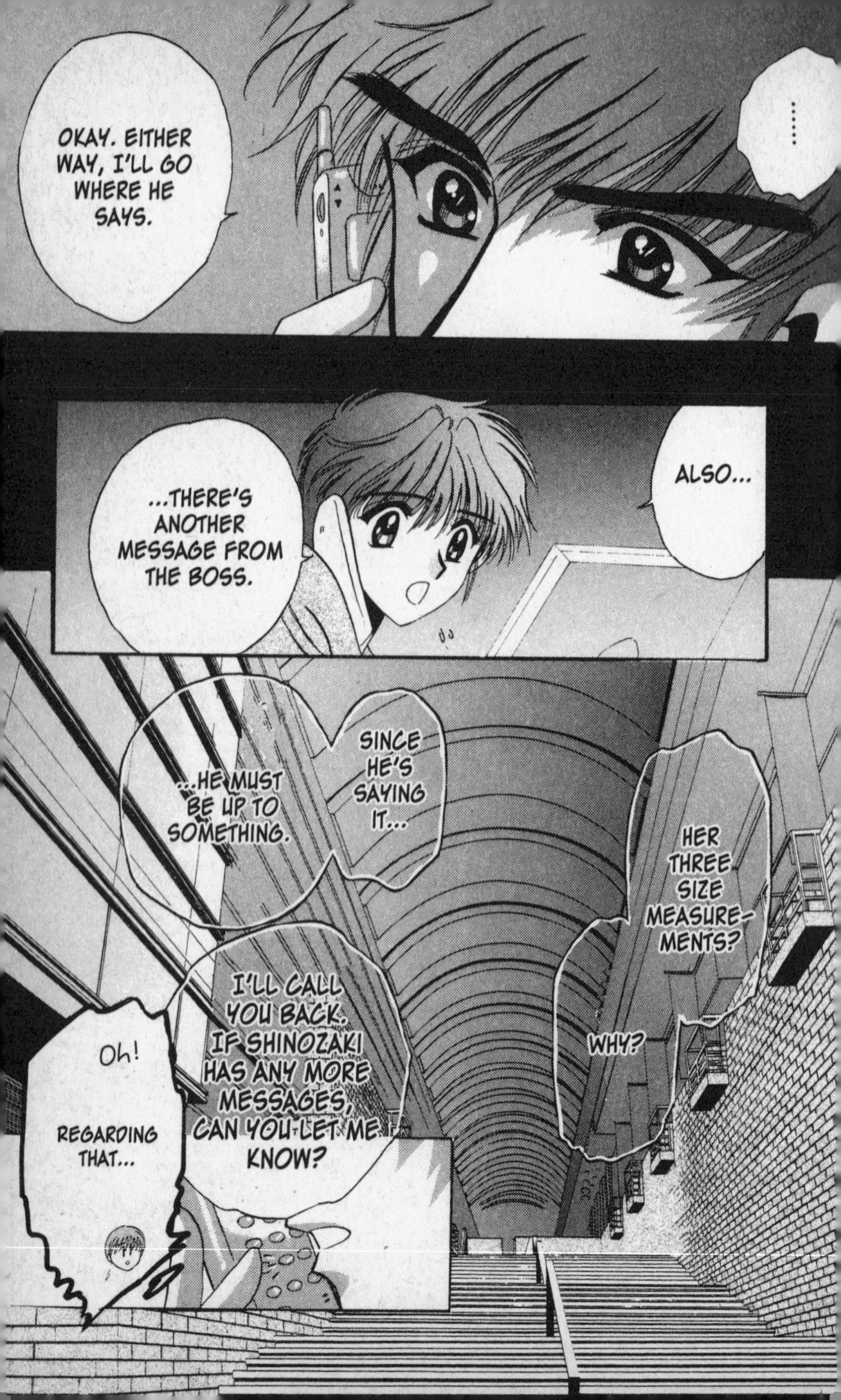
......
OKAY. EITHER WAY, I'LL GO WHERE HE SAYS.
ALSO...
...THERE'S ANOTHER MESSAGE FROM THE BOSS.
HER THREE SIZE MEASUREMENTS?
WHY?
SINCE HE'S SAYING IT...
...HE MUST BE UP TO SOMETHING.
I'LL CALL YOU BACK. IF SHINOZAKI HAS ANY MORE MESSAGES, CAN YOU LET ME KNOW?
Oh!
REGARDING THAT...

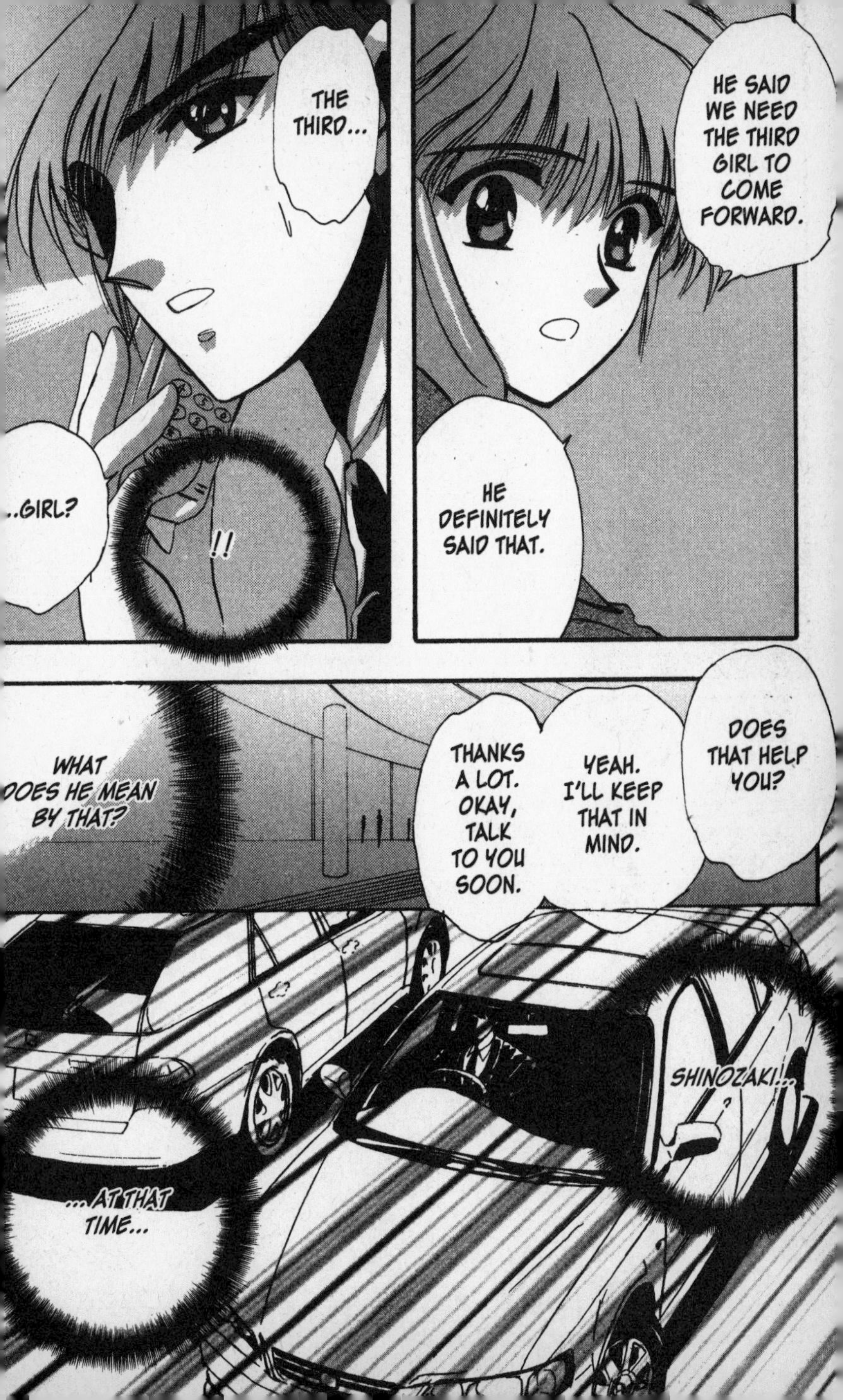
HE SAID WE NEED THE THIRD GIRL TO COME FORWARD.
HE DEFINITELY SAID THAT.
THE THIRD...
..GIRL?
!!
DOES THAT HELP YOU?
YEAH. I'LL KEEP THAT IN MIND.
THANKS A LOT. OKAY, TALK TO YOU SOON.
WHAT DOES HE MEAN BY THAT?
SHINOZAKI...
...AT THAT TIME...

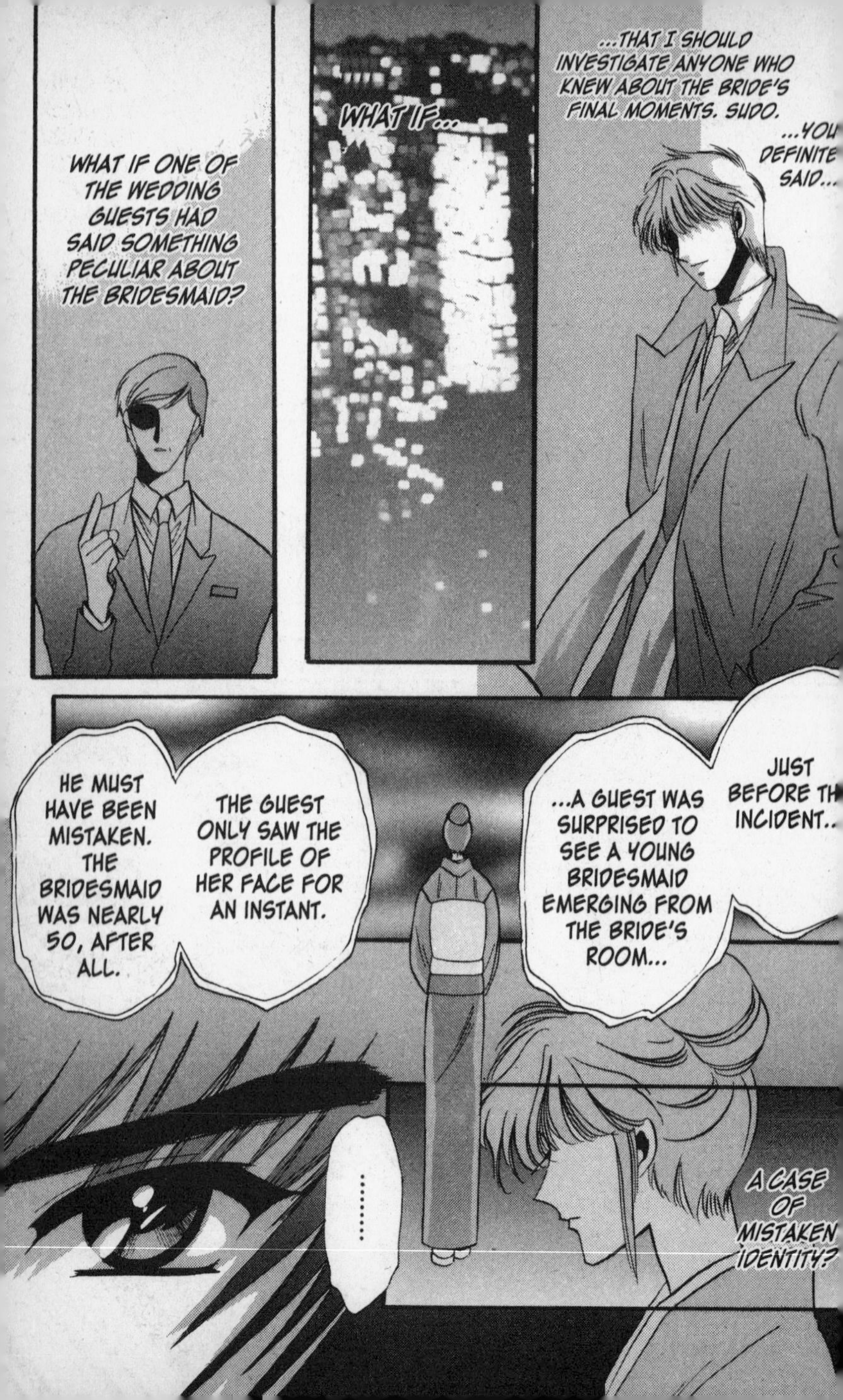
...YOU DEFINITE SAID...
...THAT I SHOULD INVESTIGATE ANYONE WHO KNEW ABOUT THE BRIDE'S FINAL MOMENTS. SUDO.
WHAT IF...
WHAT IF ONE OF THE WEDDING GUESTS HAD SAID SOMETHING PECULIAR ABOUT THE BRIDESMAID?
JUST BEFORE TH INCIDENT..
...A GUEST WAS SURPRISED TO SEE A YOUNG BRIDESMAID EMERGING FROM THE BRIDE'S ROOM...
THE GUEST ONLY SAW THE PROFILE OF HER FACE FOR AN INSTANT.
HE MUST HAVE BEEN MISTAKEN. THE BRIDESMAID WAS NEARLY 50, AFTER ALL.
A CASE OF MISTAKEN IDENTITY?
......

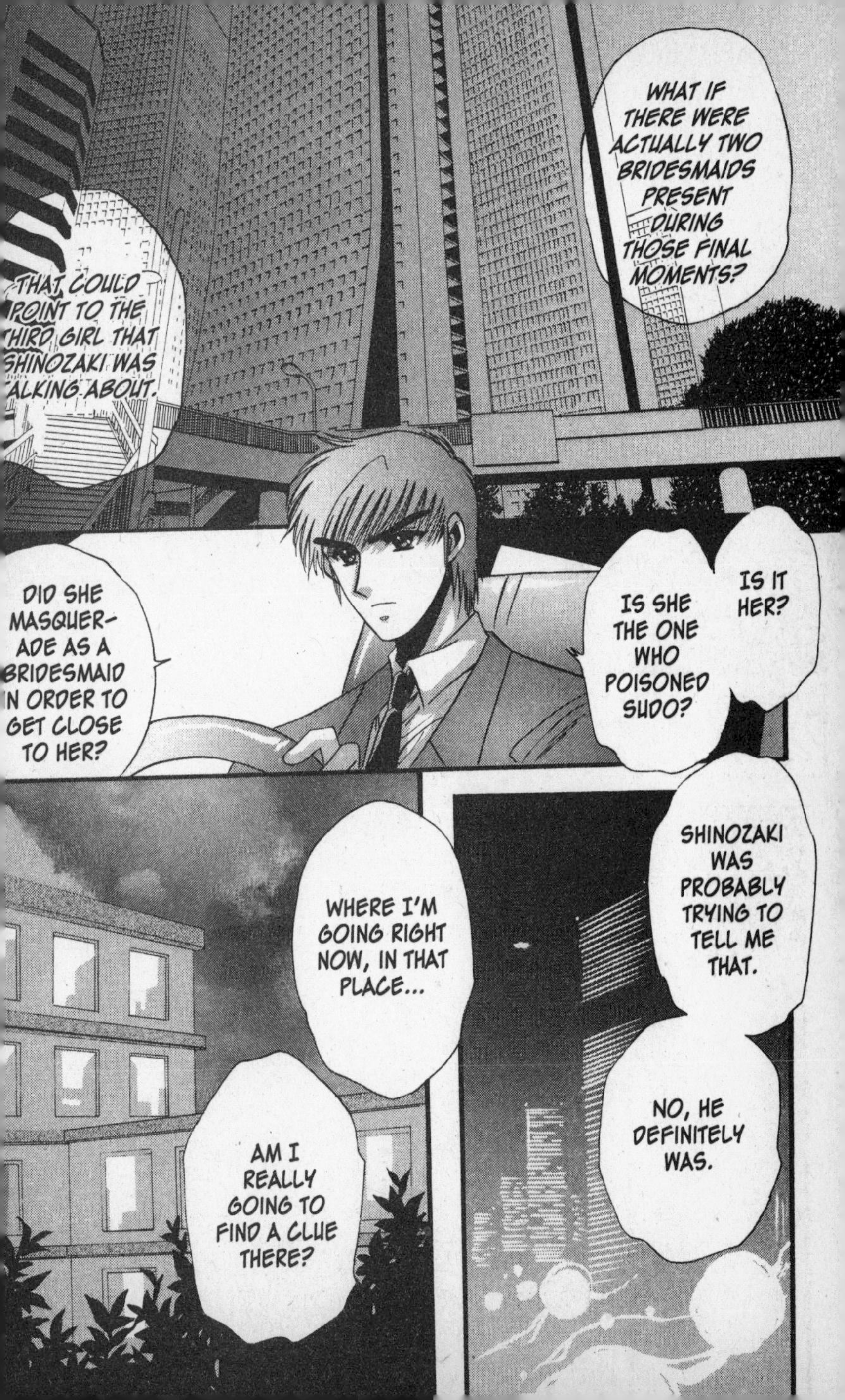
WHAT IF THERE WERE ACTUALLY TWO BRIDESMAIDS PRESENT DURING THOSE FINAL MOMENTS?
THAT COULD POINT TO THE THIRD GIRL THAT SHINOZAKI WAS TALKING ABOUT.
IS IT HER?
IS SHE THE ONE WHO POISONED SUDO?
DID SHE MASQUERADE AS A BRIDESMAID IN ORDER TO GET CLOSE TO HER?
SHINOZAKI WAS PROBABLY TRYING TO TELL ME THAT.
NO, HE DEFINITELY WAS.
WHERE I'M GOING RIGHT NOW, IN THAT PLACE...
AM I REALLY GOING TO FIND A CLUE THERE?

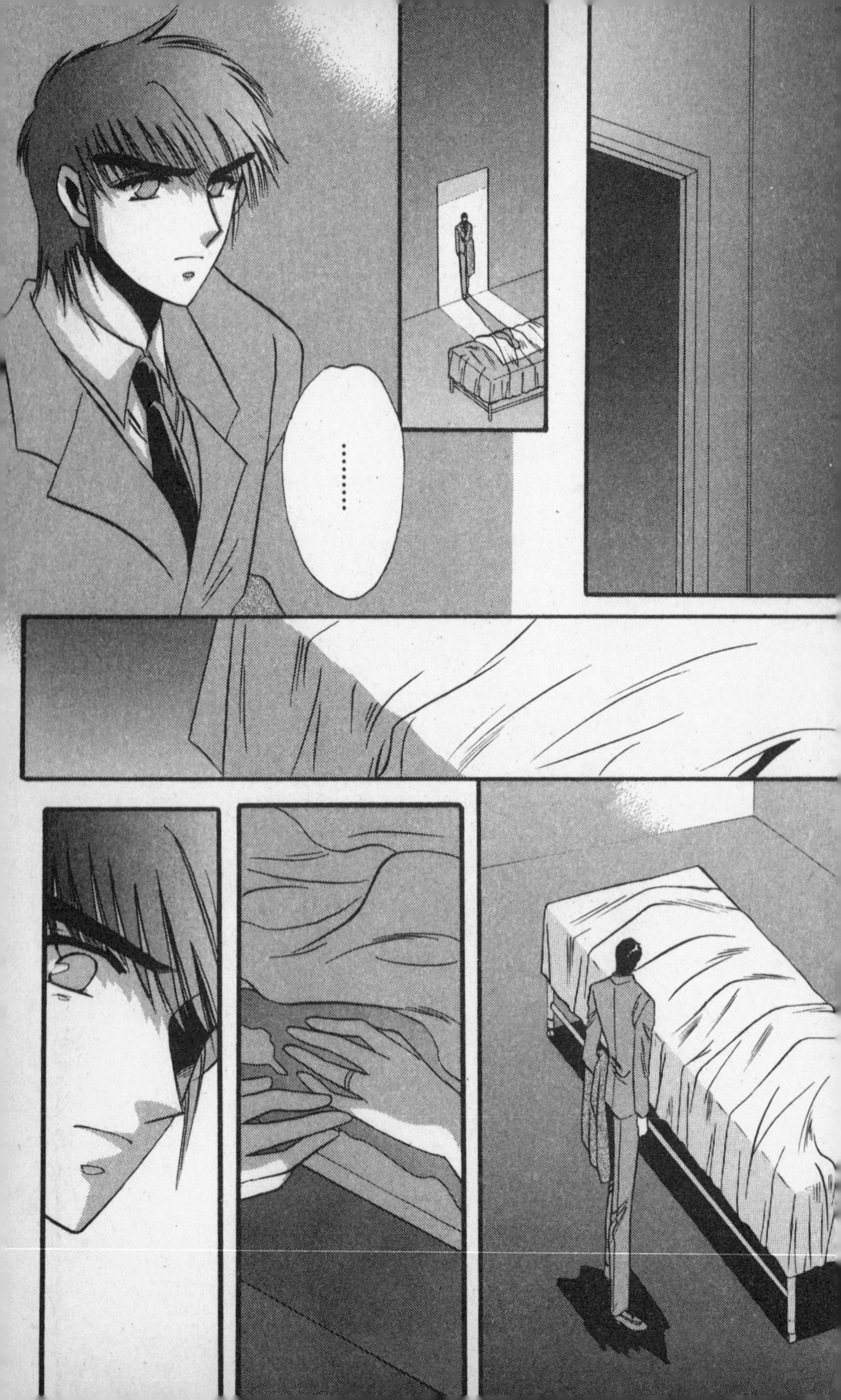

……

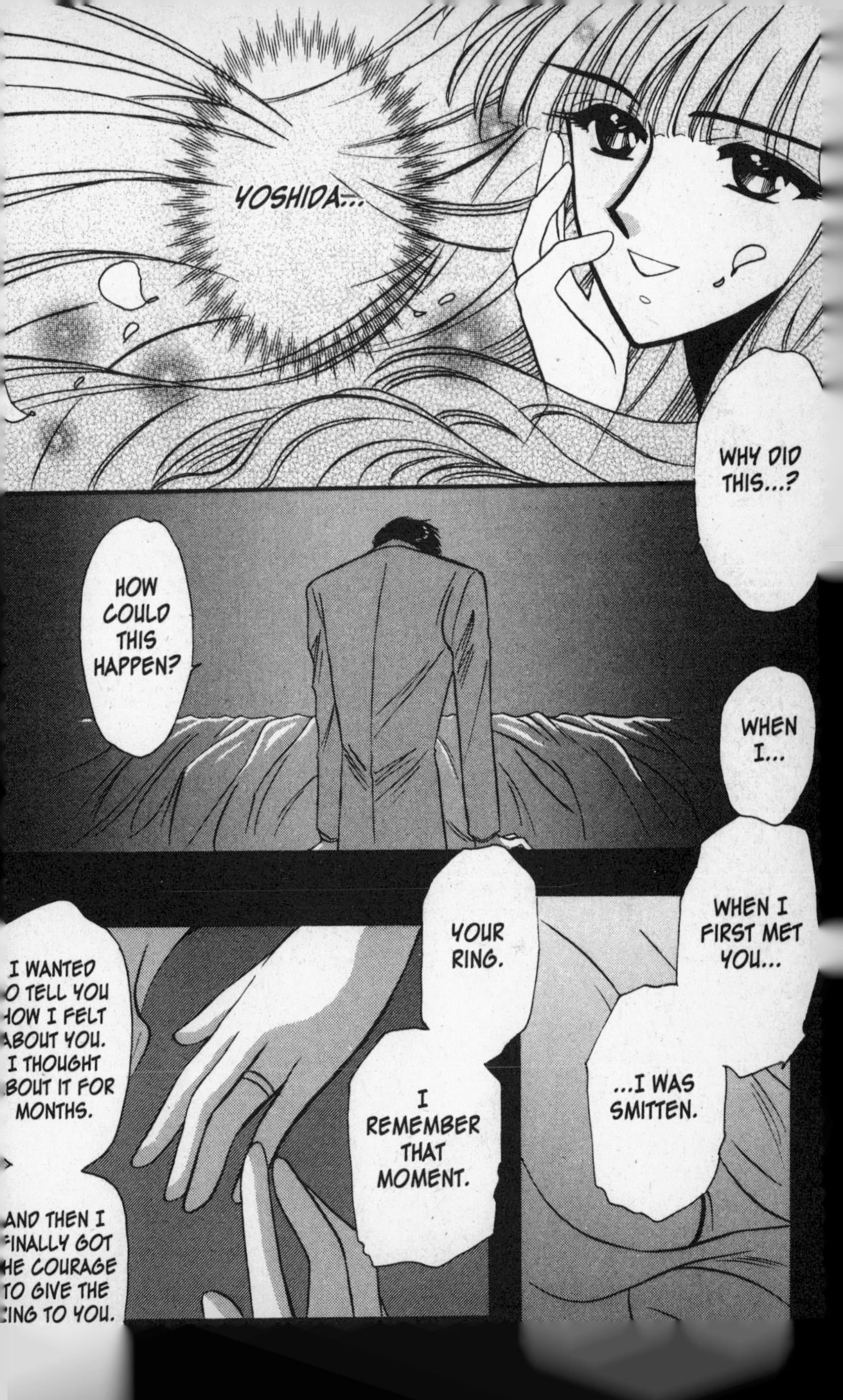
YOSHIDA...
WHY DID THIS...?
HOW COULD THIS HAPPEN?
WHEN I...
WHEN I FIRST MET YOU...
...I WAS SMITTEN.
YOUR RING.
I REMEMBER THAT MOMENT.
I WANTED O TELL YOU HOW I FELT ABOUT YOU. I THOUGHT BOUT IT FOR MONTHS.
AND THEN I FINALLY GOT HE COURAGE TO GIVE THE ING TO YOU.

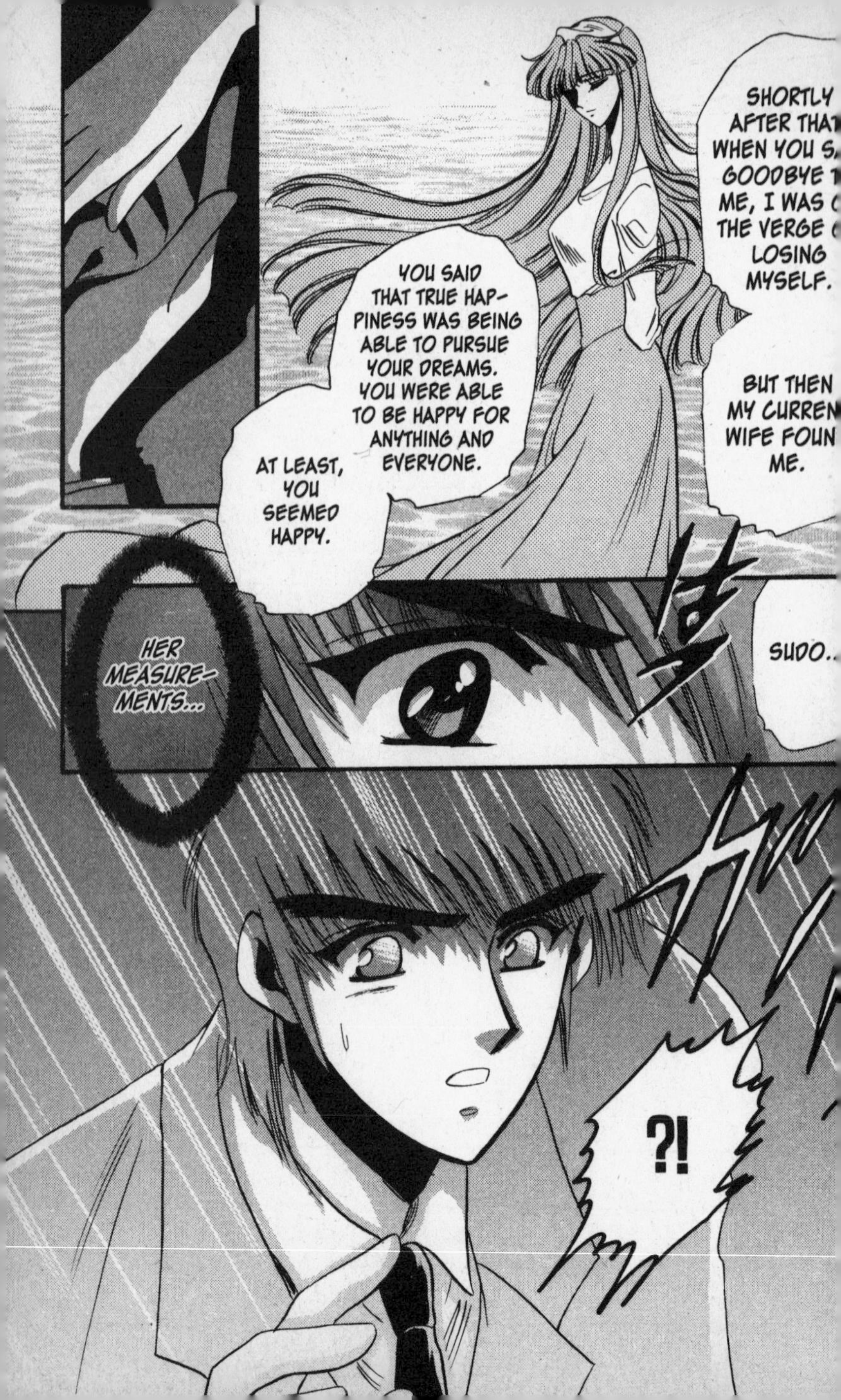
SHORTLY AFTER THAT WHEN YOU S GOODBYE T ME, I WAS THE VERGE LOSING MYSELF.
BUT THEN MY CURREN WIFE FOUN ME.
YOU SAID THAT TRUE HAPPINESS WAS BEING ABLE TO PURSUE YOUR DREAMS. YOU WERE ABLE TO BE HAPPY FOR ANYTHING AND EVERYONE.
AT LEAST, YOU SEEMED HAPPY.
SUDO..
HER MEASUREMENTS...
?!

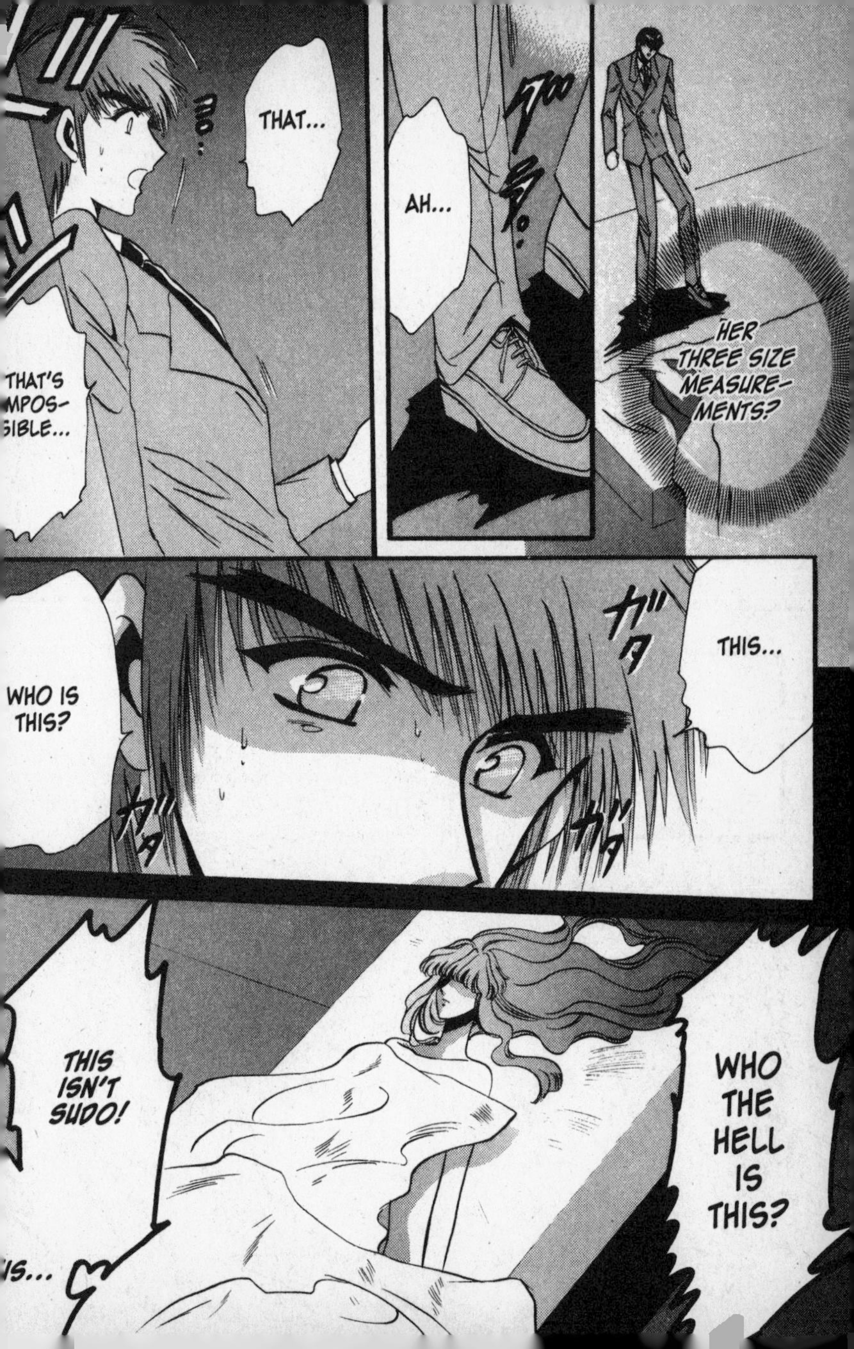

HER THREE SIZE MEASURE-MENTS?
AH...
THAT...
THAT'S MPOS-SIBLE...
THIS...
WHO IS THIS?
WHO THE HELL IS THIS?
THIS ISN'T SUDO!
IS...

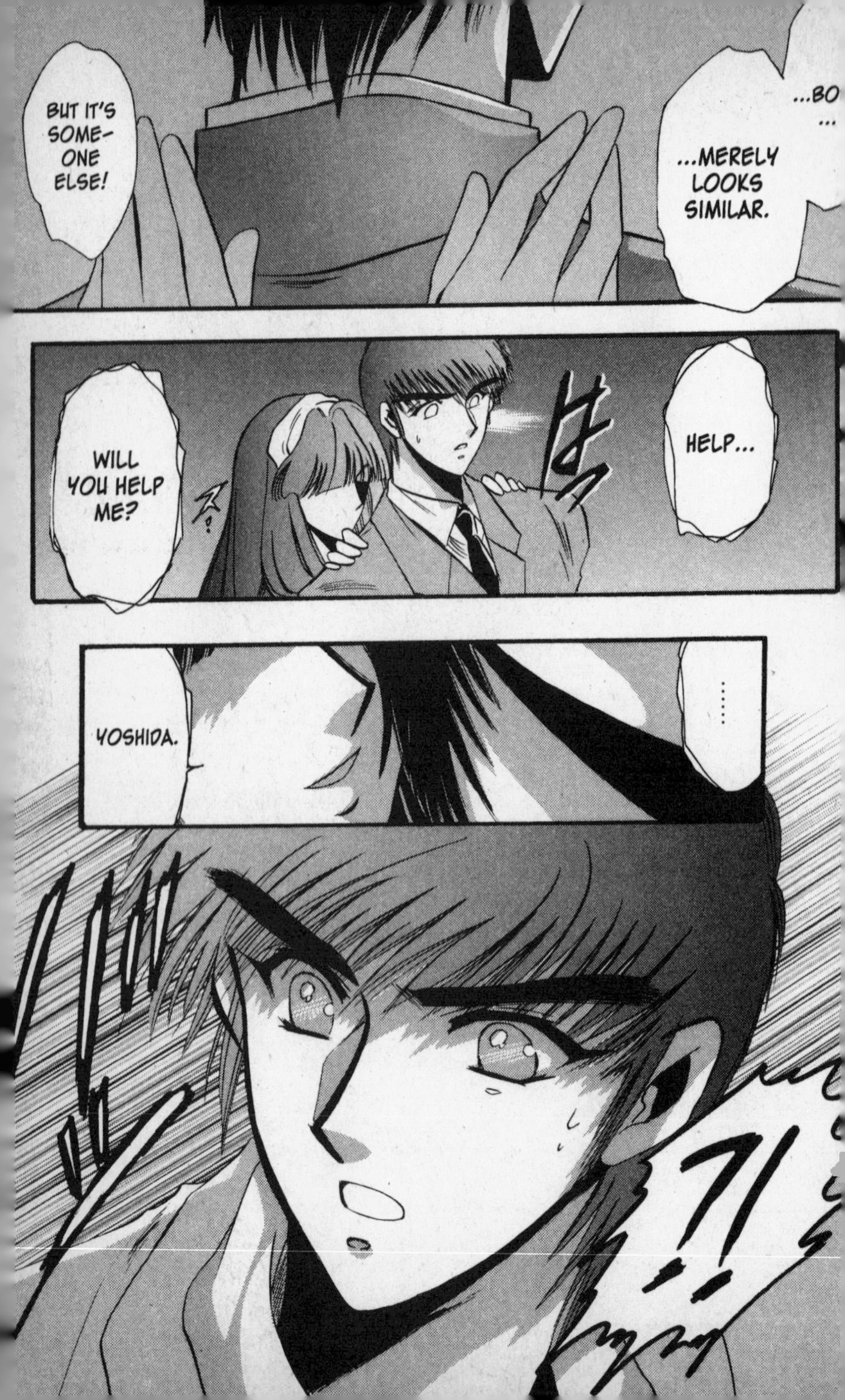
...BO
...
...MERELY LOOKS SIMILAR.
BUT IT'S SOME-ONE ELSE!
HELP...
はっ
WILL YOU HELP ME?
......
YOSHIDA.
!!

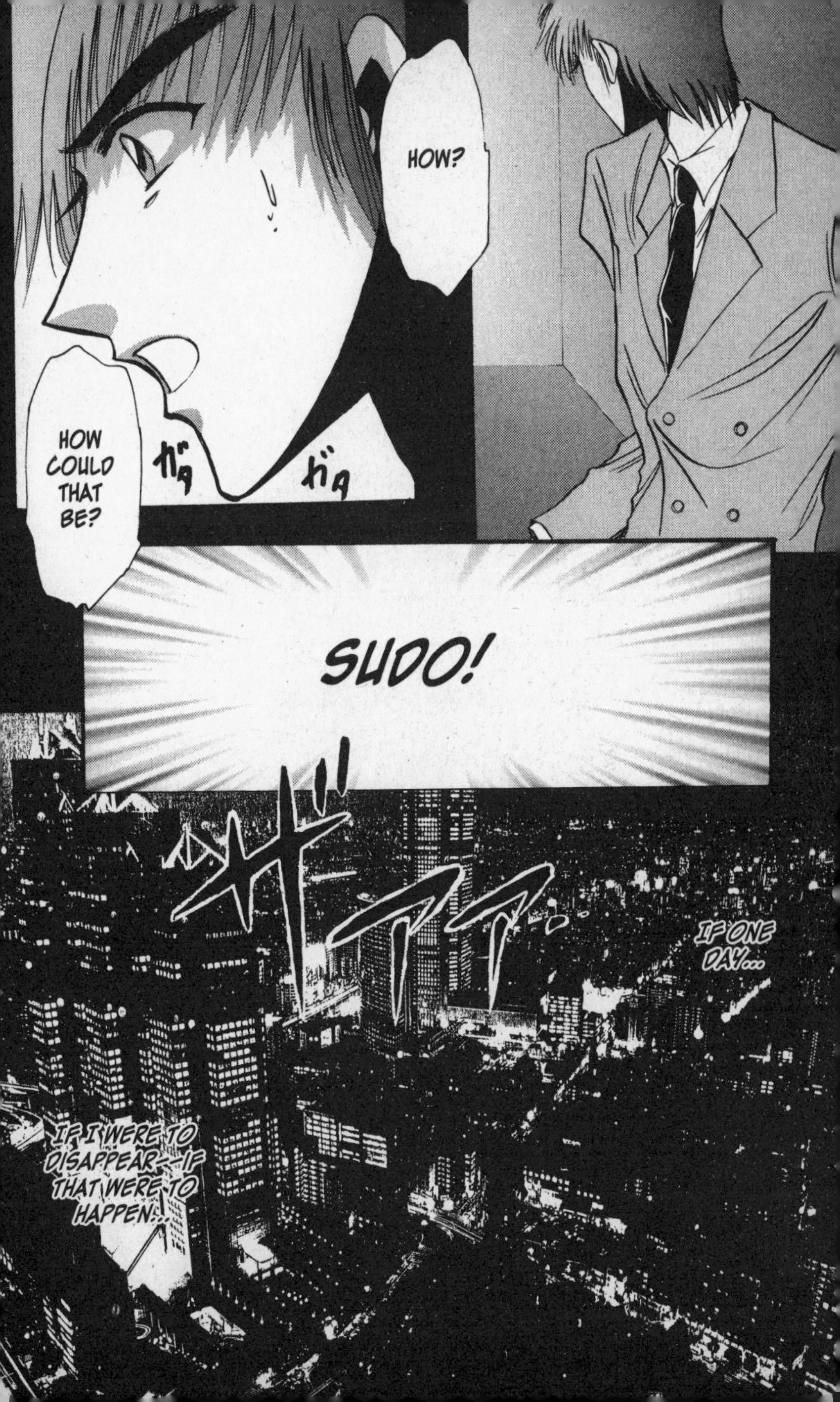
HOW?
HOW COULD THAT BE?
SUDO!
IF ONE DAY...
IF I WERE TO DISAPPEAR--IF THAT WERE TO HAPPEN...

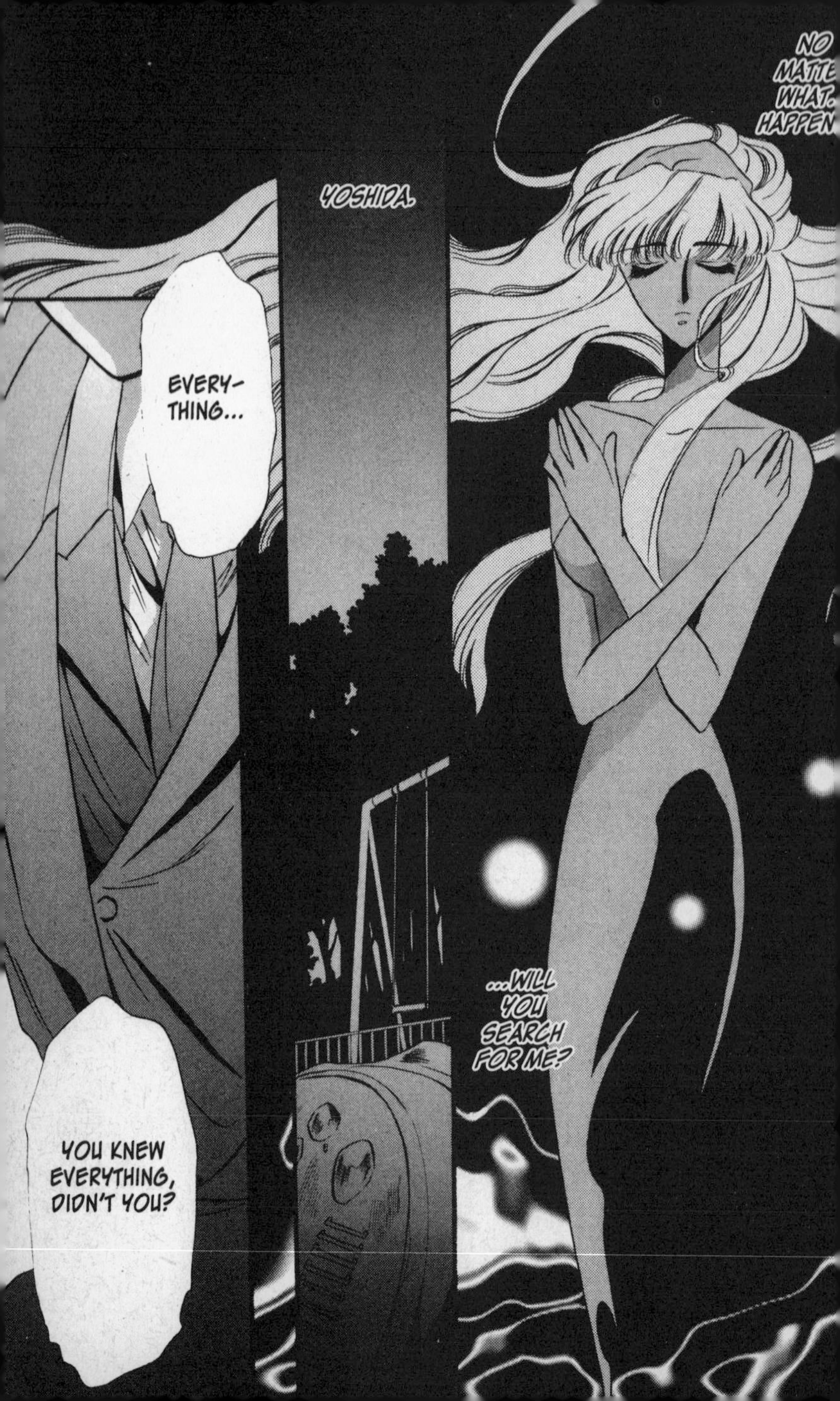
NO MATTE WHAT. HAPPEN
...WILL YOU SEARCH FOR ME?
YOSHIDA.
EVERY-THING...
YOU KNEW EVERYTHING, DIDN'T YOU?

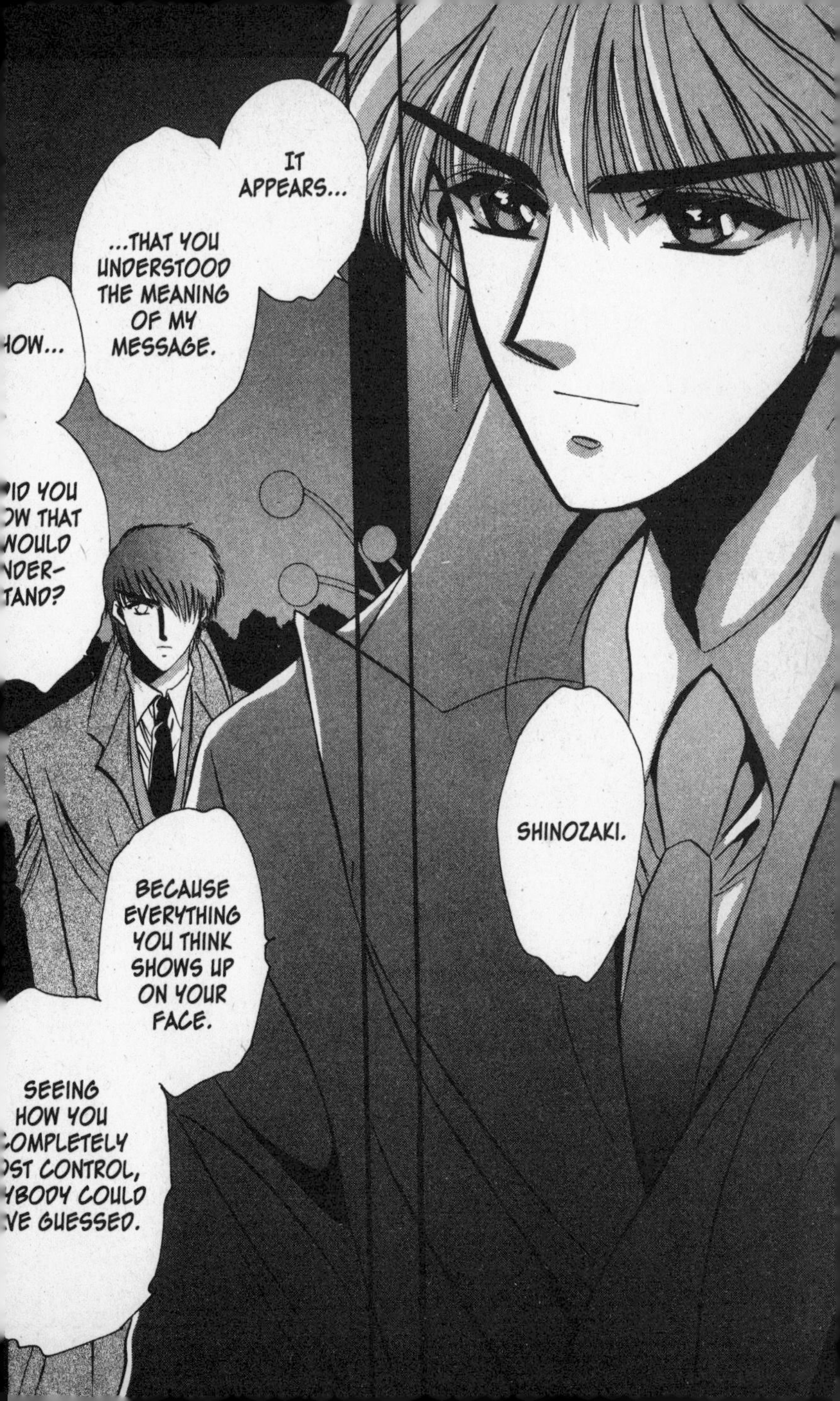
IT APPEARS...
...THAT YOU UNDERSTOOD THE MEANING OF MY MESSAGE.
IOW...
ID YOU OW THAT NOULD NDER- TAND?
SHINOZAKI.
BECAUSE EVERYTHING YOU THINK SHOWS UP ON YOUR FACE.
SEEING HOW YOU OMPLETELY ST CONTROL, YBODY COULD VE GUESSED.

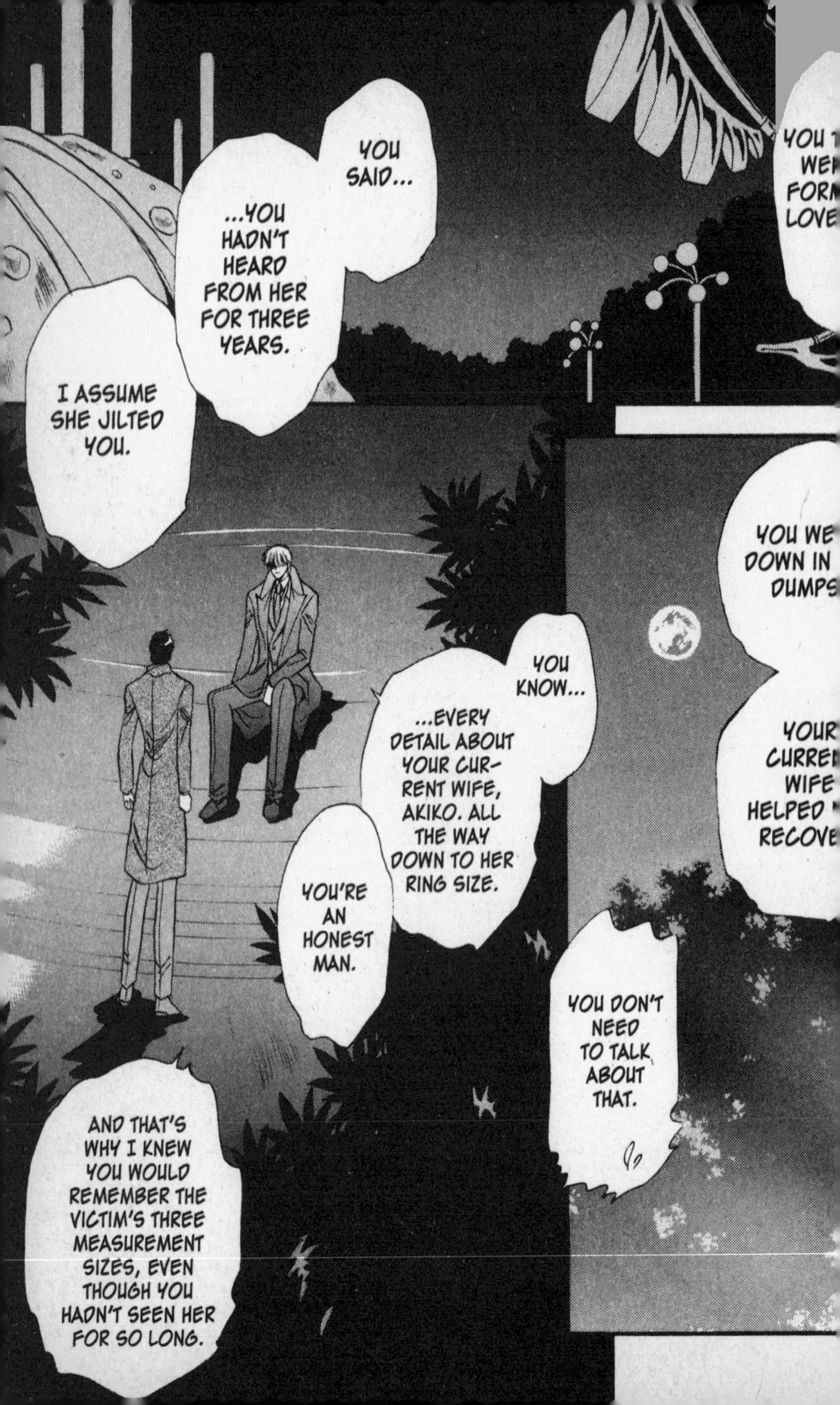

YOU T WER FORM LOVE
YOU WE DOWN IN DUMPS
YOUR CURRE WIFE HELPED RECOVE
YOU DON'T NEED TO TALK ABOUT THAT.
YOU SAID...
...YOU HADN'T HEARD FROM HER FOR THREE YEARS.
I ASSUME SHE JILTED YOU.
YOU KNOW...
...EVERY DETAIL ABOUT YOUR CUR-RENT WIFE, AKIKO. ALL THE WAY DOWN TO HER RING SIZE.
YOU'RE AN HONEST MAN.
AND THAT'S WHY I KNEW YOU WOULD REMEMBER THE VICTIM'S THREE MEASUREMENT SIZES, EVEN THOUGH YOU HADN'T SEEN HER FOR SO LONG.

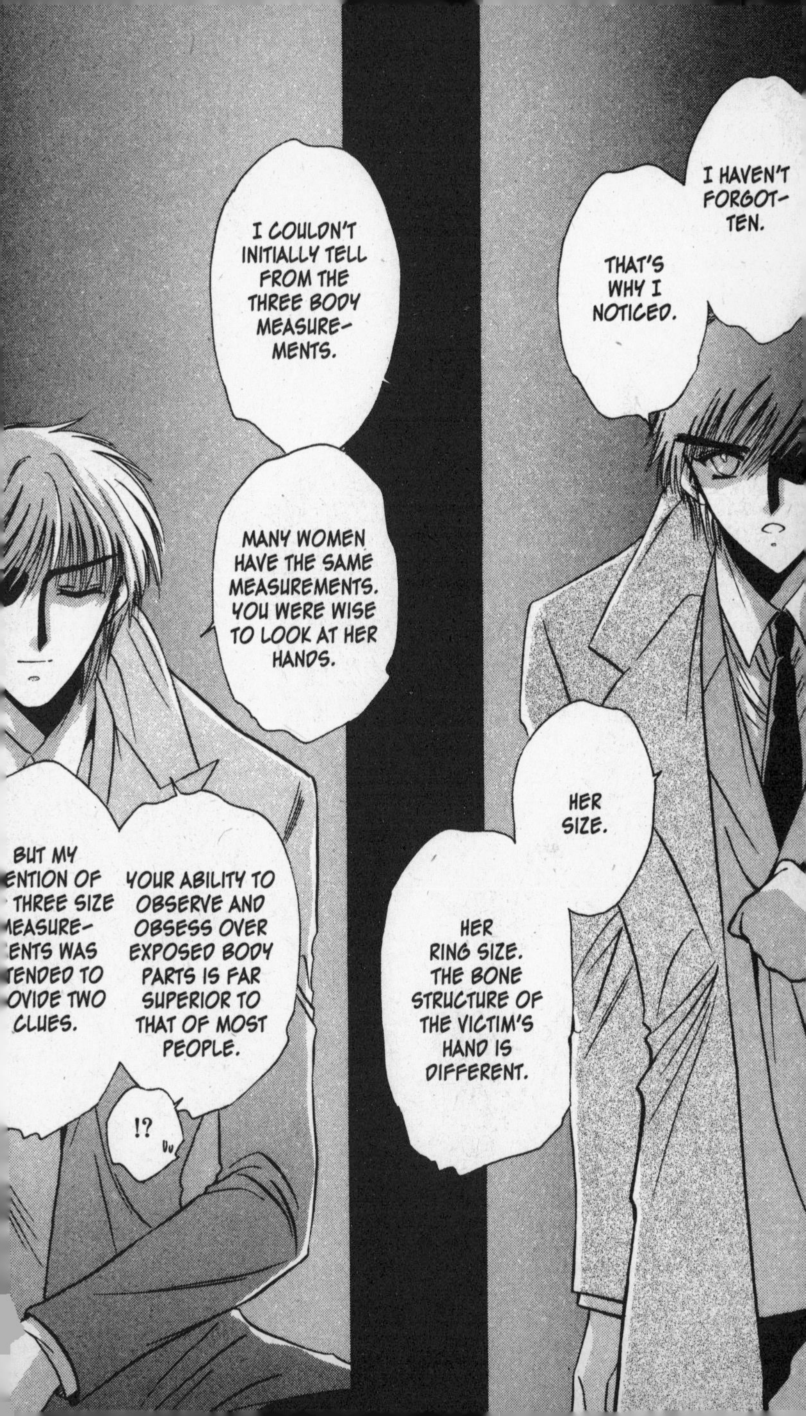
I HAVEN'T FORGOT-TEN.
THAT'S WHY I NOTICED.
HER SIZE.
HER RING SIZE. THE BONE STRUCTURE OF THE VICTIM'S HAND IS DIFFERENT.
I COULDN'T INITIALLY TELL FROM THE THREE BODY MEASURE-MENTS.
MANY WOMEN HAVE THE SAME MEASUREMENTS. YOU WERE WISE TO LOOK AT HER HANDS.
YOUR ABILITY TO OBSERVE AND OBSESS OVER EXPOSED BODY PARTS IS FAR SUPERIOR TO THAT OF MOST PEOPLE.
BUT MY ENTION OF THREE SIZE EASURE-ENTS WAS TENDED TO OVIDE TWO CLUES.
!?

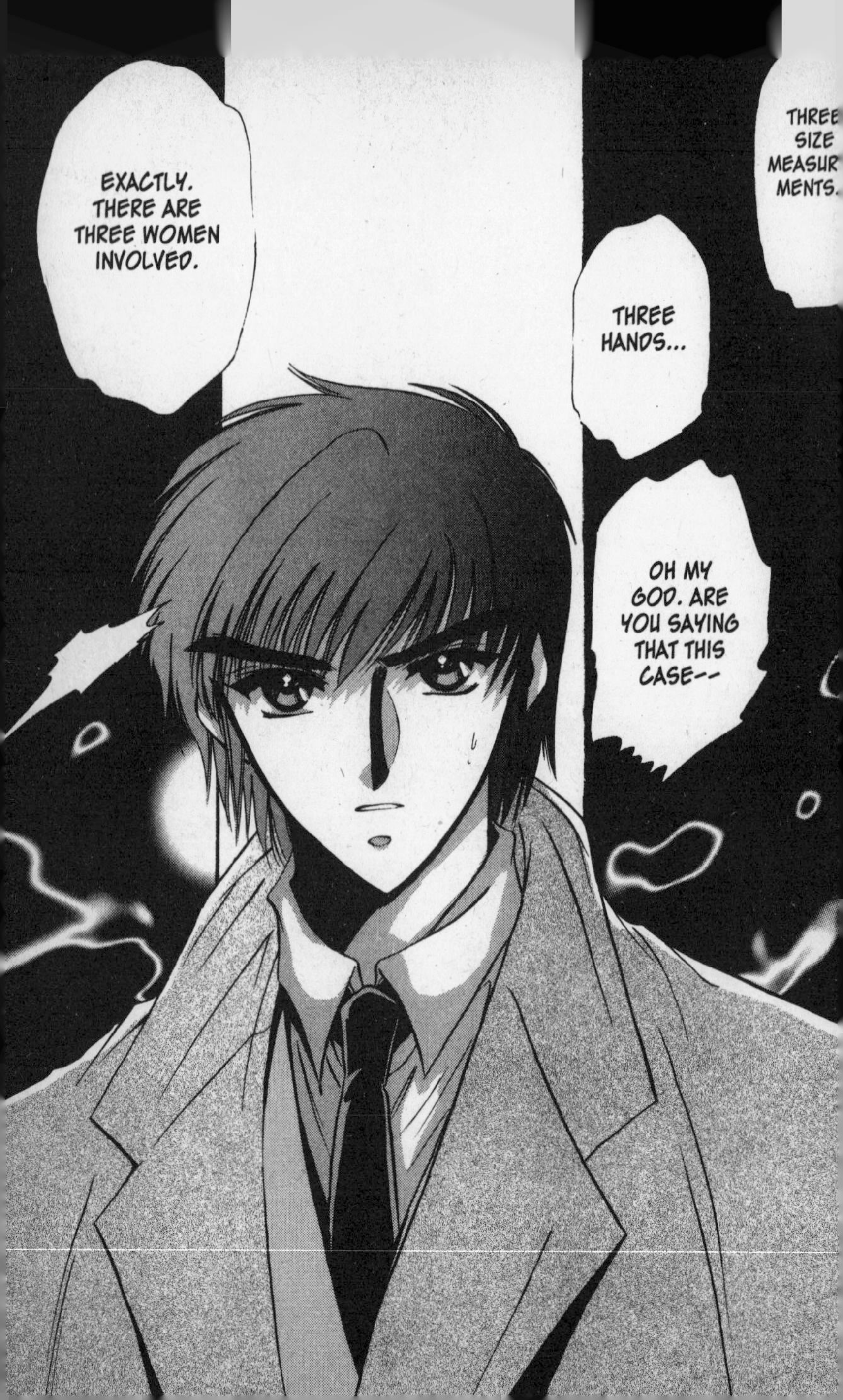
THREE SIZE MEASUR MENTS.
THREE HANDS...
OH MY GOD. ARE YOU SAYING THAT THIS CASE--
EXACTLY. THERE ARE THREE WOMEN INVOLVED.

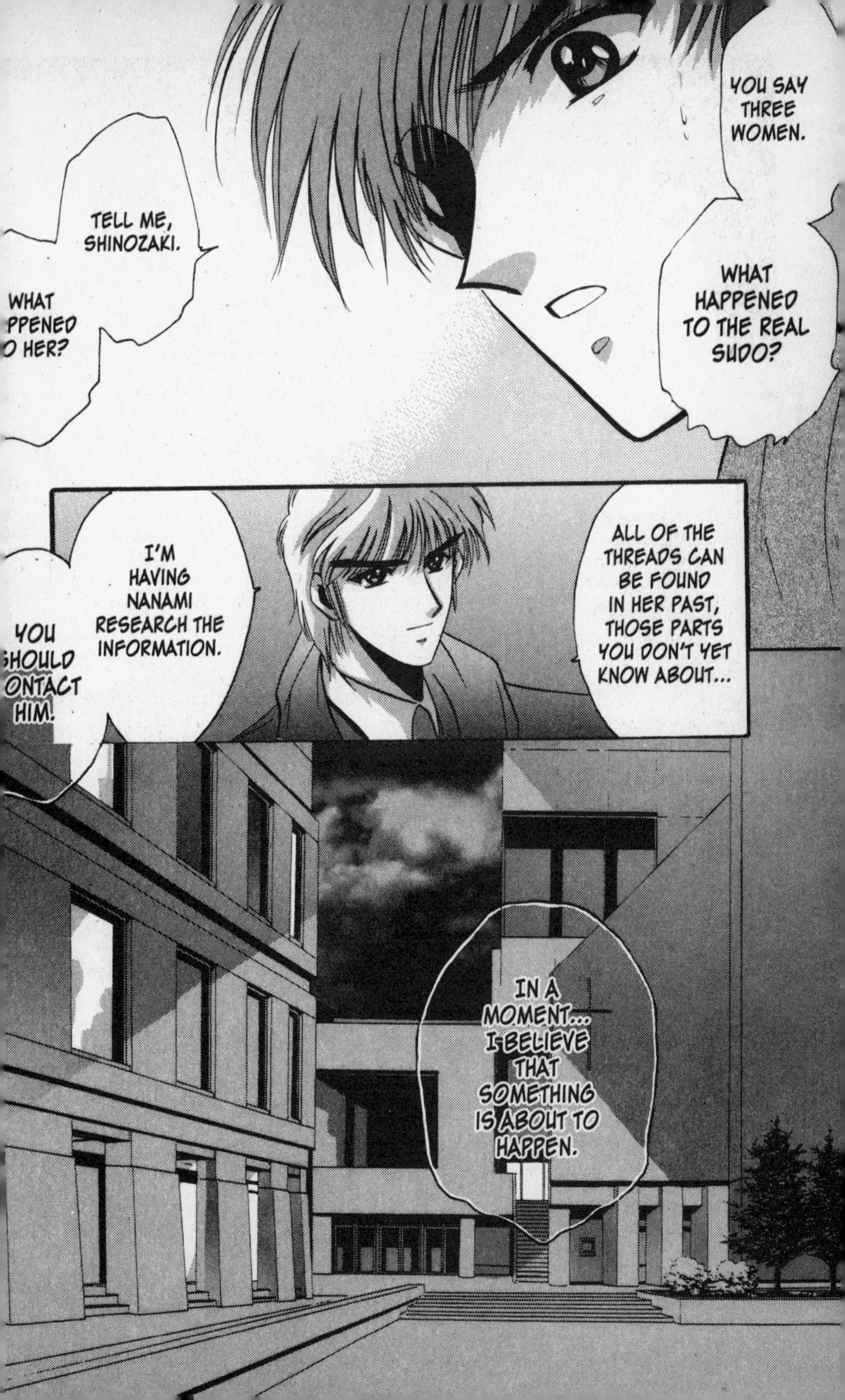
YOU SAY THREE WOMEN.
WHAT HAPPENED TO THE REAL SUDO?
TELL ME, SHINOZAKI.
WHAT PPENED O HER?
ALL OF THE THREADS CAN BE FOUND IN HER PAST, THOSE PARTS YOU DON'T YET KNOW ABOUT...
I'M HAVING NANAMI RESEARCH THE INFORMATION.
YOU HOULD ONTACT HIM.
IN A MOMENT... I BELIEVE THAT SOMETHING IS ABOUT TO HAPPEN.

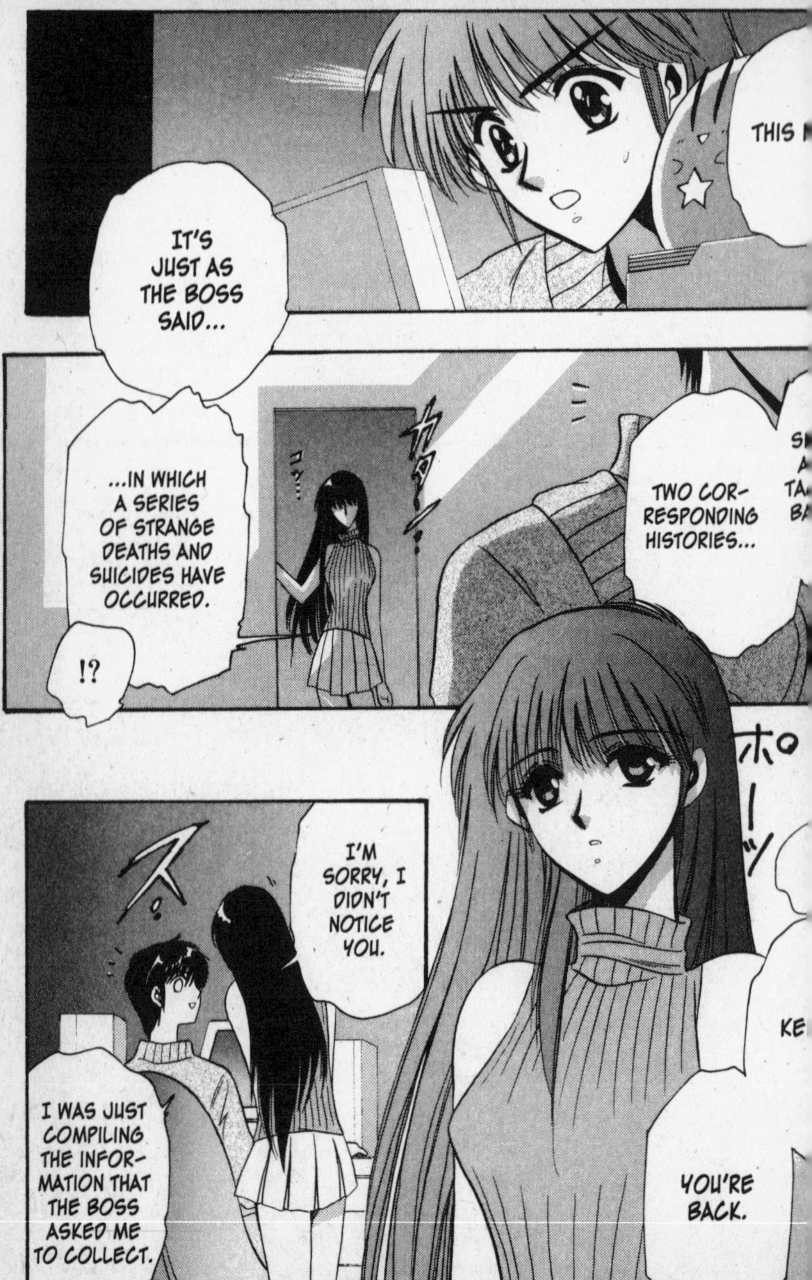
THIS
IT'S JUST AS THE BOSS SAID...
TWO COR-RESPONDING HISTORIES...
...IN WHICH A SERIES OF STRANGE DEATHS AND SUICIDES HAVE OCCURRED.
!?
YOU'RE BACK.
I'M SORRY, I DIDN'T NOTICE YOU.
I WAS JUST COMPILING THE INFOR-MATION THAT THE BOSS ASKED ME TO COLLECT.

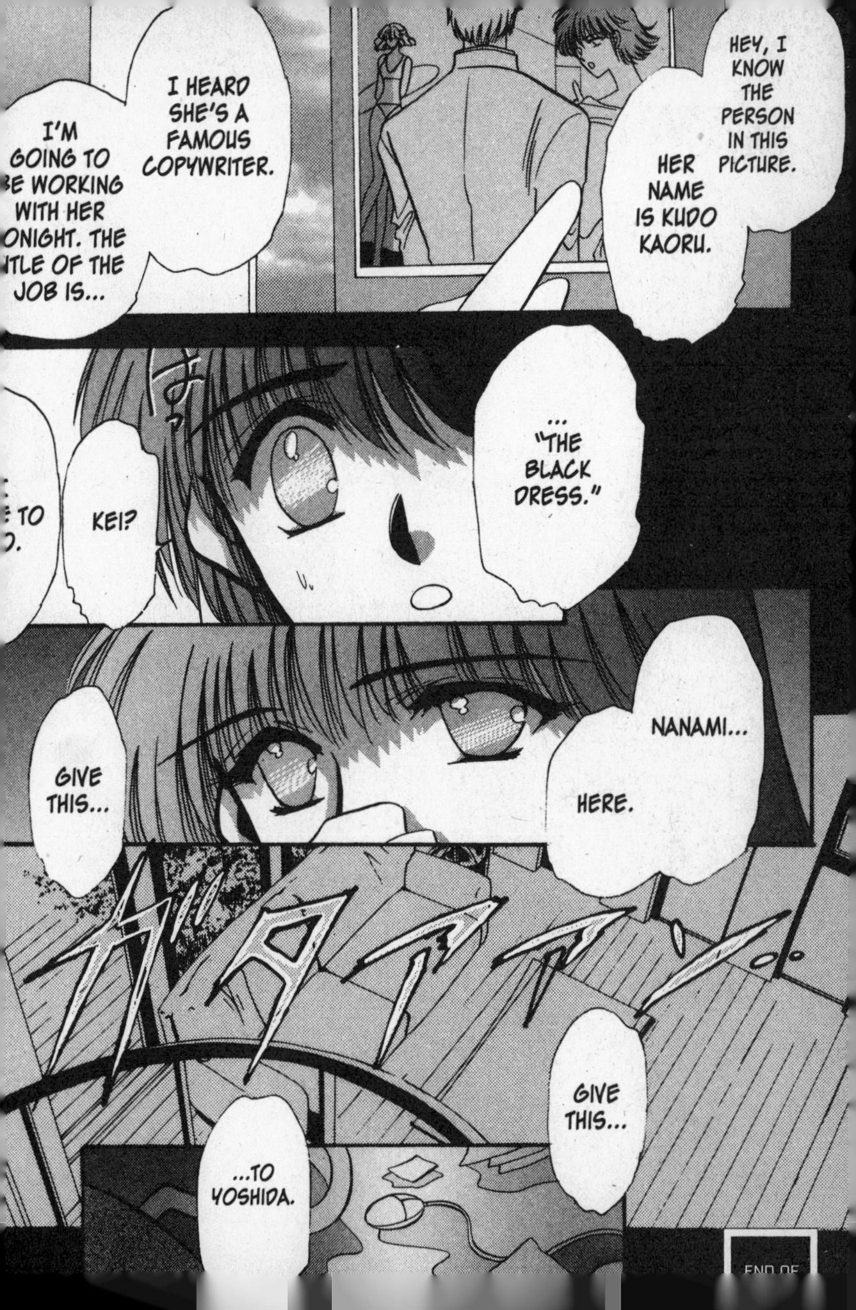
HEY, I KNOW THE PERSON IN THIS PICTURE.
HER NAME IS KUDO KAORU.
I HEARD SHE'S A FAMOUS COPYWRITER.
I'M GOING TO E WORKING WITH HER ONIGHT. THE ITLE OF THE JOB IS...
..."THE BLACK DRESS."
KEI?
NANAMI...
HERE.
GIVE THIS...
GIVE THIS...
...TO YOSHIDA.
END OF

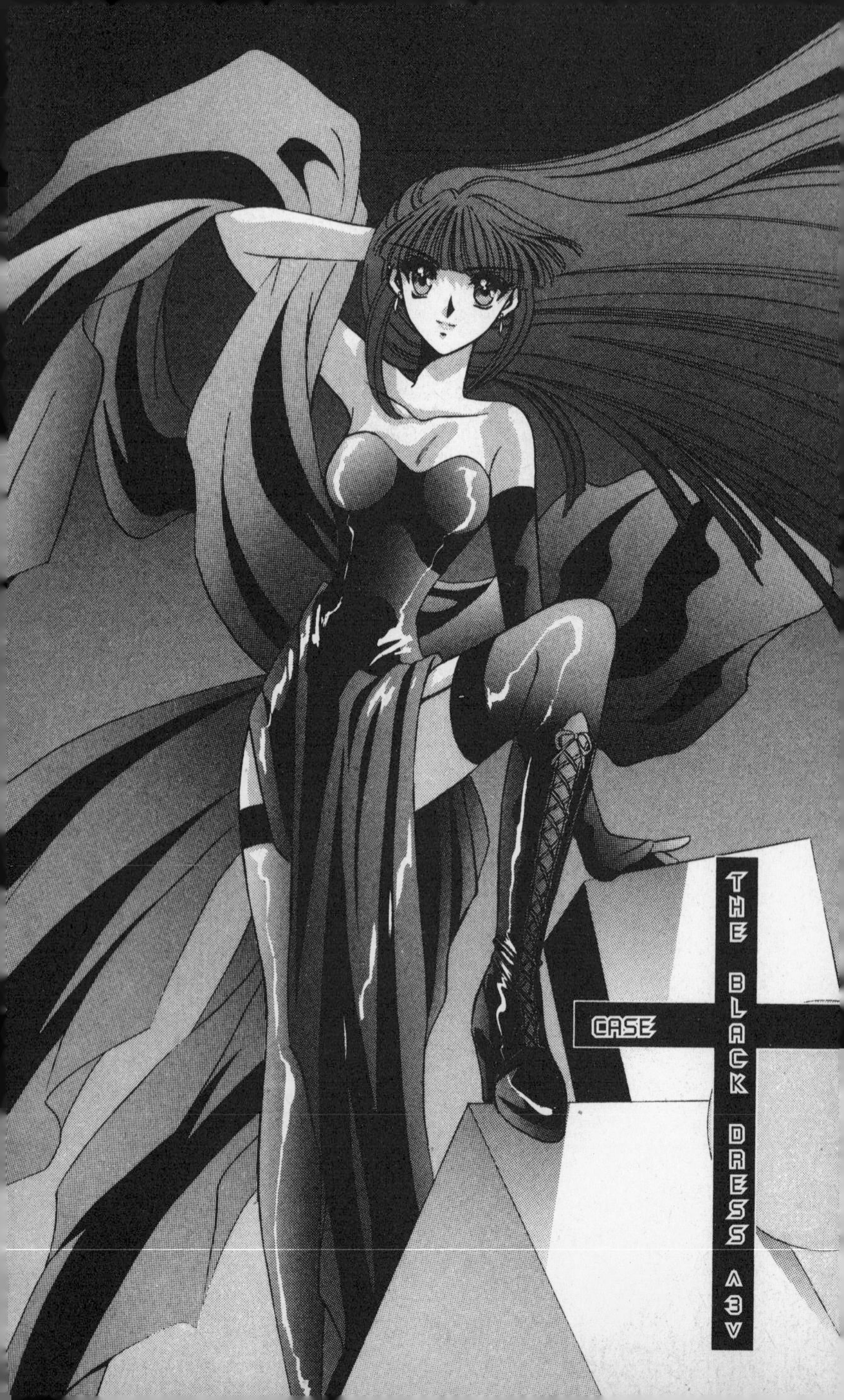
CASE
THE BLACK DRESS
<3>

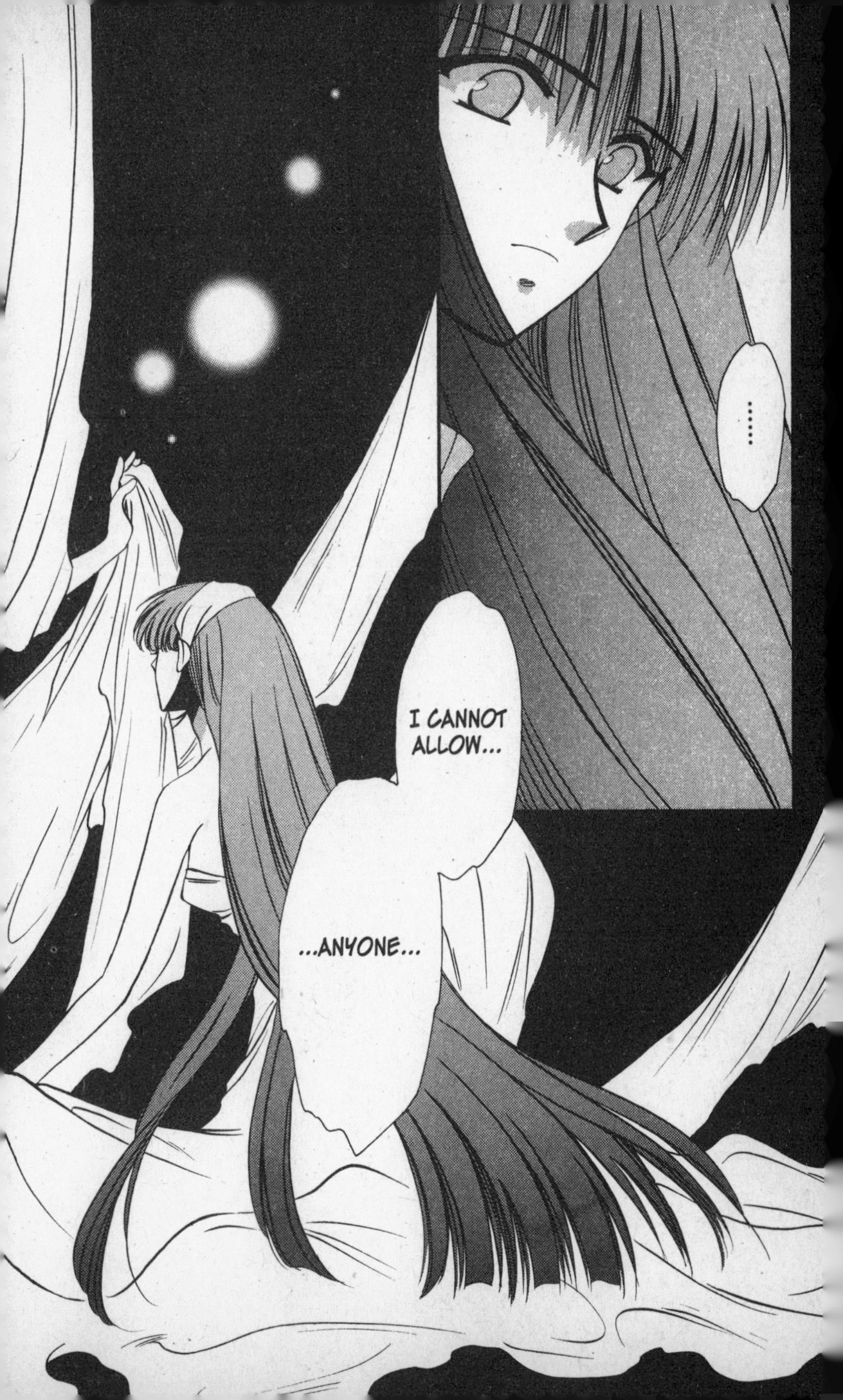
......
I CANNOT ALLOW...
...ANYONE...

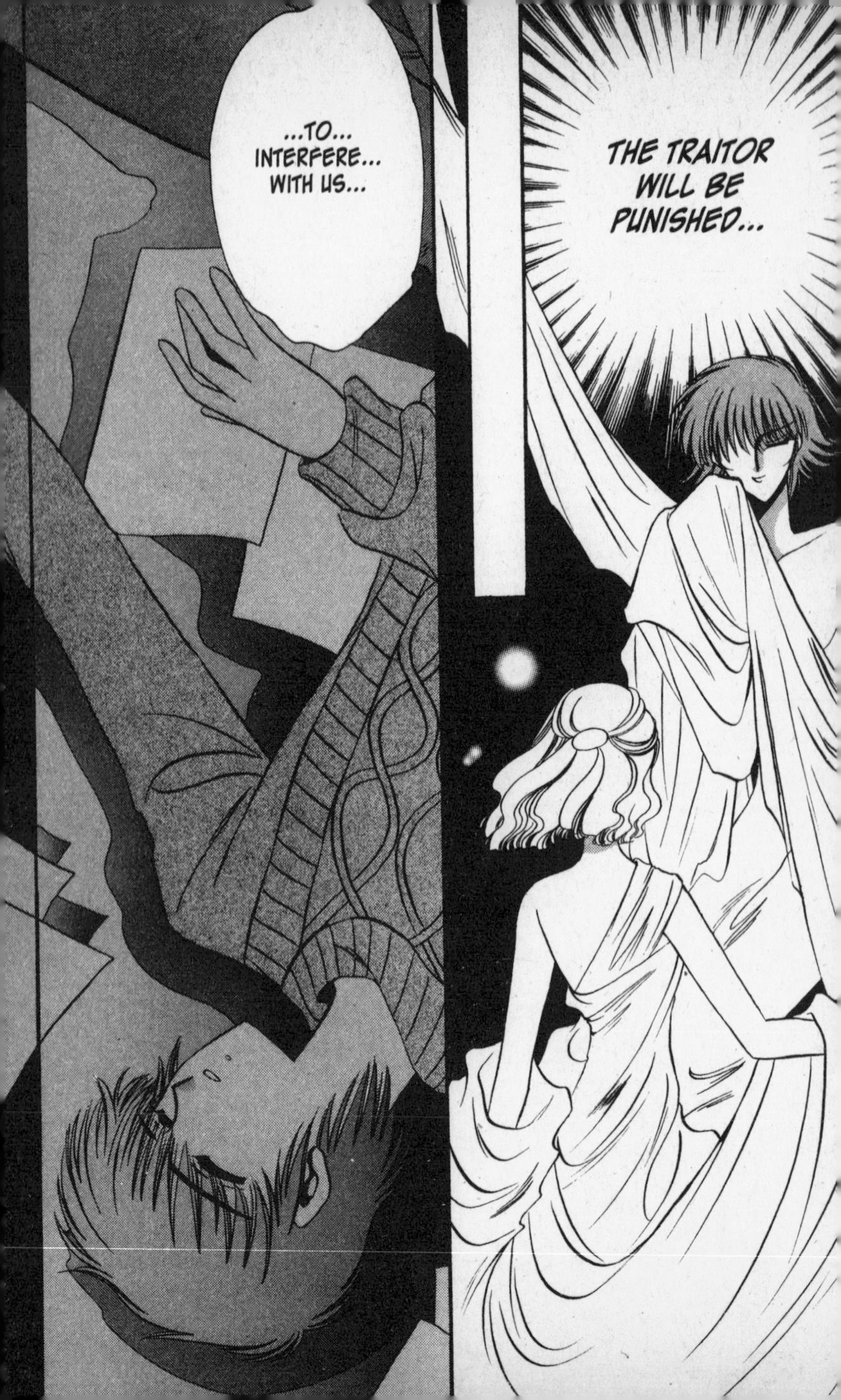
THE TRAITOR WILL BE PUNISHED...
...TO... INTERFERE... WITH US...

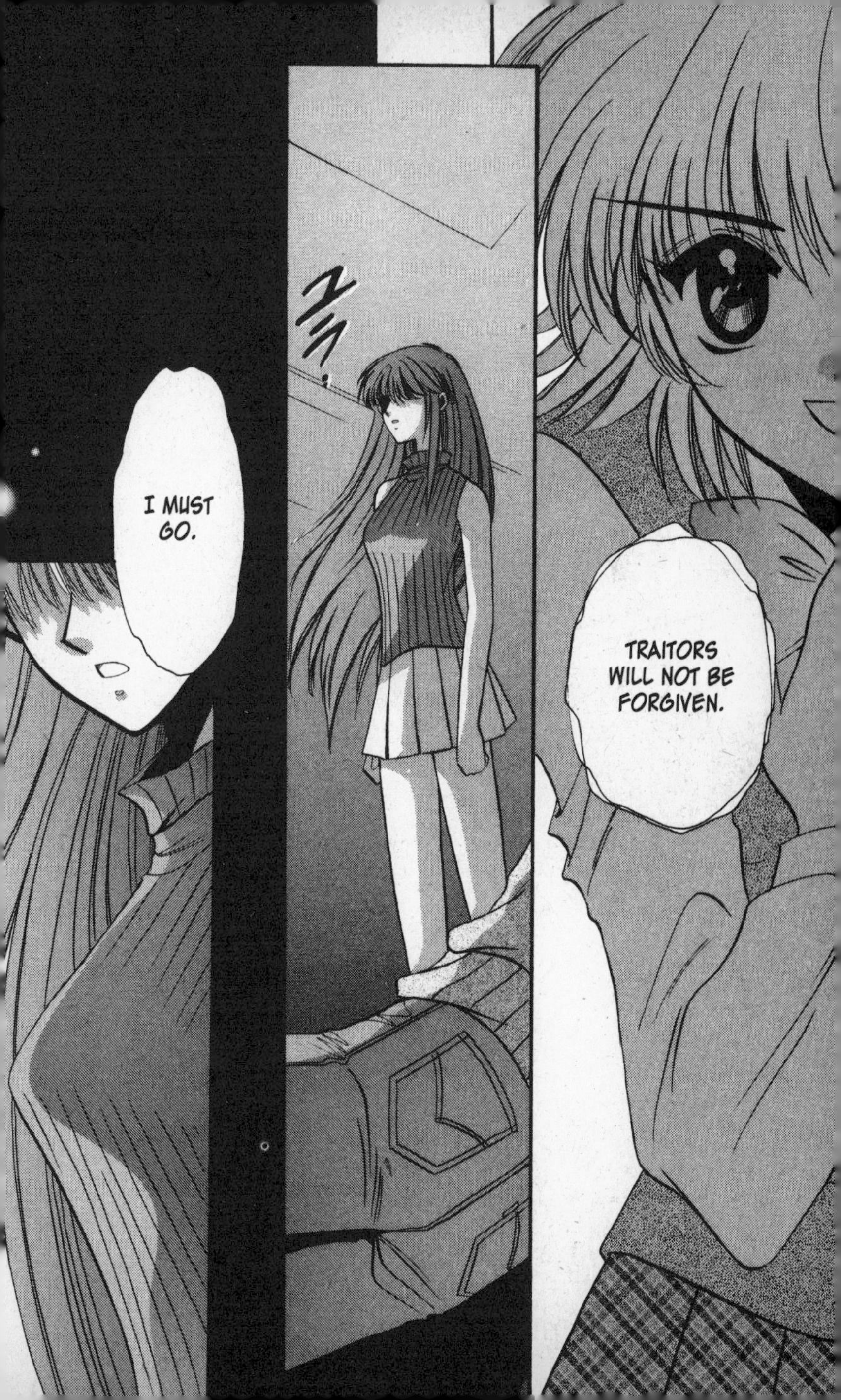
TRAITORS WILL NOT BE FORGIVEN.
I MUST GO.

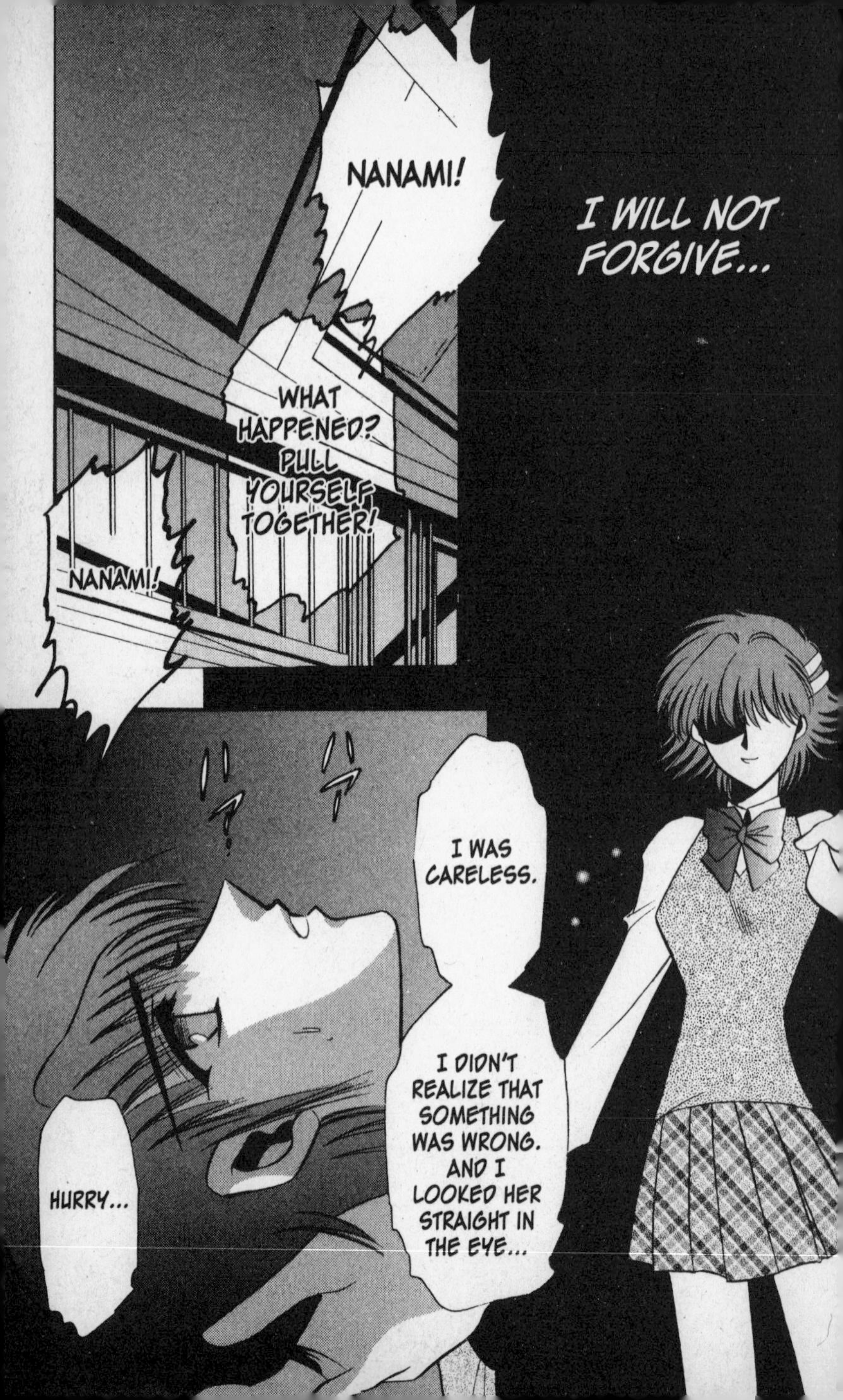
I WILL NOT FORGIVE...
NANAMI!
WHAT HAPPENED? PULL YOURSELF TOGETHER!
NANAMI!
I WAS CARELESS.
I DIDN'T REALIZE THAT SOMETHING WAS WRONG. AND I LOOKED HER STRAIGHT IN THE EYE...
HURRY...

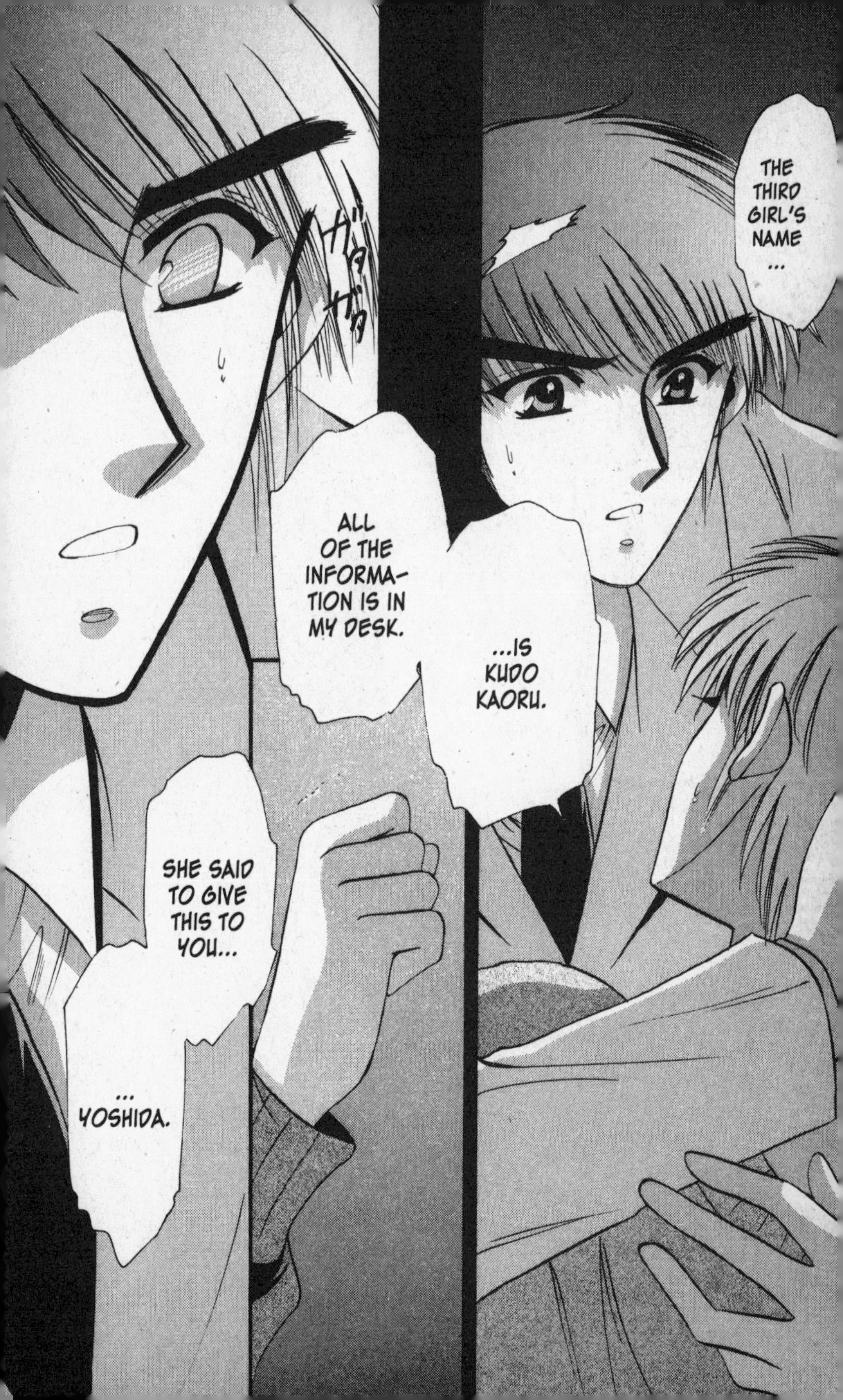
THE THIRD GIRL'S NAME ...
...IS KUDO KAORU.
ALL OF THE INFORMATION IS IN MY DESK.
SHE SAID TO GIVE THIS TO YOU...
... YOSHIDA.

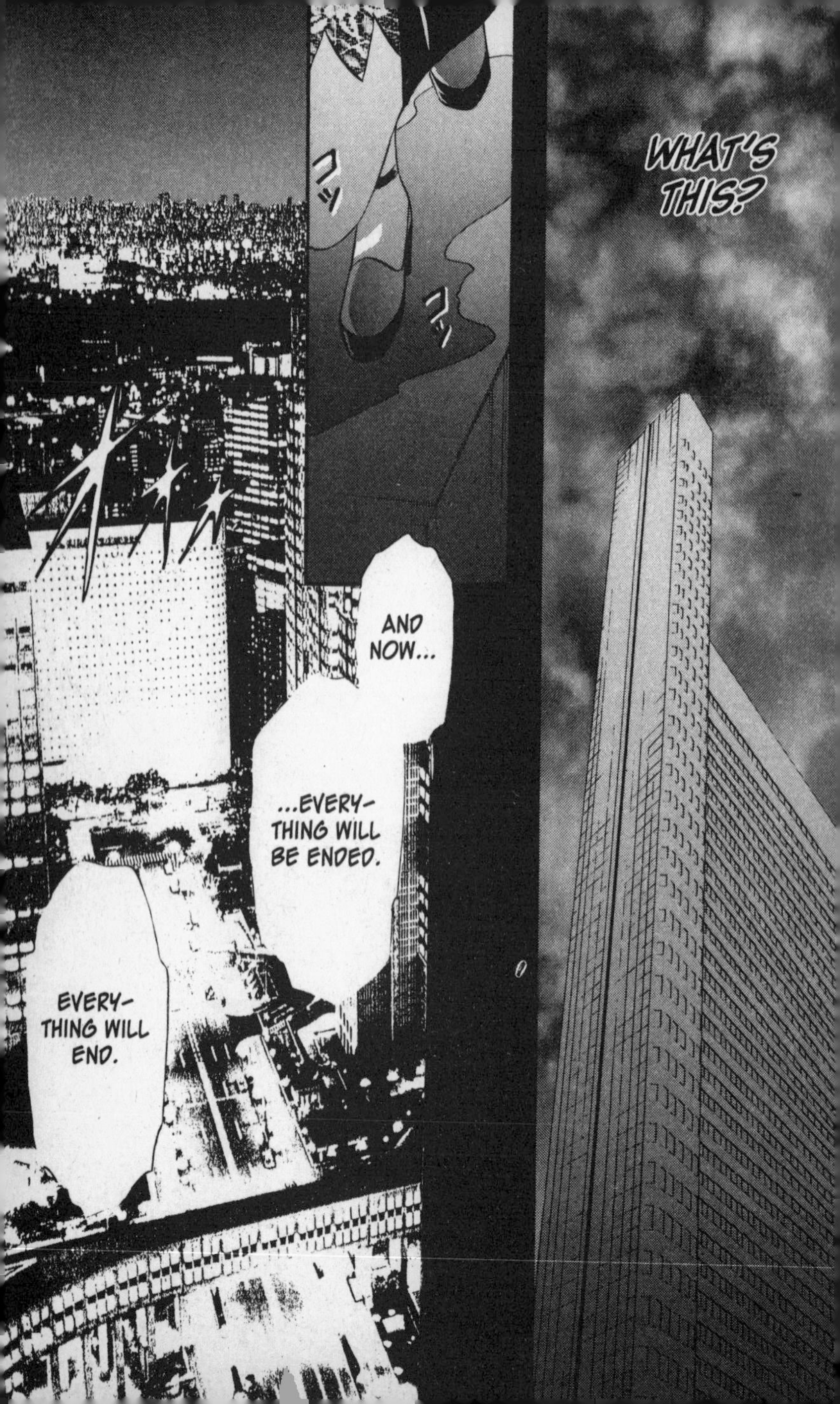
WHAT'S THIS?
AND NOW...
...EVERY-THING WILL BE ENDED.
EVERY-THING WILL END.

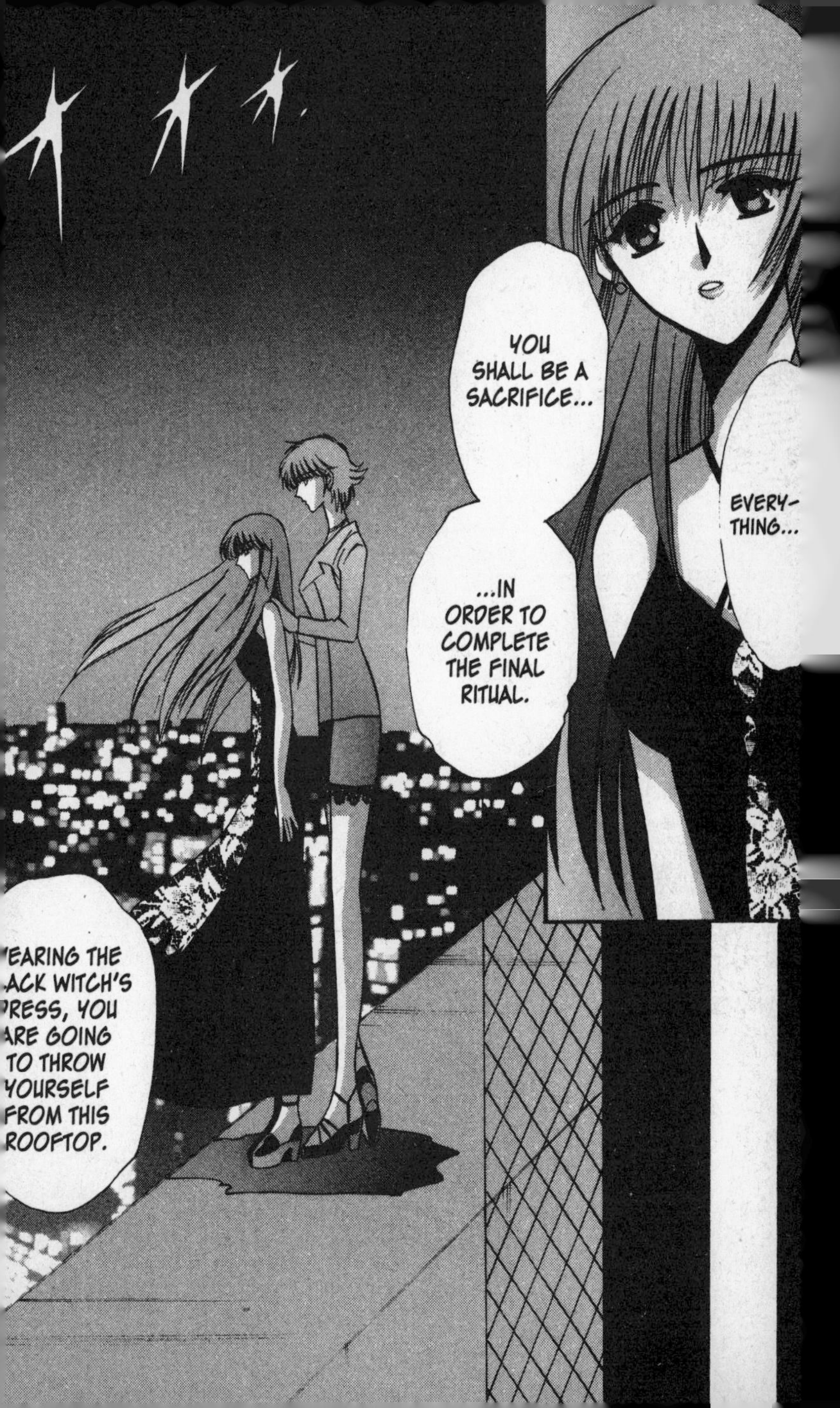
YOU SHALL BE A SACRIFICE...
...IN ORDER TO COMPLETE THE FINAL RITUAL.
EVERY-THING...
EARING THE ACK WITCH'S RESS, YOU ARE GOING TO THROW YOURSELF FROM THIS ROOFTOP.

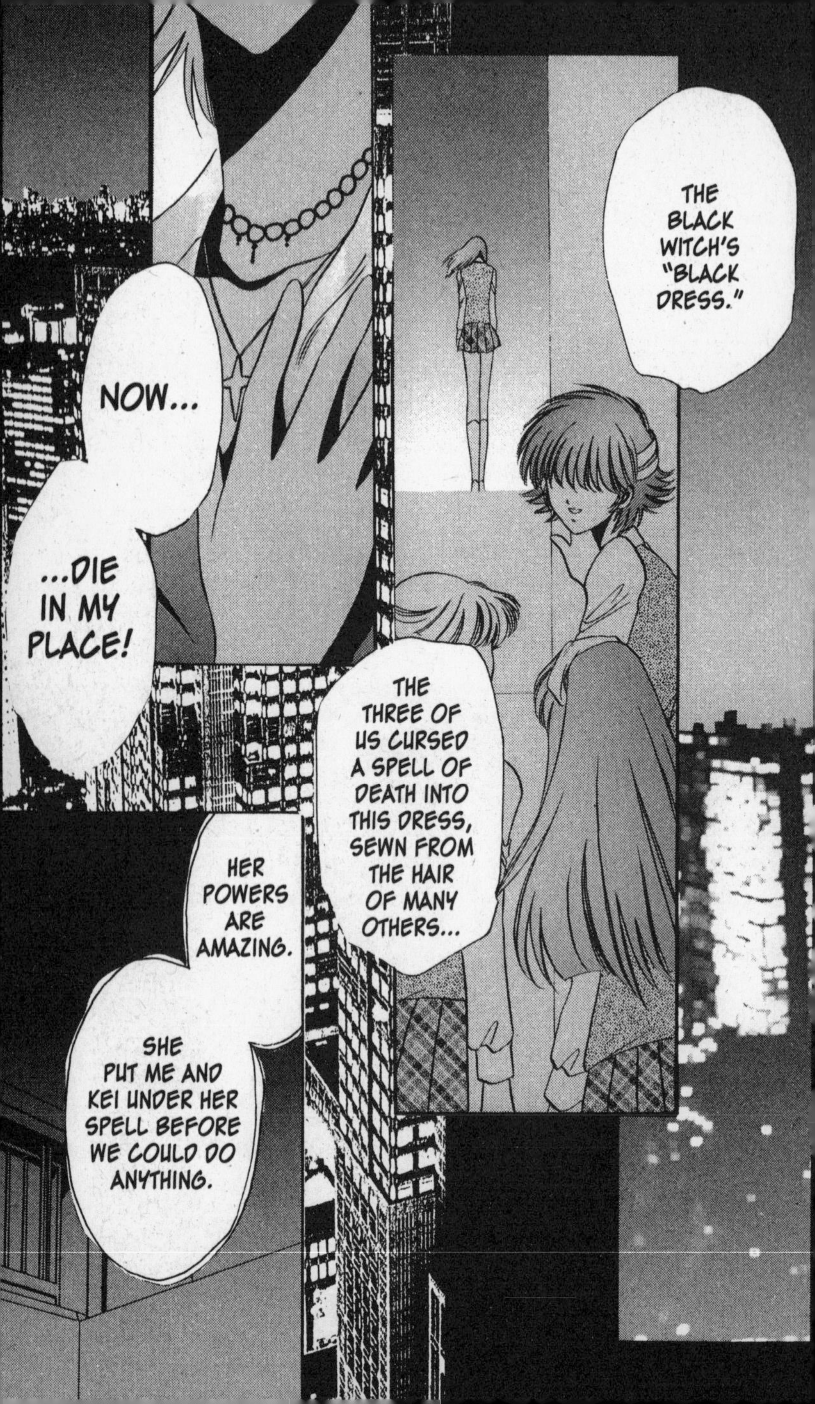
THE BLACK WITCH'S "BLACK DRESS."
THE THREE OF US CURSED A SPELL OF DEATH INTO THIS DRESS, SEWN FROM THE HAIR OF MANY OTHERS...
NOW...
...DIE IN MY PLACE!
HER POWERS ARE AMAZING.
SHE PUT ME AND KEI UNDER HER SPELL BEFORE WE COULD DO ANYTHING.

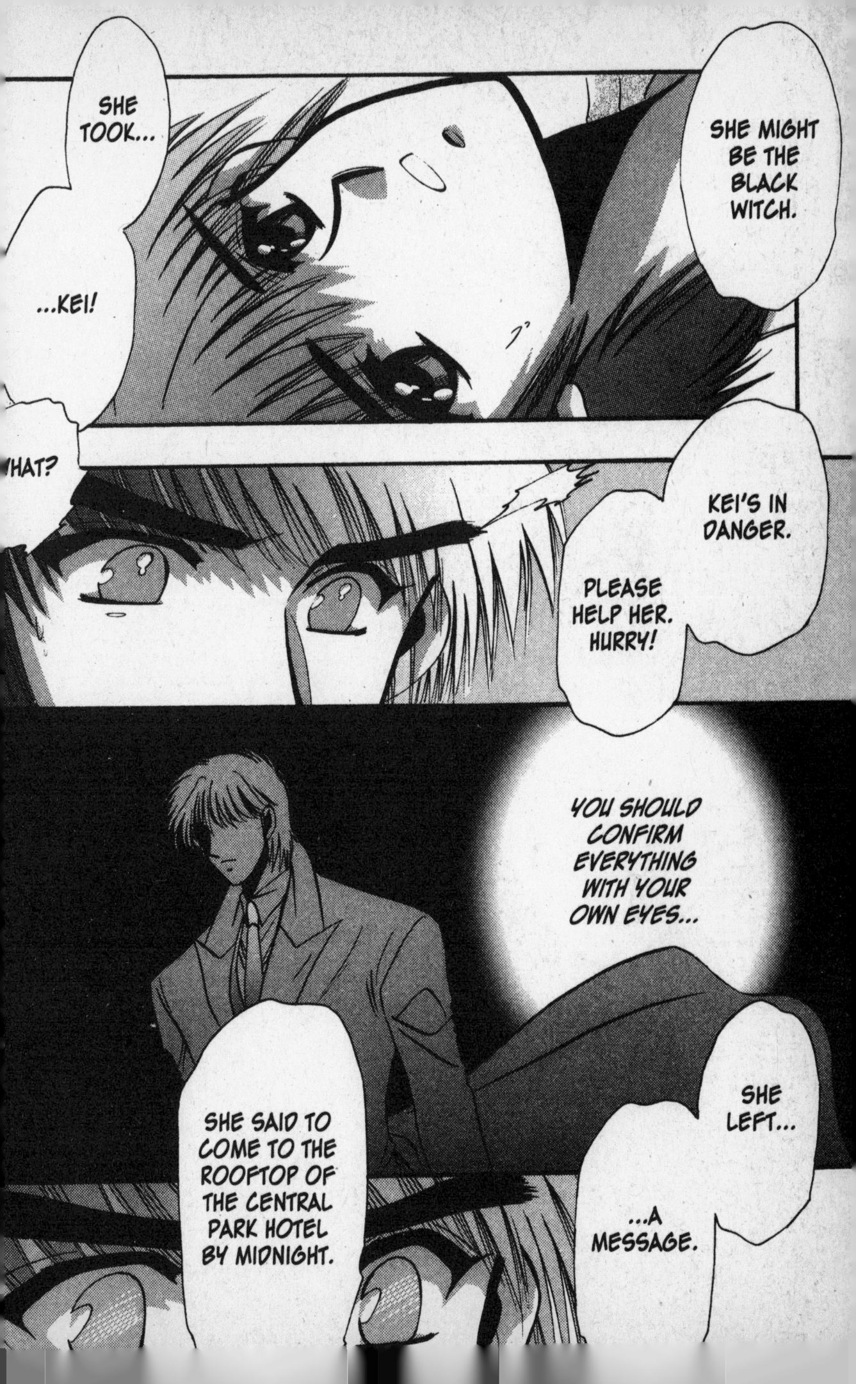
SHE MIGHT BE THE BLACK WITCH.
SHE TOOK...
...KEI!
KEI'S IN DANGER.
PLEASE HELP HER. HURRY!
YOU SHOULD CONFIRM EVERYTHING WITH YOUR OWN EYES...
SHE LEFT...
...A MESSAGE.
SHE SAID TO COME TO THE ROOFTOP OF THE CENTRAL PARK HOTEL BY MIDNIGHT.

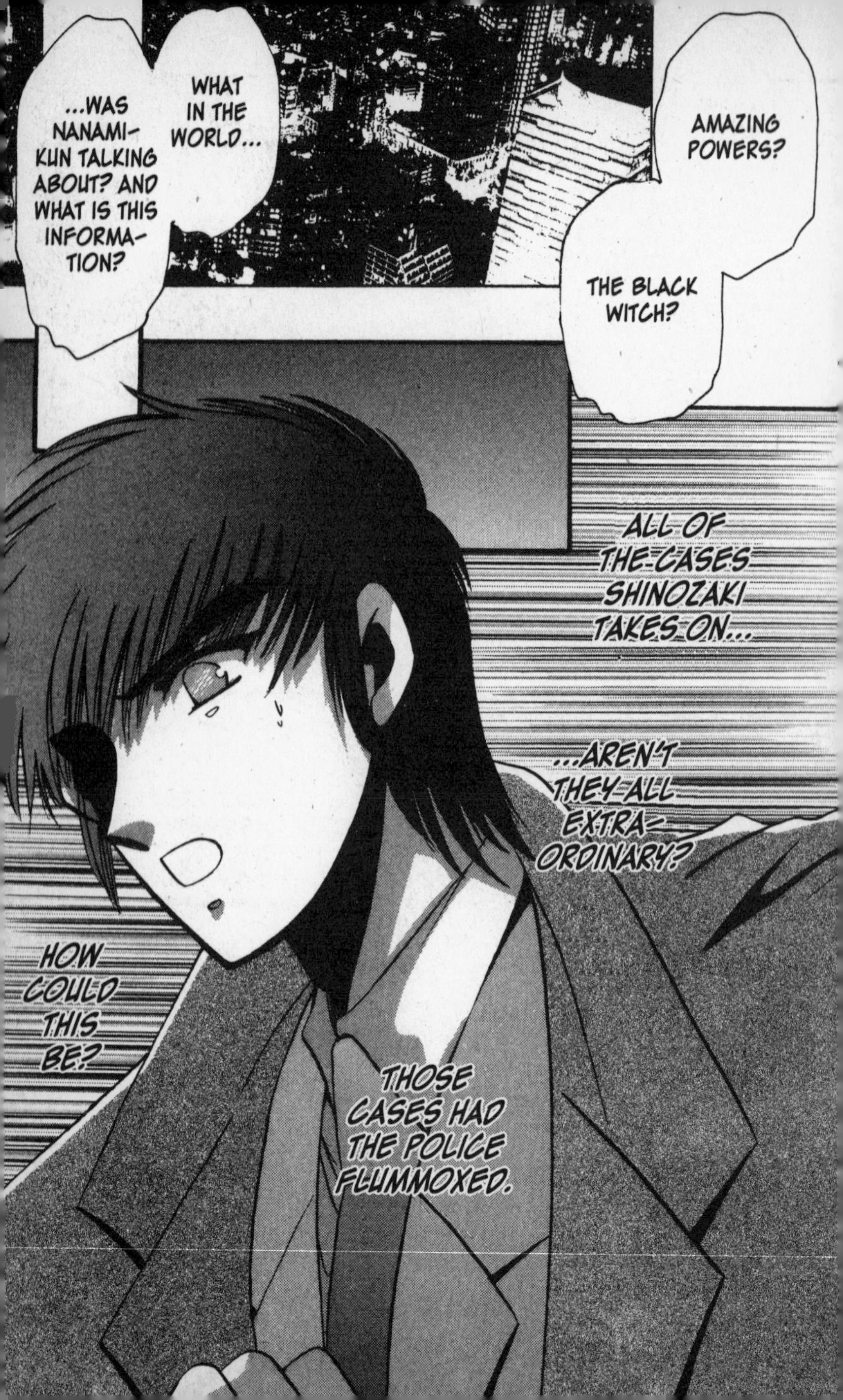
AMAZING POWERS?
THE BLACK WITCH?
WHAT IN THE WORLD...
...WAS NANAMI-KUN TALKING ABOUT? AND WHAT IS THIS INFORMATION?
ALL OF THE CASES SHINOZAKI TAKES ON...
...AREN'T THEY ALL EXTRA-ORDINARY?
THOSE CASES HAD THE POLICE FLUMMOXED.
HOW COULD THIS BE?

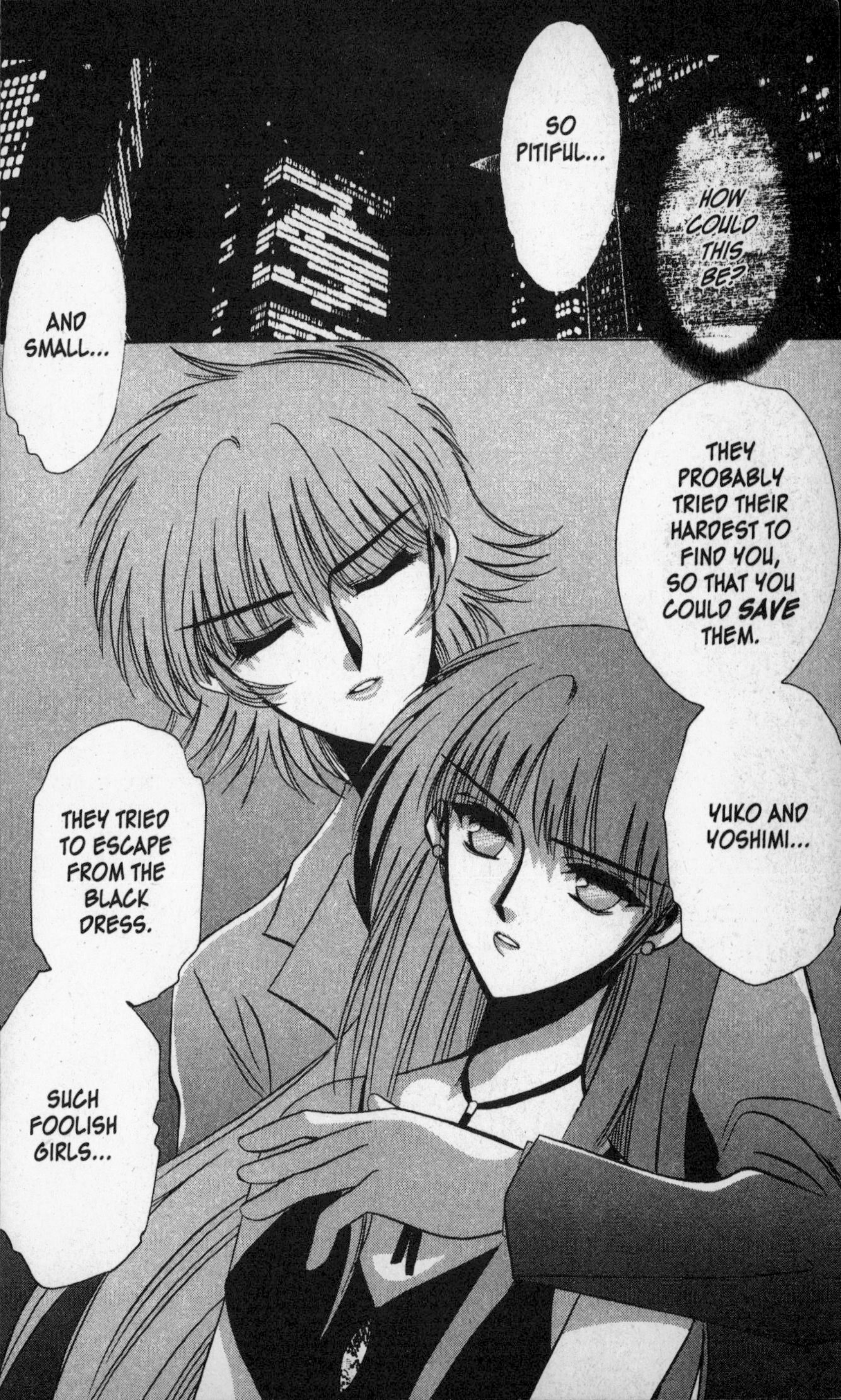
HOW COULD THIS BE?
SO PITIFUL...
AND SMALL...
THEY PROBABLY TRIED THEIR HARDEST TO FIND YOU, SO THAT YOU COULD **SAVE** THEM.
YUKO AND YOSHIMI...
THEY TRIED TO ESCAPE FROM THE BLACK DRESS.
SUCH FOOLISH GIRLS...

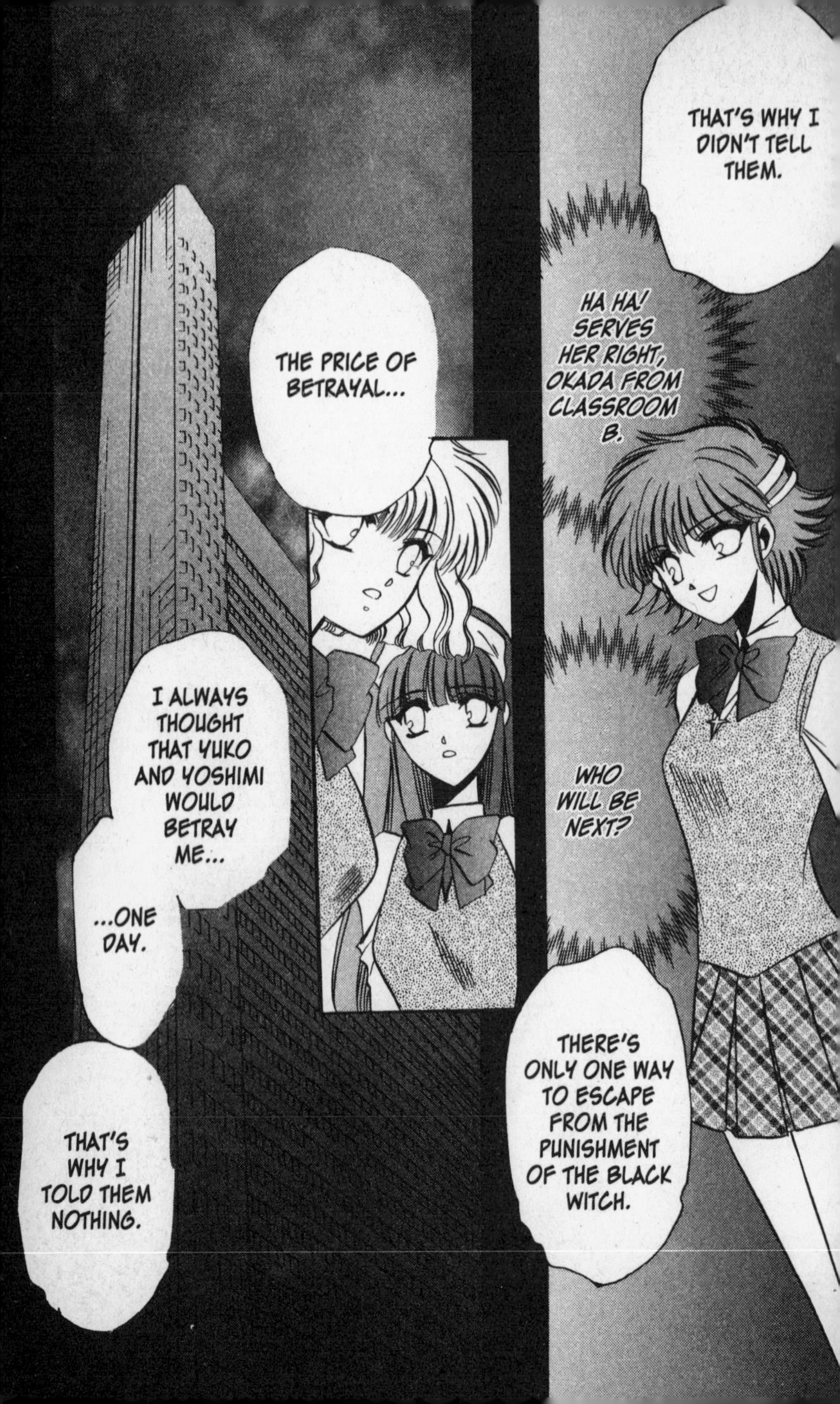
THAT'S WHY I DIDN'T TELL THEM.
HA HA! SERVES HER RIGHT, OKADA FROM CLASSROOM B.
WHO WILL BE NEXT?
THERE'S ONLY ONE WAY TO ESCAPE FROM THE PUNISHMENT OF THE BLACK WITCH.
THE PRICE OF BETRAYAL...
I ALWAYS THOUGHT THAT YUKO AND YOSHIMI WOULD BETRAY ME...
...ONE DAY.
THAT'S WHY I TOLD THEM NOTHING.

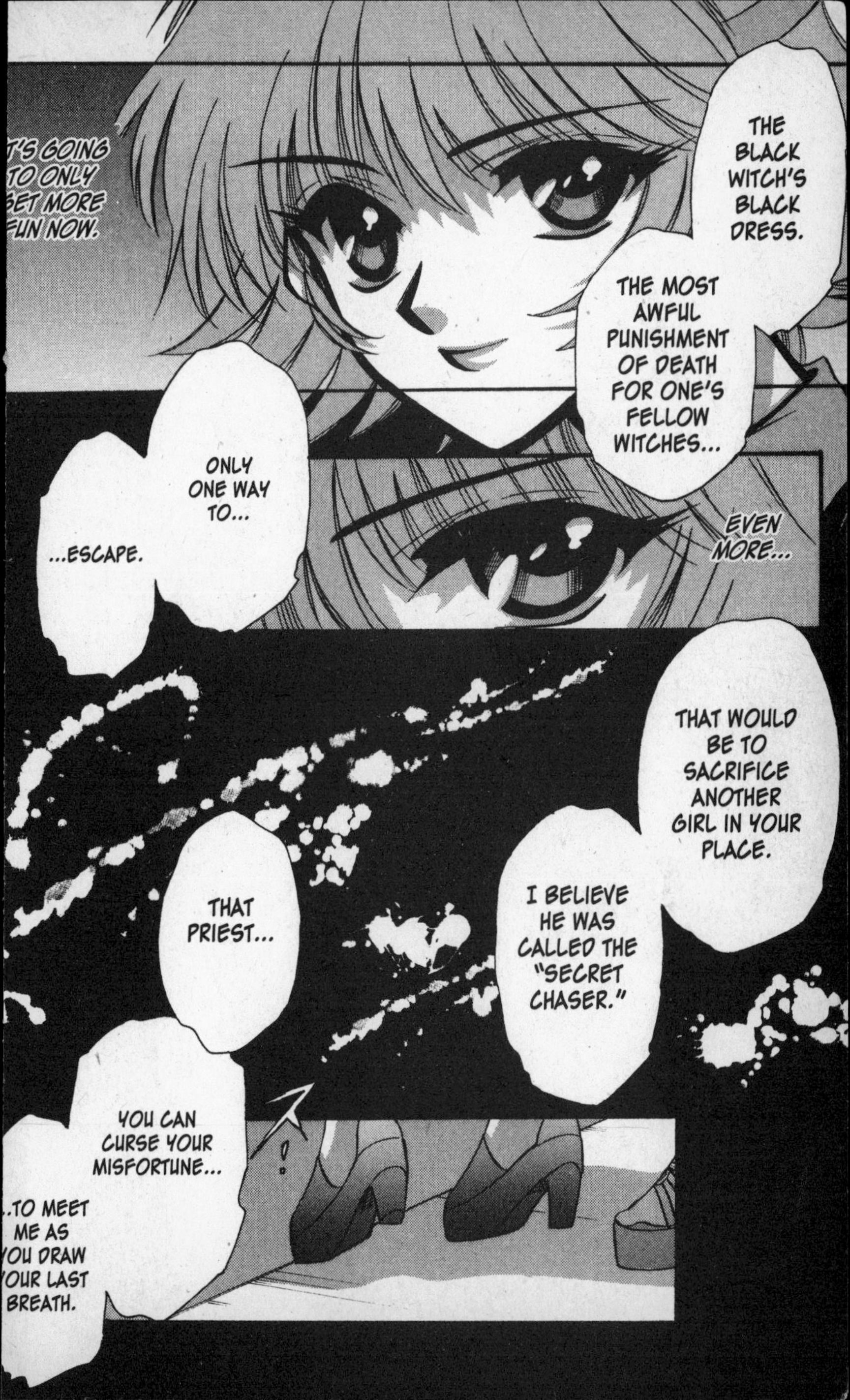
THE BLACK WITCH'S BLACK DRESS.
THE MOST AWFUL PUNISHMENT OF DEATH FOR ONE'S FELLOW WITCHES...
T'S GOING TO ONLY GET MORE FUN NOW.
EVEN MORE...
ONLY ONE WAY TO...
...ESCAPE.
THAT WOULD BE TO SACRIFICE ANOTHER GIRL IN YOUR PLACE.
I BELIEVE HE WAS CALLED THE "SECRET CHASER."
THAT PRIEST...
!
YOU CAN CURSE YOUR MISFORTUNE...
..TO MEET ME AS YOU DRAW YOUR LAST BREATH.

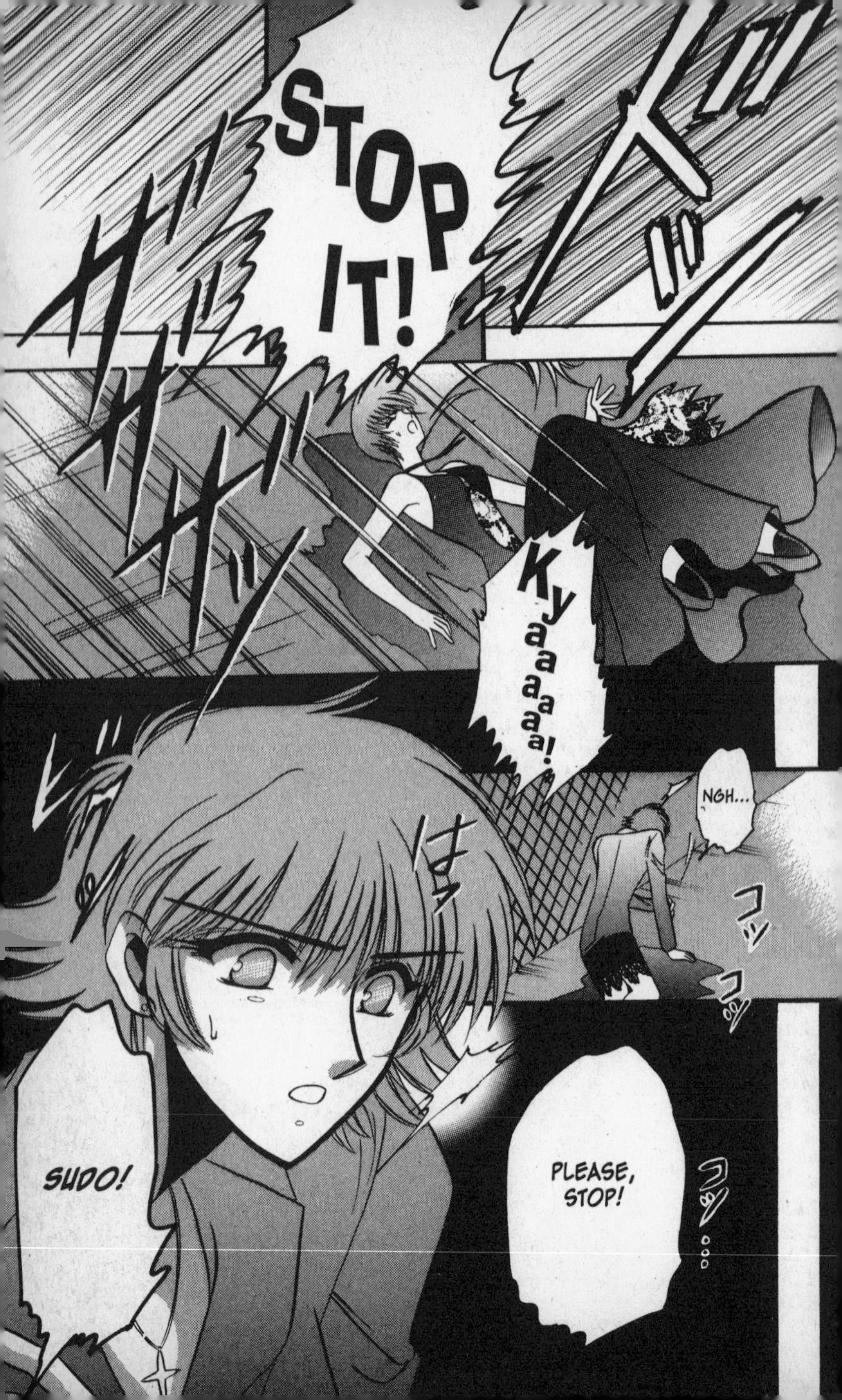
STOP IT!
Kyaaaaaa!
NGH...
PLEASE, STOP!
SUDO!

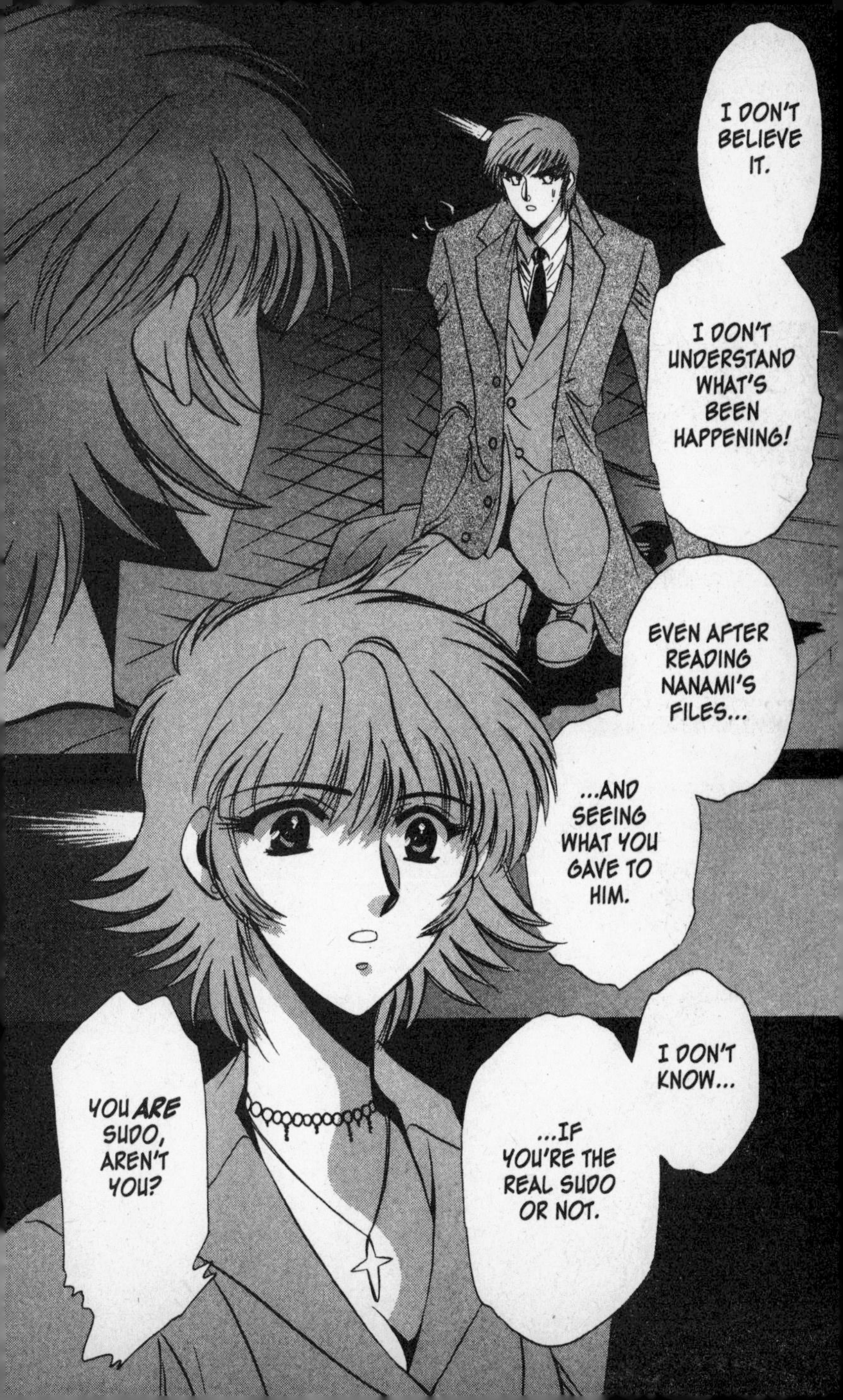
I DON'T BELIEVE IT.
I DON'T UNDERSTAND WHAT'S BEEN HAPPENING!
EVEN AFTER READING NANAMI'S FILES...
...AND SEEING WHAT YOU GAVE TO HIM.
I DON'T KNOW...
...IF YOU'RE THE REAL SUDO OR NOT.
YOU *ARE* SUDO, AREN'T YOU?

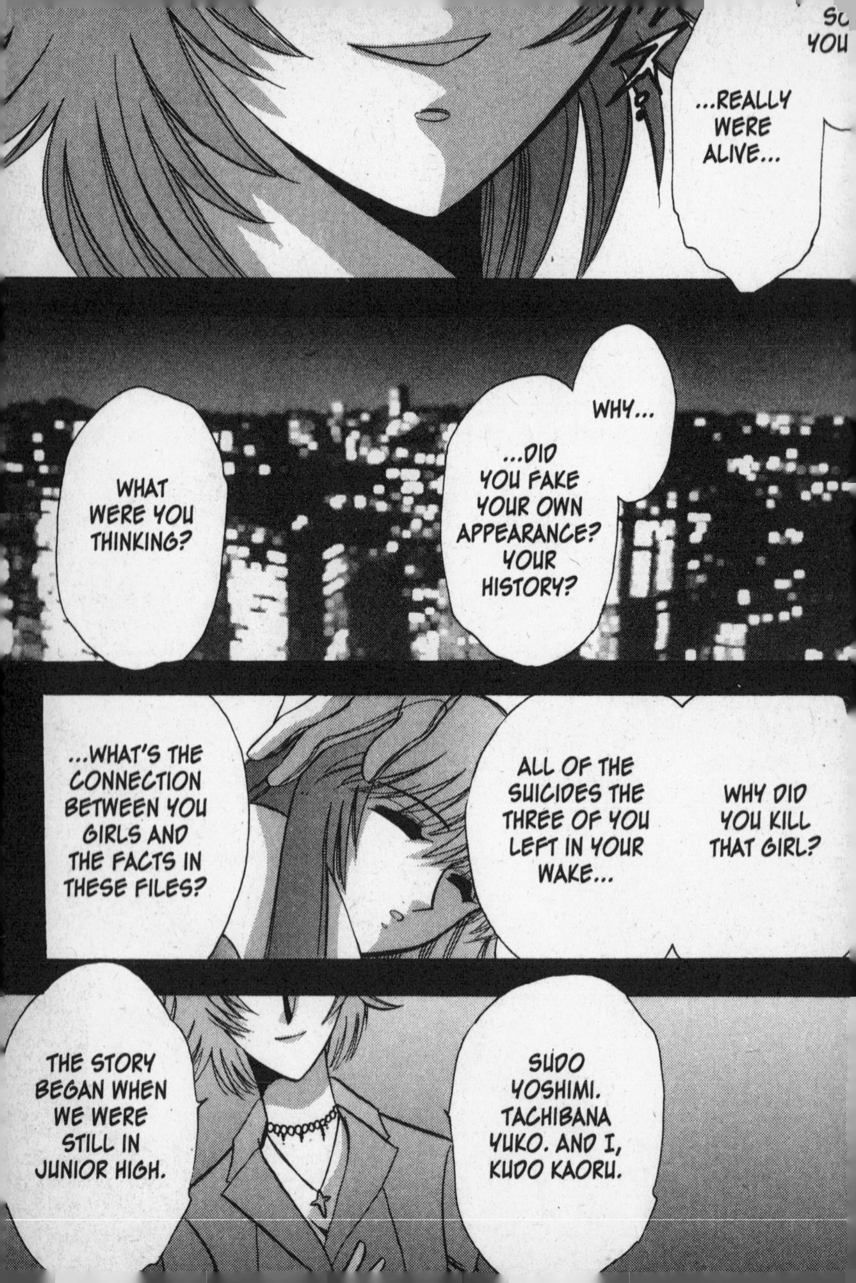
YOU
...REALLY WERE ALIVE...
WHY...
...DID YOU FAKE YOUR OWN APPEARANCE? YOUR HISTORY?
WHAT WERE YOU THINKING?
WHY DID YOU KILL THAT GIRL?
ALL OF THE SUICIDES THE THREE OF YOU LEFT IN YOUR WAKE...
...WHAT'S THE CONNECTION BETWEEN YOU GIRLS AND THE FACTS IN THESE FILES?
SUDO YOSHIMI. TACHIBANA YUKO. AND I, KUDO KAORU.
THE STORY BEGAN WHEN WE WERE STILL IN JUNIOR HIGH.

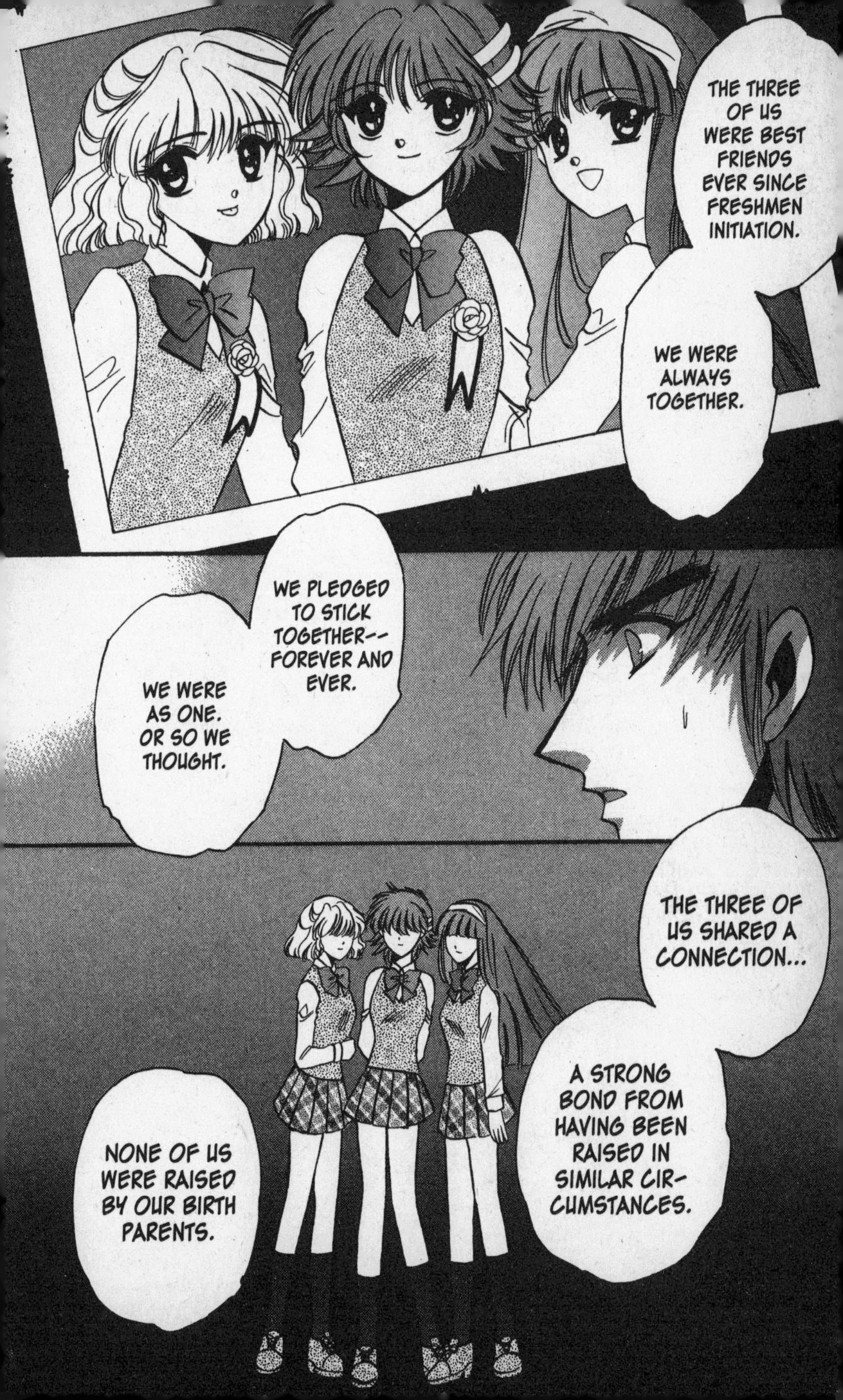
THE THREE OF US WERE BEST FRIENDS EVER SINCE FRESHMEN INITIATION.
WE WERE ALWAYS TOGETHER.
WE PLEDGED TO STICK TOGETHER-- FOREVER AND EVER.
WE WERE AS ONE. OR SO WE THOUGHT.
THE THREE OF US SHARED A CONNECTION...
A STRONG BOND FROM HAVING BEEN RAISED IN SIMILAR CIR-CUMSTANCES.
NONE OF US WERE RAISED BY OUR BIRTH PARENTS.

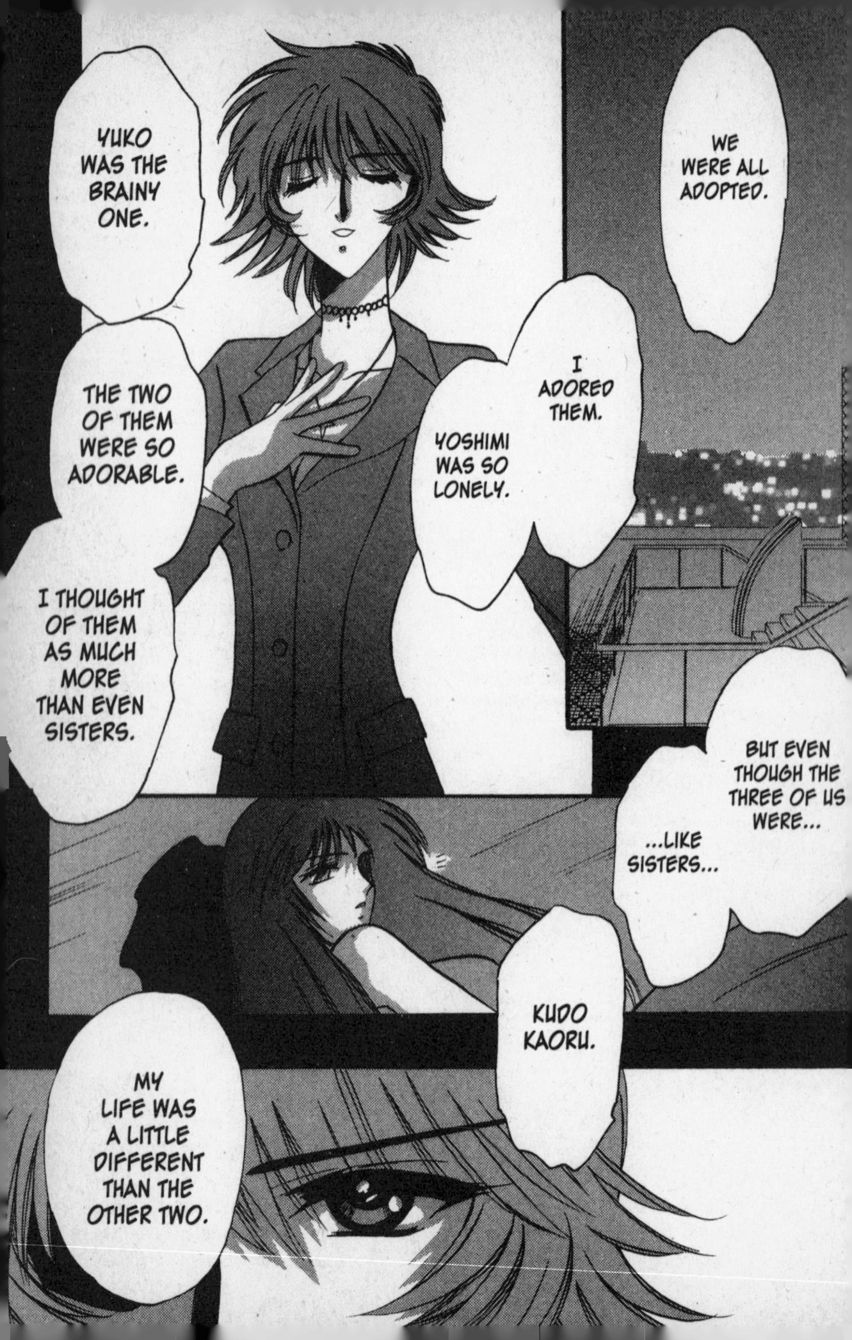
WE WERE ALL ADOPTED.
I ADORED THEM.
YOSHIMI WAS SO LONELY.
YUKO WAS THE BRAINY ONE.
THE TWO OF THEM WERE SO ADORABLE.
I THOUGHT OF THEM AS MUCH MORE THAN EVEN SISTERS.
BUT EVEN THOUGH THE THREE OF US WERE...
...LIKE SISTERS...
KUDO KAORU.
MY LIFE WAS A LITTLE DIFFERENT THAN THE OTHER TWO.

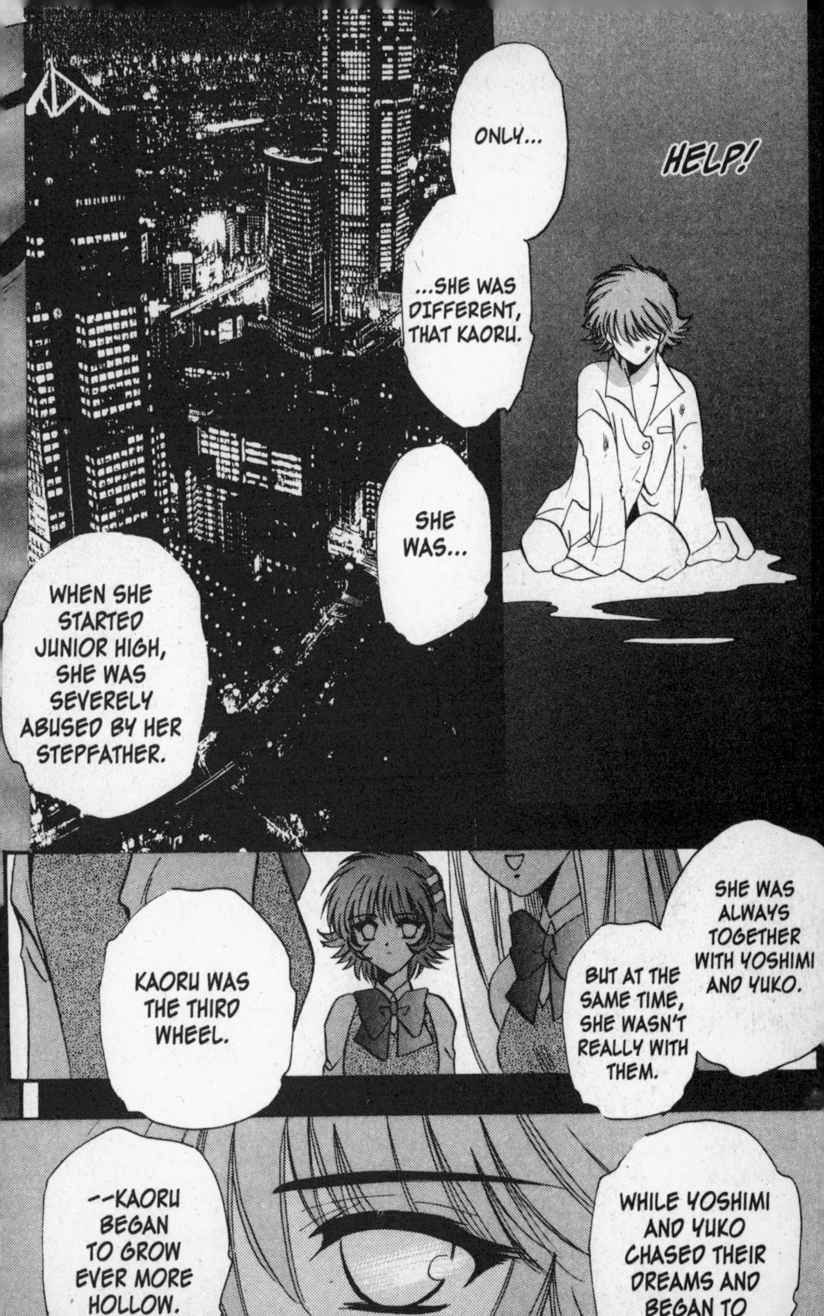
HELP!
ONLY...
...SHE WAS DIFFERENT, THAT KAORU.
SHE WAS...
WHEN SHE STARTED JUNIOR HIGH, SHE WAS SEVERELY ABUSED BY HER STEPFATHER.
SHE WAS ALWAYS TOGETHER WITH YOSHIMI AND YUKO.
BUT AT THE SAME TIME, SHE WASN'T REALLY WITH THEM.
KAORU WAS THE THIRD WHEEL.
WHILE YOSHIMI AND YUKO CHASED THEIR DREAMS AND BEGAN TO
--KAORU BEGAN TO GROW EVER MORE HOLLOW.

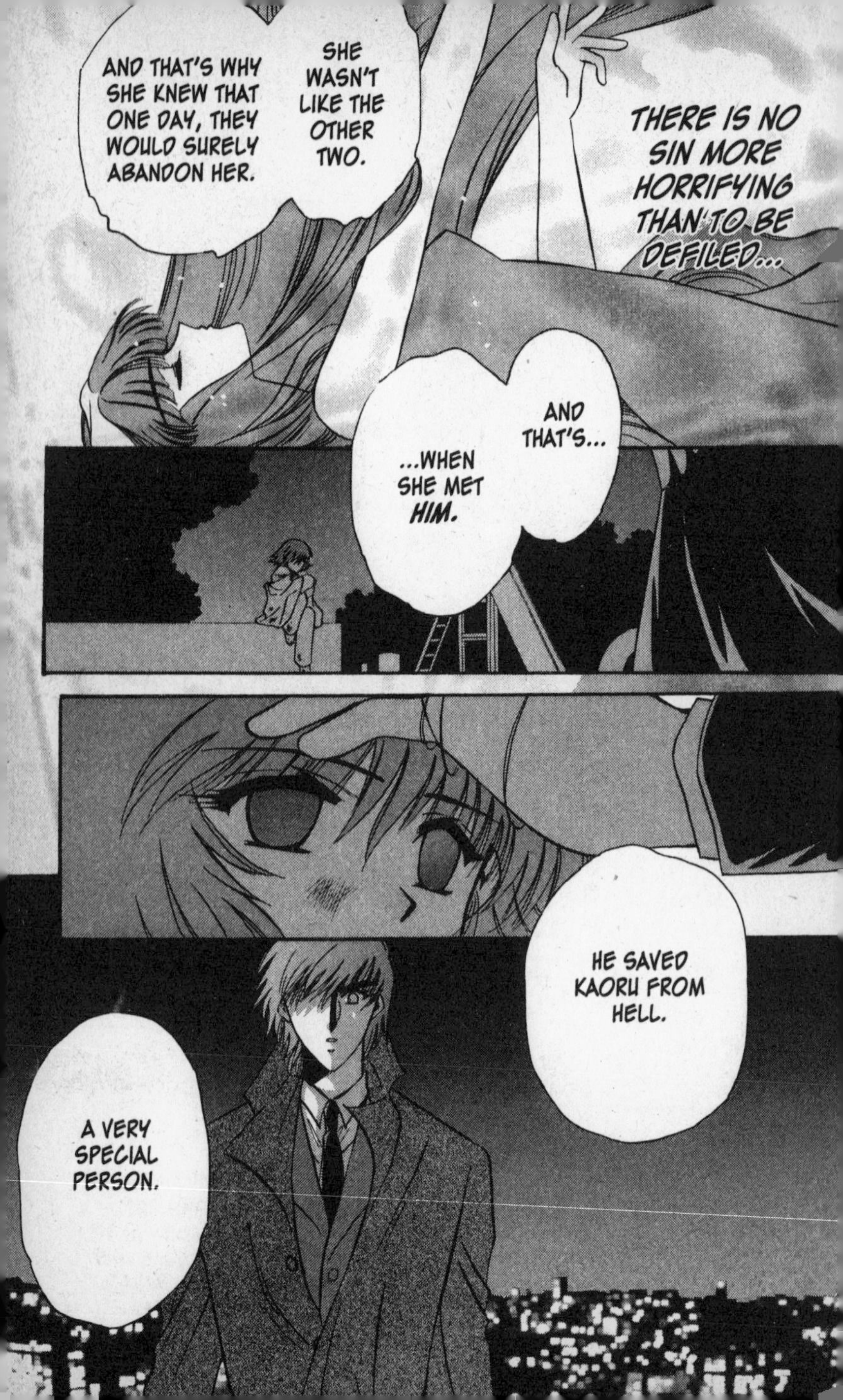
THERE IS NO SIN MORE HORRIFYING THAN TO BE DEFILED...
SHE WASN'T LIKE THE OTHER TWO.
AND THAT'S WHY SHE KNEW THAT ONE DAY, THEY WOULD SURELY ABANDON HER.
AND THAT'S...
...WHEN SHE MET *HIM.*
HE SAVED KAORU FROM HELL.
A VERY SPECIAL PERSON.

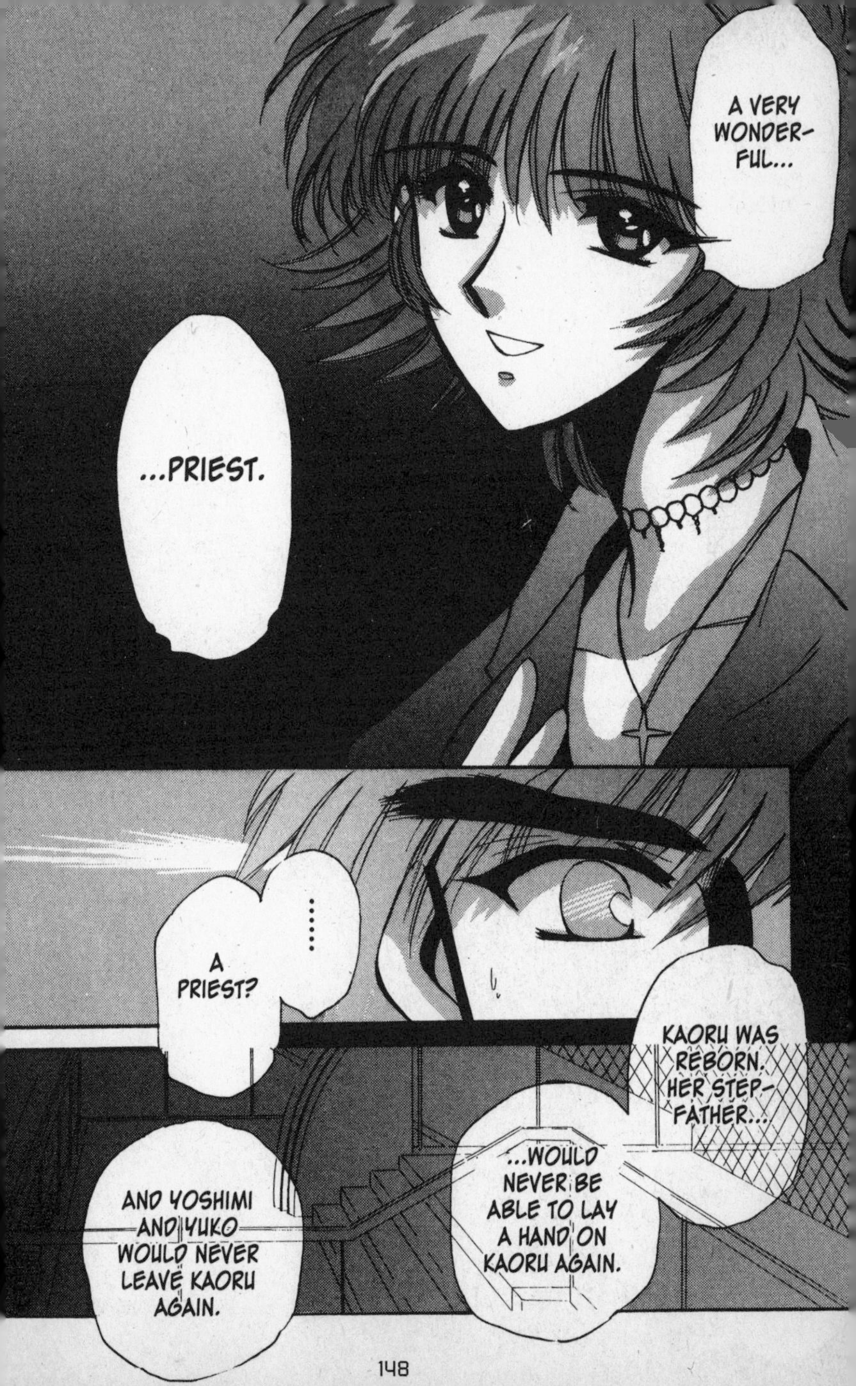

A VERY WONDER-FUL...
...PRIEST.
......
A PRIEST?
KAORU WAS REBORN. HER STEP-FATHER...
...WOULD NEVER BE ABLE TO LAY A HAND ON KAORU AGAIN.
AND YOSHIMI AND YUKO WOULD NEVER LEAVE KAORU AGAIN.

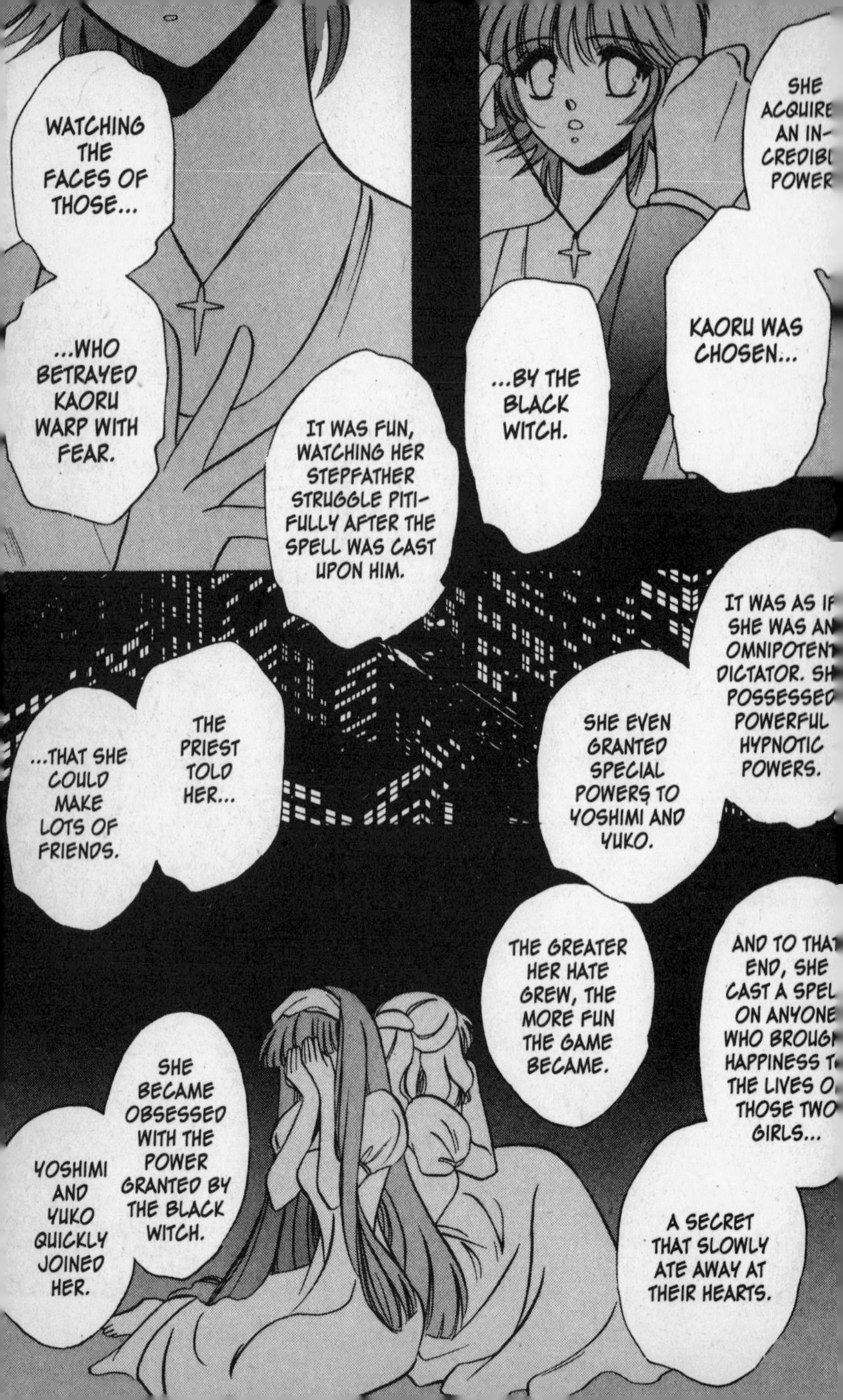
SHE ACQUIRE AN IN- CREDIBL POWER
KAORU WAS CHOSEN...
...BY THE BLACK WITCH.
WATCHING THE FACES OF THOSE...
...WHO BETRAYED KAORU WARP WITH FEAR.
IT WAS FUN, WATCHING HER STEPFATHER STRUGGLE PITI- FULLY AFTER THE SPELL WAS CAST UPON HIM.
IT WAS AS IF SHE WAS AN OMNIPOTEN DICTATOR. SH POSSESSED POWERFUL HYPNOTIC POWERS.
SHE EVEN GRANTED SPECIAL POWERS TO YOSHIMI AND YUKO.
THE PRIEST TOLD HER...
...THAT SHE COULD MAKE LOTS OF FRIENDS.
AND TO THA END, SHE CAST A SPEL ON ANYONE WHO BROUG HAPPINESS T THE LIVES O THOSE TWO GIRLS...
THE GREATER HER HATE GREW, THE MORE FUN THE GAME BECAME.
A SECRET THAT SLOWLY ATE AWAY AT THEIR HEARTS.
SHE BECAME OBSESSED WITH THE POWER GRANTED BY THE BLACK WITCH.
YOSHIMI AND YUKO QUICKLY JOINED HER.

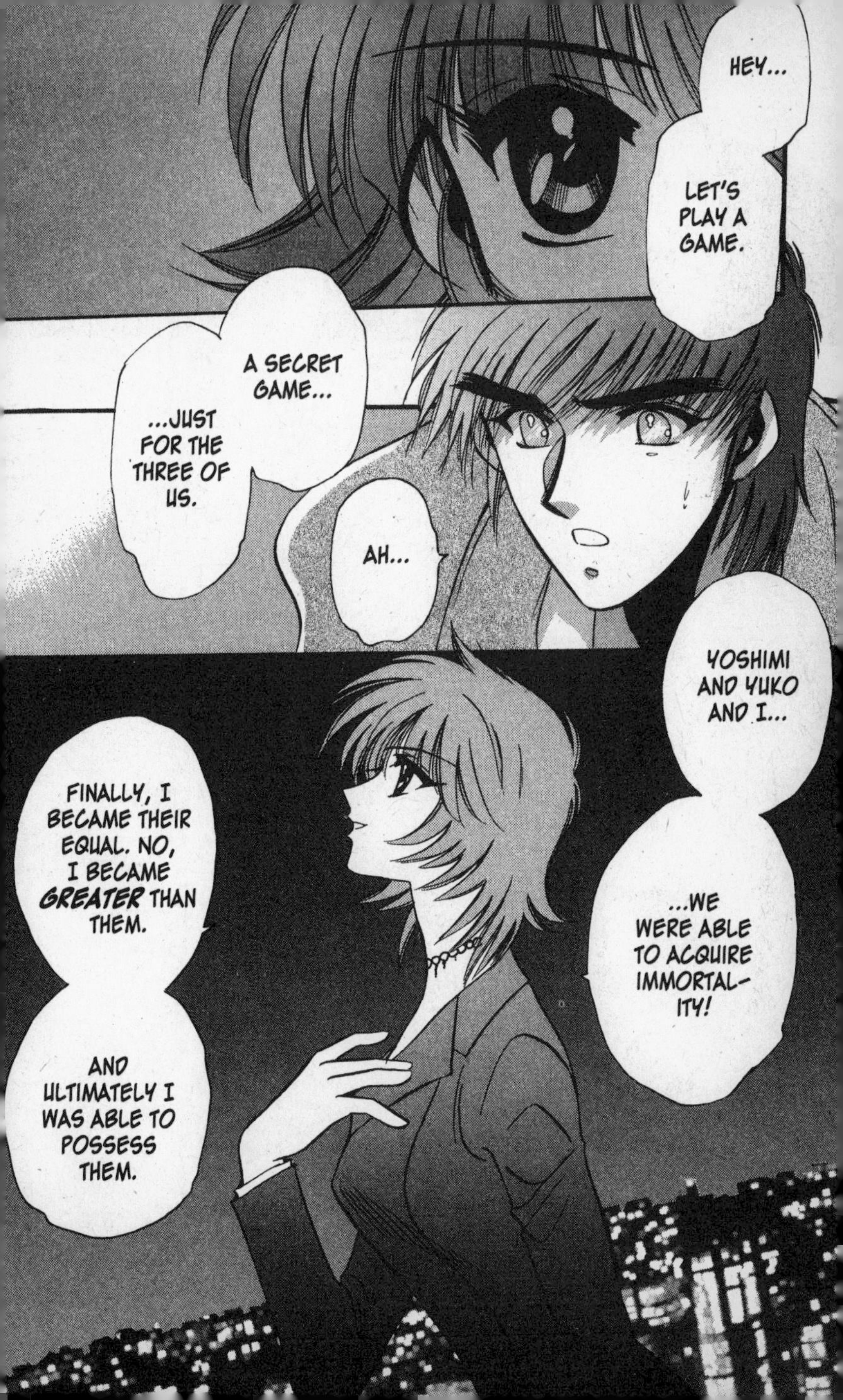
HEY...
LET'S PLAY A GAME.
A SECRET GAME...
...JUST FOR THE THREE OF US.
AH...
YOSHIMI AND YUKO AND I...
...WE WERE ABLE TO ACQUIRE IMMORTAL-ITY!
FINALLY, I BECAME THEIR EQUAL. NO, I BECAME **GREATER** THAN THEM.
AND ULTIMATELY I WAS ABLE TO POSSESS THEM.

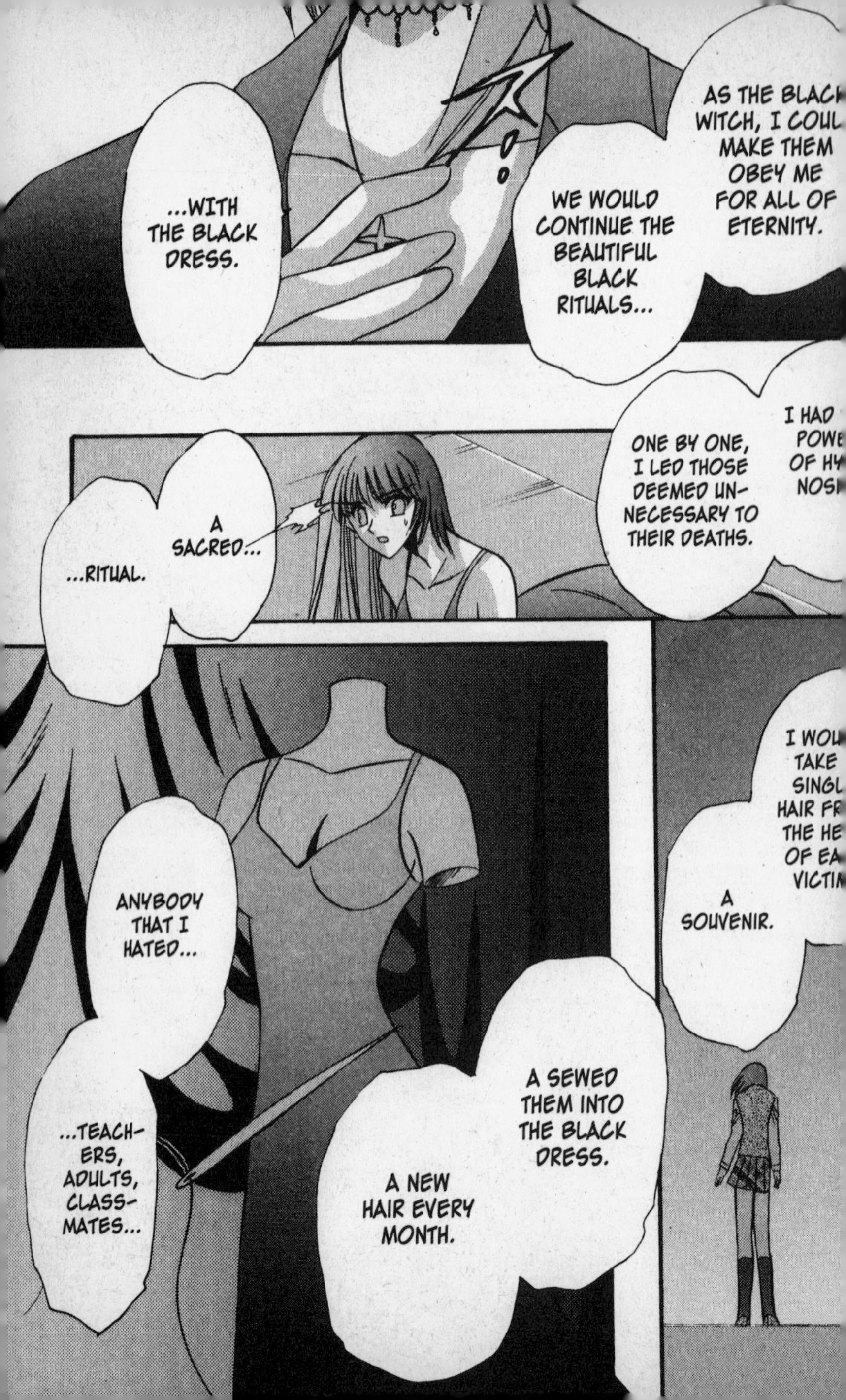
AS THE BLAC WITCH, I COUL MAKE THEM OBEY ME FOR ALL OF ETERNITY.
WE WOULD CONTINUE THE BEAUTIFUL BLACK RITUALS...
...WITH THE BLACK DRESS.
I HAD POWE OF HY NOSI
ONE BY ONE, I LED THOSE DEEMED UN-NECESSARY TO THEIR DEATHS.
A SACRED...
...RITUAL.
I WOU TAKE SINGL HAIR FR THE HE OF EA VICTIM
A SOUVENIR.
A SEWED THEM INTO THE BLACK DRESS.
A NEW HAIR EVERY MONTH.
ANYBODY THAT I HATED...
...TEACH-ERS, ADULTS, CLASS-MATES...

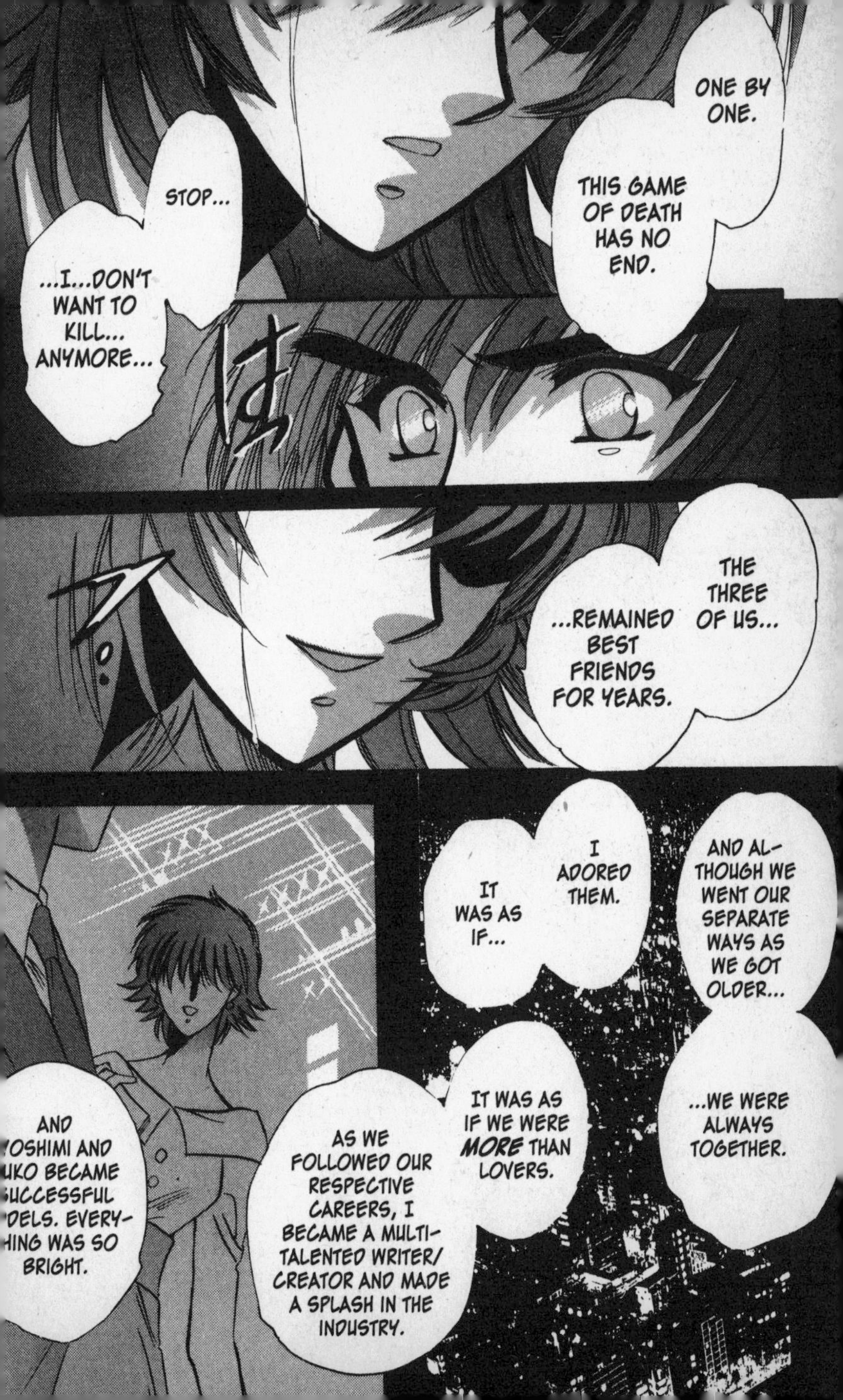
ONE BY ONE.
THIS GAME OF DEATH HAS NO END.
STOP...
...I...DON'T WANT TO KILL... ANYMORE...
は
THE THREE OF US...
...REMAINED BEST FRIENDS FOR YEARS.
AND ALTHOUGH WE WENT OUR SEPARATE WAYS AS WE GOT OLDER...
I ADORED THEM.
IT WAS AS IF...
...WE WERE ALWAYS TOGETHER.
IT WAS AS IF WE WERE *MORE* THAN LOVERS.
AS WE FOLLOWED OUR RESPECTIVE CAREERS, I BECAME A MULTI-TALENTED WRITER/ CREATOR AND MADE A SPLASH IN THE INDUSTRY.
AND OSHIMI AND UKO BECAME UCCESSFUL DELS. EVERY- HING WAS SO BRIGHT.

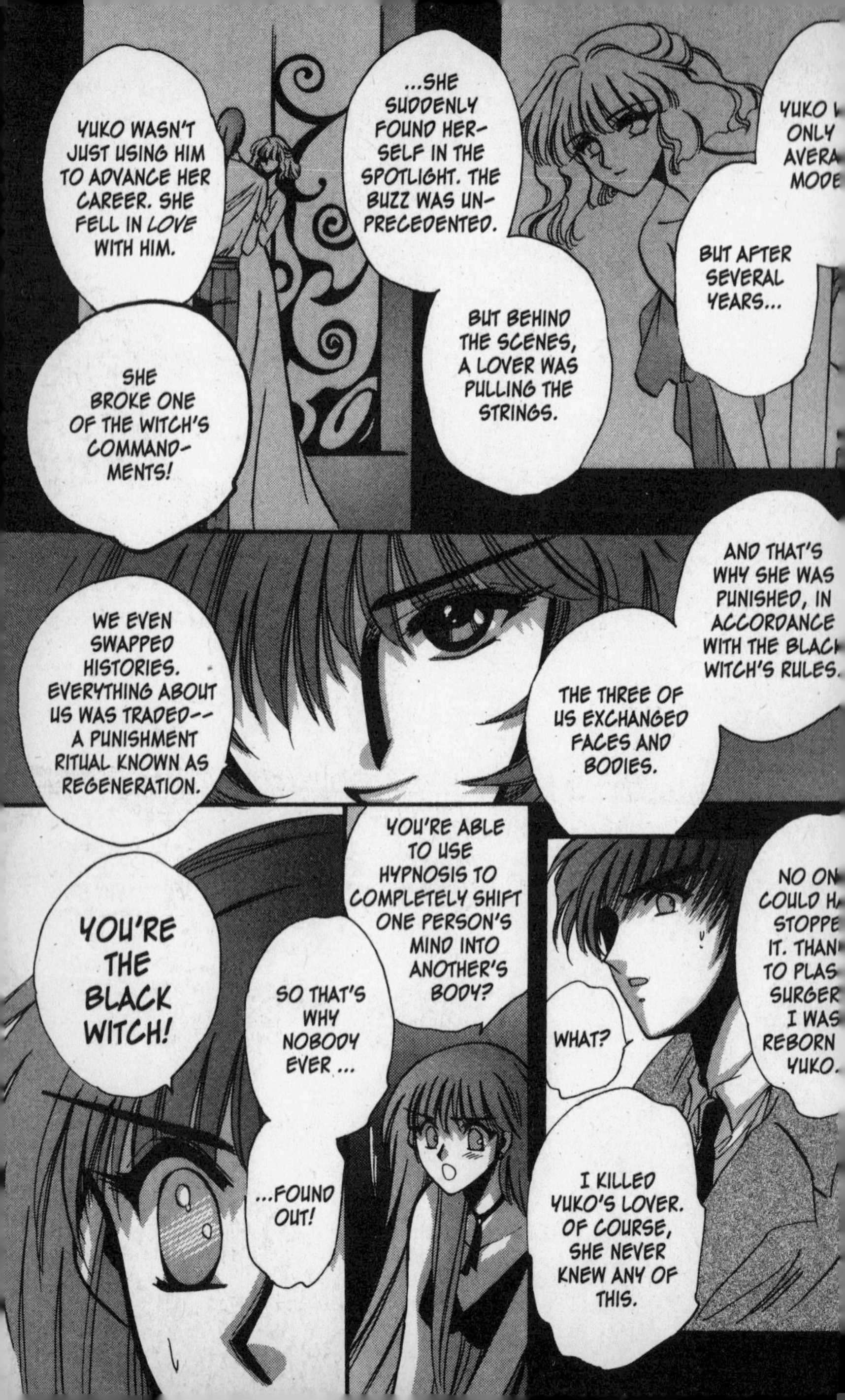
YUKO W ONLY AVERA MODE
BUT AFTER SEVERAL YEARS...
...SHE SUDDENLY FOUND HER-SELF IN THE SPOTLIGHT. THE BUZZ WAS UN-PRECEDENTED.
BUT BEHIND THE SCENES, A LOVER WAS PULLING THE STRINGS.
YUKO WASN'T JUST USING HIM TO ADVANCE HER CAREER. SHE FELL IN *LOVE* WITH HIM.
SHE BROKE ONE OF THE WITCH'S COMMAND-MENTS!
AND THAT'S WHY SHE WAS PUNISHED, IN ACCORDANCE WITH THE BLACK WITCH'S RULES.
THE THREE OF US EXCHANGED FACES AND BODIES.
WE EVEN SWAPPED HISTORIES. EVERYTHING ABOUT US WAS TRADED-- A PUNISHMENT RITUAL KNOWN AS REGENERATION.
NO ON COULD H STOPPE IT. THAN TO PLAS SURGER I WAS REBORN YUKO.
WHAT?
I KILLED YUKO'S LOVER. OF COURSE, SHE NEVER KNEW ANY OF THIS.
YOU'RE ABLE TO USE HYPNOSIS TO COMPLETELY SHIFT ONE PERSON'S MIND INTO ANOTHER'S BODY?
SO THAT'S WHY NOBODY EVER ...
...FOUND OUT!
YOU'RE THE BLACK WITCH!

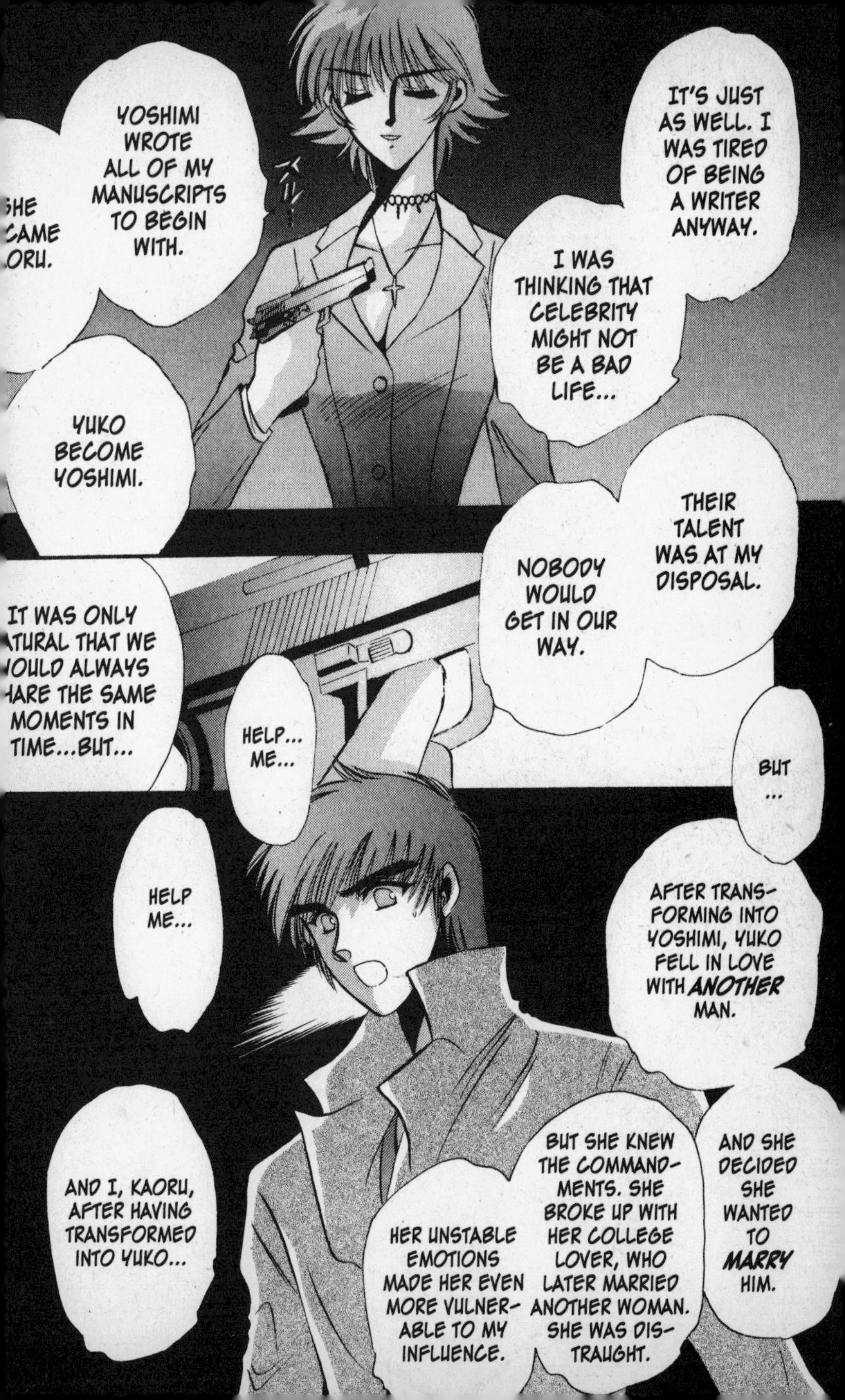
IT'S JUST AS WELL. I WAS TIRED OF BEING A WRITER ANYWAY.
I WAS THINKING THAT CELEBRITY MIGHT NOT BE A BAD LIFE...
YOSHIMI WROTE ALL OF MY MANUSCRIPTS TO BEGIN WITH.
HE CAME ORU.
YUKO BECOME YOSHIMI.
THEIR TALENT WAS AT MY DISPOSAL.
NOBODY WOULD GET IN OUR WAY.
HELP... ME...
IT WAS ONLY ATURAL THAT WE OULD ALWAYS HARE THE SAME MOMENTS IN TIME...BUT...
BUT ...
AFTER TRANS-FORMING INTO YOSHIMI, YUKO FELL IN LOVE WITH *ANOTHER* MAN.
HELP ME...
AND SHE DECIDED SHE WANTED TO *MARRY* HIM.
BUT SHE KNEW THE COMMAND-MENTS. SHE BROKE UP WITH HER COLLEGE LOVER, WHO LATER MARRIED ANOTHER WOMAN. SHE WAS DIS-TRAUGHT.
HER UNSTABLE EMOTIONS MADE HER EVEN MORE VULNER-ABLE TO MY INFLUENCE.
AND I, KAORU, AFTER HAVING TRANSFORMED INTO YUKO...

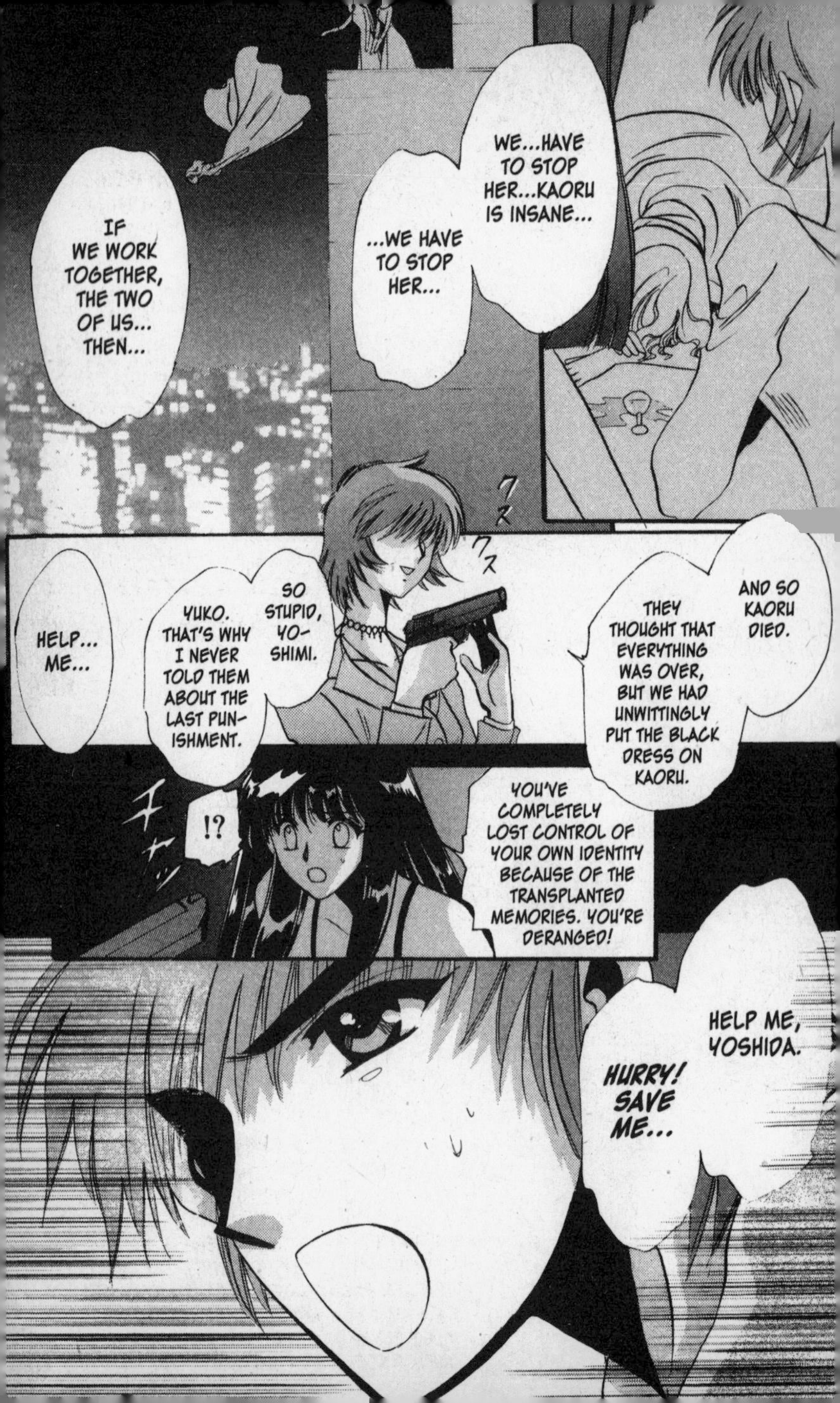

WE...HAVE TO STOP HER...KAORU IS INSANE...
...WE HAVE TO STOP HER...
IF WE WORK TOGETHER, THE TWO OF US... THEN...
AND SO KAORU DIED.
THEY THOUGHT THAT EVERYTHING WAS OVER, BUT WE HAD UNWITTINGLY PUT THE BLACK DRESS ON KAORU.
クスクス
SO STUPID, YOSHIMI.
YUKO. THAT'S WHY I NEVER TOLD THEM ABOUT THE LAST PUNISHMENT.
HELP... ME...
YOU'VE COMPLETELY LOST CONTROL OF YOUR OWN IDENTITY BECAUSE OF THE TRANSPLANTED MEMORIES. YOU'RE DERANGED!
!?
HELP ME, YOSHIDA.
HURRY! SAVE ME...

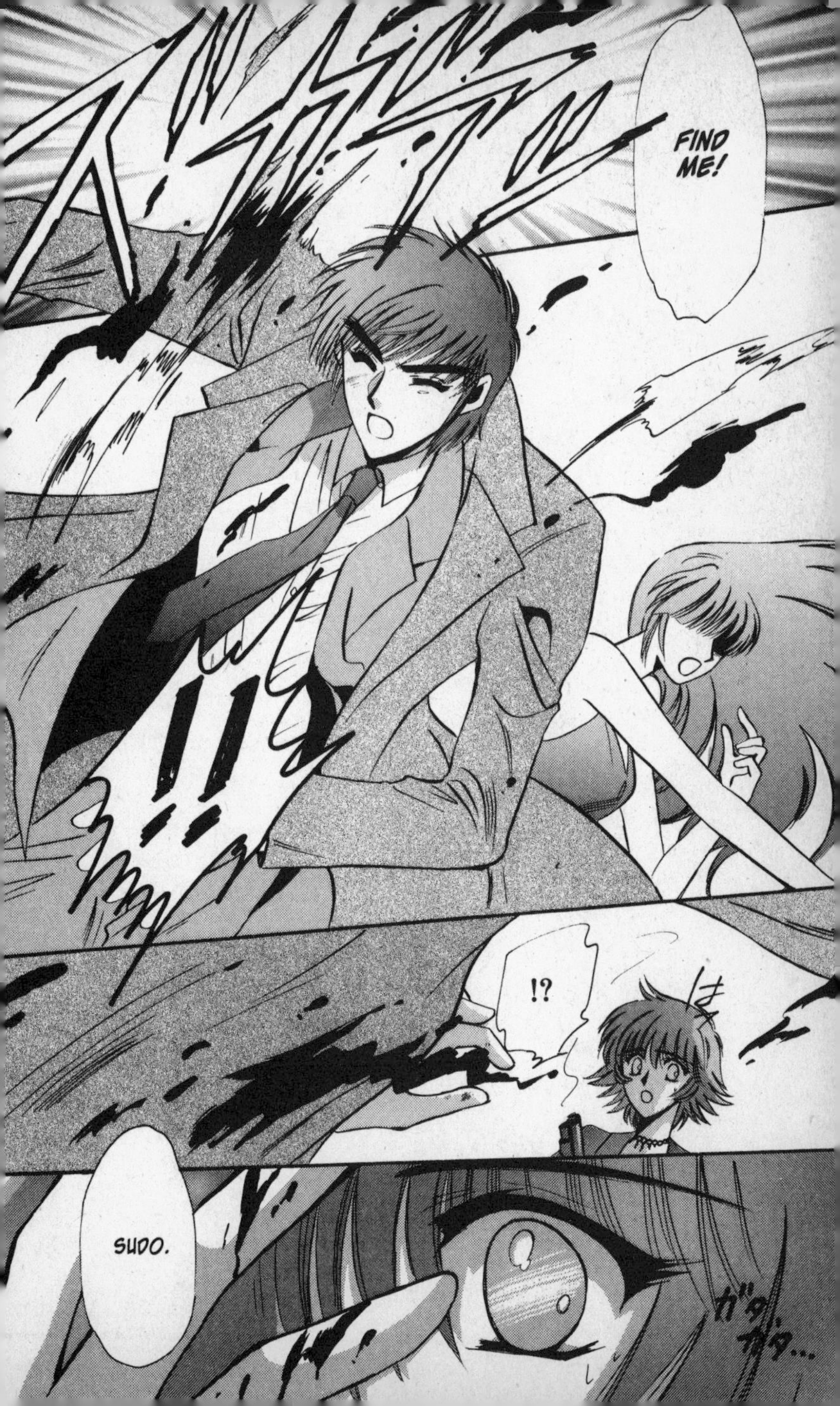
FIND ME!
!?
は
SUDO.
ガタ ガタ...

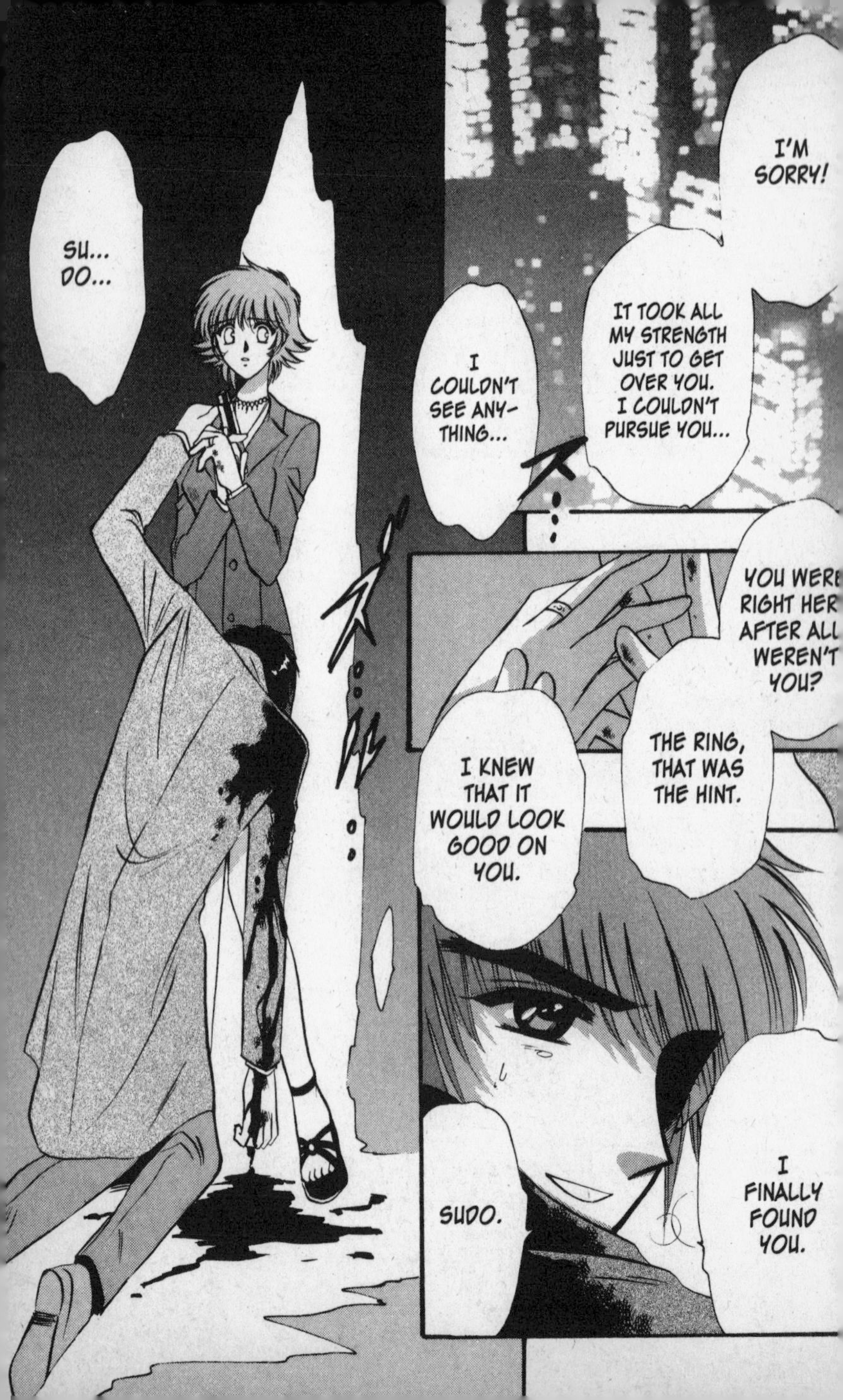
I'M SORRY!
IT TOOK ALL MY STRENGTH JUST TO GET OVER YOU. I COULDN'T PURSUE YOU...
I COULDN'T SEE ANY-THING...
YOU WERE RIGHT HER AFTER ALL WEREN'T YOU?
THE RING, THAT WAS THE HINT.
I KNEW THAT IT WOULD LOOK GOOD ON YOU.
I FINALLY FOUND YOU.
SUDO.
SU... DO...

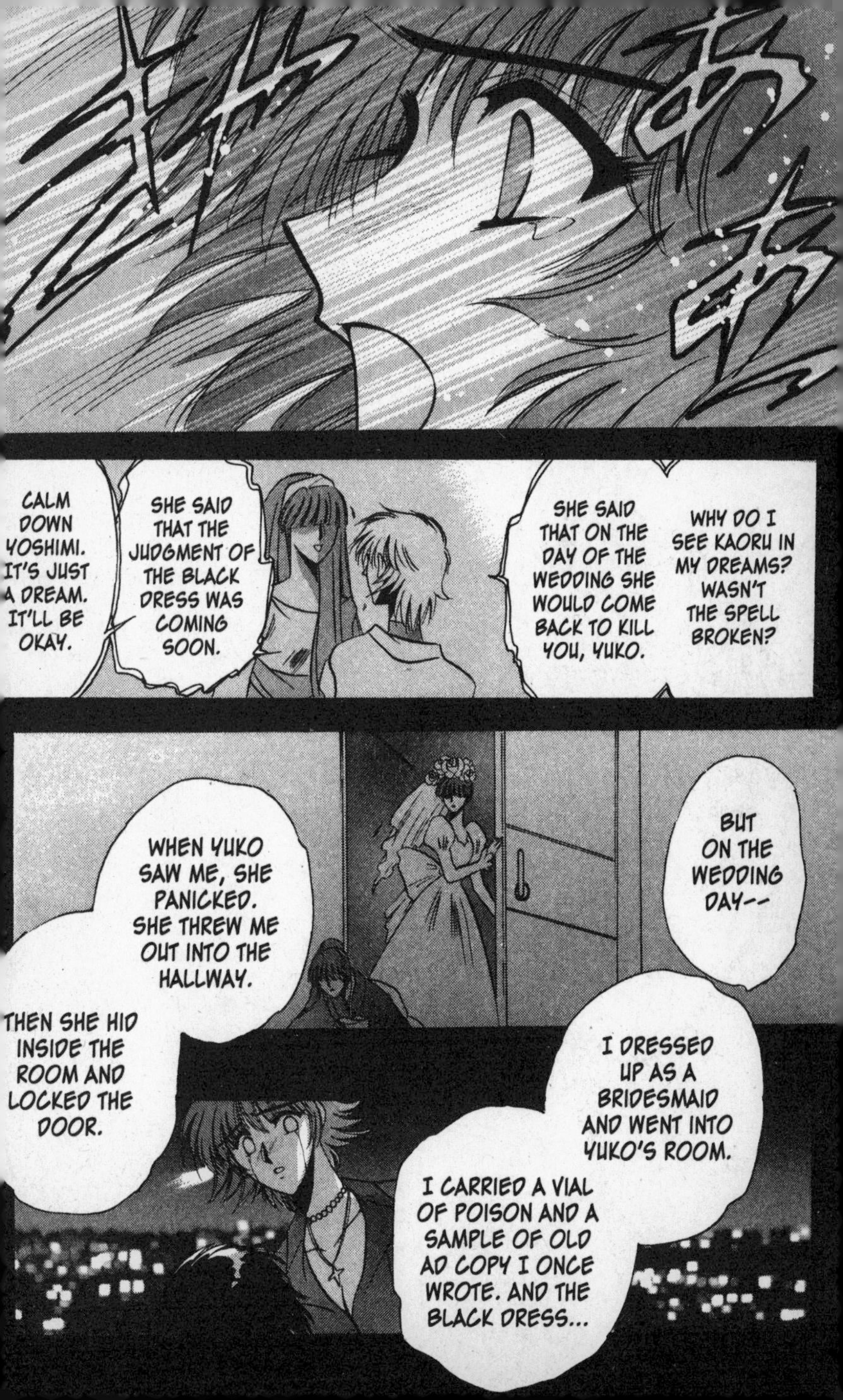
WHY DO I SEE KAORU IN MY DREAMS? WASN'T THE SPELL BROKEN?
SHE SAID THAT ON THE DAY OF THE WEDDING SHE WOULD COME BACK TO KILL YOU, YUKO.
SHE SAID THAT THE JUDGMENT OF THE BLACK DRESS WAS COMING SOON.
CALM DOWN YOSHIMI. IT'S JUST A DREAM. IT'LL BE OKAY.
BUT ON THE WEDDING DAY--
WHEN YUKO SAW ME, SHE PANICKED. SHE THREW ME OUT INTO THE HALLWAY.
THEN SHE HID INSIDE THE ROOM AND LOCKED THE DOOR.
I DRESSED UP AS A BRIDESMAID AND WENT INTO YUKO'S ROOM.
I CARRIED A VIAL OF POISON AND A SAMPLE OF OLD AD COPY I ONCE WROTE. AND THE BLACK DRESS...

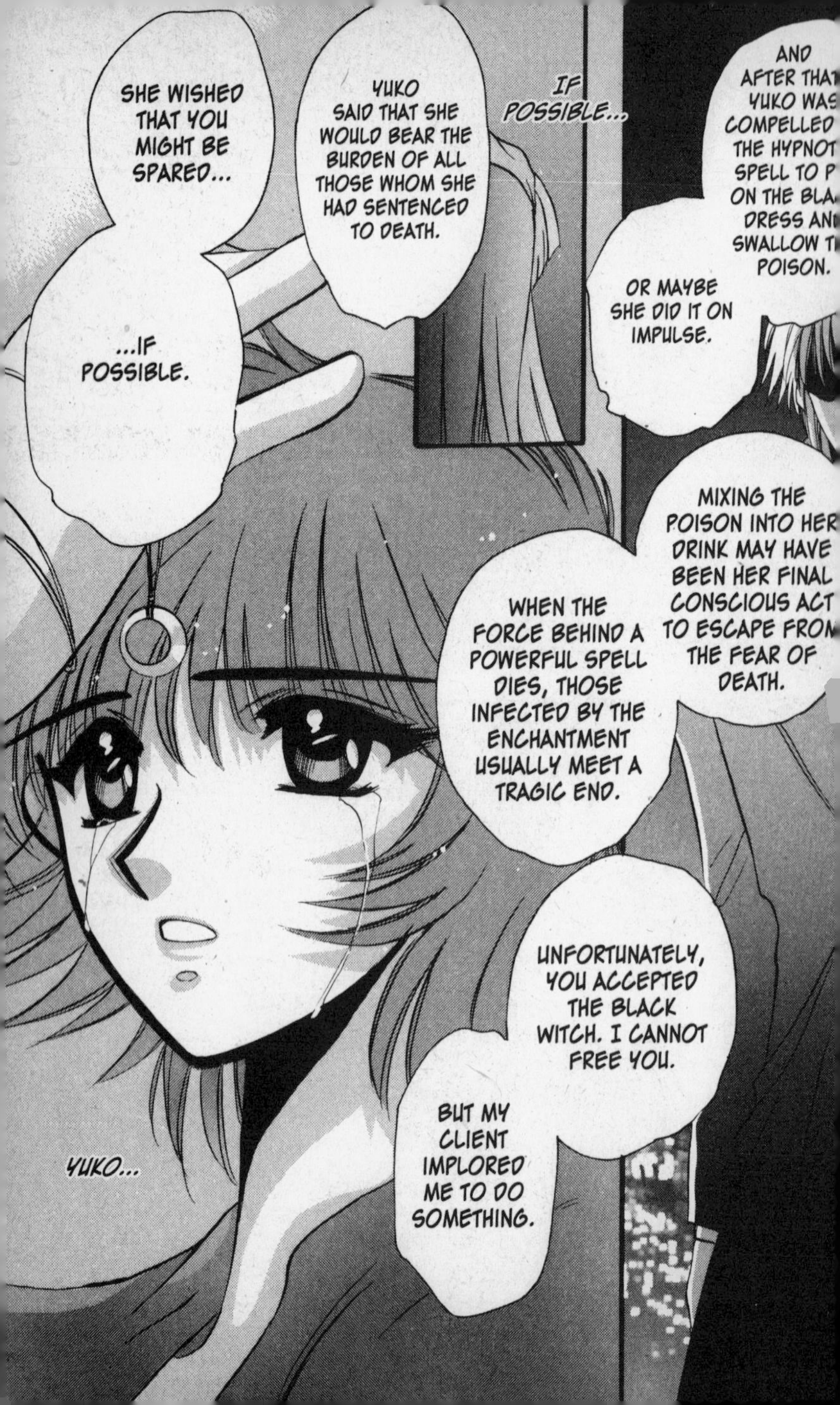
AND AFTER THA YUKO WAS COMPELLED THE HYPNOT SPELL TO P ON THE BLA DRESS AN SWALLOW T POISON.
OR MAYBE SHE DID IT ON IMPULSE.
IF POSSIBLE...
YUKO SAID THAT SHE WOULD BEAR THE BURDEN OF ALL THOSE WHOM SHE HAD SENTENCED TO DEATH.
SHE WISHED THAT YOU MIGHT BE SPARED...
...IF POSSIBLE.
MIXING THE POISON INTO HER DRINK MAY HAVE BEEN HER FINAL CONSCIOUS ACT TO ESCAPE FROM THE FEAR OF DEATH.
WHEN THE FORCE BEHIND A POWERFUL SPELL DIES, THOSE INFECTED BY THE ENCHANTMENT USUALLY MEET A TRAGIC END.
UNFORTUNATELY, YOU ACCEPTED THE BLACK WITCH. I CANNOT FREE YOU.
BUT MY CLIENT IMPLORED ME TO DO SOMETHING.
YUKO...

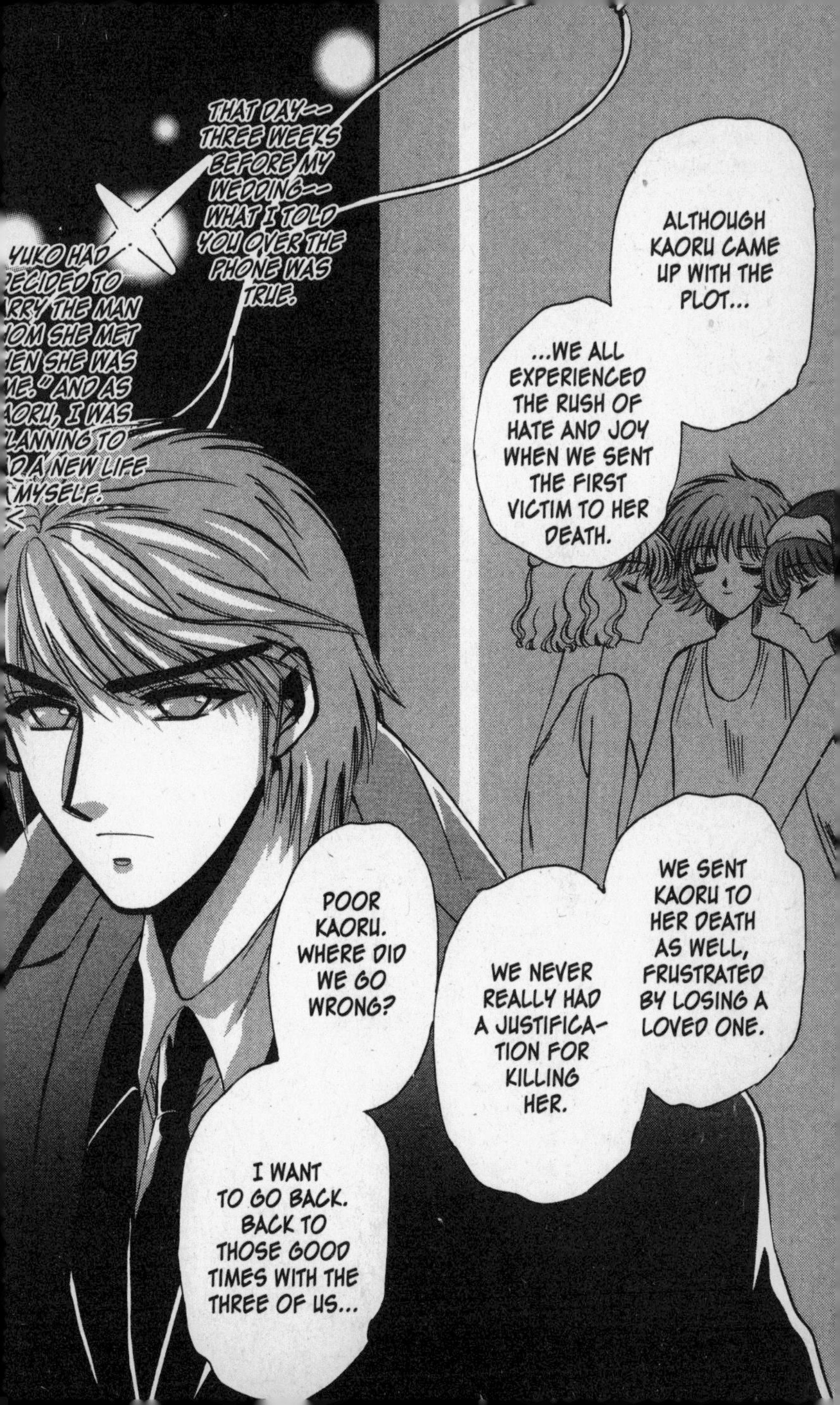
ALTHOUGH KAORU CAME UP WITH THE PLOT...
...WE ALL EXPERIENCED THE RUSH OF HATE AND JOY WHEN WE SENT THE FIRST VICTIM TO HER DEATH.
THAT DAY-- THREE WEEKS BEFORE MY WEDDING-- WHAT I TOLD YOU OVER THE PHONE WAS TRUE.
YUKO HAD ECIDED TO ARRY THE MAN HOM SHE MET HEN SHE WAS ME." AND AS AORU, I WAS LANNING TO D A NEW LIFE MYSELF.
WE SENT KAORU TO HER DEATH AS WELL, FRUSTRATED BY LOSING A LOVED ONE.
WE NEVER REALLY HAD A JUSTIFICATION FOR KILLING HER.
POOR KAORU. WHERE DID WE GO WRONG?
I WANT TO GO BACK. BACK TO THOSE GOOD TIMES WITH THE THREE OF US...

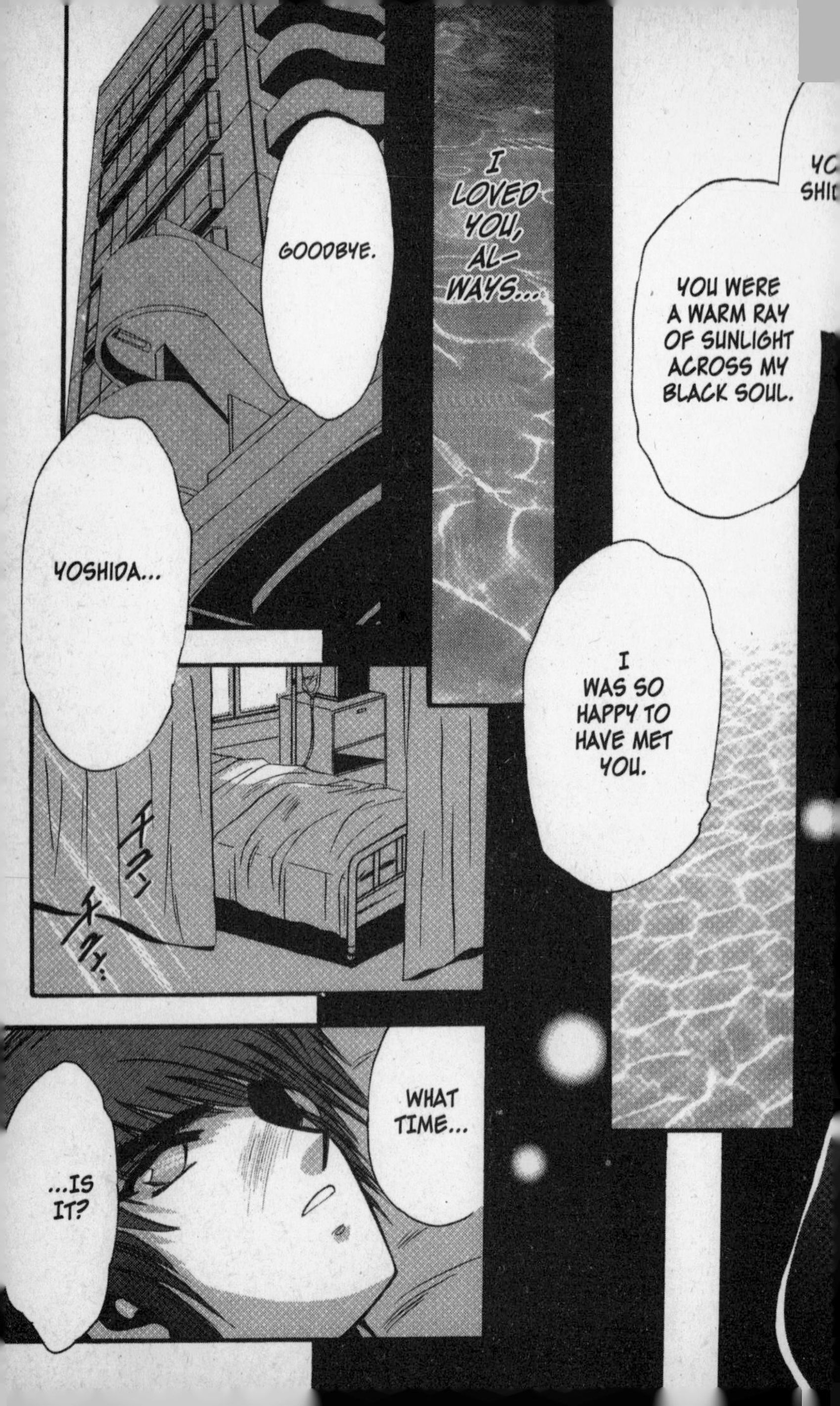
YOU WERE A WARM RAY OF SUNLIGHT ACROSS MY BLACK SOUL.
I WAS SO HAPPY TO HAVE MET YOU.
I LOVED YOU, AL-WAYS...
GOODBYE.
YOSHIDA...
WHAT TIME...
...IS IT?

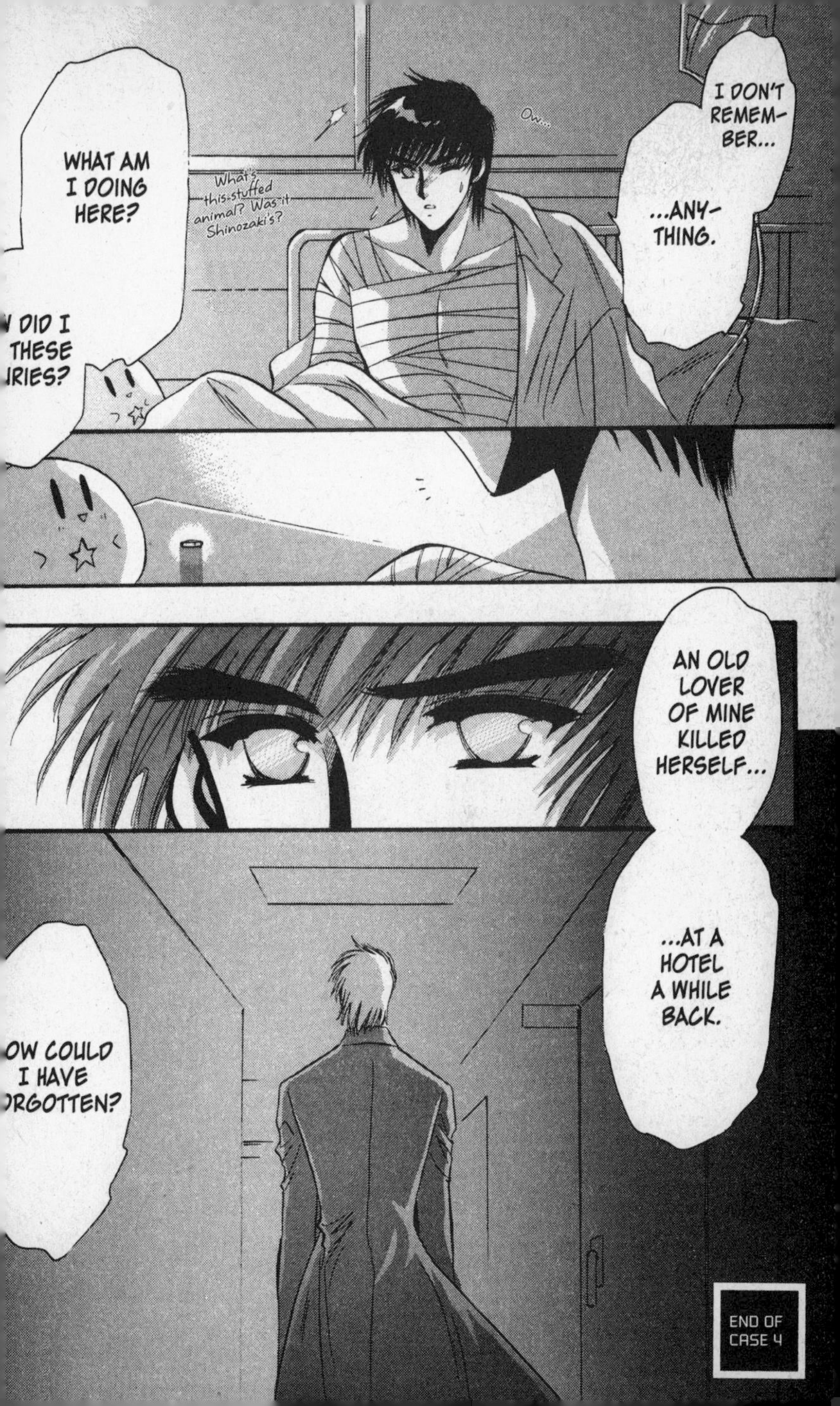
I DON'T REMEMBER... ...ANYTHING.
Ow...
What's this stuffed animal? Was it Shinozaki's?
WHAT AM I DOING HERE?
DID I THESE IRIES?
AN OLD LOVER OF MINE KILLED HERSELF...
...AT A HOTEL A WHILE BACK.
OW COULD I HAVE RGOTTEN?
END OF CASE 4

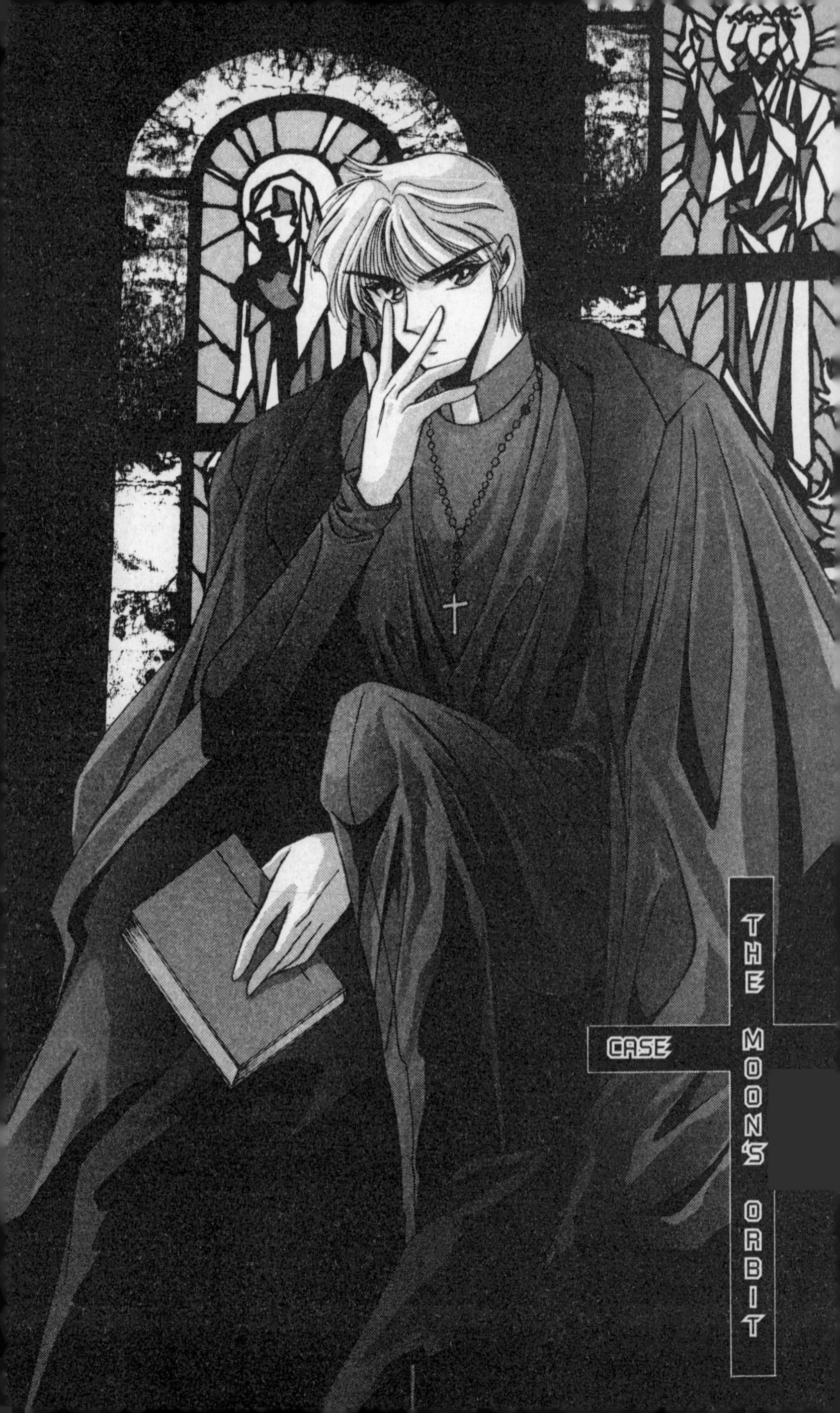
CASE
THE MOON'S ORBIT

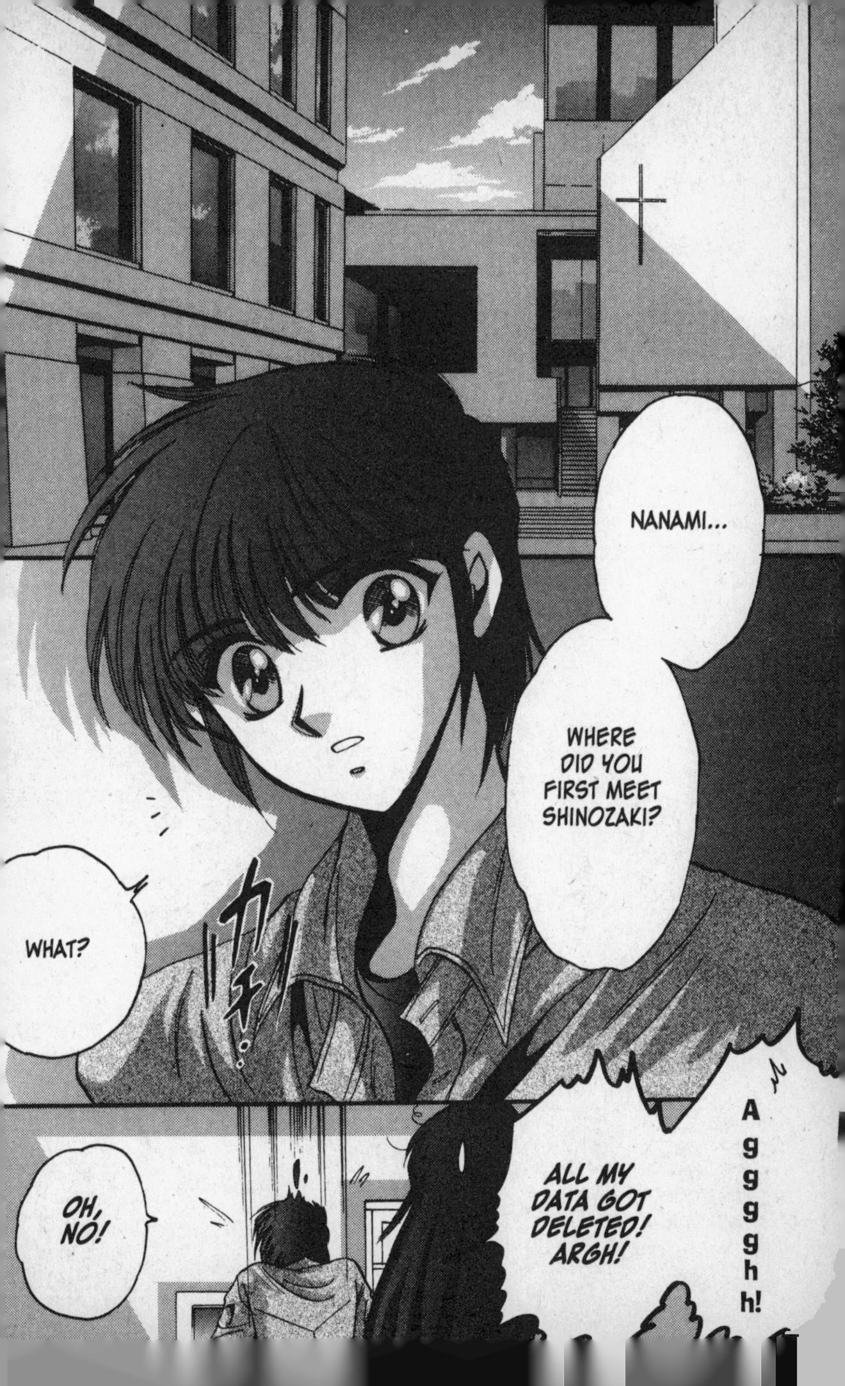
NANAMI...
WHERE DID YOU FIRST MEET SHINOZAKI?
カチ
WHAT?
Aggggh!
ALL MY DATA GOT DELETED! ARGH!
OH, NO!

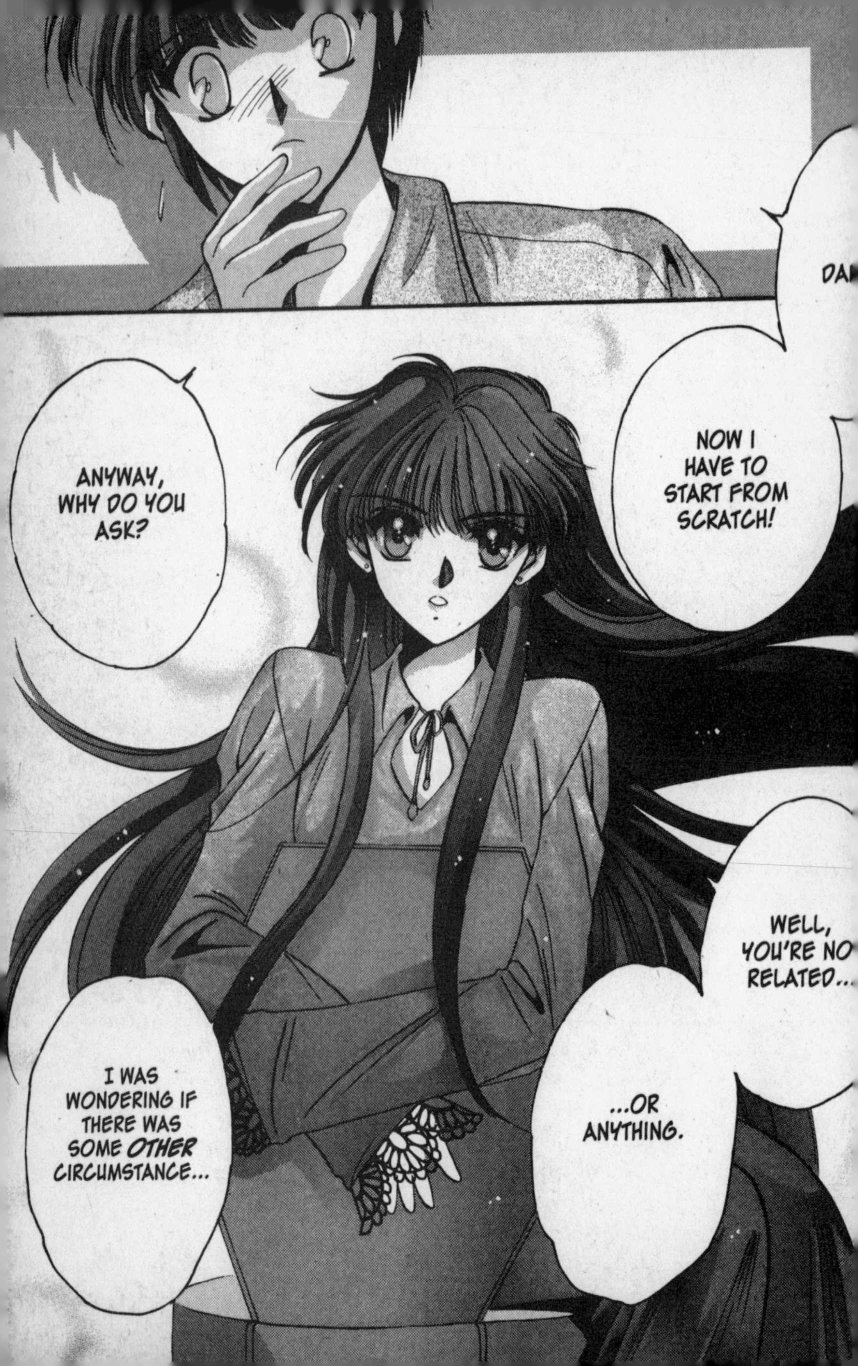
NOW I HAVE TO START FROM SCRATCH!
ANYWAY, WHY DO YOU ASK?
WELL, YOU'RE NO RELATED...
...OR ANYTHING.
I WAS WONDERING IF THERE WAS SOME *OTHER* CIRCUMSTANCE...

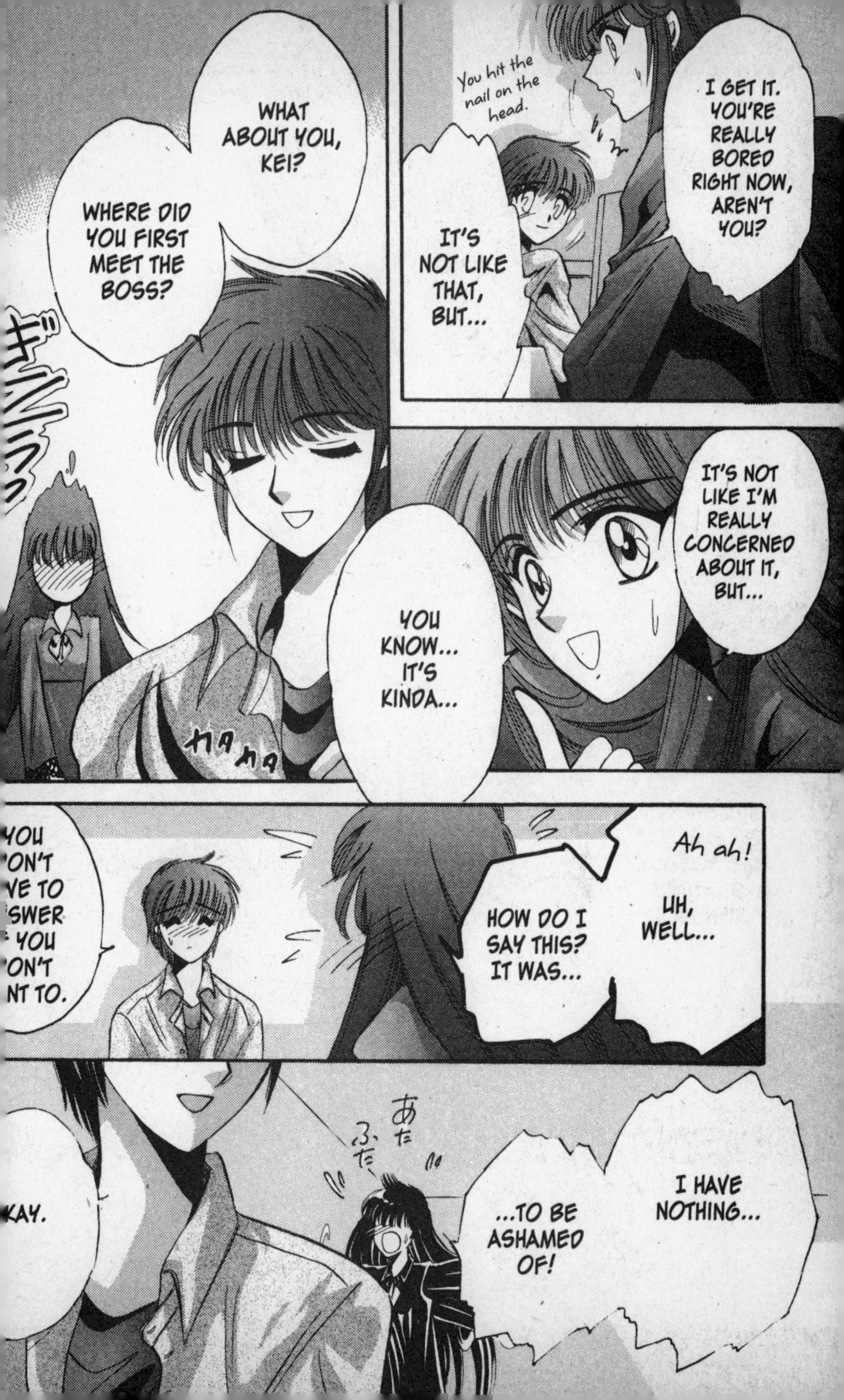

I GET IT. YOU'RE REALLY BORED RIGHT NOW, AREN'T YOU?
You hit the nail on the head.
IT'S NOT LIKE THAT, BUT...
IT'S NOT LIKE I'M REALLY CONCERNED ABOUT IT, BUT...
YOU KNOW... IT'S KINDA...
WHAT ABOUT YOU, KEI?
WHERE DID YOU FIRST MEET THE BOSS?
Ah ah!
UH, WELL...
HOW DO I SAY THIS? IT WAS...
YOU ON'T VE TO SWER YOU ON'T NT TO.
I HAVE NOTHING...
...TO BE ASHAMED OF!
あたふた
KAY.

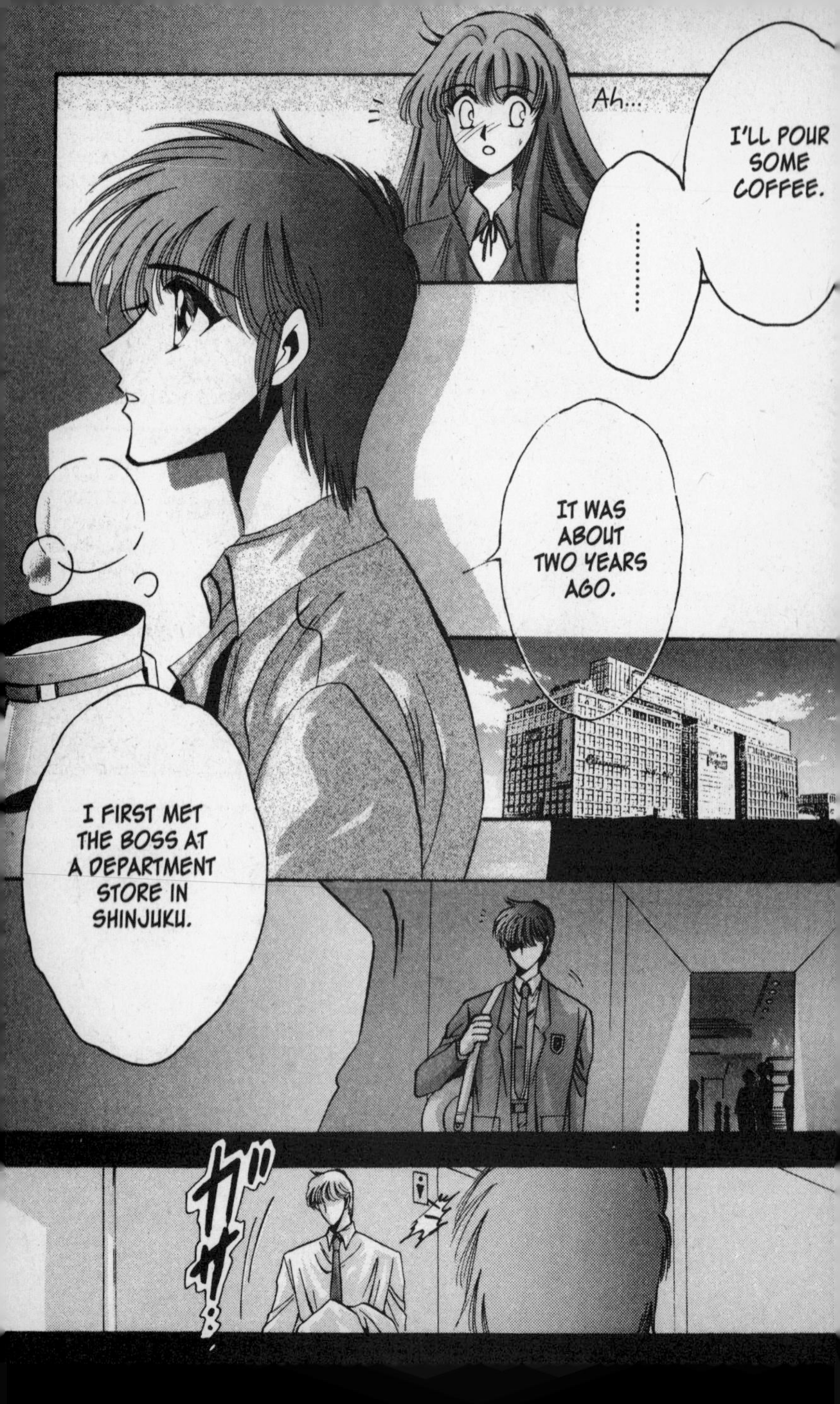

I'LL POUR SOME COFFEE.
Ah...
......
IT WAS ABOUT TWO YEARS AGO.
I FIRST MET THE BOSS AT A DEPARTMENT STORE IN SHINJUKU.
ガザ!!

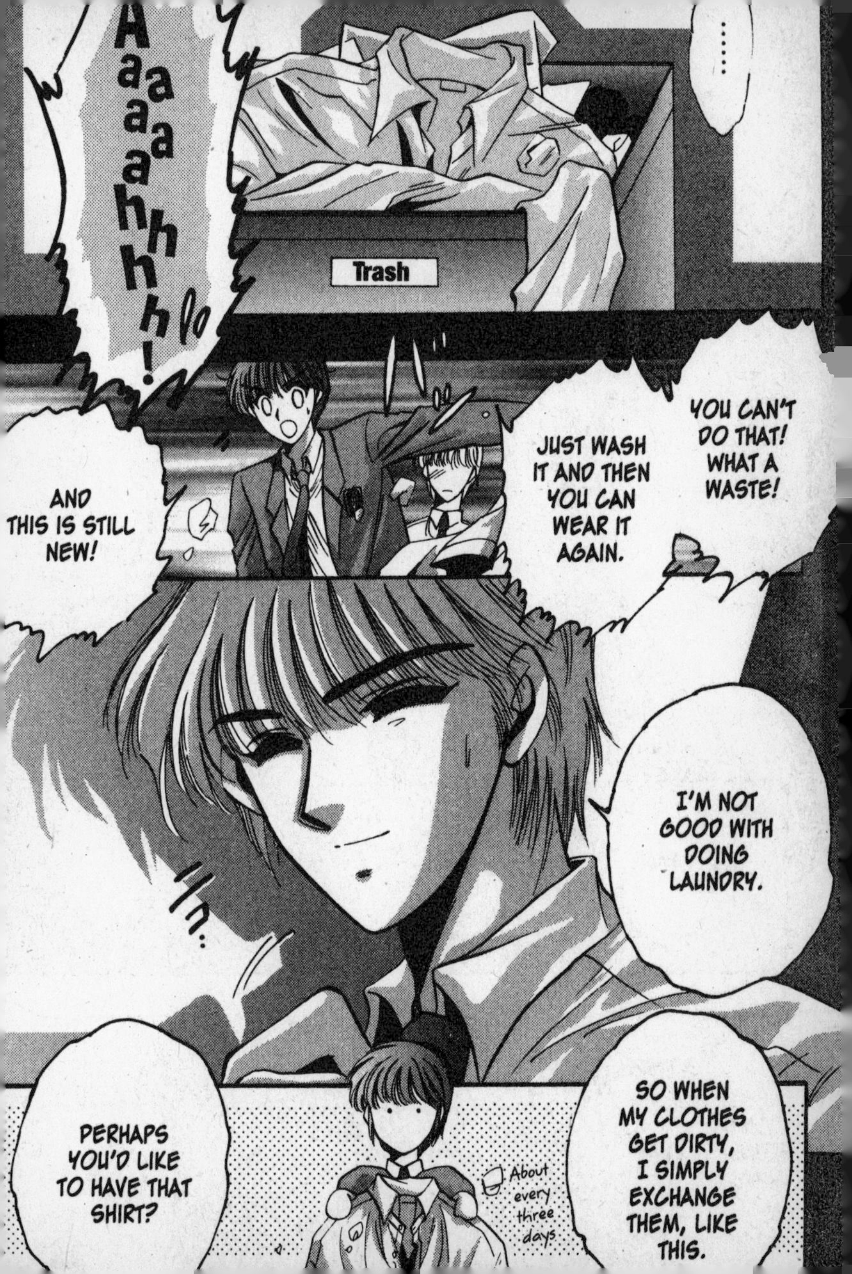
……
Trash
Aaaaaahhhh!
YOU CAN'T DO THAT! WHAT A WASTE!
JUST WASH IT AND THEN YOU CAN WEAR IT AGAIN.
AND THIS IS STILL NEW!
I'M NOT GOOD WITH DOING LAUNDRY.
SO WHEN MY CLOTHES GET DIRTY, I SIMPLY EXCHANGE THEM, LIKE THIS.
About every three days
PERHAPS YOU'D LIKE TO HAVE THAT SHIRT?

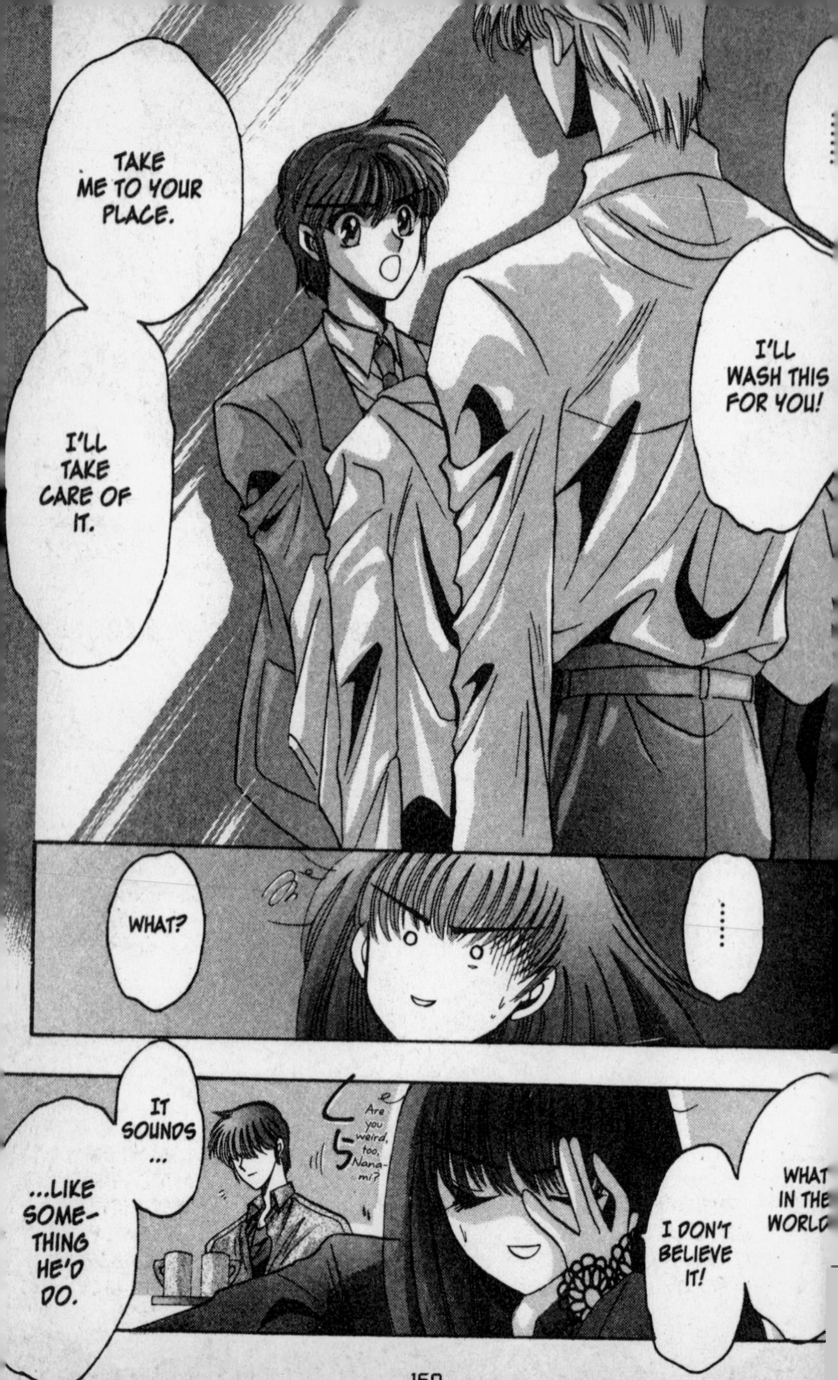
I'LL WASH THIS FOR YOU!
TAKE ME TO YOUR PLACE.
I'LL TAKE CARE OF IT.
......
WHAT?
WHAT IN THE WORLD
I DON'T BELIEVE IT!
Are you weird, too, Nana-mi?
IT SOUNDS...
...LIKE SOME-THING HE'D DO.

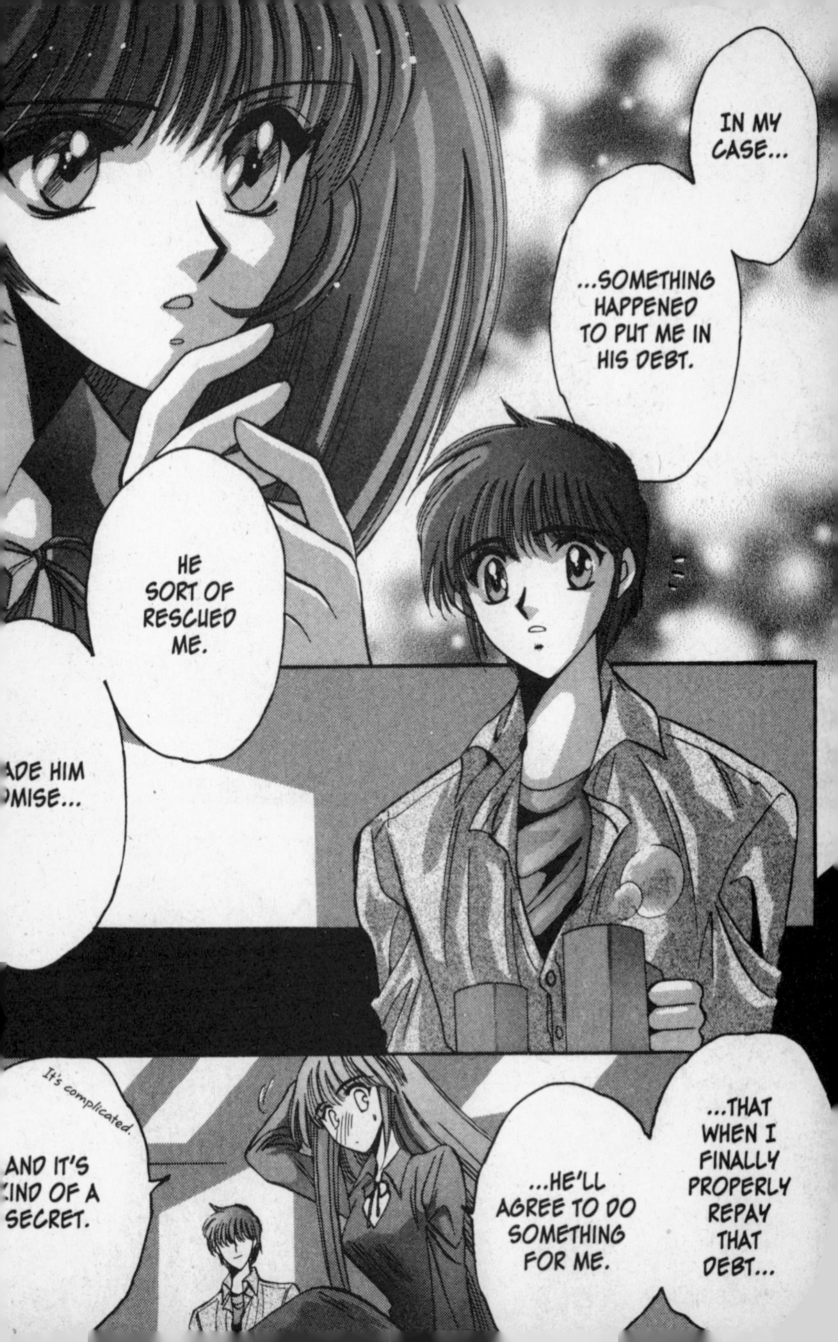
IN MY CASE...
...SOMETHING HAPPENED TO PUT ME IN HIS DEBT.
HE SORT OF RESCUED ME.
ADE HIM MISE...
...THAT WHEN I FINALLY PROPERLY REPAY THAT DEBT...
...HE'LL AGREE TO DO SOMETHING FOR ME.
It's complicated.
AND IT'S IND OF A SECRET.

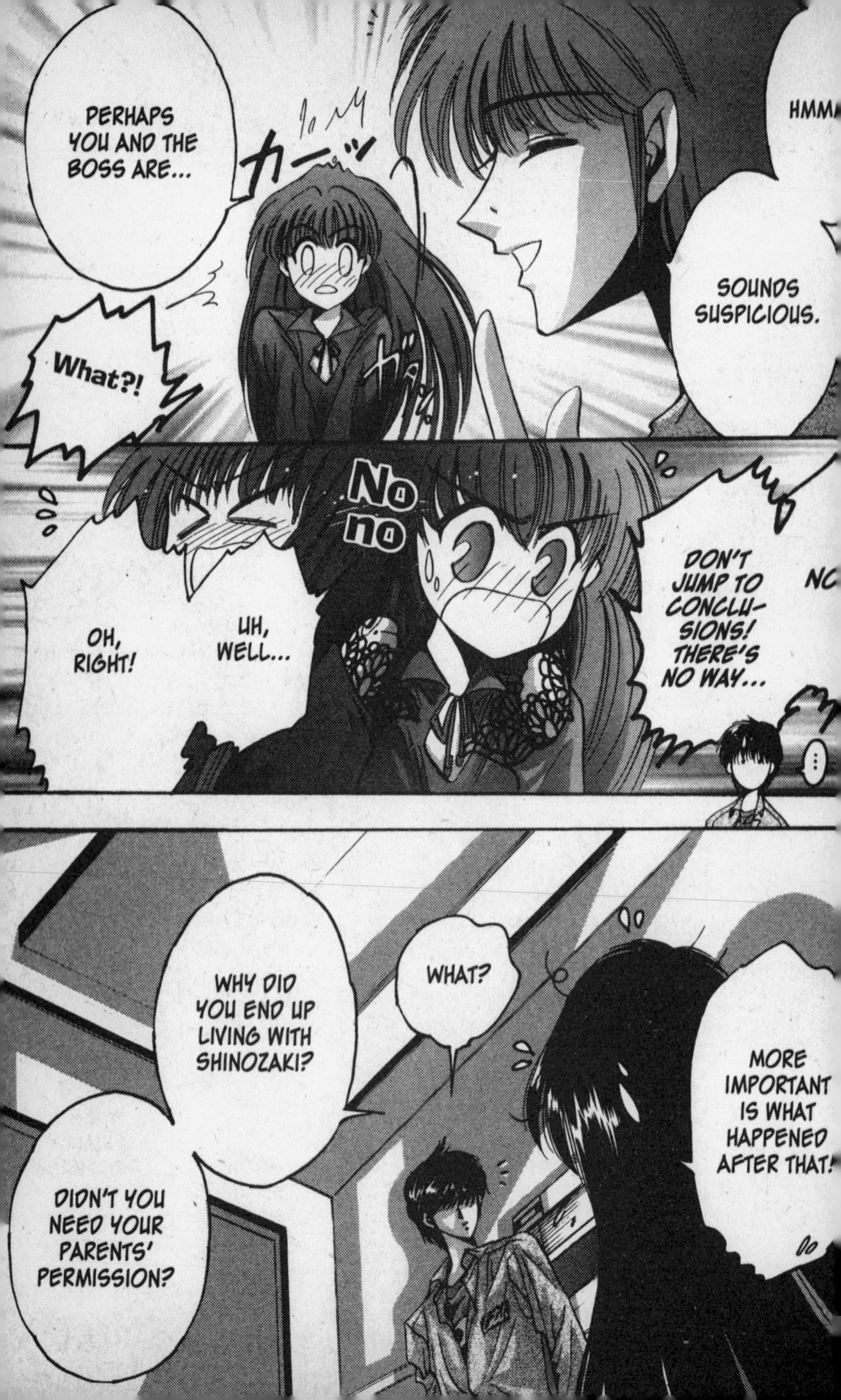
HMM
SOUNDS SUSPICIOUS.
PERHAPS YOU AND THE BOSS ARE...
カーッ
What?!
DON'T JUMP TO CONCLUSIONS! THERE'S NO WAY...
...
No no
UH, WELL...
OH, RIGHT!
MORE IMPORTANT IS WHAT HAPPENED AFTER THAT!
WHAT?
WHY DID YOU END UP LIVING WITH SHINOZAKI?
DIDN'T YOU NEED YOUR PARENTS' PERMISSION?

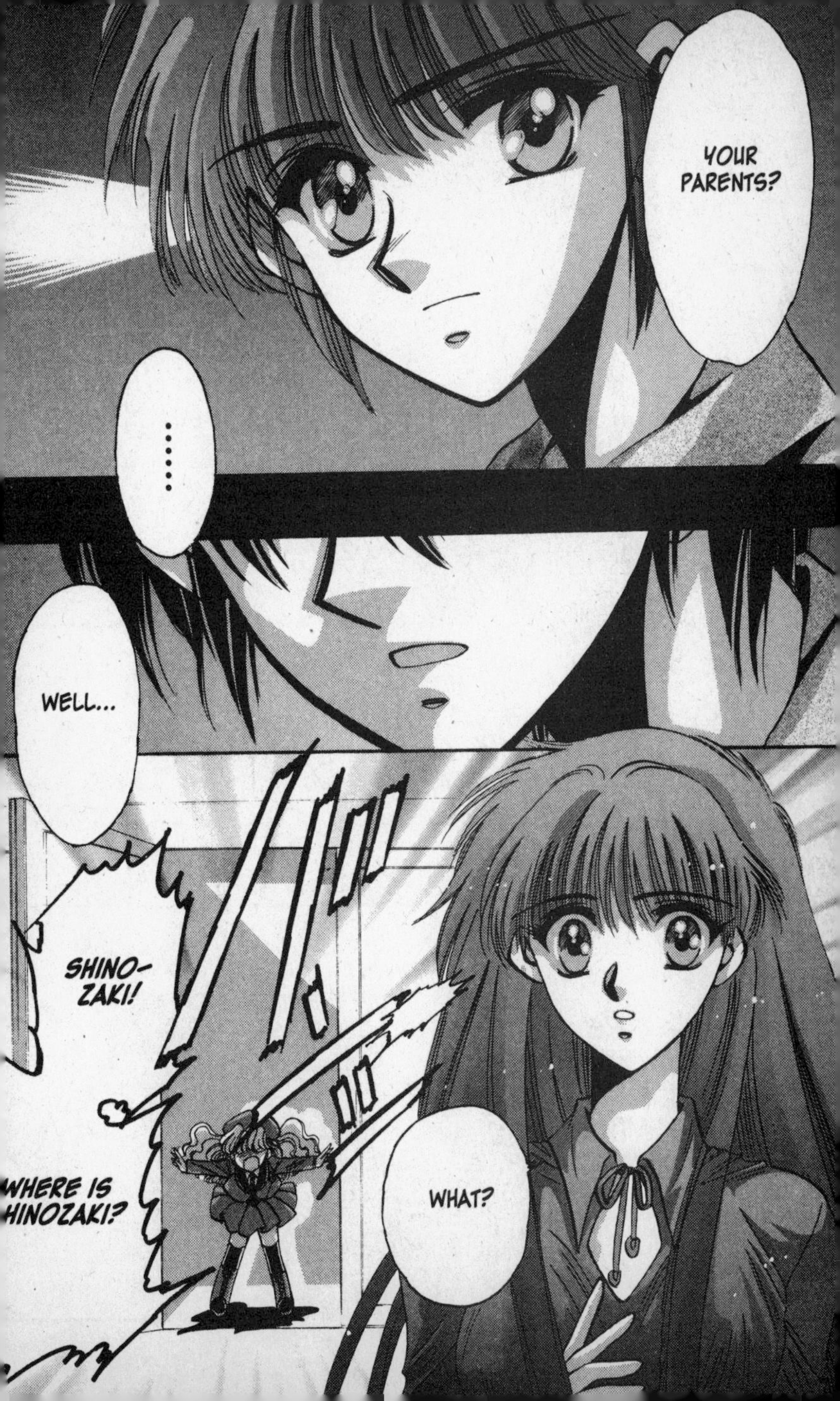
YOUR PARENTS?
......
WELL...
SHINO-ZAKI!
WHAT?
WHERE IS HINOZAKI?

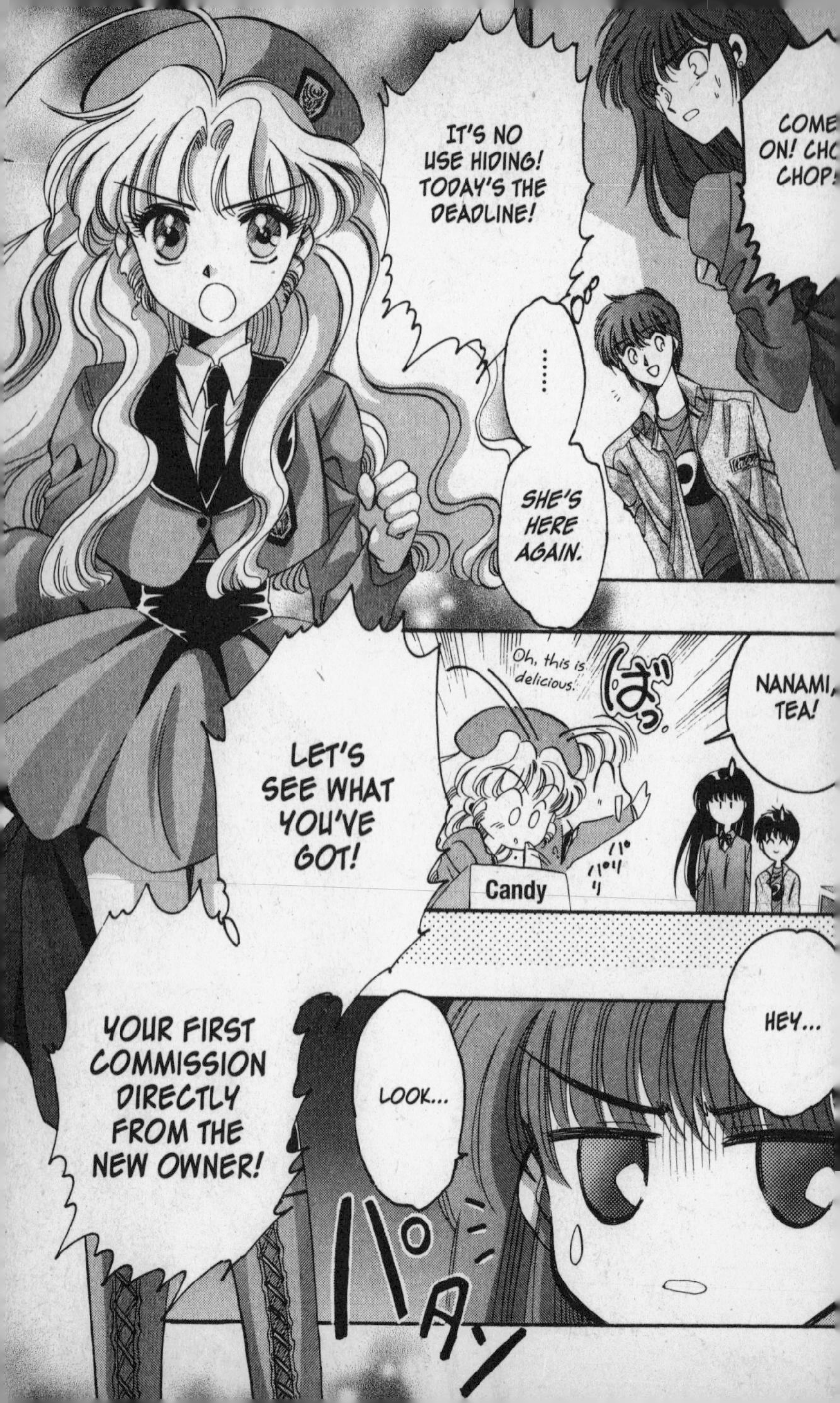
COME ON! CHO CHOP!
IT'S NO USE HIDING! TODAY'S THE DEADLINE!
......
SHE'S HERE AGAIN.
NANAMI, TEA!
ぱっ
Oh, this is delicious.
Candy
LET'S SEE WHAT YOU'VE GOT!
HEY...
LOOK...
パッ
YOUR FIRST COMMISSION DIRECTLY FROM THE NEW OWNER!

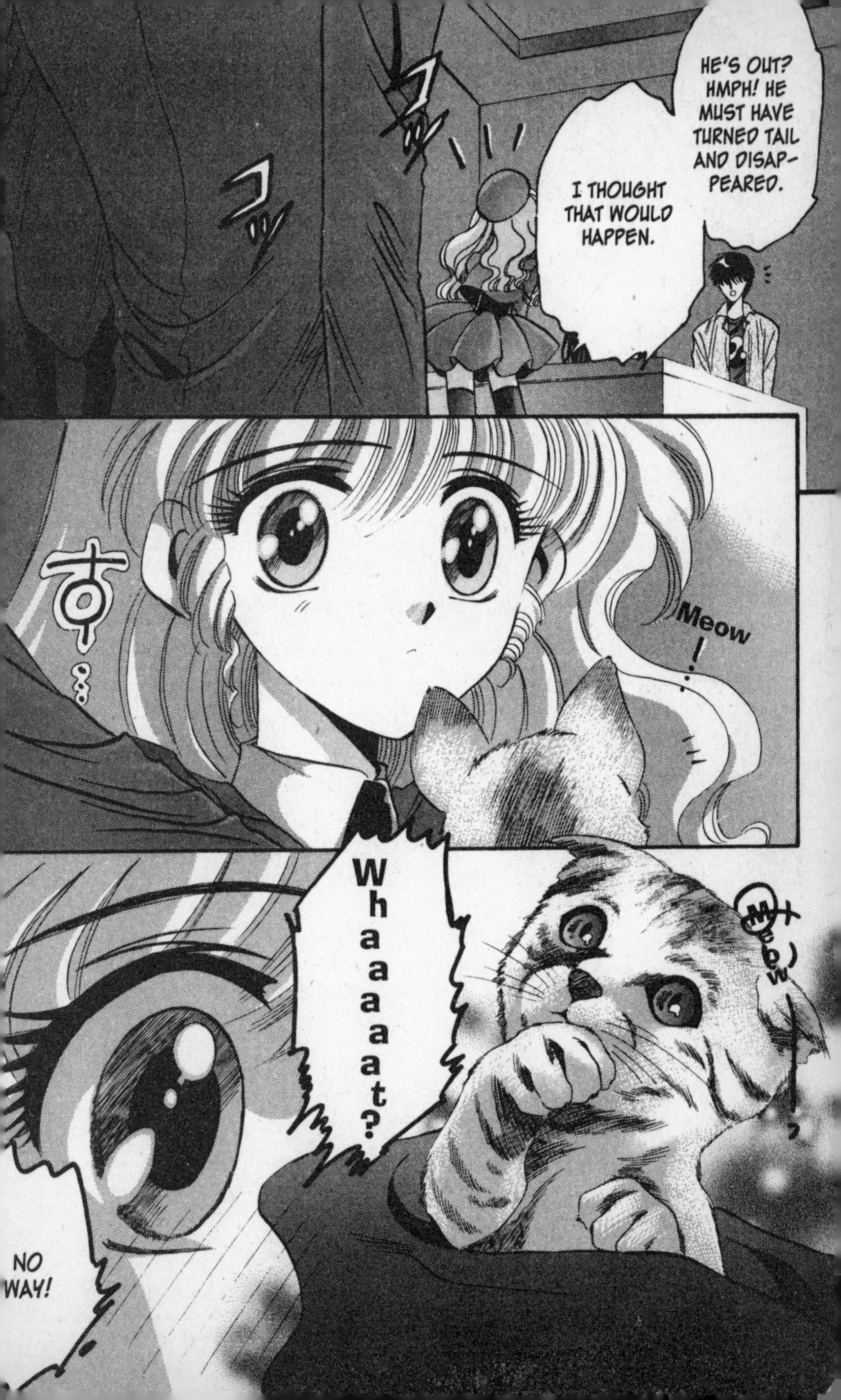
HE'S OUT? HMPH! HE MUST HAVE TURNED TAIL AND DISAP-PEARED.
I THOUGHT THAT WOULD HAPPEN.
Meow!
Meow
Whaaaaat?
NO WAY!

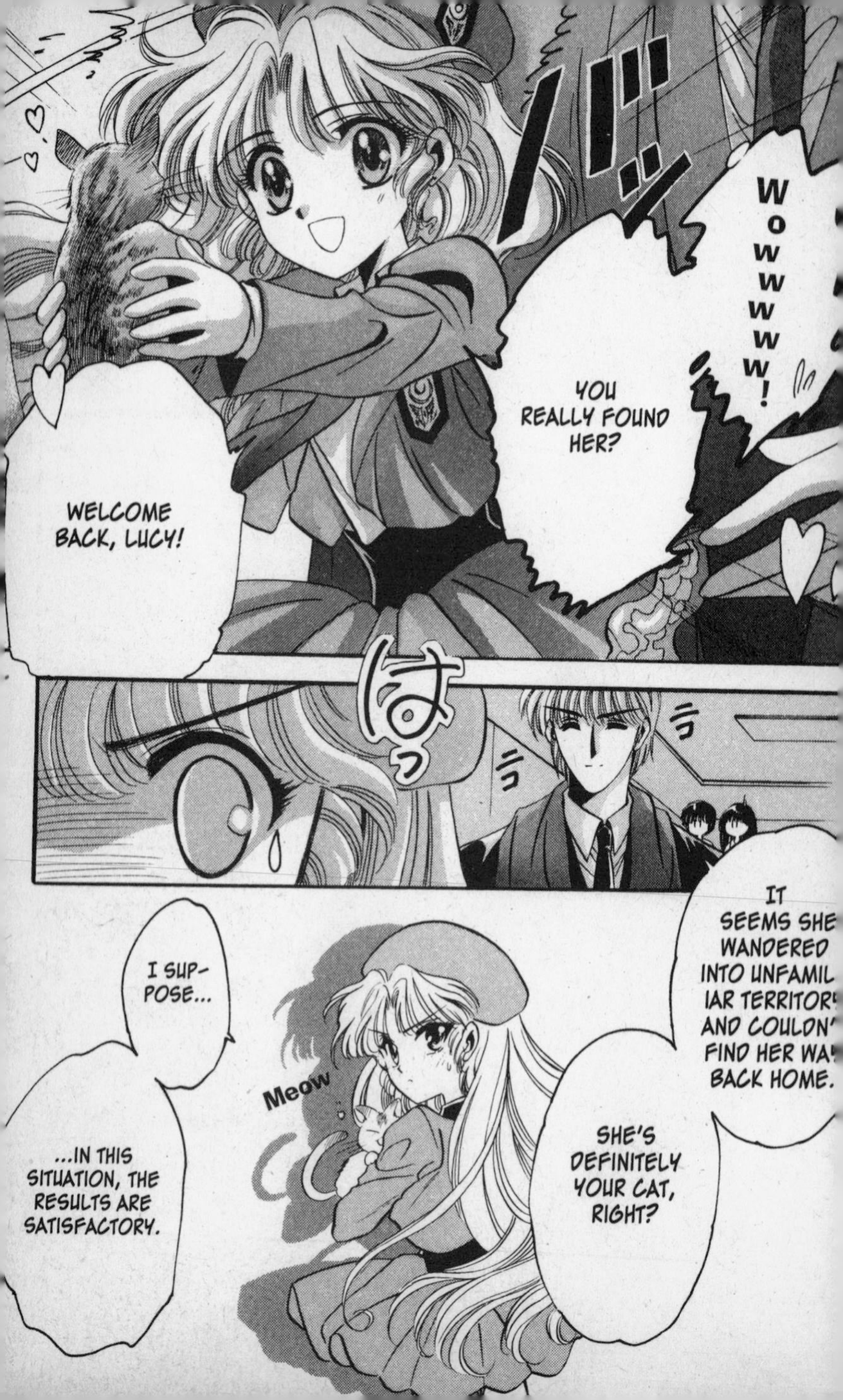
Wowwwwww!
YOU REALLY FOUND HER?
WELCOME BACK, LUCY!
はっ
IT SEEMS SHE WANDERED INTO UNFAMIL IAR TERRITOR AND COULDN FIND HER WA BACK HOME.
SHE'S DEFINITELY YOUR CAT, RIGHT?
Meow
I SUP-POSE...
...IN THIS SITUATION, THE RESULTS ARE SATISFACTORY.

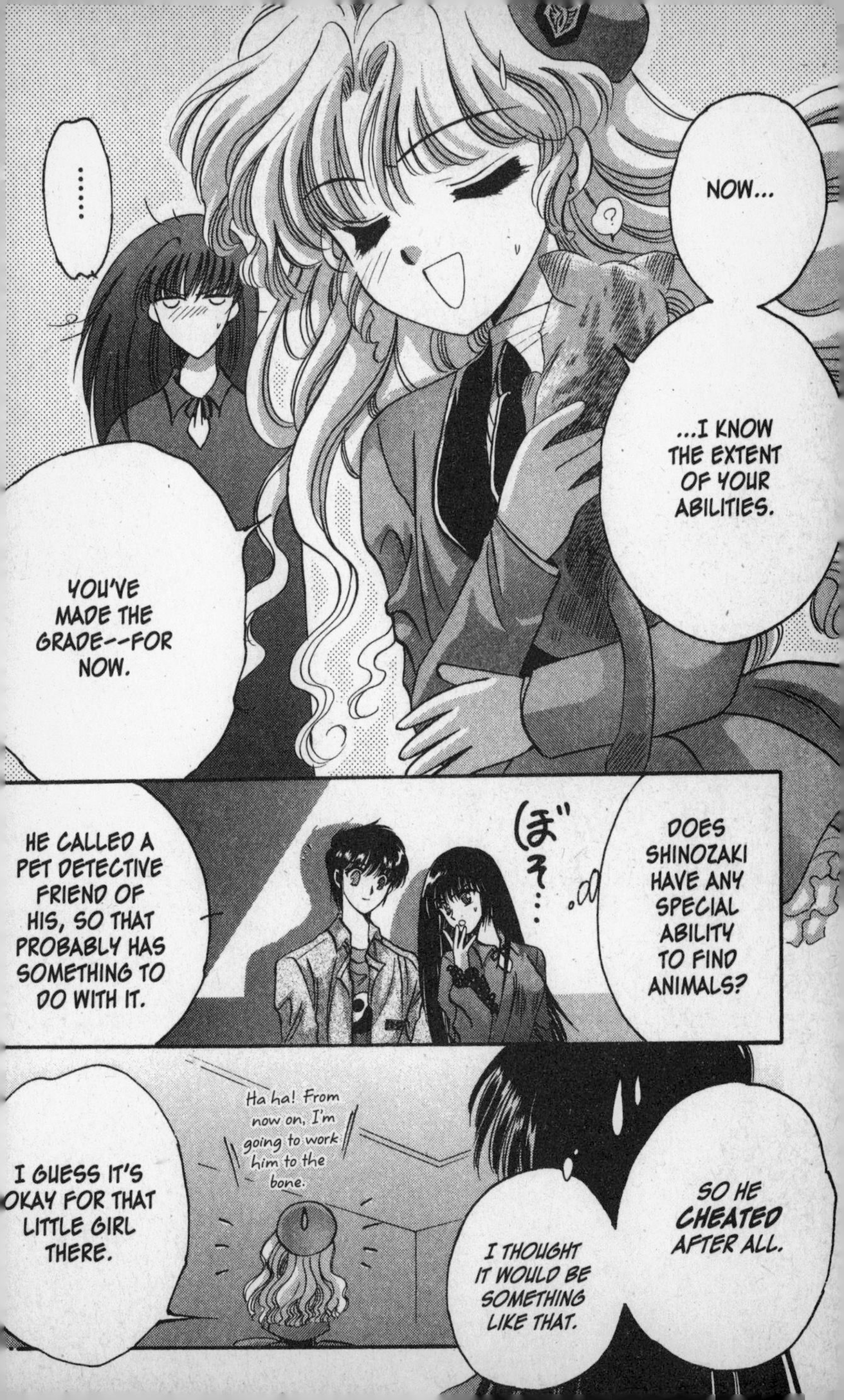
NOW...
...I KNOW THE EXTENT OF YOUR ABILITIES.
YOU'VE MADE THE GRADE--FOR NOW.
......
DOES SHINOZAKI HAVE ANY SPECIAL ABILITY TO FIND ANIMALS?
ぼそ…
HE CALLED A PET DETECTIVE FRIEND OF HIS, SO THAT PROBABLY HAS SOMETHING TO DO WITH IT.
SO HE **CHEATED** AFTER ALL.
I THOUGHT IT WOULD BE SOMETHING LIKE THAT.
Ha ha! From now on, I'm going to work him to the bone.
I GUESS IT'S OKAY FOR THAT LITTLE GIRL THERE.

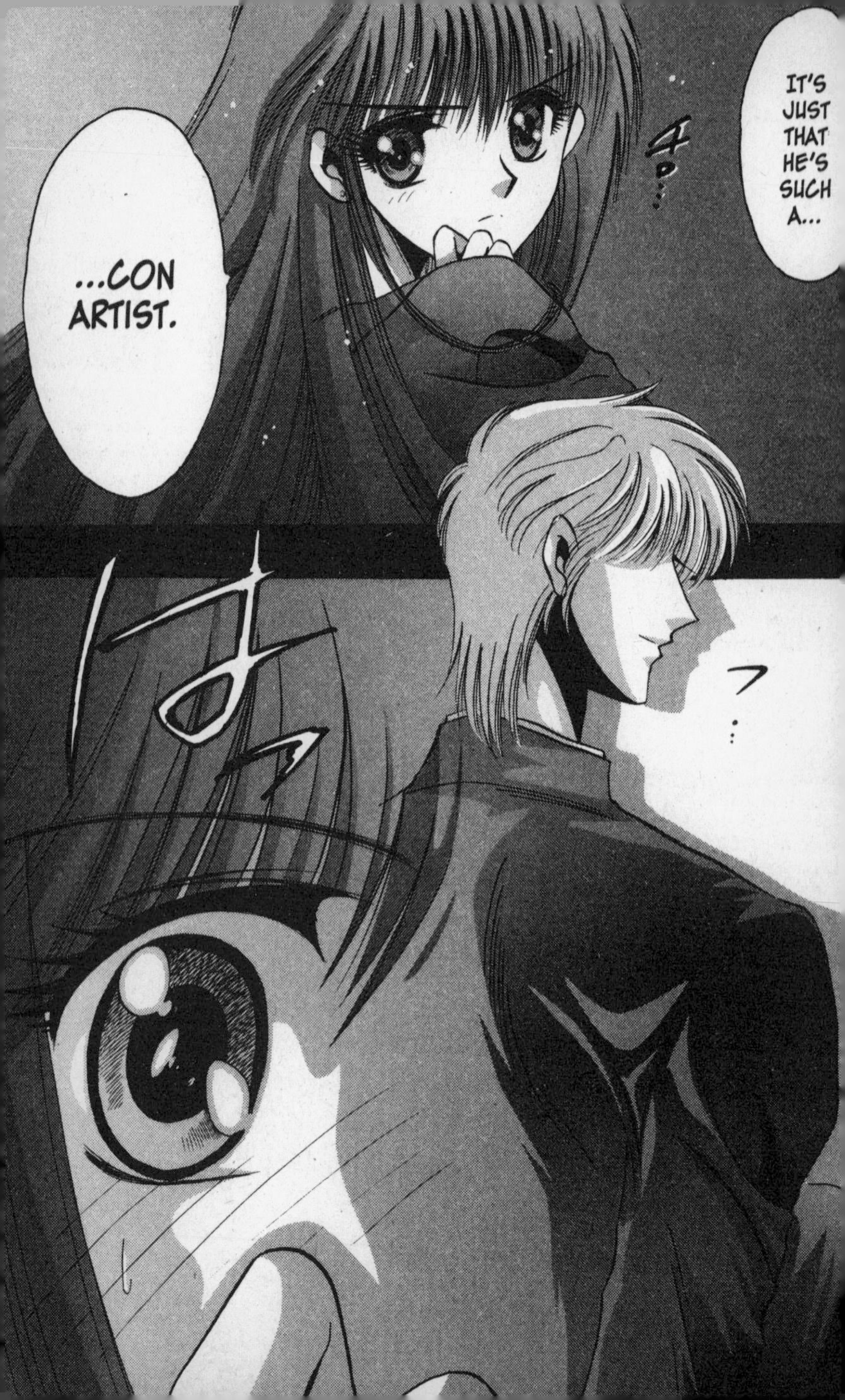
IT'S JUST THAT HE'S SUCH A...
...CON ARTIST.

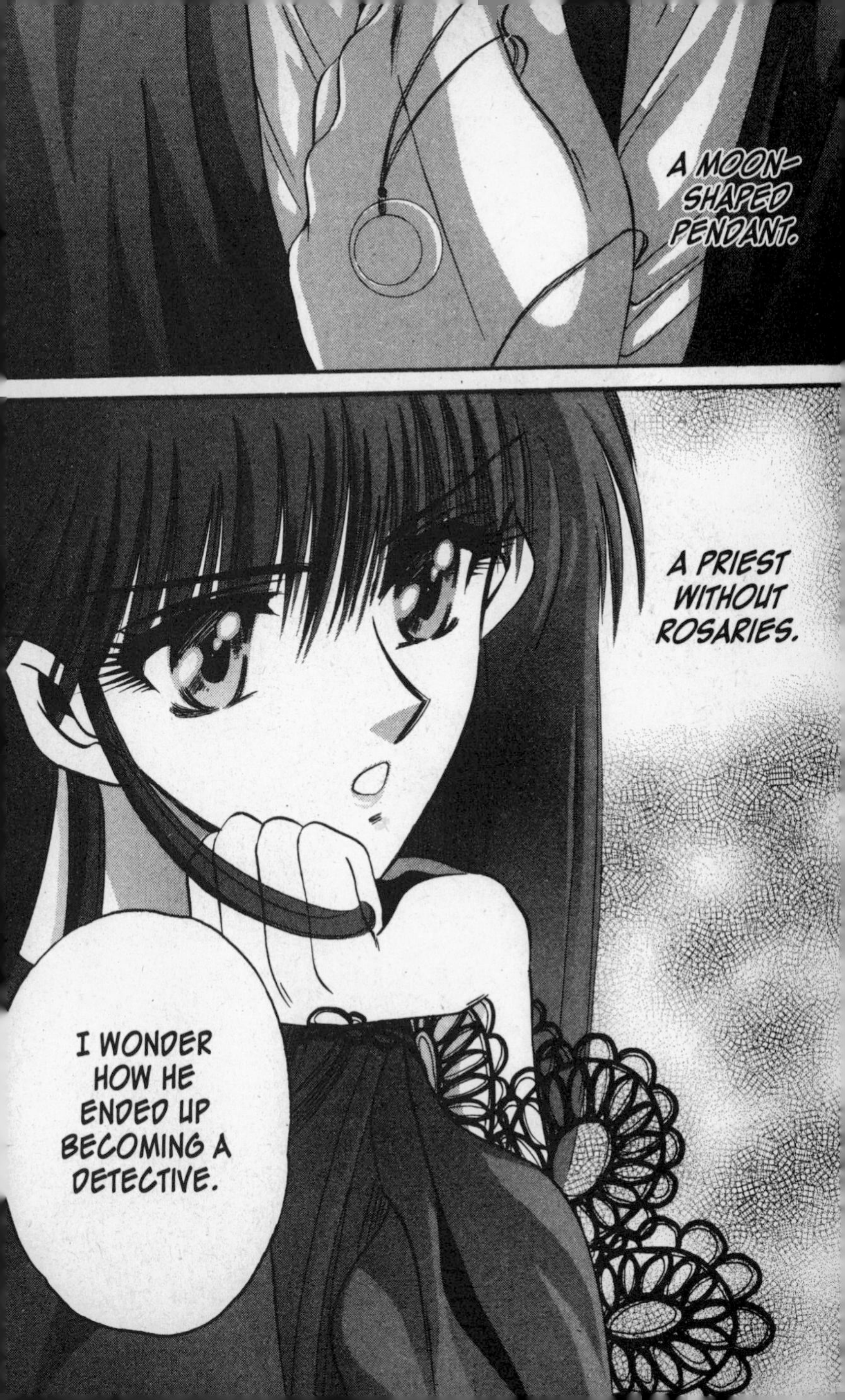
A MOON-SHAPED PENDANT.
A PRIEST WITHOUT ROSARIES.
I WONDER HOW HE ENDED UP BECOMING A DETECTIVE.

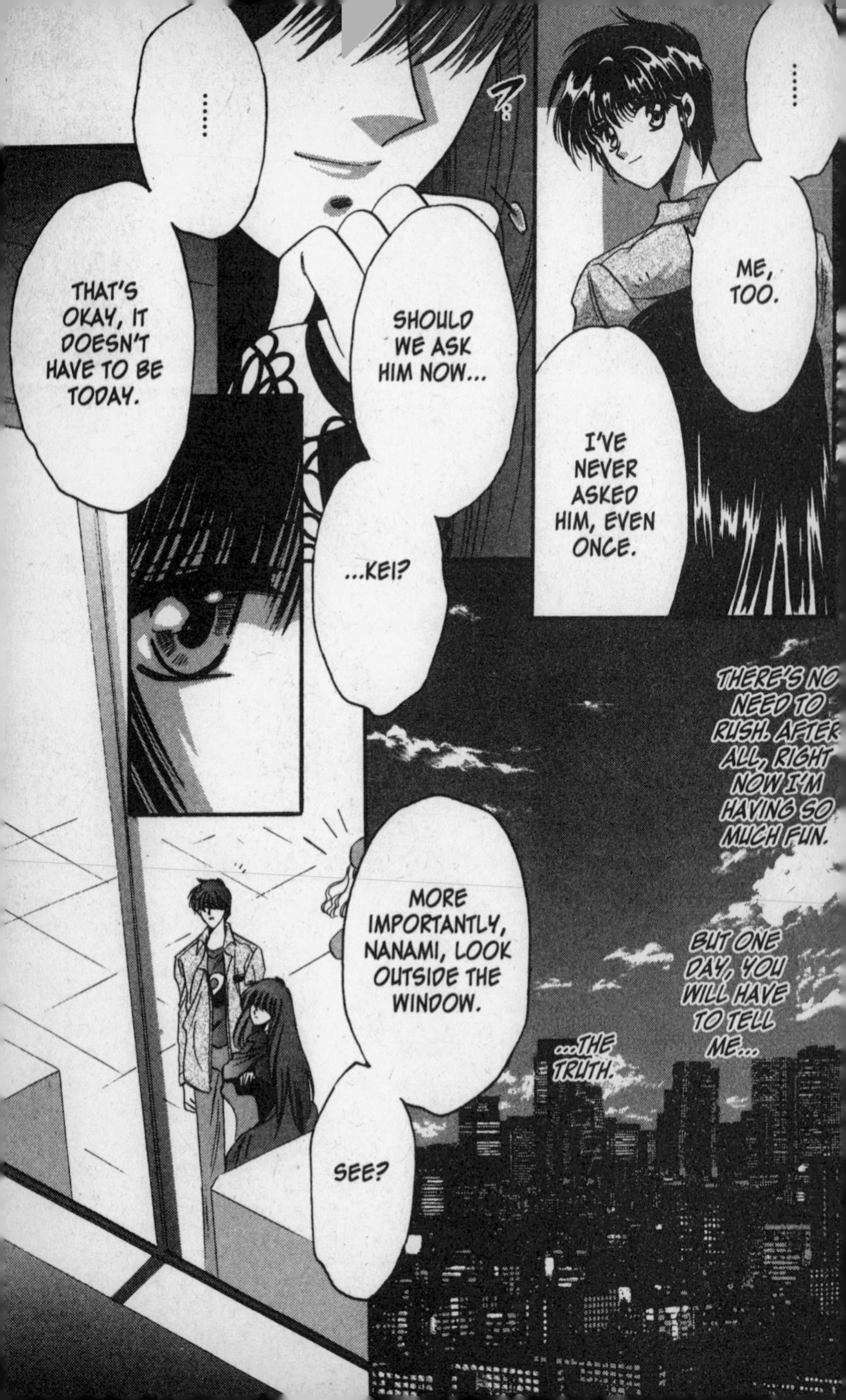
......
ME, TOO.
I'VE NEVER ASKED HIM, EVEN ONCE.
SHOULD WE ASK HIM NOW...
......
THAT'S OKAY, IT DOESN'T HAVE TO BE TODAY.
...KEI?
THERE'S NO NEED TO RUSH. AFTER ALL, RIGHT NOW I'M HAVING SO MUCH FUN.
BUT ONE DAY, YOU WILL HAVE TO TELL ME...
...THE TRUTH.
MORE IMPORTANTLY, NANAMI, LOOK OUTSIDE THE WINDOW.
SEE?

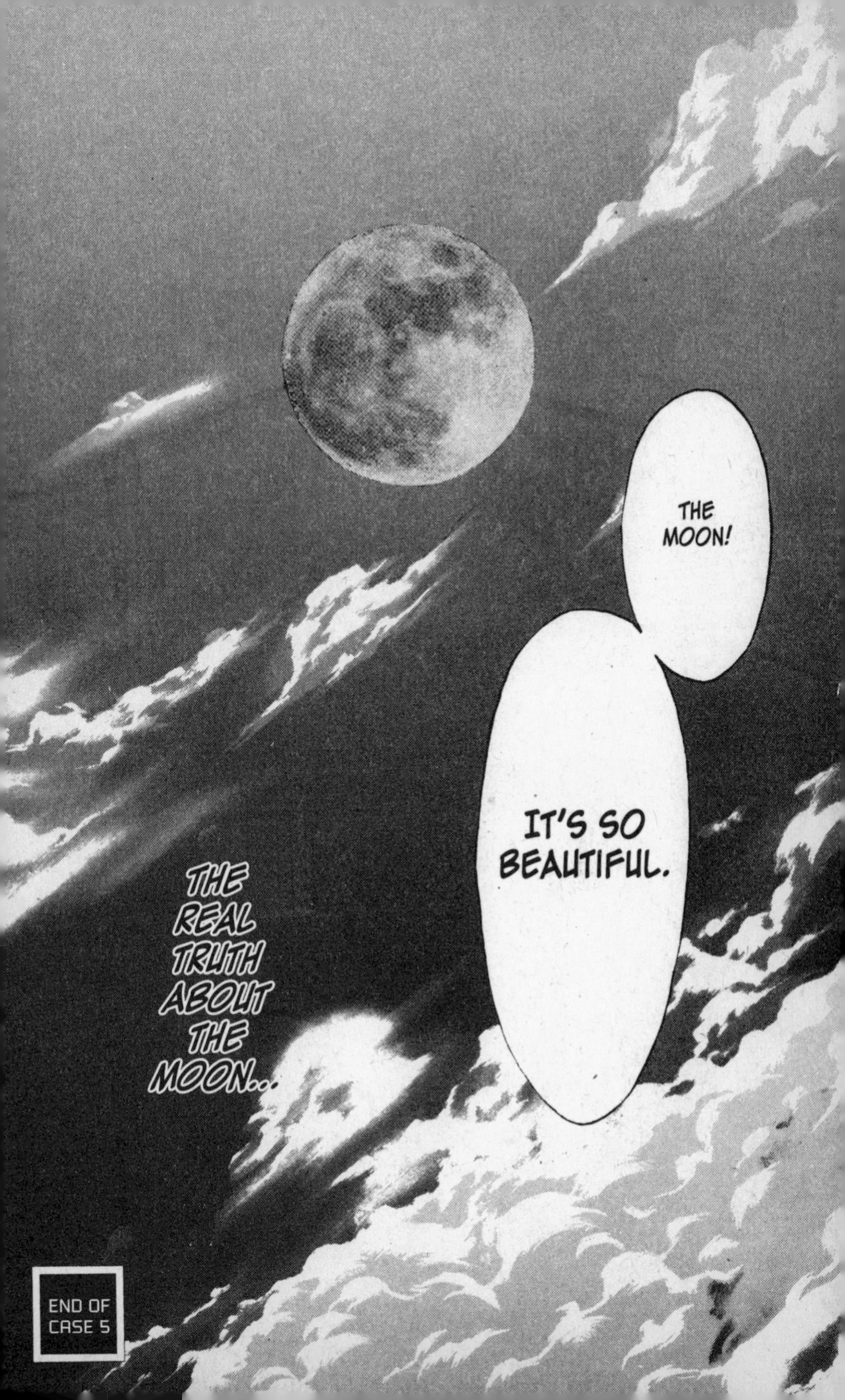
THE MOON!
IT'S SO BEAUTIFUL.
THE REAL TRUTH ABOUT THE MOON...
END OF CASE 5

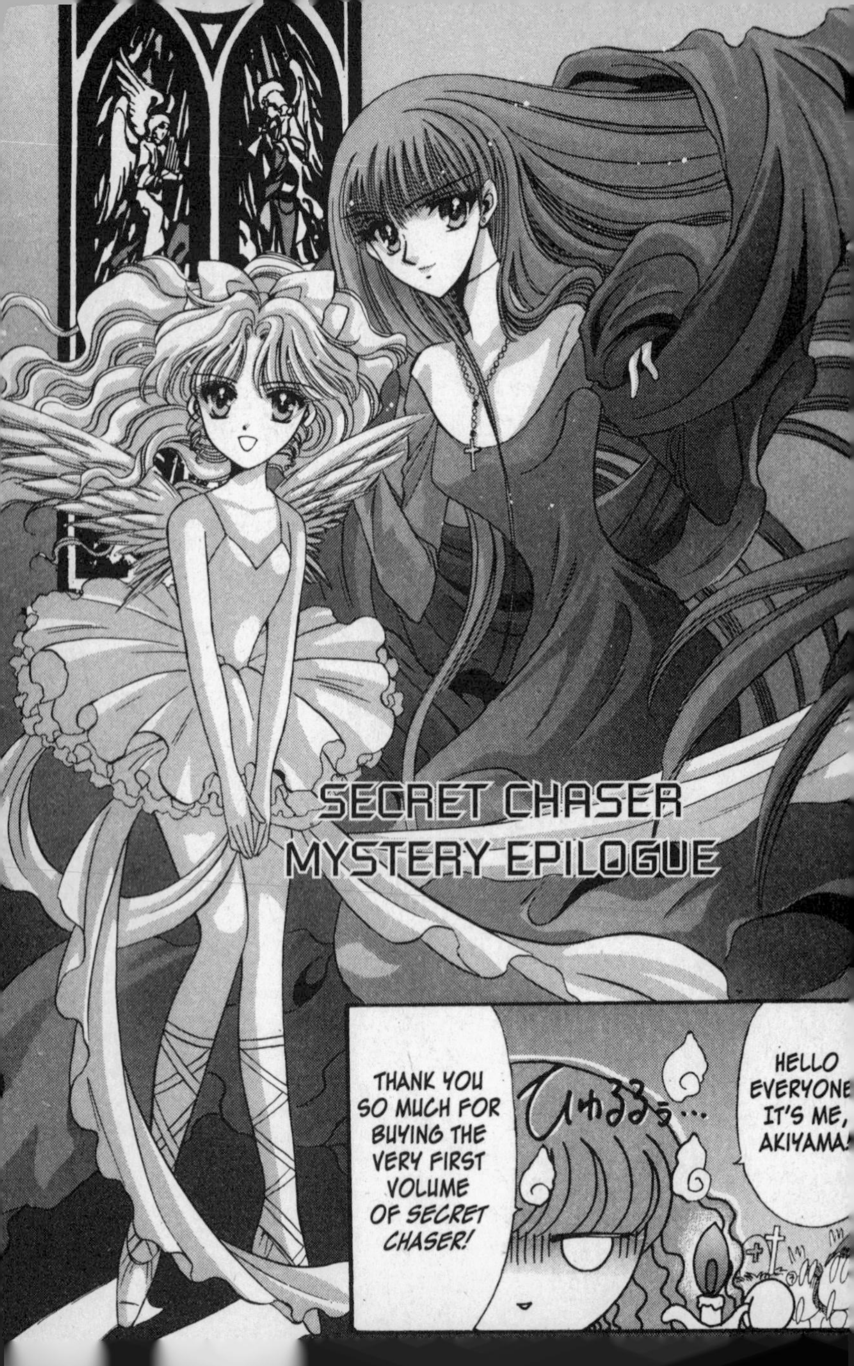
SECRET CHASER
MYSTERY EPILOGUE
HELLO EVERYONE IT'S ME, AKIYAMA!
ひゅるるる…
THANK YOU SO MUCH FOR BUYING THE VERY FIRST VOLUME OF SECRET CHASER!

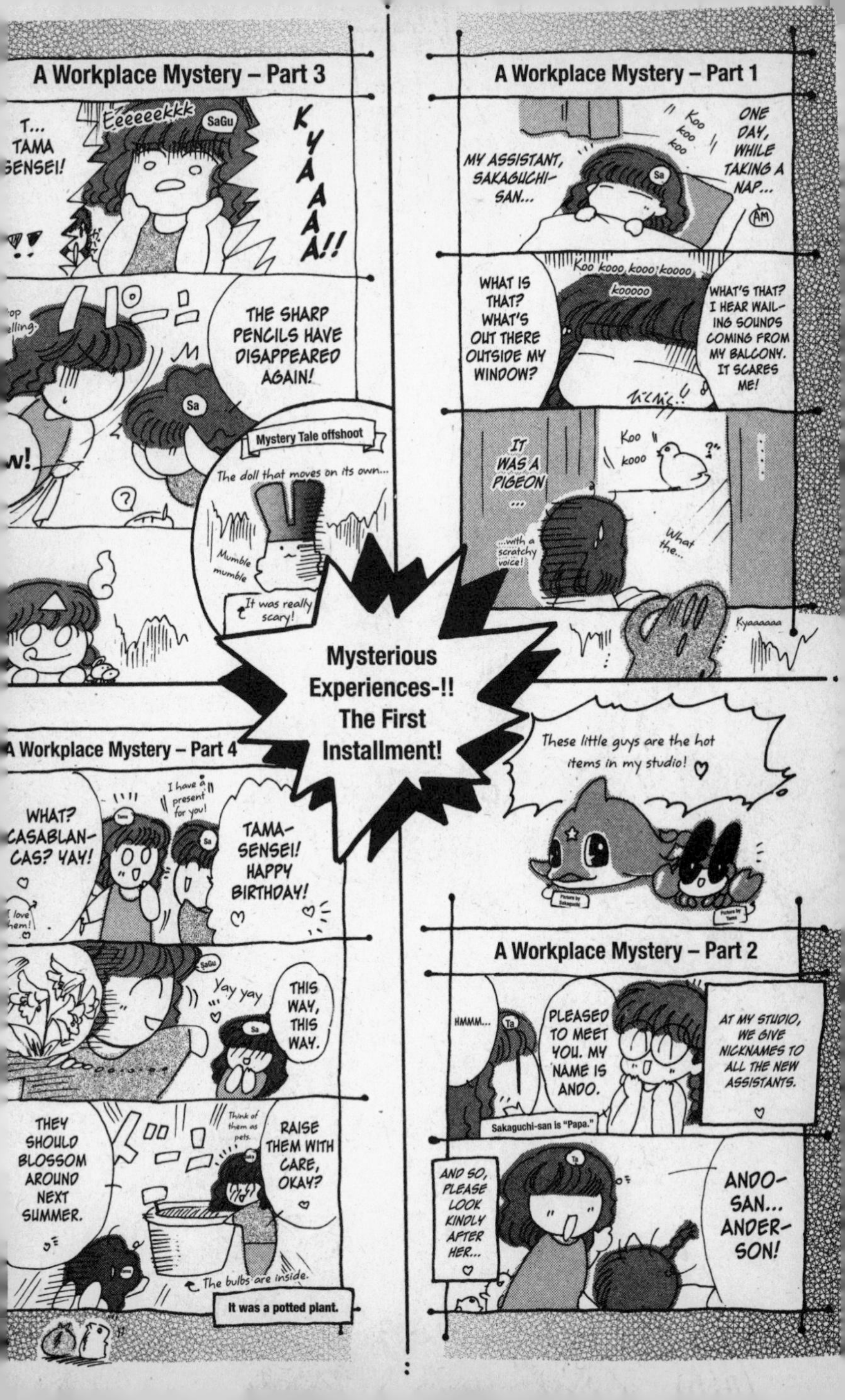
Mysterious Experiences-!! The First Installment!
A Workplace Mystery – Part 1
ONE DAY, WHILE TAKING A NAP...
AM
Koo koo koo
MY ASSISTANT, SAKAGUCHI-SAN...
Sa
WHAT'S THAT? I HEAR WAILING SOUNDS COMING FROM MY BALCONY. IT SCARES ME!
Koo kooo kooo koooo kooooo
WHAT IS THAT? WHAT'S OUT THERE OUTSIDE MY WINDOW?
Koo kooo
IT WAS A PIGEON...
...with a scratchy voice!
What the...
Kyaaaaaa
These little guys are the hot items in my studio!
Picture by Sakaguchi
Picture by Tama
A Workplace Mystery – Part 2
AT MY STUDIO, WE GIVE NICKNAMES TO ALL THE NEW ASSISTANTS.
PLEASED TO MEET YOU. MY NAME IS ANDO.
HMMM...
Ta
Sakaguchi-san is "Papa."
ANDO-SAN... ANDERSON!
Ta
AND SO, PLEASE LOOK KINDLY AFTER HER...
A Workplace Mystery – Part 3
KYAAAAA!!
Eeeeeekkk
SaGu
T... TAMA SENSEI!
THE SHARP PENCILS HAVE DISAPPEARED AGAIN!
Sa
Mystery Tale offshoot
The doll that moves on its own...
Mumble mumble
It was really scary!
A Workplace Mystery – Part 4
TAMA-SENSEI! HAPPY BIRTHDAY!
I have a present for you!
Sa
Tama
WHAT? CASABLANCAS? YAY!
THIS WAY, THIS WAY.
Yay yay
SaGu
Sa
RAISE THEM WITH CARE, OKAY?
Think of them as pets.
THEY SHOULD BLOSSOM AROUND NEXT SUMMER.
The bulbs are inside.
It was a potted plant.

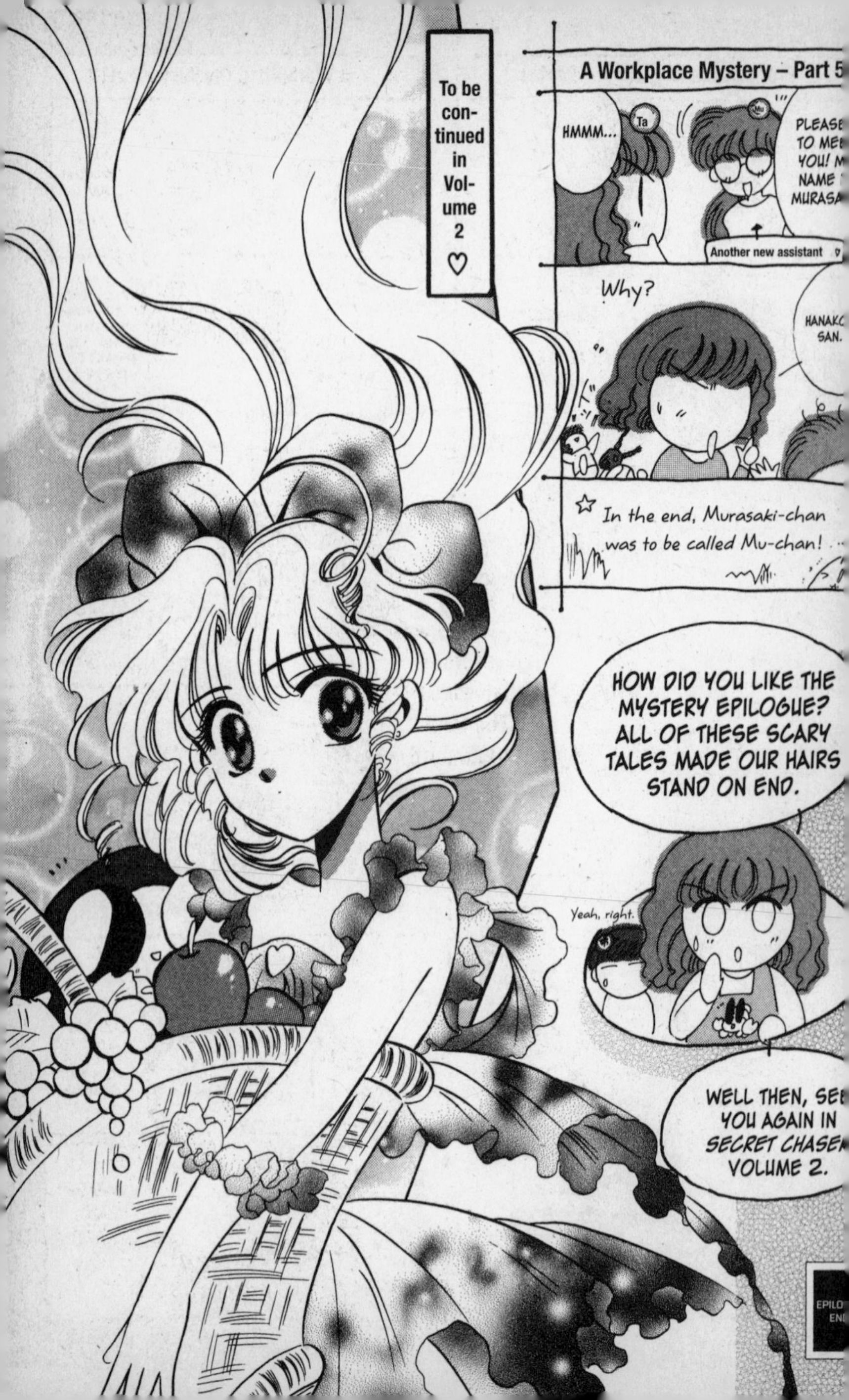
A Workplace Mystery – Part 5
PLEASE TO ME YOU! M NAME MURASA
Mu
HMMM...
Ta
Another new assistant
HANAK SAN.
Why?
In the end, Murasaki-chan was to be called Mu-chan!
HOW DID YOU LIKE THE MYSTERY EPILOGUE? ALL OF THESE SCARY TALES MADE OUR HAIRS STAND ON END.
Yeah, right.
WELL THEN, SE YOU AGAIN IN SECRET CHASE VOLUME 2.
EPILO EN
To be continued in Volume 2 ♡

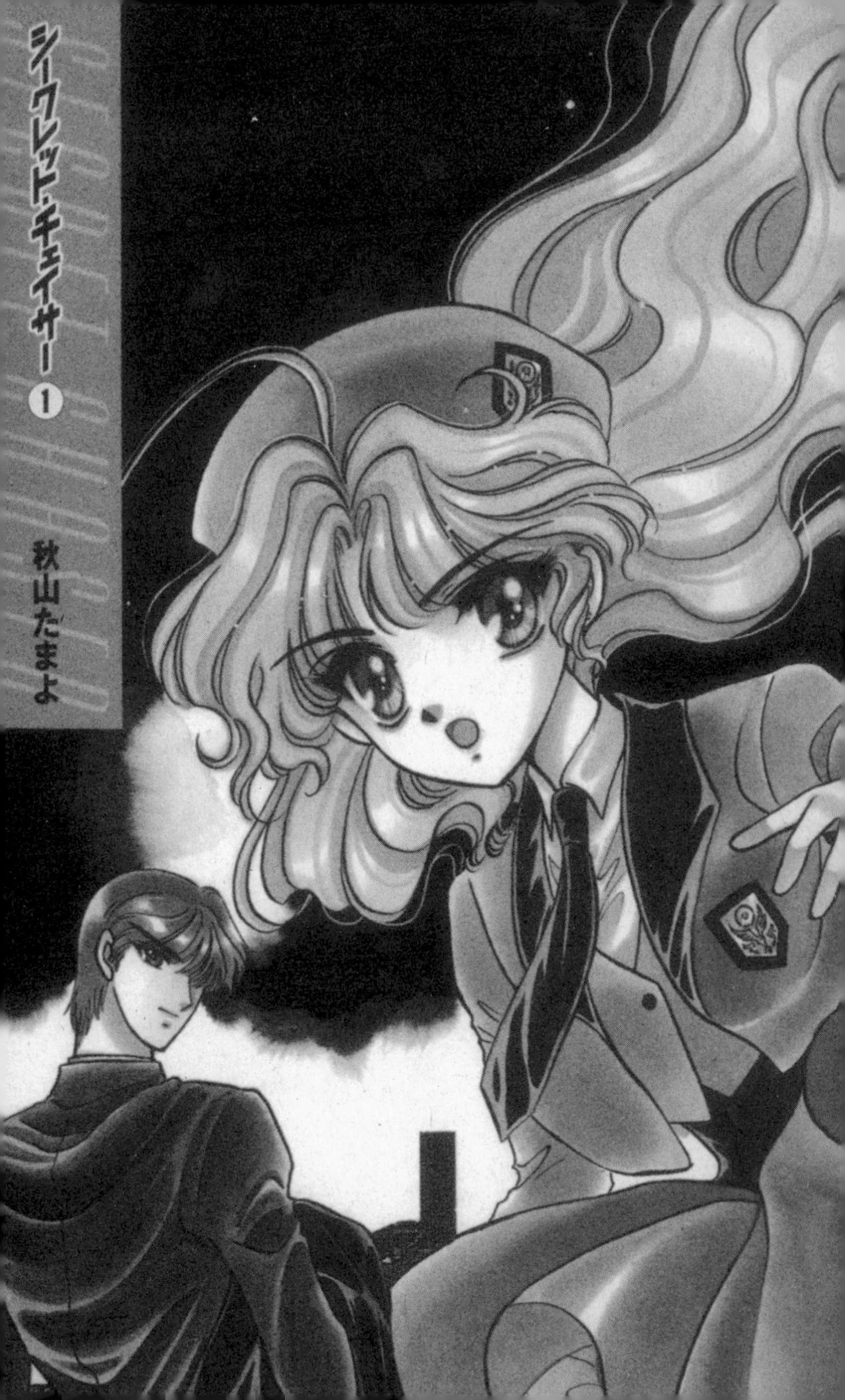
シークレット・チェイサー①
秋山たまよ

In the next volume of

SECRET CHASER

Shinozaki's next case involves a reclusive, rich orphan in need of companionship. Her name is Shiori Seijo, heir to the powerful Seijo corporation. But Shiori is plagued by horrible nightmares, as well as a strange condition that has rendered one of her eyes blood red. The question is: what ca Shinozaki and Aileen do for the young girl? And what about the old woman caretaker with traces of blood on her hands?

Unravel the mysteries along with the
Secret Chaser in volume 2!

TOKYOPOP SHOP

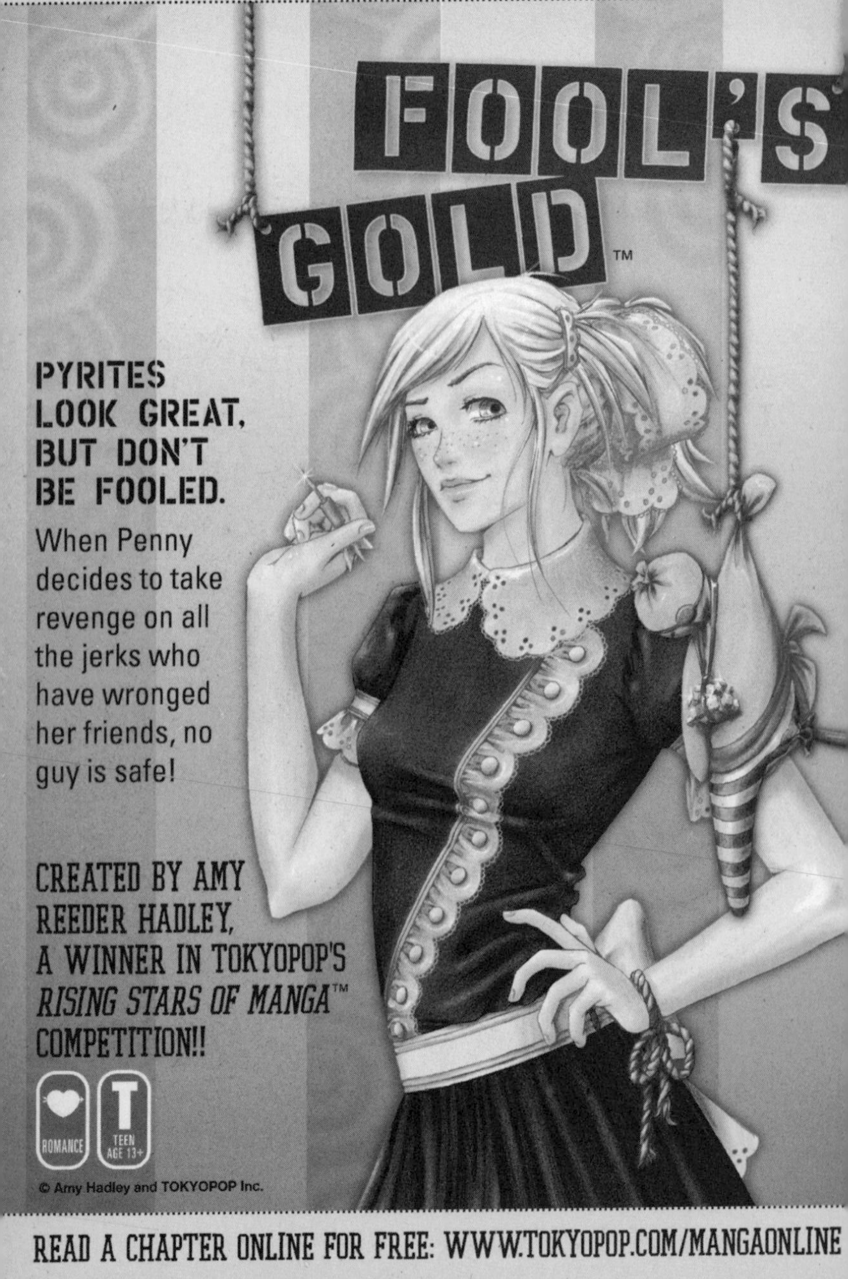

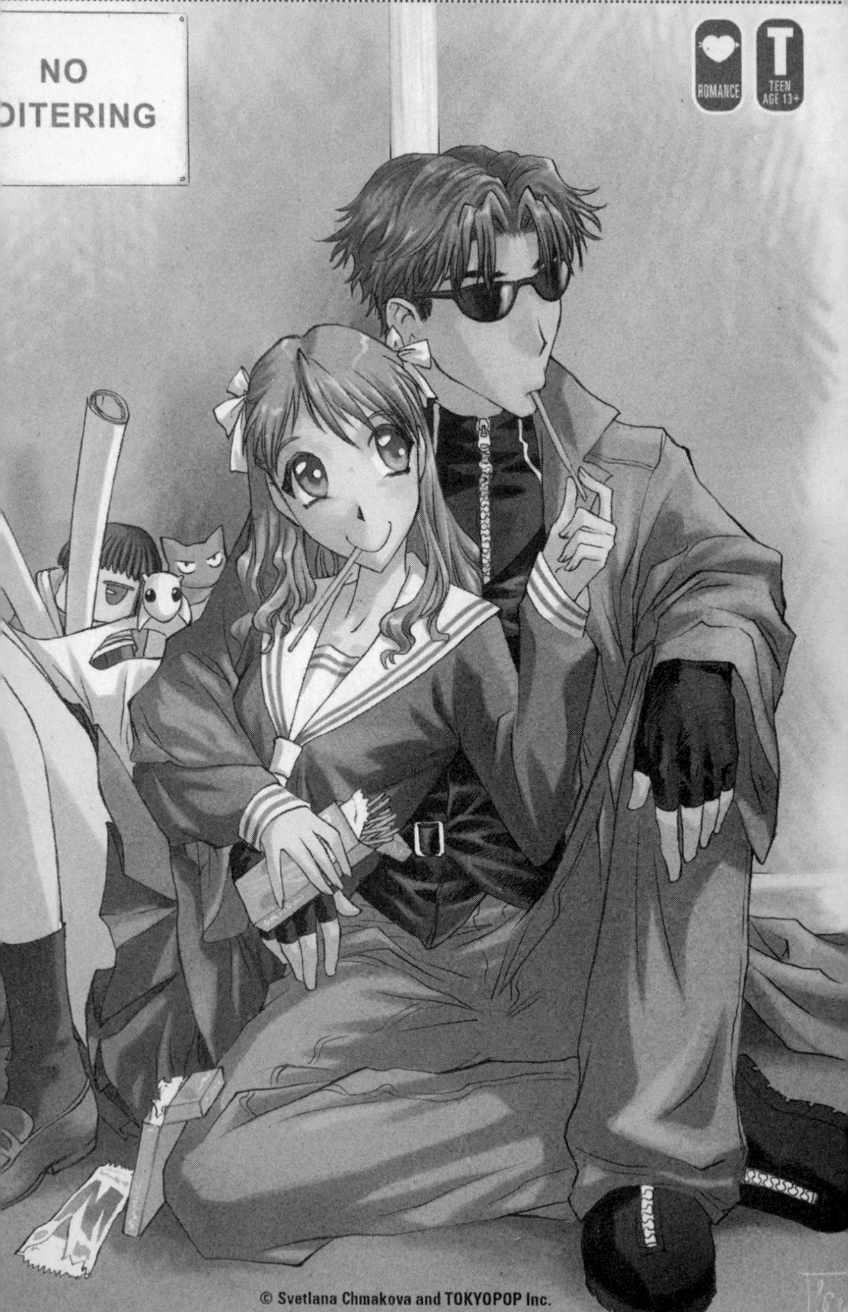
NO
OITERING
ROMANCE
T
TEEN
AGE 13+

DRAMACON™

Sometimes even two's a crowd.

When Christie settles in the Artist Alley of her first-ever anime convention, she only sees it as an opportunity to promote the comic she has started with her boyfriend. But conventions are never what you expect, and soon a whirlwind of events sweeps Christie off her feet and changes her life. Who is the mysterious cosplayer who won't even take off his sunglasses indoors? What do you do when you fall in love with a guy who is going to be miles away from you in just a couple of days?

CREATED BY SVETLANA CHMAKOVA!
"YOU CAN'T AVOID FALLING UNDER ITS CHARM." -IGN.COM

READ AN ENTIRE CHAPTER ONLINE FOR FREE:
WWW.TOKYOPOP.COM/MANGAONLINE

STOP!

This is the back of the book.
ou wouldn't want to spoil a great ending!

his book is printed "manga-style," in the authentic Japanese right-to-left
rmat. Since none of the artwork has been flipped or altered, readers
et to experience the story just as the creator intended. You've been
sking for it, so TOKYOPOP® delivered: authentic, hot-off-the-press,
nd far more fun!

DIRECTIONS

1
2
3
4
5
6
7
8
9
10

If this is your first time reading manga-style, here's a quick guide to help you understand how it works.

It's easy... just start in the top right panel and follow the numbers. Have fun, and look for more 100% authentic manga from TOKYOPOP®!

100% AUTHENTIC MANGA

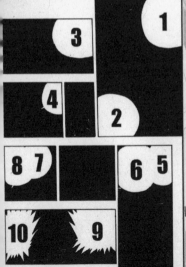

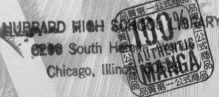